This book explores the remarkable sustained growth rates of the East Asian continent over the last 50 years. The only continent where countries have exhibited widespread success in moving out of the ranks of lower income countries is Asia. What accounts for this success? The authors explore the role of outward oriented policies, including both openness to trade and foreign investment. They find that trade and growth reinforce each other, and that foreign investment also plays a role. However, contrary to received wisdom pushing the concept of "export-led" growth, they do not find that exporting in a causal sense always leads to higher growth — the evidence seems to point more in the opposite direction (that growth engenders export activity).

These prominent authors, both at the University of Colorado, also get heterogeneous effects on causality between foreign investment, exports and growth. While there are strong associations running in both directions for the first generation of Asian countries (Korea, Singapore, Taiwan), these linkages are not significant when examining the second generation (Malaysia, Indonesia, Philippines, China). In the second half of the book, they examine how technology policy has helped Asia's growth, and also explore the implications of Asia's rise for North American economies. These series of studies are written by two authors with deep roots in Asia, who are at the frontier of their profession. This is an insightful and provocative book!

— Professor Ann E. Harrison
Dean and Bank of America Chair
Haas School of Business, University of California, Berkeley

The Pacific Basin is the region where economic dynamism is most acutely observed in the world. The authors identify the short as well as long run nature of time series with their superb expertise in Asian economics, mathematical economics and econometrics. They not only clarify the time series structures of interdependence among countries with international trade and investments, but also reveal the strategic interactions among macroeconomic policies of exports, foreign direct investment and economic growth in East and Southeast Asian economies.

— Professor Koichi Hamada
Fellow, Econometric Society
Tuntex Emeritus Professor of Economics
Department of Economics (Economic Growth Center), Yale University

Advanced Research on Asian Economy and Economies of Other Continents – Vol. 11

Development Strategies of Open Economies

Cases from Emerging East and Southeast Asia

Advanced Research on Asian Economy and Economies of Other Continents
(ISSN: 1793-0944)

Series Editor: HOON Hian Teck
                  (Singapore Management University, Singapore)

The escape from the Malthusian trap dating from the Industrial Revolution in the eighteenth century began in Europe and its North American offshoots and spread to different parts of the world. Technological diffusion from these frontier economies enabled Japan, then the East Asian economies of Hong Kong, Singapore, South Korea and Taiwan and, somewhat later, China and India to experience catch-up growth. Yet, there are signs that the pace of innovation that propelled the engine of growth in the frontier economies has slowed down. The growth slowdown has been accompanied by widening income disparities and weaker labour market performance. What are the economic and non-economic forces that are likely to shape the evolution of the global economy in the twenty-first century? What type of institutions and policy measures would reinvigorate economic dynamism and bring about economic inclusion? With the end of catch-up growth, what are the challenges and opportunities facing Singapore and the other East Asian economies?

Published

Vol. 11   *Development Strategies of Open Economies: Cases from Emerging East and Southeast Asia*
            by Frank S. T. Hsiao (University of Colorado, Boulder, USA) &
            Mei-Chu Wang Hsiao (University of Colorado, Denver, USA)

Vol. 10   *Economic Dynamism, Openness, and Inclusion: How Singapore Can Make the Transition from an Era of Catch-up Growth to Life in a Mature Economy*
            by Hian Teck Hoon (Singapore Management University, Singapore)

Vol. 9   *Economic Development of Taiwan: Early Experiences and the Pacific Trade Triangle*
            by Frank S. T. Hsiao (University of Colorado, Boulder, USA) &
            Mei-Chu Wang Hsiao (University of Colorado, Denver, USA)

Vol. 8   *Resilient States from a Comparative Regional Perspective: Central and Eastern Europe and Southeast Asia*
            by Bafoil François (Sciences Po Paris, France)

Vol. 7   *EU-Asia and the Re-Polarization of the Global Economic Arena*
            edited by Lars Oxelheim (Lund University, Sweden & Research Institute of Industrial Economics, Sweden)

More information on this series can also be found at http://www.worldscientific.com/series/araeeoc

Advanced Research on Asian Economy and Economies of Other Continents – Vol. 11

Development Strategies of Open Economies

Cases from Emerging East and Southeast Asia

Frank S T Hsiao
University of Colorado, Boulder, USA

Mei-Chu Wang Hsiao
University of Colorado, Denver, USA

World Scientific

NEW JERSEY · LONDON · SINGAPORE · BEIJING · SHANGHAI · HONG KONG · TAIPEI · CHENNAI · TOKYO

Published by

World Scientific Publishing Co. Pte. Ltd.

5 Toh Tuck Link, Singapore 596224

USA office: 27 Warren Street, Suite 401-402, Hackensack, NJ 07601

UK office: 57 Shelton Street, Covent Garden, London WC2H 9HE

Library of Congress Cataloging-in-Publication Data

Names: Hsiao, Frank S. T., author. | Hsiao, Mei-Chu Wang, author.

Title: Development strategies of open economies : cases from emerging East and Southeast Asia / Frank S.T. Hsiao, Mei-Chu Wang Hsiao.

Description: New Jersey : World Scientific, [2019] | Series: Advanced research on Asian economy and economies of other continents ; volume 11 | Includes bibliographical references and index.

Identifiers: LCCN 2019020531 | ISBN 9789811205408

Subjects: LCSH: Economic development--East Asia--Case studies. | Economic development--Southeast Asia--Case studies. | East Asia--Economic policy. | Southeast Asia--Economic policy.

Classification: LCC HC460.5 .H75 2019 | DDC 338.95--dc23

LC record available at https://lccn.loc.gov/2019020531

British Library Cataloguing-in-Publication Data

A catalogue record for this book is available from the British Library.

For any available supplementary material, please visit
https://www.worldscientific.com/worldscibooks/10.1142/11416#t=suppl

Desk Editor: Shreya Gopi

Typeset by Stallion Press
Email: enquiries@stallionpress.com

Printed in Singapore

In loving memory of our parents

Brief Contents

Contents

Part II. The United States and Emerging East and Southeast Asia   195

List of Figures

List of Tables

Sources of the Chapters

The various sources of each chapter are listed below. For the final published sources, copyright permissions for reprinting in this book were granted from the publishers of the papers as specified below. All papers were reformatted for consistency and uniformity for publication in this book.

Part I. Emerging East and Southeast Asian Economies: Exports, FDI, and Growth

1. "Tests of Causality and Exogeneity between Exports and Economic Growth: The Case of Asian NICs," *Journal of Economic Development,* Mei-Chu Wang Hsiao, **12** (2), 143–159, December 1987. Copyright (1987) with permission for reprint from Professor Sung Y. Park, Editor (2018), *Journal of Economic Development.*

    This paper was one of the earliest papers on causality analysis in the economic literature. It was originally presented at the North American Annual Meeting of the Econometric Society, Dallas, Texas, December 1984.

2. "The Chaotic Attractor of Foreign Direct Investment — Why China? A Panel Data Analysis." *Journal of Asian Economics* **15** (4), August 2004, 641–670. Copyright (2004), with permission for reprint from Elsevier Publishing.

    This paper was originally presented at the joint session of the American Economic Association/American Committee of East

Asian Studies (AEA/ACAES) at the 2004 Annual Allied Social
Science Association (ASSA) meetings, January, San Diego, CA.
It was also given at the seminar at the Department of Eco-
nomics, University of Colorado Denver and Health Science Center
(UCDHSC), January 2004; Institute of Economics, Academia
Sinica, Taipei, Taiwan, July 2004. The paper was published as one
of the four papers in special issue on "China's Economic Presence:
Implications for the Asia Pacific Region" edited by Richard
Hooley and Frank S.T. Hsiao, *Journal of Asian Economics,* 15,
2004, Introduction, pp. 607–611. The comments on this paper by
Michael Plummer and T. Srinivasan were also published in the
same issue of *Journal of Asian Economics.*

3. "FDI, Exports, and GDP in East and Southeast Asia — Panel
   Data versus Time-Series Causality Analyses." *Journal of Asian
   Economics* **17** (6), December 2006, 1082–1106. Copyright (2006),
   with permission for reprint from Elsevier Publishing.

   This paper was originally presented at the International Conference on Korea and the World Economy, V, held at Seoul, Korea,
   July 2006. It was also presented at the UCDHSC Economics
   Department Seminar, October 2006; Taipei International Conference on *Growth and Development in Global Perspective,* Institute
   of Economics, Academia Sinica, Taipei, Taiwan, July 2004. For
   many years, the paper had been one of the most downloaded
   papers of *Journal of Asian Economics* since its publication.

4. "Panel Causality Analysis on FDI-Exports-Economic Growth
   Nexus in First and Second Generation ANIEs" (Frank S. T.
   Hsiao with Yongkul Won). *The Journal of Korean Economy* **9**
   (2), August 2008, 237–267. Copyright (2008), with permission for
   reprint from Professor Sung Jin Kang, Editor (2018), *Korea and
   the World Economy* (formerly *the Journal of Korean Economy*).

   This is a shortened and revised version of the monograph
   written for a funded project, *FDI Inflows, Exports and Economic
   Growth in First and Second generation ANIEs: Panel Data
   Causality Analyses,* Yongkul Won, Frank S.T. Hsiao, and Doo
   Yong Yang. Korea Institute for International Economic Policy,
   Seoul, South Korea, February 2008, 86 pp.

5. "The IT Revolution and Macroeconomic Volatility in Newly Developed Countries: ARCH/GARCH — VAR Approaches," paper presented at the Joint International Conference of American Committee for Asian Economic Studies (ACAES) and the Rimini Centre for Economic Analysis (RCEA), Rimini, Italy, 29–31 August, 2008.

The original paper was presented at the International Conference on Korea and the Global Economy, II, University of Washington, Seattle, August 2003; the University of Colorado Denver (UCDHSC) Economics Department Seminar, November 2007; the 8th Annual Missouri Economics Conference, University of Missouri–Columbia, MO, March 2008.

Part II. The United States and East and Southeast Asia

6. "The Impact of the U.S. Economy on the Asia-Pacific Region — Does it Matter?" (with Akio Yamashita), *Journal of Asian Economics* **14** (2), April 2003, 219–241. Copyright (2003), with permission for reprint from Elsevier Publishing.

This paper was originally presented at the joint AEA/ACAES Session at the 2003 ASSA Annual Meeting at Washington, DC, January 2003. It was translated into Japanese by Akio Yamashita with permission from the publisher, Elsevier Publishing, "America Keizai ga Ajia-Taiheiyo Chieki ni Ataeru Eikyo - Sorewa Jyuyo de Aruka?" in *Ryukoku University Kei-ei Gaku Ronshyu* (*Ryukoku University Journal of Management*), Vol. 43, Nos. 3 and 4, March 2004, 27–48.

7. "Gains from Policy Coordination between Taiwan and the United States — On the Games Governments Play," in *Asia-Pacific Economies: 1990s and Beyond, Research in Asian Economic Studies*, Eds. M. Dutta and R. Shiratori, Vol. 5, Greenwich, CT: JAI Press, Inc., 1994, Chapter 17, 239–264. Copyright (1994), with permission for reprint from Elsevier Publishing.

This paper was originally presented at the Fifth Biennial Conference on The United States–Asia Economic Relations, jointly sponsored by the American Committee of Asian Economic Studies

(ACAES) and the Tokai University, Tokyo, Japan, June 1991. It was also presented at the Otaru University of Commerce, Otaru, Japan, June 1991; Chung-Hua Institute for Economic Research (CIER), Taipei, Taiwan, January 1992; Central Bank of China (Taiwan), Taipei, Taiwan, January 1992; Hong Kong Baptist University, May 1992; The general session of the 1993 Econometric Society Far Eastern Annual Meeting at the Chung-Hua Institute for Economic Research (CIER), Taipei, Taiwan, June 1993.

8. "International Policy Coordination with a Dominant Player — The Case of the United States, Japan, Taiwan, and Korea," in *Journal of Asian Economics*, **6** (1), Spring 1995, 29–52. Copyright (1995), with permission for reprint from Elsevier Publishing.

   This paper was originally presented at the Sixth Biennial Conference on United States–Asia Economic Relations, sponsored by the American Committee of Asian Economic Studies (ACAES) and the Brandeis University, Waltham, MA, May 1994. The paper was also presented at the Post-Conference Workshop on *New Frontiers in Economic Theory,* the 1993 Econometric Society Far Eastern Annual Meeting at the Chung-Hua Institute for Economic Research, Taipei, Taiwan, June 1993; the First Conference on *Pacific Basin Business, Economics and Finance,* Rutgers University, New Jersey, April 1993.

About the Authors

Frank S. T. Hsiao received his BA and MA in Economics from the National Taiwan University, Taipei, Taiwan, and MA and PhD (1967) in Economics from the University of Rochester, Rochester, NY. He was Visiting Assistant Professor (1967–69), Assistant Professor (1967–69), Associate Professor (1969–75), and Professor (1975–2007) in the Department of Economics at the University of Colorado Boulder.

He taught undergraduate and graduate courses on *Mathematical Economics (Statics and Dynamics)*, *Economic Statistics*, and *Microcomputer Applications in Economics*. From his lecture notes, he has published books on *Game Theory using Microcomputers* (coauthored with Y. Umehara, in Japanese, Tokyo, Japan: Nihon Hyoronsha, 1999, 220 pp.) and *Economic and Business Analysis-Quantitative Methods using Spreadsheets* (World Scientific, 2011, 669 pp.). Recently, his research interests resulted in joint publication, with Mei-Chu Wang Hsiao, of collected essays on *Economic Development of Taiwan-Early Experiences and the Pacific Trade Triangle* (World Scientific, 2015, 599 pp.), among three other books.

His research interests include economic growth and development, quantitative methods in economics, and comparative studies on Taiwanese economy with other Asian countries and the United States. He has published extensively in leading professional journals, including *American Economic Review, Journal of Political Economy, Journal of Finance, Southern Economic Journal, Metroeconomica,* and others. He has also coauthored research papers in many journals, including *World Development, Review of Development Economics, Journal of Asian Economics, Journal of the Asia Pacific Economy, Journal of Korean Economy, and Journal of Productivity Analysis.*

His expertise has been recognized nationally and internationally through many lectures at universities and institutes in the USA, Japan, the Netherlands, Italy, Mexico, Taiwan, South Korea, Malaysia, Thailand, Hong Kong, and China. He was a Fulbright-Hays Research Fellow at Hitotsubashi University and National Taiwan University, and was a visiting scholar at the Fairbank Center for East Asian Research of Harvard University and the Hoover Institute of Stanford University. He was also an oversees visiting scholar at the Korea Development Institute; Academia Sinica, Taiwan, Chung-Hua Institution for Economic Research in Taiwan; Kansai University, Nagoya University, and the International Centre for the Study of East Asian Development (ICSEAD) in Japan.

He was a Senior Editor (1991–2007) and an Associate Editor (2007–19) of the *Journal of Asian Economics.* Currently, he is Professor Emeritus of Economics at the Department of Economics, University of Colorado at Boulder (2007–), and serves on the Advisory Council of the American Committee of Asian Economic Studies (ACAES).

Mei-Chu Wang Hsiao, Professor Emerita of Economics, University of Colorado at Denver, earned her MA and PhD (1967) in Economics from the University of Rochester, Rochester, NY. She received her BA in Accounting and Banking from National Taiwan University. She was an Assistant Professor at New York University (1967–69), and was then appointed as Assistant Professor, Associate Professor and Professor, Professor Emerita (2008–) in the Department of Economics at the University of Colorado Denver. She taught undergraduate and graduate courses in *Econometrics, Statistics, Mathematical Economics, and Development Economics.* Prior teaching positions include those at University of Colorado at Boulder and National Taiwan University.

Her research interests are concentrated on the econometric analyses of time-series and panel data, the study of trade strategies, economic development and growth of East and Southeast Asia, and their trade relations with the United States and Japan. She was a visiting scholar at the Hoover Institution of Stanford University, the International Centre for the Study of East Asian Development (ICSEAD) in Japan, National Taiwan University, the Institute of Economics at Academia Sinica in Taiwan, and the Chung-Hua Institution for Economic Research in Taiwan. Her research interests also resulted in recent joint publications of books with Frank S.T. Hsiao on *Economic Development of Taiwan-Early Experiences and the Pacific Trade Triangle* (World Scientific, 2015, 599 pp.) and on *Economic Development of Emerging East Asia: Catching Up of Taiwan and South Korea* (Anthem Press, 2017, 326 pp.).

Her professional publications include papers in *World Development, Review of Development Economics, Journal of Economic Development, Journal of Asian Economics, Energy Economics, Journal of the Asia Pacific Economy, Southern Economic Journal*, etc., and chapters in books and conference proceedings on Asian economic studies. She presented numerous research papers at national and international economic conferences and economic research institutes in the United States, Japan, Italy, the Netherlands, Taiwan, South Korea, Hong Kong, Malaysia, and Thailand.

About the Contributors

Yongkul Won, Professor of Economics, Department of Economics, and a former Dean of the College of Economics and Public Affairs (CEPA), University of Seoul, Seoul, South Korea. He received his BA and MA from Seoul National University, and he earned his PhD in Economics in 1995 from Indiana University, Bloomington, USA. His fields of research are International Economics and Development Macroeconomics. He has published papers in *European Economic Review, Korean Economic Review*, and *Seoul Journal of Economics*, among others. His recent publications include "Regulation and Service Exports: Theoretical and Empirical Analyses," in the *Korean Economic Review* (with Gilseong Kang, 2016).

Akio Yamashita, Professor of Economics, School of Business, Ryukoku University, Kyoto, Japan. He served as the Dean of the College of Business for several years and stepped down in 2018. His recent interest is in the microcomputer applications in economic research and teaching, especially related to the use of Maxima (Open-Source Computer Algebra System). He published papers in *Ryukoku University Journal of Management*, and other journals. His latest publications include *Economic Analysis using Maxima* (in Japanese), Kyoto, Japan: Koyo Shobo Publisher, 2014.

Acknowledgments

In the preparation of the chapters in this book, we are grateful to the original publishers of our papers, the *Journal of Korean Economy*, *Korea and the World Economy*, and the Elsevier Publishing Company, as listed in the Sources of Papers section, for granting copyright permissions to reprint the papers, and to Ms. Jeanne Brewster of the Copyright Clearance Center for advising us on matter related to copyright search and application. Our sincere appreciation goes to Dean Ann E. Harrison of University of California Berkeley and Professor Koichi Hamada of Yale University for writing thoughtful blurbs for the book. Professor Hamada also suggested that a concluding chapter for this book might be appropriate.

We have a long list of economists and organizations to thank for helping us by providing statistical data and references for our research. We are particularly grateful to the Council of Economic Planning and Development, Executive Yuan, Taiwan, for sending us, for many years, the *Taiwan Statistical Data Book* and the monthly *Taiwan Economic Forum* (formerly, *Industry of Free China*). The Central Bank of China (Taiwan) and the Bank of Taiwan also sent us many years of *Taiwan Economic and Financial Statistics Monthly* and *the Journal of Bank of Taiwan* for our research. These publications were particularly valuable since Taiwan's statistical data are not available from almost all the international organizations. The comprehensive economic time-series dataset on East and Southeast Asian countries compiled and distributed by the International Centre for the Study of East Asian Development (ICSEAD), Kitakyushu, Japan, were also very valuable for our work.

We are also very fortunate for having been acquainted with many teachers, students, and friends. At different stages of writing this book, we were especially benefited from M. Jan Dutta, Steve Beckman, Kyoo-Hong Cho, Bagestani Hamid, Cheng-Few Lee, Sheng-Cheng Hu, Hyun-Hoon Lee, Joseph C. Lee, Michael Luzius, Angus Maddison, Naci Mocan, Robert McNown, Motoaki Moriya, Kazuo Nishimura, Sukrisno Njoto, Masao Oda, Changsuh Park, Michael Plummer, Eric D. Ramstetter, Hiroshi Setooka, Yoshio Shimizu, Jaw-Yann Twu, Masaru Uzawa, Henry Wan, Jr., Yongkul Won, Akio Yamashita, Kenji Yamamoto, Tzong-shian Yu, and Kevin Zhang, among many others. We are grateful for their data collection, advices, and friendship. Naturally, all errors of commission and omission are ours.

The Dean's Office of the Leeds School of Business, University of Colorado Boulder, Professor Kai R. Larsen, Ms. Brenda Engle, and many faculty members provided us an excellent environment to work on this book. We are also appreciative of Professor Hian Teck Hoon, the new editor of the well-established World Scientific Book Series on *Advanced Research on Asian Economy and Economies of Other Continents*, for including this book in the series. Many staff members of the editorial office of the World Scientific, especially Ms. Shreya Gopi and Mr. Balasubramanian Shanmugam, spent long time to see this book published. We are thankful for their patience and advices.

This being our third book on Asian economic development, as in the previous books, we wish to express our sincere and deep gratitude to our parents, who saw the importance of having us receive the best education we could. We also wish to express our profound appreciation to our teachers, in particular, Professors Ronald W. Jones, Lionel W. McKenzie, and Richard N. Rosette, Hugh Rose, Sho-Chieh Tsiang, Shu-Ren Yang, and Mo-huan Hsing, among others, who taught us rigorous economic analyses; to Professor Alexander Eckstein, who encouraged and helped Frank study at Rochester; and to our children, Edward and Victoria, for their patience and understanding throughout our research and teaching careers.

Introduction and Overview
of Chapters

The economies of East and Southeast Asia have been growing for almost half a century. They are expected to grow amid the slowing down in Chinese and American markets, the uncertainty in the European Union and the United States, the conflicts in the Near and Middle East, and the stagnation in Latin America.

Economic Growth of Emerging East and Southeast Asia

The almost half a century of high and sustained growth of Asian economies is unprecedented in modern Asian history. In 1979, a report by the Organization of Economic Cooperation and Development (OECD) defined the Newly Industrializing Countries (NICs) as those countries "whose share in world industrial output and in world exports of manufactures has increased rapidly since the early 1960s and particularly during the 1970s" (OECD, 1979, p. 6). Ten NICs were identified in the report: the four "Asian NICs" — South Korea (hereafter, Korea), Taiwan, Singapore, and Hong Kong; Portugal, Spain, Yugoslavia, and Greece in Southern Europe; and Brazil and Mexico in the Americas. After more than a decade, it turned out that only the four NICs in Asia, along with Spain and Portugal, which were already in the OECD group, remained as NICs (WDR, 1992, p. 245). In 1988, during the G7 Summit at Toronto, the four Asian NICs were the only four economies in the world that achieved and maintained long-run rapid modern economic growth, and they were renamed as the Newly Industrializing Economies (NIEs). By 1996, Korea was admitted to the OECD. Taiwan should have followed suit, but Taiwan was prevented by the China factor.

The rapid and sustained growth of the NIEs spilled over to China after China opened its coastal cities in 1985, especially after Deng Xiaoping's southern tour in early 1992 (Chapter 2). China quickly joined the group of the NIEs after its admission to the WTO in 2001. The growth trend has also spread to the Southeast Asian countries, especially the ASEAN-4 — Indonesia, Malaysia, Thailand, and the Philippines. They are called the second-generation NIEs (Chapter 4).

In 1993, the World Bank (1993) dubbed the Asian economic growth as *The East Asian Miracle*. It pointed out that "From 1965 to 1990 the twenty-three economies of East Asia grew faster than all other regions of the world. Most of this achievement is attributable to seemingly miraculous growth in just eight economies": Japan, Korea, Taiwan, Singapore, Hong Kong, and "the three newly industrializing economies (NIEs) of Southeast Asia, Indonesia, Malaysia, and Thailand." It called these eight economies the "High-Performing Asian Economies" (HPAEs) (World Bank, 1993, p. 1). In this book, we have added China and the Philippines to convert it to 10 economies when we discuss the economic development of emerging East and Southeast Asia (Chapters 3–6), or the economic take-off stage of the Asia-Pacific Region.

Another quarter century has passed since the 1993 study by the World Bank on the "East Asian Miracle," and the "miracle" is continuing according to "Asia's Growth Far from Finished" (Fensom, 2015; Hsiao, 2016). In recent years, their gross domestic product (GDP) and GDP per capita have grown dramatically (Hsiao and Hsiao, 2017, Chapter 9), the economies have shifted to the manufacturing and services, and poverty have been reduced drastically, thanks mainly to the information technology and computer (ITC) revolution (Chapters 4–6). The development has been helped by their strong propensity for learning from the advanced countries, especially from Japan and the United States (Hsiao and Hsiao, 2017).

In a recent study (Hsiao and Hsiao, 2017, Chapter 9), in terms of GDP per capita in purchasing power parity (PPP), we found that the four Asian NIEs and the four ASEAN countries, along with China and India and, to a lesser degree, Japan, have been growing steadily since 1980, especially Taiwan and Korea. "East Asia and Pacific accounted for almost two-fifths of global growth in 2015, more than twice the combined contribution of all other developing regions" (World Bank, 2016). Their "growth ... is expected to be from 6.5% in 2015 to 6.3% in 2016 and 6.2% in 2017–2018" (World Bank, 2016). Thus, East and Southeast Asia are still the most economically active areas in the world (IMF, 2014), and they are expected to continue to the end of this decade.

In fact, according to the prediction by the Intelligence Unit of *The Economist*, "Asian economies ... took their share of global GDP from 26% to 32% between 2000 and 2014. ... Asia's rise will continue up to 2050 ... , by 2050 it will account for 53% of global GDP" (EIU, 2015, p. 4).

The rapid and resilient economies and the strategic location of the Asia-Pacific region have attracted the attention of economists, politicians, researchers, and the business community. Many books and journal articles have been written about the economies of the region. The United States is now trading more with Asia than with Europe. The economic dynamics of the ever-growing Asia-Pacific region necessitate the United States to adopt a "rebalancing strategy" or "pivot" toward Asia and to propose the Trans-Pacific Partnership (TPP) and the Free Trade Area of Asia-Pacific (FTAAP) before the current US administration.

Although the new Trump Administration decided not to join the TPP or FTAAP, the original members of the TPP, led by Japan, Australia, and Singapore, forged ahead in March 2018 without the participation of the US and formed TPP-11, also known as the Comprehensive and Progressive Agreement for TPP (CPTPP). At the same time, the Trump Administration rolled out the Free and Open Indo-Pacific Strategy (IPS), including India, to promote "free, fair, and reciprocal trade relations." On the other hand, the China-backed Regional Comprehensive Economic Partnership (RCEP) was launched in 2012 with 16 member countries, but by 2018, it was still in the negotiating stage and evolving slowly.

In any case, the CPTPP, the RCEP, or the IPS are all aimed at opening the economies wider and promoting regional trade and foreign direct investment (FDI) among the member countries for further economic growth. While it is not clear which one will prevail in the future, a new era of the Asia-Pacific economic integration, prosperity, and economic growth through foreign trade and investment is emerging.

Trade, Foreign Direct Investment, and Growth in Open Economic Development

In the macroeconomics of a closed economy without foreign trade, the economy produces gross domestic product GDP (in US dollars) in a year. GDP is spent by the households (as consumption (C)), by firms (as investment (I)), and by government (as government expenditure (G)). Thus, GDP $= C + I + G$.

In an open economy, however, the firms also produce for exports (X), and the spending in C, I, and G above also includes imported goods and services. We denote the total spending on imported goods and services as M. Imports are not produced by the country in question. Therefore, in the foreign sector of the GDP, we deduct imports M from exports X to have net exports $X - M$ and add it to the macroeconomic equation of GDP in an open economy. The net exports, $X - M$, is also called the balance of trade $(B = X - M)$. In developing countries, trade in services is generally very small, that is, statistically not significant. Thus, in this book, we generally consider trade in goods, depending on the data sources.

Furthermore, under an open economy, a country may receive foreign investment (F) to produce goods in the country. Thus, we have

$$\text{GDP} = C + I + G + F + (X - M). \tag{1}$$

In fact, foreign investment consists of direct and indirect foreign investments. Direct foreign investment (DFI) is investment in new facilities or mergers and acquisitions of firms in the hosting countries by foreign nationals or firms, while indirect portfolio investment (PI) is foreign investment through purchasing of shares of the hosting country. More accurately, the former is called inward foreign direct investment (IFDI) and the latter is called inward foreign indirect investment (IFII).

Naturally, in an open economy, people in their home country may also invest in a foreign country directly or indirectly. In this case, we have outward foreign direct investment (OFDI) or outward foreign indirect investment (OFII), which is also called outward portfolio investment (OPI).

Since this book deals with the emerging East and Southeast Asia in which stock markets are not developed or are small in the early emerging development stage, and the domestic firms are not large enough, or are still too small, to invest in foreign countries, we only consider inward FDI, namely, IFDI or simply FDI, and denote it as F in the first part of this book.

Thus, in order not to spread our studies too wide and too thin, in the first part of this book, we are interested in the three basic development strategies of the open economies: exports (X), IFDI (F), and economic growth, namely, GDP.

Growth Relations in Open Economic Development

In the international trade literature, the first three terms on the right-hand side of Eq. (1) is called domestic absorption[1] A, where A is given by $A = C + I + G$. Thus, GDP $= A + F + (X - M)$. For simplicity and symmetry, we write GDP as Y. Now, taking the total differential on both sides, dividing both sides by Y, and rearranging, we have

$$\frac{dY}{Y} = \frac{A}{Y}\frac{dA}{A} + \frac{F}{Y}\frac{dF}{F} + \frac{X}{Y}\frac{dX}{X} - \frac{M}{Y}\frac{dM}{M}, \tag{2}$$

---

[1]Goods "absorbed" by domestic expenditure. Thus, the trade balance $X - M$ is the difference of GDP and $(A + F)$, and it will increase if GDP increases faster than domestic absorption and FDI.

where d is differential, dA/A, dF/F, dX/X, and dM/M are growth rates of absorption, FDI, exports, and imports, respectively. The coefficient of each growth rate (namely, $A/Y \equiv w_A$, $F/Y \equiv w_F$, $X/Y \equiv w_X$, and $M/Y \equiv w_M$) is the weight of each variable in GDP, and the coefficients sum to 1.

Thus, the growth rate of GDP equals to the weighted average of the growth rates of all the variables, weighted by the proportion of the value of each variable in GDP.

Since $dY/Y = d\ln Y$, Eq. (2) may also be written as

$$d\ln Y = w_A d\ln A + w_F d\ln F + w_X d\ln X - w_M d\ln M.$$

For a discrete analysis, the differential d in $d\ln Y$ may be replaced by difference Δ as $\Delta \ln Y$, where $\Delta \ln Y$ is the logarithmic difference of Y between consecutive time periods (namely, $\Delta \ln Y = \ln Y_t - \ln Y_{t-1}$). Similar replacement can be done for the other logarithmic variables A, F, X, and M. As we will see in this book, this transformation enables us to interpret the results of econometric analysis using vector autoregression (VAR).

For an open economy of a developing country (for that matter, even a developed country), FDI (F) and Trade (T) (in this book, we emphasize exports (X),[2] but not imports, M, to avoid a collinearity problem in regression analysis, at least for the first approach[3]) are

---

[2]Note that, as in a macroeconomics textbook, consumption and investment are functions of GNP. The intersection (Keynesian cross) of the supply curve Y on the left and the demand curve on the right determines the equilibrium GDP, Y. The left and right variables adjust each other *ex ante* (before the event) to reach equilibrium, and the impact of C or X on Y, for a linear function, is measured by consumption multipliers, etc.

Statistically, the data are *ex post* (after the event), and the equality of both sides of (1) always holds identically ($\equiv$). Thus, for the national income account statistics published by the Bureau of Statistics in bookkeeping, both sides of Eq. (1) balance exactly.

[3]Imports of capital goods can indirectly promote technological transfer and economic growth. However, to increase imports, the country must earn foreign currencies from exports. Thus, imports are of secondary importance. Furthermore, since, ideally, imports should be balanced against exports, imports and exports are often linearly correlated, presenting the collinearity problem in econometric analysis. Thus, we consider exports (X) in this book.

considered the important catalysts for economic growth and development. They are commonly called TIG for simplicity. In fact, FDI is regarded as an important means of technological transfer, stimulating domestic investment and human capital development. International trade also stimulates domestic investment, efficient production, and globalization of developing countries. The importance of TIG for open economies, whether developing or developed countries, has been pointed out by various international economic organizations and policy-oriented politicians and economists as evidenced by numerous entries in Google Search or other search engines.[4] The topics of the relations among TIG as development strategies are certainly still currently important and up-to-date for all the open economies.

In the studies among TIG, much less known is the reversed relations of the impact of GDP on exports or FDI. Intuitively, by switching the sides of Y and F or Y and X, in Eq. (1), that is, making F or X the dependent variable and Y the independent variable, we may also see that the growth of Y also affects the growth of F or X. For example, a growing GDP means a growing domestic market or growing industrial activities. This, in turn, will attract inward FDI and increase exports.

Interdependency of the Three Strategies

Thus, the three variables are mutually interdependent and influence each other. In the jargon of econometrics, there is an endogeneity problem among these three variables, as discussed specifically in detail in Chapter 3. It is not clear which variable influences which variable. We submit that, for the academics as well as for the policy makers, it is important to understand causality and intensity of

---

[4]The importance of trade, investment, and growth (TIG) can be seen from the general discussions and reports on websites. The most recent papers and reports include OECD (2015), Samans and Melendez-Ortiz (2016), Udo (2017), UNESCAP (2017), Eckardt, Mishra, and Dinh (2018), CSEA (2018), Government of Canada (2018), etc. All these recent papers show the importance of the topics of this book. Yet, very few books take up the three variables (TIG) simultaneously and study the interaction of TIG academically using econometric methods of causality analysis.

causality (in terms of statistical significance) among each variable or among a group of variables.

For example, the development policy makers in an open economy need to know which sector to emphasize: the foreign sector (trade and FDI) or the domestic sector (GDP), and among the foreign sectors, which factor to emphasize, trade or FDI. These are the problems of causality and the intensity of causality. Our analysis shows the direction of policy making mostly by using the causality analysis in econometrics.

The policy makers also like to know what the historical trend (time-series) is of each variable in TIG, how each pair of two variables (there are three pairs in TIG) are causally related, and then how all three variables interact with one another, what the intensity or importance of such interaction(s) is, and what the **historical trend** of these three variables in each and all countries is. Finally, the policy makers also like to know what the causal directions among each of the three pairs of the variables are or what the causal relations among all the three variables are, etc. This is very important information for policy makers or for any economist. To our knowledge, no book deals with these topics systematically directly or indirectly, and uniquely graphically, in the context of development strategies in open economies.

Thus, the main objective of the first part of this book, and the unique contribution of this book, is to analyze the interactions between these three strategic variables for economic development — exports, FDI, and GDP, namely, the TIG — empirically as well as theoretically and econometrically in the context of emerging East and Southeast Asian countries.

Naturally, openness may risk economic volatility from other countries. Regional trade and investment can be enhanced by reducing friction and volatility through government-to-government trade agreements or coordination. This is another development strategy of open economies among the emerging countries. The second part of this book introduces the role of the United States in the Asia-Pacific region. We then found that, so far as our data are concerned, the monetary policy coordination among the small and large countries does not work. This theoretical discussion of policy coordination is a prelude to the more comprehensive models of free trade agreements (FTA) that were developed later during the last decade of the previous century. After fitting data into the model, we give a plausible justification that monetary policy coordination, to our surprise, does not benefit much for both large and small countries in terms of gain in GDP. The policy makers need to know the problem and its background.

About this Book

This book is a collection of our papers published mostly during the two decades at the turn of the century (1987–2008), the period economists generally consider the emergence of the Asia-Pacific century and the rapid development of the econometric method of causality. As mentioned above, the major players among countries have been the four Asian NIEs and the Association of Southeast Asian Nations (ASEAN), or ASEAN-4, along with China and Japan. The book covers the economic and econometric analysis of these 10 countries, individually or collectively.

In contrast to the mostly descriptive statistical analysis of the World Bank's *The East Asian Miracle* (1993) and most of the literature on economic development, we first use the time-series data to present the descriptive data of exports, FDI, and GDP of each country. We then use quantitative and econometric analyses throughout the book systematically, and like the World Bank, we provide future policy implications for economic development based on our econometric analysis of the three strategic variables — namely, exports, FDI, and GDP — taken individually or collectively, for a country or a group of countries.

We examine these three most important macroeconomic variables in open economies, with emphasis on the impacts of ITC revolution (Chapters 3–6). The book shows how other developing countries in other continents, especially those in Africa and Latin America, can learn from the historical experiences of Asian NIEs and ASEAN4 by studying these three strategic variables. It also explores the possibility of policy coordination among East Asian countries with the USA and Japan.

Since this book is about what we can learn from the historical experiences of emerging Asian NIEs and ASEAN4, the data we use were necessarily taken from the time these countries were "emerging" at various stages of development. Thus, what the book tries to present is "positive economics" (Lipsey, 2008), as well as "normative economics." It is positive economics since what we would like to extract from our analysis are theories and modus operandi which are universal for the emerging open developing countries in this age of globalization, using the historical experiences of Asian NIEs and ASEAN4. As such, our findings should not depend on the specific period of the data we have taken. In other words, the specific time frame of the analysis should not be a problem.

Naturally, the book also presents an aspect of "normative economics," as we would like to rank the importance of economic policies or outcomes for policy recommendations. Thus, this book provides valuable paradigms of economic development for Latin and African countries, and as such, the book is valuable for these emerging developing countries from the economic take-off stage to the mature stage.

Although the chapters were written individually, and the topics were selected based on what we thought were the most important at the time of writing, all chapters are, as explained in the first part of the Introduction and the abstract of each chapter, related to each other very closely and cohesively. They are timely collected in one volume on similar themes for comprehensive understanding of emerging Asian economies, and they are arranged systematically with the level of explanation proceeding from simple to more complex econometric and economic analyses.

For more quantitatively oriented readers or students, we have added new expository appendixes in the book. Thus, this book can also be a supplement to the World Bank's book or any textbook on economic growth and development. As such, it can be a textbook or a reference for graduate or upper undergraduate courses in economics, business, quantitative analysis, applied econometrics, and as a reference for researchers and policy makers at various stages of research.

The book is unique as it provides the first quantitative and comparative analyses of regional economies, economic growth, real and financial linkages, and causality among the strategic economic variables of the open economies in the Asia-Pacific region.

Moreover, countries may invigorate exports and FDI through better cooperation among governments, like current FTA or regional trade agreements like the TPP or the RCEP, which were non-existent or not popular during the writing of these chapters. As a prelude to trade agreements, we have explored the possibility of monetary policy coordination among East Asian countries with the USA and Japan. We believe we have derived a plausible interpretation of why policy coordination was not popular or even possible. Thus, the book will also contribute to the scholarship on the regional studies and cooperation of East and Southeast Asia.

The time-series analysis presented in the book includes unit root tests, cointegration, error correction, Granger causality tests, Sims' exogeneity test, and panel data analysis along with the descriptive statistics. These topics were new (advanced) in econometrics at the time of our writing. They are now standard subjects in many, if not all, undergraduate and introductory graduate econometrics classes as evidenced in Dougherty (2007), Gujarati and Porter (2010), Hill, Carter, Griffiths, and Judge (2000), and Woodridge (2003).

As with any statistical/econometric studies, some of the statistical tests are based on the large sample properties (like the t-test of significance of a sample mean with the unknown population variance), and the studies require a large sample. This is impossible for macroeconomic data like those on GDP, FDI, exports, and imports, etc. Thus, the readers should be aware of the assumptions and limitations made on the econometric analysis and the interpretation of the test results. Nevertheless, it appears that our test results in this book generally yield very reasonable policy interpretations consistent with our economic reasoning and the actual observations.

In each chapter, as shown by the sections inside the chapter, the first several sections explain the relevant economic conditions in detail, with extensive literature review, to enable the reader's understanding of the background of the countries and the objectives

of the chapter. We then explain the need for the use of certain econometric models and the sources of data in detail. Finally, we illustrate
the results of quantitative analysis graphically, acknowledging the
limits of the model and analysis. The conclusion then explores policy
implications of the analysis.

For some inquisitive readers, we have redrawn figures and tables
in this book so that they are more user-friendly, and we have added
several expository notes in the appendixes of this book to help
readers understand the methods of mathematical derivation. While
the quantitative analysis used in several chapters of this book requires
a certain level of econometrics and mathematics, the readers who are
not interested in the quantitative analysis may quickly glance over
the quantitative part and go directly to the concluding remarks on
policy implications of the chapter without a loss of understanding.

This is the third book in the sequel of our research on Asian
Economic Development. We started from the country study of
*Economic Development of Taiwan: Early Experiences and the Pacific
Trade Triangle* (Hsiao and Hsiao, 2015). We expanded our analysis
to *Economic Development of Emerging East Asia: Catching up of
Taiwan and South Korea* (Hsiao and Hsiao, 2017), dealing with
the long-run catching up process and convergence of the two newly
developed countries in East Asia to Japan and the United States.
This book then extends our previous two studies from economic
development of emerging East Asia to that of emerging East and
Southeast Asia, with emphasis on macroeconomic development
strategies and policy implications of open economies.

As in the previous volumes, for those who are interested in our
econometric analysis, we provide the detailed sources of data and
references in each chapter. All the tables and figures are constructed
using Microsoft Excel. We believe that the various methods and
arrangements of statistical data into Excel tables and figures in this
book are also unique and innovative.

The econometrics software programs used in this book were the
EViews software (see www.EViews.com/home.html) for the first six
chapters and the *Micro TSP* program (version 7) for Chapters 7
and 8. Naturally, *EViews* may also be used for these two chapters.

Some data sources may not be readily accessible or even be available. For practice and practical purposes, data can be easily generated by using the methods in Hsiao (2011, pp. 182, 350, 494, 526) applying the random number generating function from the widely and easily available Microsoft Excel program and by referring to the descriptive statistics given in the chapter.

Overview of Chapters

Part I. Emerging East and Southeast Asian Economies — Exports, FDI, and Growth

The first half of the book analyzes the interdependence and interaction among trade/exports, FDI, and economic growth (TIG) of the East and Southeast Asian countries. The second half discusses the role of the United States in Asia and the possibility of policy coordination between the USA and the East Asian countries in this interdependent world.

It is well known that Korea and Taiwan are two countries that had similar historical background before World War II, and developed very closely and rapidly after the war (Hsiao and Hsiao, 2017). It is often claimed that the rapid growth of these two countries has benefited from the export-promotion policy, namely that exports cause economic growth through their impact on the GDP. On the other hand, there are also studies indicating economic growth itself promotes exports, as higher GDP will stimulate imports, and to pay for imports, a country must increase exports to earn the foreign currencies. Hence, the causality between exports and economic growth is one of the controversies in economics.

In this book, we first explore the causality (to be precise, Granger causality, see Appendix 3B of Chapter 3) between exports and economic growth among the Asian NICs in Chapter 1. In fact, Chapter 1 is one of the very early papers in the economic literature, which applies causality and exogeneity tests between exports and GDP for Asian NICs. The Sims' exogeneity test shows that, unlike the general perception that exports may unidirectionally cause GDP, there is a strong bidirectional causality between exports and GDP, indicating both factors influence each other.

In addition to exports strategy, the other important external factor influencing economic growth is inward FDI. It is also an important strategy to promote economic development. There is a vast amount of literature discussing the pros and cons of encouraging FDI to promote economic growth. In view of the importance of FDI in China in the 1990s, Chapter 2 uses panel data to analyze why FDI was attracted, especially from Asian NICs (Korea, Taiwan, Hong Kong, and Singapore) and Japan, to China despite several negative predictions of China's future, while other countries were starving for FDI (thus, we call China a "strange attractor" of FDI).

Few readers are aware of the fact that at the beginning of the Chinese development, FDI in China depended on small- and medium-sized enterprises (SMEs) from Taiwan and Hong Kong, not the large companies from the USA and EU (we submit this observation was new). However, the FDI from Asian NIEs were very small, especially the FDI from Taiwan, which was only US $1 million per case. This implies that, as per development policy, a developing country should not be biased against, or even exclude, small-scale FDI.

On the other hand, we also show in Chapter 2 why Taiwanese investment in China was rational, as it was the smallest per case among other countries. Thus, the Taiwanese FDI took into account its political risk in China, implying the rational expectation of the Taiwanese firms. We also discussed the cultural similarity and geological proximity, and we use panel data analysis to verify our observations.

It is natural to combine these three strategic variables discussed in the previous two chapters — exports, FDI, and GDP, namely, TIG, the three basic macroeconomic variables — simultaneously in an econometric model. This will give us a better picture of the role and interaction of these macroeconomic variables. Chapter 3 studies all three variables systematically for eight emerging East and Southeast Asian economies (China, Korea, Taiwan, Hong Kong, Singapore, Malaysia, the Philippines, and Thailand). After examining the interactions among these three variables in each country, we use both time-series analysis and panel data analysis to compare the results.

The results indicate that since the time-series analysis of each country gives vastly different Granger causality relations, so we conclude that the panel data causality analysis is a superior method of analysis. We also found very useful policy implications from our analysis. In the appendixes of this chapter, for the first time in the economic literature, we give a macroeconomic foundation of using a VAR analysis with regard to TIG, and we explain it in detail along with the method of Granger causality in the appendixes.

Instead of examining individual countries, the econometric analysis may use panel data causality analysis for groups of East and Southeast Asian countries. Noting the different developmental stages of these economies, Chapter 4 supplements the three-variable panel data causality analysis of Chapter 3 to seven Asia-Pacific ANIEs. This is accomplished by constructing a panel of the first-generation ANIEs (Taiwan, Korea, and Singapore) and a panel of the second-generation ANIEs (Malaysia, the Philippines, Thailand, and China). We then combine the two panels into one panel.

The panel VAR Granger causality tests show that the first-generation ANIEs have bidirectional causality relations for all three strategic variables, but only weak causality relations between exports and GDP for the second-generation ANIEs. Thus, we conclude that the stage of development does matter in the causality relations among the three variables. As such, a different government policy is required. The policy implication from this analysis is that the developing country should adopt the export-promotion policy before encouraging inward foreign investment promotion policy.

Chapter 5 extends and expands the analysis of previous chapters and studies the impact of the recent IT revolution on the New Economy of the three Asian NICs, namely, Taiwan, Korea, and Singapore. Here, the economies have interacted with each other through the real linkages of exports and FDI, and they have also interacted through the financial linkage of stock prices. Instead of using the level or the first differences, the model uses volatilities of seven macroeconomic variables: GDP, stock price index, consumer price index, exchange rate, interest rate, narrow money supply (M1), and merchandise exports. The volatilities of variables are measured by the square roots of conditional variances that are generated by the Generalized Autoregressive Conditional Heteroskedasticity (ARCH/GARCH) procedure.

While we have found that the causality among variables differs among countries, the panel data analysis indicates that stock market volatility can cause instability of the exchange rate, GDP, and money supply. Thus, the important policy implication of this finding is that, instead of using the classical thinking of money and finance as a "veil," the government should pay closer attention to the international impact of stock markets.

Part II. The United States and Emerging East and Southeast Asia

The bulk of the US foreign trade has shifted from Europe to Asia during the past two decades. The US trade and investment play an important role in Asia. The US initiation of "rebalancing" in the Asia-Pacific region of the last US administration and recent trade dispute between the USA and China indicate the importance of this region for the USA and the world economy. Hence, studies of the East and Southeast Asian economies and politics could not ignore the impact of the US economy on Asia-Pacific economies. This is another area, in addition to the impact of the recent IT revolution, the 1993 World Bank study needed to emphasize. Hence, Chapters 6–8 in Part II of this book examine the role of the USA in the Asia-Pacific economies and the possibility of policy coordination between the emerging small countries, Taiwan and Korea, and the developed large countries, the US and Japan in Asia.

Chapter 6 evaluates the interdependence between the US economy and Asian economies due to the recent IT revolution. Our tests of four countries — Taiwan, Korea, Japan, and China — show no significant unidirectional causality from the US GDP to that of the four countries, but the US stock price will cause stock market instability in these countries except China. Thus, in general, government stabilization policy in these Asian countries should pay close attention to the external impact from the USA on the stock market, which academic economists tend to ignore.

In view of the spread of instability among nations in this interrelated and interactive world, in an ideal situation, a country may want to coordinate its economic policy with that of the other countries to mitigate, or even eliminate, economic instability, and all countries could reap benefits. Thus, Chapters 7 and 8 introduce a Mundell–Fleming–Dornbusch type two-country game-theoretic model to examine the gain from monetary policy coordination. This is done first between Taiwan and the United States (Chapter 7). We then expand the method in Chapter 7 to study the effect of policy coordination between Taiwan and Korea (small countries) on the one hand and Japan and the United States (large countries) on the other (Chapter 8). We would like to know whether small countries and/or the large countries can benefit from economic policy coordination.

Chapters 7 and 8 present our game-theoretic empirical studies, which are unique in the literature in terms of the theoretical model, country studies, and econometric and simulation analysis. Our results show that policy coordination does not benefit small countries and seems to have no effect for large countries. The results are similar in a larger model in Chapter 8 when we consider a group of small countries (represented by Taiwan and South Korea) and large countries (represented by the United States and Japan). Our analysis gives a plausible justification that monetary policy coordination does not benefit much for both large and small countries in terms of gain in GDP. The policy makers need to know why. Thus, while more studies are needed, it appears that the neoclassical free competition among countries may still be the best modus operandi for all the countries.

Since our research was done some decades ago, the last chapter, Chapter 9, re-evaluates our research results from broader vantage points of current global economy as well as the evolution of economic policy and recent advancement of development strategies and financial development. We show that the results of our research on development strategies of open economies based on the emerging East and Southeast Asia are still very much applicable and illuminative for the researchers and policy makers in this age of globalization.

We have shown the sequence of our studies and their interrelation among the chapters in this Introduction. The topics presented in this book are strongly policy-oriented. Our policy analysis is statistically rigorous, based on statistical inference. The beginning of each chapter has a more detailed abstract of the contents. For students and young researchers, this book may serve as an example of writing research papers in regional studies, as we have received many requests for more information and questions about the papers collected in this volume, especially those in Part I on the time-series and panel data analysis.

References

CSEA (2018). Research Area: Trade, Investment and Growth (TIG), The Center for the Study of the Economies of Africa (CSEA) downloaded in June 2018 from http://cseaafrica.org/trade-investment-and-growth-tig/.

Dougherty, Christopher (2007). *Introduction to Econometrics* (3rd edn., Chapters 12–14). London: Oxford University Press.

Eckardt, Sebastian, Deepak Mishra, and Viet Tuan Dinh (2018). Vietnam's manufacturing miracle: Lessons for developing countries, Brookings Institute. Downloaded in June 2018 from https://www.brookings.edu/blog/future-development/2018/04/17/vietnams-manufacturing-miracle-lessons-for-developing-countries/.

Economist Intelligence Unit (EIU) (2015). *Long-term Macroeconomic Forecasts, Key Trends to 2050. A Special Report from the Economist Intelligence Unit.* Downloaded on 30 July 2016, from http://pages.eiu.com/rs/783 XMC194/images/LongtermMacroeconomicForecasts_KeyTrends.pdf. Relocated to https://espas.secure.europarl.europa.eu/orbis/sites/default/files/g enerated/document/en/Long-termMacroeconomicForecasts_KeyTrends.pdf (January, 2020).

Fensom, Anthony (2015). Asia's Growth Far from Finished: The Region Is Still the World's Engine of Economic Growth. *The Diplomat*, 12 August 2015. Based on an interview with Duncan-Innes Ker of EIU. Downloaded in July 2016 from the website, http://thediplomat.com/2015/08/asias-growth-far-f rom-finished/.

Government of Canada (2018). Canada-Asia Trade and Investment for Growth Program, downloaded in June 2018, from http://international.gc.ca/world -monde/issues_development-enjeux_developpement/priorities-priorites/whe re-ou/brochure.aspx?lang=eng.

Gujarati, Damodar N. and Dawn C. Porter (2010). *Essentials of Econometrics* (4th edn., Chapter 12). New York, NY: McGraw-Hill Irwin.

Hill, R. Carter, William E. Griffiths and George G. Judge (2000). *Undergraduate Econometrics* (2nd edn., Chapters 16 and 17). New York, NY: John Wiley & Sons, Inc.

Hsiao, Frank S. T. (2011). *Economic and Business Analysis: Quantitative Methods using Spreadsheets.* Singapore: World Scientific Publishing.

Hsiao, Frank S. T. (2016). How Bad Is Taiwan's Economy? Compared to other Economies around the World, Taiwan is doing just fine. Featured Article in *The Diplomat*, 22 July. Downloaded in August 2018 from https://thediplom at.com/2016/07/how-bad-is-taiwans-economy/.

Hsiao, Frank S. T. and Mei-Chu Wang Hsiao (2015). *Economic Development of Taiwan-Early Experiences and the Pacific Trade Triangle.* Singapore: World Scientific Publishing, 600 pp.

Hsiao, Frank S. T. and Mei-Chu Wang Hsiao (2017). *Economic Development of Emerging East Asia—Catching Up of Taiwan and South Korea.* London: Anthem Press, 326 pp; Cambridge University Press Cambridge Core 2018.

IMF (2014). *Regional Economic Outlook: Asia and Pacific—Sustaining the Momentum: Vigilance and Reforms.* Washington, D.C.: International Monetary Fund. Downloaded in May 2015 from http://www.imf.org/ external/pubs/ft/reo/2014/apd/eng/areo0414.htm. Relocated to https:// www.imf.org/en/Publications/REO/APAC/Issues/2017/02/23/Sustaining-the-Momentum-Vigilance-and-Reforms (January, 2020).

Lipsey, Richard G. (2008). Positive economics. In *The New Palgrave Dictionary of Economics* (2nd edn.), L. E. Blume and S. N. Durlauf (Eds.). London: Palgrave Macmillan.

OECD (1979). *The Impact of the Newly Industrializing Countries on Production and Trade in Manufactures.* Report by the Secretary-General. Paris: OECD.

OECD (2015). How to connect trade, investment and development. OECD Forum. Downloaded in June 2018, from http://www.oecd.org/trade/connect-trade-investment-development.htm. Relocated to http://www.oecd.org/forum/oe cdyearbook/connect-trade-investment-development.htm (January, 2020).

Samans, Richard and Ricardo Melendez-Ortiz (2016). How can trade and investment underpin growth? *World Economic Forum.* 22 January 2016. Downloaded in November 2017 from https://www.weforum.org/agenda/2 016/01/a-new-agenda-for-global-growth-through-trade-and-investment.

Udo, Bassey (2017). ECOWAS, WTO urge more trade, investment for economic growth. 3 November *Premium Times*, 25 June 2018. (ECOWAS, Economic Community of West African States). Downloaded in June 2018 from https://www.premiumtimesng.com/business/business-news/248269-ec owas-wto-urge-trade-investment-economic-growth.html.

UNESCAP (2017). *Asia-Pacific Trade and Investment Report: Channeling Trade and Investment into Sustainable Development.* NY: United Nations Economic and Social Commission for Asia and the Pacific. Downloaded in June 2018 from https://www.unescap.org/publications/APTIR2017.

Woodridge, Jeffrey M. (2003). *Introductory Econometrics, A Modern Approach* (Chapter 18). Ohio: Thompson/South Western.

World Bank (1992). *World Development Report, 1992.* London: Oxford University Press.

World Bank (1993). *The East Asian Miracle, Economic Growth and Public Policy,* A World Bank Policy Research Report. London: Oxford University Press.
World Bank (2016). East Asia-Pacific Economic Update, April 2016: Growing Challenges. Key findings, downloaded in July 2016 from the website http://www.worldbank.org/en/region/eap/publication/east-asia-pacific-economic-update. Relocated to https://openknowledge.worldbank.org/bitstream/handle/10986/24015/9781464809064.pdf (January, 2020).

Part I

Emerging East and Southeast Asian Economies — Exports, FDI, and Growth

Chapter 1

Tests of Causality and Exogeneity between Exports and Economic Growth — The Case of Asian NICs

Abstract

This chapter presents a detailed econometric investigation using Sims' unidirectional exogeneity test and Granger's causality test to detect the existence and the directions of causality between exports and GDP for the four rapidly developing Asian newly industrializing countries (NICs): Hong Kong, South Korea, Singapore, and Taiwan. In general, our analysis shows that the two tests did not yield the same causal implications for each country. The Sims' test indicates a feedback relationship while the Granger's test indicates no causal relation between the exports and GDP, except for Hong Kong where both tests indicate a unidirectional causality from GDP to exports without feedback. Thus, our results from Sims' test strongly indicate that the rapid economic growth of the Asian NICs is not only achieved with the export promotion policy but also derived from the domestic growth of industries and import substitution.

Keywords: Exports and GDP; Granger causality analysis; economic development; Korea and Taiwan

1.1   Introduction

The opposing views of trade as an "engine" of growth or a "hand-maiden" of growth are well known. For example, Lewis (1980) asserts that trade serves as an "engine" of growth for developing countries that is, the growth of developing countries has depended on their exports to the developed countries. Thus, slower growth in developed countries effects on the growth of developing countries. On the other hand, Kravis (1970) and Riedel (1984) suggest that trade is more likely a "handmaiden" of growth, rather than an "engine"; thus, the recent world recession should not have much effect on the growth of developing countries. In recent years, the phenomenal growth of Japan and the newly industrializing countries (NICs) with their exports promotion policies during 1960s and 1970s (OECD, 1979), the pessimistic prospects for the NICs due to the world recession, and the rise of protectionism in Western countries after the second oil shock (1979–1980) have revived interest in the study of the relationship between trade and economic development.

In many previous studies, the relationship between exports and economic growth has been quantitatively analyzed by Spearman's rank correlation and/or ordinary least-squares (OLS) regression analysis (e.g. Emery, 1983; Feder, 1983; Riedel, 1984). From the econometric point of view, all the above studies were based on the *a priori* assumption that exports are an exogenous variable in the growth equation and no causality tests were offered. However, it is well known that a high degree of correlation does not necessarily imply causation, and a meaningful econometric model requires support from causality tests between variables. Recently, Jung and Marshall have applied Granger's test to examine the direction of causality between the growth rates of exports and GNP for 37 developing countries. Their statistical results show no strong support for the export promotion hypothesis.

The main purpose of this chapter is to apply Sims' unidirectional exogeneity test (Sims, 1972) and Granger's causality test (Granger, 1969) to detect the existence and the direction of causality between exports and GDP for the four Asian NICs: South Korea, Hong Kong, Singapore, and Taiwan. These four countries are widely recognized as the countries which have achieved rapid growth with vigorous export promotion during the past two decades. They also have more or less similar economic conditions, production technology, and social and cultural background compared with other developing countries outside the group (Hsiao and Hsiao, 1983). For these reasons, it is of great interest to study the exports–economic growth relationship for the Asian NICs using the recently developed econometric methods.

Although Sims' test and Granger's test have been applied in econometric studies of other fields (e.g. Schnitzel, 1983), they are seldom used and compared in the study of the relationship between trade and economic growth. In addition, we are able to use the exact Durbin–Watson test and non-parametric run-test to detect the existence of the first-order autoregressive errors, AR(1), in OLS regression residuals. We then apply the maximum likelihood Cochrane–Orcutt iterative procedure to estimate the equations to correct autocorrelated errors. Box–Pierce's Q-statistic is also employed to test for the acceptance of causal model specifications.

In Section 1.2, we specify the causal models between exports and GDP[1] for Granger's test and Sims' test. In Section 1.3, we describe the data sources, variables, and double-log regression functions. In Section 1.4, we explain the econometric procedures used in estimation. In Section 1.5, we present, analyze, and compare the empirical results obtained from the two causality tests. Some concluding remarks are given in Section 1.6.

1.2 Causal Models between Exports and GDP

The basic idea of Granger's causality (Granger) between any two variables X and Y is that X (the right-hand-side independent variable) causes Y (the left-hand-side dependent variable) in a regression equation, if the part of current Y that cannot be explained by the past values of Y is explained by the past values of X. Thus, in the context of the exports–GDP relationship, the Granger's causality

---

[1]The GDP is used instead of GNP, as the growth variable, because GDP is considered as a better measurement for internal economic activities.

test involves estimation of the following two distributed lag regression equations:

$$Y(t) = \alpha + \sum_{i=1}^{m} a(i)Y(t-i) + \sum_{i=1}^{m} b(i)E(t-i) + u(t), \quad (1.1)$$

$$E(t) = \beta + \sum_{i=1}^{m} c(i)Y(t-i) + \sum_{i=1}^{m} d(i)E(t-i) + v(t), \quad (1.2)$$

where $Y(t)$ is the GDP variable at time t ($t = 1, 2, \ldots, n$), $E(t)$ is the exports variable at time t, i denotes the lagged period, m is the predetermined length of lag variables, α and β are constant terms, $a(i)$, $b(i)$, $c(i)$, and $d(i)$ are coefficients, and $u(t)$ (or $v(t)$) is an uncorrelated series of disturbances.

According to Granger's definition of causality, E causes Y if the past values of E in Eq. (1.1), namely, $E(t-1), E(t-2), \ldots, E(t-m)$ taken as a group of additional explanatory variables, have joint significant influence on $Y(t)$, but the past values of Y in Eq. (1.2), namely, $Y(t-1), Y(t-2), \ldots, Y(t-m)$, taken as a group of additional explanatory variables, have no joint significant influence on $E(t)$.

On the other hand, Y causes E if the past values of Y in Eq. (1.2) have joint significant influence on $E(t)$, but the past values of E in Eq. (1.1) have no joint significant influence on $Y(t)$. Lastly, if the past values of E in Eq. (1.1) have joint significant influence on $Y(t)$, and at the same time, the past values of Y in Eq. (1.2) also have joint significant influence on $E(t)$, then there is a bidirectional feedback relationship between Y and E.

Sims proposed an exogeneity test for the existence of unidirectional causality (Sims). According to Sims, if the causality runs one way from the current and past values of some list of exogenous variables to a given endogenous variable, then in a regression of the endogenous variable on future, current, and past values of the exogenous variables, the future values of the exogenous variables should have zero coefficients.

Thus, the application of Sims' test to the case of exports and GDP involves estimation of the following two distributed lag regression equations:

$$Y(t) = a + \sum_{i=-k}^{m} b(i)E(t-i) + e(t), \qquad (1.3)$$

$$E(t) = c + \sum_{i=-k}^{m} d(i)Y(t-i) + w(t), \qquad (1.4)$$

where $Y(t)$, $E(t)$, i, and m denote the same variables as in Eqs. (1.1) and (1.2), $-k$ denotes the lead length of future values of a variable, a and c are constant terms, $b(i)$ and $d(i)$ are coefficients, and $e(t)$ (or $w(t)$) is an uncorrelated series on disturbances.

Thus, E is exogenous to (or causes) Y if the future values of E in Eq. (1.3), namely, $E(t+1), E(t+2), \ldots, E(t+k)$, taken as a group of additional explanatory variables, have no joint significant influence on $Y(t)$. That is, the estimates of $b(i)$'s for $i = -1, \ldots, -k$ in Eq. (1.3) are jointly insignificantly different from zero. Y is exogenous to (or causes) E if the future values of Y in Eq. (1.4), namely, $Y(t+1), Y(t+2), \ldots, Y(t+k)$, taken as a group of additional explanatory variables, have no joint significant influence on $E(t)$. That is, the estimates of $d(i)$'s for $i = -1, \ldots, -k$ in Eq. (1.4) are jointly insignificantly different from zero. If the estimates of $b(i)$'s and $d(i)$'s for $i = -1, \ldots, -k$, are both insignificant, then there is a feedback relationship between Y and E. If the estimates of $b(i)$'s and $d(i)$'s, for $i = -1, \ldots, -k$, are both significant, then there is no causality relation between Y and E.

1.3   Data, Variables, and Double-Log Functions

The statistical data available for the Asian NICs differ slightly in sample size. Annual data from 1960 to 1982 for South Korea and Taiwan, from 1961 to 1982 for Hong Kong, and from 1966 (Singapore became an independent nation in 1965) to 1982 for Singapore were collected. GDP (in USD million) and GDP price deflators (1975 is the base year) were collected from *National Accounts Statistics* yearbooks published by the United Nations, except that Taiwan's GDP was collected from *Statistical Yearbook of the Republic of China*, and GDP price deflators were calculated using the data from *Taiwan Statistical Data Book*, all published by the government in Taiwan.[2] Export data (in USD million) were collected from *Direction of Trade Statistics* yearbooks published by the International Monetary Fund, except that Taiwan's data for 1977 to 1982 were collected from the *Statistical Yearbook* quoted above.

Export price deflators for Hong Kong and South Korea were collected from *National Accounts Statistics yearbooks*. Since there were no export price deflator for Singapore and Taiwan, Singapore's price deflators for manufacturing industries and Taiwan's wholesale price indexes were used as the proxy for their exports price deflators. The GDP and export data are then calculated in real terms.

The functional form often used in the estimation of exports–GDP relationship is a double-natural logarithmic function of the level values of variables, that is, $Y = \ln(\text{real GDP})$ and $E = \ln(\text{real exports})$ in Eqs. (1.1)–(1.4). The main advantage of using a double-log function is that the estimated regression coefficients are the constant elasticity-coefficients with respect to the independent variables. Therefore, we choose to use double-log functions of real GDP and real exports in all Eqs. (1.1)–(1.4). The computer program used is the *SHAZAM Econometrics Computer Program* for IBM-PC/AT microcomputers (White, 1978; White and Horsman, 1985).

1.4   Estimation Methods

Theoretically, the length of distributed lags, m-periods, and leads, k-periods, in Eqs. (1.1)–(1.4) should be long. In practice, however, each additional lag period will cause a loss of one sample point in the estimation process. To avoid the serious loss of data information, we

---

[2]Since 1978, Taiwan has not been a member of the United Nations (UN), and the UN and international Monetary Fund (IMF) have not published statistical data for Taiwan. The *Statistical Yearbook of the Republic of China* and *Taiwan Statistical Data Book* are the official statistical data sources for Taiwan published by the government. The format of statistical tables, definition of terms, and survey methods used in the yearbooks are essentially the same as those used by other countries in the UN and IMF statistical yearbooks.

assign $m = k = 3$ for all equations, except in the case of Singapore where we assign $m = k = 2$ due to a smaller sample size.[3]

For Granger's test, we apply OLS to estimate the coefficients in Eqs. (1.1) and (1.2) for each of the Asian NICs. Since Eqs. (1.1) and (1.2) include the lagged dependent variables as independent variables, it is inappropriate to use the Durbin–Watson d-statistic to test for AR(1) errors. Hence, we have tried to compute Durbin's h-statistic (Judge *et al.*, 1985). However, the values of the h-statistic cannot be computed in all cases, due to the necessity of taking the square root of a negative value in the formula.

Instead, two alternative tests are used: First, a non-parametric run-test is applied to test for general serial correlation (Gujarati, 1978). At the 5% significance level, the results from the run-test show that there is no autocorrelation in OLS residuals in all cases. Second, the Box–Pierce's Q-statistic is also calculated for each of the residual series.[4] Column Q in Table 1.1 reports the calculated Q-values. They range between 1.396 and 11.602. All Q-values are below the critical χ^2 value, 15.987, at the 10% significance level. Thus, the Q-test indicates that we could accept the null hypothesis that the residual series is white-noise and the model specification is thus acceptable for all cases. Hence, the OLS estimates of Eqs. (1.1) and (1.2) are used in the Granger's causality test.

On the other hand, for Sims' test, we first apply the OLS to estimate Eqs. (1.3) and (1.4) and also calculate the probability-value of exact Durbin–Watson d-statistic to test for the existence of AR(1) errors in each regression (Judge *et al.*, 1985).[5] The calculated probability values range between 0.00002 and 0.035 in most cases, except for 0.074 in Singapore's Eq. (1.3), 0.099 in Singapore's Eq. (1.4), and 0.133 in Hong Kong's Eq. (1.4).

---

[3]Jung and Marshall have used two lagged periods in the Granger's causality test.

[4]See Box–Jenkins and Pindyck-Rubinfeld (also see Appendix 1A).

[5]See White and Horsman. The calculated probability value of exact Durbin–Watson d-statistic is the probability of rejecting the null hypothesis that there is no positive AR(1) error.

Thus, at the 10% significance level, the exact Durbin–Watson test indicates that we could not accept the null hypothesis of no positive AR(1) errors in all cases, except Hong Kong's Eq. (1.4).[6] This implies that the existence of AR(1) errors violates the OLS assumption of zero covariance among the disturbances, and the OLS formulas for the variances of the estimators no longer hold. Without correction, we would be unable to test the hypothesis accurately. To correct this problem, we then use the maximum likelihood Cochrane–Orcutt iterative procedure to estimate equations with the first-order autoregressive scheme (Beach and MacKinnon, 1978; Judge *et al.*, 1982). We also calculate Box–Pierce's Q-statistic for each of the residual series estimated from maximum likelihood AR(1) regression.

Column Q in Table 1.2 reports the calculated Q-values. Except for Taiwan's Eq. (1.3), the Q-values range between 3.392 and 12.771. They are below the critical χ^2 value, 14.684, at the 10% significance level. The Q-value for Taiwan's Eq. (1.3) is 18.769, which is below the critical value, 21.666, at the 1% significance level. Thus, the Q-test indicates that we could accept the null hypothesis that the residual series is white-noise and the model specification is acceptable in all cases. Hence, the results of maximum likelihood Cochrane–Orcutt estimation of Eqs. (1.3) and (1.4) are used in the Sims' causality test.

1.5   Empirical Results of the Two Causality Tests

Table 1.1 presents the estimated coefficients, t-ratios, R^2 of Eqs. (1.1) and (1.2), F-statistics,[7] and the causal directions indicated by

---

[6]Only in this Hong Kong case, the problem of first-order autoregressive errors may be considered not serious.

[7]See Kmenta (1986, p. 418). The values of F-statistic were calculated from the formula:

$$F = [(R_Q^2 - R_K^2)/(1 - R_Q^2)][(n - Q)/(Q - K)],$$

where R_Q^2 is the value of R^2 for the regression equation with additional explanatory variables, while R_K^2 is the value of R^2 for the regression equation without the additional explanatory variables, n is the number of observations used in the estimation, Q is the number of coefficients in the regression equation with additional explanatory variables, and K is the number of coefficients in the regression equation without additional explanatory variables.

Table 1.1: OLS Regression Coefficients for Granger's Test

Equation (1)										Causality
a(1)	a(2)	a(3)	b(1)	b(2)	b(3)	Const.	R2	n	Q	F
HK 0.969	0.341	-0.424	0.117	-0.354	0.332	0.268	0.989	19	1.396	0.661
(3.30)	*(0.92)*	*(1.10)*	*(0.39)*	*(0.98)*	*(1.30)*	*(0.56)*				**E –/–>Y**
0.914	0.338	-0.25					0.056	0.987	19	
(3.40)	*(0.97)*	*(0.89)*					*(0.20)*			
0.682	-0.086	0.119	-0.027	0.139	-0.024	2.195	0.994	20	5.547	1.538
Kor *(2.30)*	*(0.25)*	*(0.48)*	*(0.22)*	*(0.85)*	*(0.20)*	*(0.20)*	*(2.00)*			**E –/–>Y**
0.946	0.031	0.005					0.264	0.992	20	
(4.10)	*(0.10)*	0.020)					*(1.20)*			
1.489	-0.519		0.018	-0.007			0.248	0.998	15	5.434	0.000
Sgp *(6.00)*	*(2.10)*		*(0.62)*	*(0.34)*.			*(0.59)*			**E –/–>Y**
1.494	-0.511						0.184	0.998	15	
(6.50)	*(2.30)*						*(1.20)*			
0.448	0.012	0.219	0.23	-0.018	-0.056	1.849	0.996	20	7.136	1.64
Twn *(0.92)*	*(0.02)*	*(0.70)*	*(2.00)*	*(0.13)*	*(0.48)*	*(1.50)*				**E –/–>Y**
1.318	-0.363	0.019					0.303	0.995	20	
(4.60)	*(0.89)*	*(0.08)*					*(1.80)*			

Equation (2)										Causality
c(1)	c(2)	c(3)	d(1)	d(2)	d(3)	Const.	R2	n	Q	F
HK 0.19	-0.095	0.575	0.66	-0.616	0.382	-0.753	0.996	19	####	5.156
(0.9)	*(0.36)*	*(2.1)*	*(3.1)*	*(2.4)*.	*(2.2)*	*(2.2)*				**Y —>E**
			1.121	-0.551	0.415	0.275	0.99	19		
			(4.8)	*(1.6)*	*(1.8)*	*(1.2)*				
Kor -0.666	0.044	-0.075	0.882.	-0.379	0.621	6.223	0.997	20	4.401	2.241
(1.2)	*(0.07)*	*(0.16)*	*(3.8)*	*(1.2)*	*(2.7)*	*(3.0)*				**Y –/–>E**
			0.937	-0.4	0.381	0.954	0.996	20		
			(4.1)	*(1.3)*	*(1.8)*	*(4.0)*				
Sgp -1.3	2.724		0.314	-0.025		-5.761	0.933	15	3.259	1.098
(0.36)	*(0.77)*		*(1.0)*	*(0.08)*		*(0.94)*				**Y –/–>E**
			0.562	0.28		1.603	0.918	15		
			(2.2)	*(1.2)*		*(2.6)*				
Twn -2.35	0.047	1.827	1.514	-0.043	-0.253	3.118	0.991	20	5.308	1.992
(1.7)	*(0.03)*	*(2.0)*	*(4.4)*	*(0.11)*	*(0.74)*	*(0.87)*				**Y –/–>E**
			1.114	-0.359	0.191	0.609	0.987	20		
			(4.7)	*(1.0)*	*(0.83)*	*(2.6)*				

Notes: The absolute values of the estimated t-ratios are in parentheses. At the 5% (or 10%) significance level, the critical value for $F(3, 12)$ is 3.49 (or 2.61), for $F(3, 13)$ is 3.41 (or 2.56), and for $F(2, 10)$ is 4.10 (or 2.92). The Box–Pierce's Q-statistic was calculated from the first 10 lags of the autocorrelation coefficients for each residual series. The critical value of the Q-test is $\chi^2(df = 10) = 15.987$ at the 10% significance level.

Granger's test. In Eq. (1.1), the F-statistic is used here to test the null hypothesis that there is no joint significant influence from the past values of exports on current GDP, that is, to test H_o: $b(1) = b(2) = b(3) = 0$ against the alternative that H_o is not true (see Kmenta, 1986). All F-values in Eq. (1.1), 0.661, 1.538, 0, and 1.64, are below their respective critical values, $F(3, 12) = 2.61$, $F(3, 13) = 2.56$, $F(2, 10) = 2.92$, and $F(3, 13) = 2.56$, at the 10% significance level. Thus, the F-test shows that we could accept the null hypothesis in all cases. This result implies that the past values of exports do not cause the current GDP, and so the hypothesis of exports-oriented growth policy in the Asian NICs is not supported by the empirical results from Granger's test.

On the other hand, in Eq. (1.2), the F-statistic is used here to test the null hypothesis that there is no joint significant influence from the past values of GDP on current exports, that is, to test H_o: $c(1) = c(2) = c(3) = 0$ against the alternative that H_o is not true. In the case of Hong Kong, the F-value, 5.156, is greater than the critical value, $F(3, 12) = 3.49$, at the 5% significance level. Thus, in Hong Kong's case, the F-test shows that we could not accept the null hypothesis, and the causality runs from GDP to current exports. For the other three Asian NICs, the F-values, 2.241, 1.098, and 1.992, are below their respective critical values, $F(3, 13) = 2.56$, $F(2, 10) = 2.92$, and $F(3, 13) = 2.56$, at the 10% significance level. Thus, in the cases of South Korea, Singapore, and Taiwan, the F-test shows that we could accept the null hypothesis, that is, the past values of GDP do not cause current exports. It is rather surprising and disappointing to find that, using Granger's test, there is no evidence of causality from either direction between exports and GDP in the cases of South Korea, Singapore, and Taiwan.

Table 1.2 presents the estimated coefficients, t-ratios, R^2 of Eqs. (1.3) and (1.4), F-statistics, and the causal direction indicated by Sims' test. In Eq. (1.3), the F-statistic is used here to test the null hypothesis that there is no joint significant influence from future values of exports on current GDP, that is, to test H_o: $b(-3) = b(-2) = b(-1) = 0$. In the case of Hong Kong, the F-value, 5.079, is greater than the critical value, $F(3, 8) = 4.07$, at the 5% significance level. The F-test shows that we could not accept the null hypothesis. Thus, in Hong Kong's case, exports are not exogenous to the current GDP.

In the other three Asian NICs, the F-values, 0.634, 1.732, and 0.706, are below their respective critical values, $F(3, 9) = 2.81$, $F(2, 7) = 3.26$, and $F(3, 9) = 2.81$, at the 10% significance level. In these three cases, the F-test shows that we could accept the null hypothesis. Thus, exports are exogenous to (or causes) the current GDP. Note that, in Singapore's case, although the F-test is insignificant, the t-ratio of coefficient $b(-2)$ is large; thus, the causality direction suggested by the F-test may be in doubt. The sum of the coefficients of current and past exports represents the long-run export elasticity; therefore, we have calculated and presented it in the column "Sum of $b(i)$" in Table 1.2. The long-run export elasticities are 0.315, 0.322, and 0.509 for South Korea, Singapore, and Taiwan, respectively.

On the other hand, in Eq. (1.4), the F-statistic is used here to test the null hypothesis that there is no joint significant influence from future values of GDP on current exports, that is, to test H_o: $d(-3) = d(-2) = d(-1) = 0$ against the alternative that H_o is not true. In all four cases, the F-values, 0.229, 0.976, 0.110, and 1.600, are below their respective critical values, $F(3, 8) = 2.92$, $F(3, 9) = 2.81$, $F(2, 7) = 3.26$, and $F(3, 9) = 2.81$, at the 10% significance level. Hence, F-test shows that we could accept the null hypothesis in all four cases. Thus, GDP is exogenous to (or causes) current exports.

Note again that, in Singapore's case, although the F-test is insignificant, the t-ratios of the coefficients of current and past income variables are all very low; thus, the result of causality test may not be accurate. Since the sum of the coefficients of current and past income represents the long-run income elasticity, we have calculated and presented it in the column "Sum of $d(i)$" in Table 1.2. The long-run income elasticities are 1.233, 2.770, 2.466, and 1.913 for Hong Kong, South Korea, Singapore, and Taiwan, respectively.

When we compare the causal directions indicated from the two tests, we find that only in the case of Hong Kong, both causality

Table 1.2: AR(1) Regression Coefficients for Sims' Test

Equation (3)

	b(-3)	b(-2)	b(-1)	b(0)	b(1)	b{2}	b(3)	Const.	b(i)	R2	n	Q	F	Causality
HK	0.727	-0.248	0.622	-0.407	0.244	-0.290	0.241	0.986		0.992	16	7.843	5.079	
	(4.6)	(1.4)	(3.4)	(1.9)	(1.3)	(1.6)	(1.4)	(2.5)						E is not exog to Y
				0.251	0.318	0.006	0.287	1.610		0.976	16			
				(0.93)	(1.3)	(0.02)	(1.1)	(2.0)						
Kor	0.000	-0.159	-0.139	0.182	-0.038	0.299	0.109	8.065		0.993	17	12.32	0.634	
	(0.0)	(1.4)	(1.3)	(1.6)	(0.41)	(3.0)	(1.1)	(20)						E is exog to Y
				0.189	-0.078	0.203	0.001	7.370	0.315	0.991	17			
				(2.0)	(0.89)	(2.3)	(0.02)	(31)	(1.75)					
Sgp	-	0.220	0.060	0.064	0.047	0.056	-	4.726		0.991	13	4.405	1.732	
	-	(3.9)	(1.8)	(1.9)	(1.4)	(1.8)	-	(18)						E is exog to Y
				0.095	0.126	0.101	-	5.950	0.322	0.986	13			
				(3.1)	(4.7)	(3.4)	-	(27)	(6.44)					
Twn	0.072	-0.036	-0.020	0.268	0.109	0.087	0.035	5.253		0.998	17	18.77	0.706	
	(1.8)	(0.84)	(0.47)	(6.4)	(2.8)	(2.2)	(0.95)	(33)						E is exog to Y
				0.262	0.101	0.099	0.047	5.325	0.509	0.998	17			
				(6.4)	(2.4)	(2.3)	(1.2)	(41)	(6.19)					

Equation (4)

	d(-3)	d(-2)	d(-1)	d(0)	d(1)	d(2)	d(3)	Const.	b(i)	R2	n	Q	F	Causality
HK	0.109	-0.254	0.029	0.029	0.020	0.038	1.074	-2.055		0.993	16	3.392	0.229	
	(0.66)	(1.2)	(0.13)	(1.0)	(0.07)	(0.16)	(5.1)	(6.3)						Y is exog to E
				0.104	-0.043	0.046	1.126	-1.972	1.233	0.992	16			
				(0.57)	(0.18)	(0.18)	(5.3)	(6.9)	(2.76)					
Kor	0.923	0.863	0.314	1.331	0.351	-0.632	-0.185	-21.540		0.992	17	6.627	0.976	
	(1.3)	(1.3)	(0.48)	(1.8)	(0.53)	(1.0)	(0.25)	(11)						Y is exog to E
				1.879	0.814	-0.287'	0.364	-19.200	2.770	0.989	17			
				(2.6)	(1.2)	(0.45)	(0.5)	(6.9)	(2.00)					
Sgp	-	-3.482	5.603	1.525	-5.788	4.450	-	-10.912		0.930	13	4.002	0.110	
	-	(0.75)	(0.55)	(0.12)	(0.55)	(0.92)	-	(3.2)						Y is exog to E
				5.015	-6.638	4.089	-	-12.526	2.466	0.928	13			
				(1.2)	(0.92)	(1.0)	-	(4.3)	(0.27)					
Twn	-0.056	0.334	0.823	2.446	-0.865	-1.026	0.263	-10.220		0.997	17	12.771	1.600	
	(0.16)	(0.78)	(2.1)	(6.6)	(2.2)	(2.2)	(0.78)	(13)						Y is exog to E
				2.942	-0.728	-0.698	0.397	-9.914	1.913	0.995	17			
				(7.1)	(1.6)	(1.4)	(1.1)	(12)	(2.19)					

Notes: The absolute values of the estimated t-ratios are in parentheses. At the 5% (or 10%) significance level, the critical value for $F(3,8)$ is 4.07 (or 2.92), for $F(3,9)$ is 3.86 (or 2.81), and for $F(2,7)$ is 4.74 (or 3.26). The Box–Pierce's Q-statistic was calculated from the first 10 lags of the autocorrelation coefficients for each residual series. The critical values of the Q-test for the AR(1) model are $\chi^2(\mathrm{df}=9)=14.684$ at the 10% significance level and 21.666 at the 1% significance level.

tests yielded the same result of a unidirectional causality from GDP to exports without feedback. In the cases of South Korea and Taiwan, the two larger and faster growing countries among the Asian NICs, the two causality tests yielded different results. Sims' test indicates a feedback relationship between exports and GDP, while Granger's test indicates no causal relationship between exports and GDP. In the case of Singapore, the newest and smallest country among the Asian NICs, Sims' test indicates a feedback relationship between exports and GDP with some undesirable t-ratios for the estimated coefficients, while Granger's test indicates no causal relationship between exports and GDP.

1.6 Concluding Remarks

Like many other empirical analyses, the results of a causality test between two variables, either with Granger's test or Sims' test, strongly depend on the data, the functional forms chosen, and the econometric techniques used in the analysis. Using the same set of data from the individual Asian NICs, the Granger's and Sims' causality tests have different causal implications. One common finding from the two tests shows a lack of support for the hypothesis of unidirectional causality from exports to GDP.

On the other hand, if we may call the economic policy of stimulating GDP to induce export increase as the "domestic growth policy," then our test results for Hong Kong even suggest that rapid growth has been not so much a result of the export promotion policy as of the domestic growth policy. Thus, the intuitive experience suggested by the export-led development theory cannot be supported in this empirical study.

This finding is also consistent with that of Jung and Marshall whose conclusion is based on Granger's causality test, which, unlike ours, is applied to the relationship between GNP growth rates and export growth rates for most developing countries.

The results of our Sims' test enable us to go beyond and state that there exists a feedback relation between exports and growth for South Korea and Taiwan, the two larger and faster growing countries among the Asian NICs. Thus, our results strongly indicate that, at least for these two countries, rapid economic growth is not only achieved with the export promotion policy but also derived from the domestic growth of industries and import substitution. We may conclude that the developing countries can learn from the experience of the major Asian NICs to achieve their economic growth by the policies of both export promotion and domestic growth.

This is hardly a surprising recommendation. It, nevertheless, contains many valid points. It is still true that, in addition to the export promotion policy, a country should strive for domestic growth through efficient use of its limited resources to develop more efficient manufacturing industries, utilizing relatively low-cost labor, and creating a stable political and social environment to attract foreign capital and technology.

Naturally, it is theoretically preferable to investigate not only the causality relation between exports and GDP but also other relations involving imports, industrial production, etc. However, rather than complicating the model, we feel that our presentation here may highlight the relation of the two most important policy variables — exports and GDP, which are especially suited for causality tests. We hope that, using our present results, a full-scale model may be constructed in the future.

Appendix 1A

According to Box and Jenkins (1970) and Pindyck and Rubinfeld (1976),

$$Q = n \sum_{k=1}^{N} r_k^2,$$

where n = the length of residual series, K = the length of lags (we assigned $K = 10$ in this study), and

$$r_k = \frac{\sum u(t)u(t-k)}{\sum u(t)^2},$$

which is the kth estimated autocorrelation coefficient.

Acknowledgments

An earlier version of this chapter was presented at the North American Annual Meeting of the Econometric Society at Dallas, Texas, in 28–30 December 1984. The author is indebted to a referee, Professor Robert McNown, and Dr. Eric Ramstetter for their valuable comments and suggestions. All errors that remain are mine.

References

Beach, C. and J. MacKinnon (1978). A maximum likelihood procedure for regression with autocorrelated errors. *Econometrica* **46** (1), 51–58.

Box, G. E. P. and G. M. Jenkins (1970). *Time Series Analysis: Forecasting and Control*. New York: Holden-Day.

Emery, R. F. (1983). The relation of exports and economic growth. *Kyklos* **20** (2), 470–486.

Feder, G. (1983). On exports and economic growth. *Journal of Development Economics* **12** (1–2), 59–73.

Granger, C. W. J. (1969). Investigating causal relations by econometric models and cross-spectral methods. *Econometrica* **37** (3), 424–438.

Gujarati, D. (1978). *Basic Econometrics*. New York: McGraw-Hill.

Hsiao, F. S. T. and M. C. W. Hsiao (1983). Some development indicators of Taiwan: A comparative study. *Journal of Economic Development* **8** (1), 45–58.

Judge *et al.* (1982). *Introduction to the Theory and Practice of Econometrics*. New York: John Wiley and Sons.

Judge *et al.* (1985). *The Theory and Practice of Econometrics* (2nd edn.). New York: John Wiley and Sons.

Jung, W. S. and P. J. Marshall (1985). Exports, growth and causality in developing countries. *Journal of Development Economics* **18** (1), 1–12.

Kmenta, J. (1986). *Elements of Econometrics* (2nd edn.). New York: Macmillan.

Kravis, I. B. (1970). Trade as a handmaiden of growth: Similarities between the nineteenth and twentieth centuries. *The Economic Journal* **80** (320), 850–872.

Lewis, W. A. (1980). The slowing down of the engine of growth. *American Economic Review* **70** (4), 555–564.

OECD (1979). *The Impact of the Newly Industrializing Countries on Production and Trade in Manufactures*. Paris: OECD.

Pindyck, R. S. and D. L. Rubinfeld (1976). *Econometric Models and Economic Forecasts*. New York: McGraw-Hill.

Riedel, J. (1984). Trade as the engine of growth in developing countries, revisited. *The Economic Journal* **94** (373), 56–73.

Sims, C. A. (1972). Money, income, and causality. *American Economic Review* **62** (4), 540–552.

Schnitzel, P. (1983). Testing for the direction of causation between the domestic monetary base and the Eurodollars system. *Weltwirtschaftliches Archiv* **119** (4), 616–629.

White, K. J. (1978). A general computer program for econometric methods-Shazame. *Econometrica* **46** (1), 239–240.

White, K. J. and N. G. Horsman (1985). *SHAZAM: The Econometrics Computer Program User's Reference Manual*. Vancouver: University of British Columbia.

Chapter 2

The Chaotic Attractor of Foreign Direct Investment — Why China?
A Panel Data Analysis

Abstract

One of the key growth factors is foreign direct investment (FDI). In this chapter, we explain that China, one of Asia's newly developing countries, is an "attractor" of FDI because its FDI inflows increased steadily in the 1990s and the early 2000s even though the world FDI inflows have decreased considerably. It is indeed "strange" or "chaotic" since its rates of FDI return are below the world average and predictions of China's economic crisis or collapse are abundant. We find that Hong Kong and Taiwan are predominant players (40–60% of total FDI), followed by the United States and the EU, and the size of investment is generally very small. The concept of the China Circle should be expanded to the East Asia Circle, which is experienced by Taiwan and Korea in earlier decades. We also consider some important characteristics, including regional distribution, geographic proximity, and cultural similarity of these neighboring countries. To avoid spurious regressions, we use panel unit root and cointegration tests developed in the last few years. The data are taken from around 1986 to 2002, and the results from panel data regressions explain our observations quite satisfactorily.

Keywords: FDI in China; determinants of FDI; economic crisis in China; cultural similarity; panel unit roots and cointegration tests

2.1 Introduction

A "chaotic attractor," also called a "strange attractor," is a mathematical term referring to a special set to which dynamic trajectories converge (are attracted). These trajectories are sensitive to initial conditions in that two nearby trajectories follow essentially different paths after a short time (strange), and their paths cannot be predicted (chaotic) (Gabisch and Lorenz, 1989). This chapter uses the term figuratively, and, as a first step, investigates its statistical implications. In examining the world trend of foreign direct investment (FDI), we have found that despite a considerable decrease in world FDI inflows in almost every region and country in the past two years, the inflows to China[1] have increased considerably (attractor), despite the dire institutional defects, corruption, and numerous predictions of upcoming collapse of the Chinese economy (strange). Thus, the future of FDI inflows to China cannot be predicted (chaotic).

As we will review in the following, in recent years there have been a few papers and book chapters dealing with China's inward FDI. However, our chapter differs from the current literature in several respects. First, instead of simply listing the data, we classify China's FDI inflows in a comprehensive and meaningful way. In particular, the inclusion of Taiwan in the group of Asian developed countries enables us to better understand the nature of China's FDI inflows and to relate the success of China with that of Taiwan and Korea in the 1980s. Second, we try to explain large FDI inflows to China despite its perceived crisis and low rates of return on investment, which are inconsistent with the business and economic sense. Third, we pointed out that, probably due to great risk factors, the average

---

[1]In this paper, China means the China Proper, or the Chinese mainland, separate from Hong Kong and Macao.

size of FDI per case is generally small for investors not only from advanced Asian countries and Hong Kong, but also from the United States and EU. Fourth, we emphasize the most recent development, 1990–2002, the period during which China fully opened its domestic market.

Fifth, instead of dealing with a large cross-section of heterogeneous countries, after a careful discussion, we concentrate our studies on five countries, which have invested heavily in China. In particular, we include Taiwan as well as Hong Kong in our studies, as these two economies constitute over 60 percent of China's FDI. Either due to data collection or political ideology, Taiwanese investment in China has been generally ignored in the literature on FDI in China. Sixth, in order to avoid spurious regressions, this chapter draws upon advances in panel data analysis developed in the last few years. It combines testing for unit roots and cointegration from time-series with power from cross-section to form a panel data analysis. Finally, for the first time in the literature, our panel data fixed effects model can explain both the conventional determinants of FDI and the perceived economic and political crisis in China.

In Section 2.2, we first show the world trend of FDI inflows to the developed and developing countries and various regions, especially Southern and Southeast Asian countries, using the detailed UNCTAD data. In Section 2.3, we explain why China has been a "strange" attractor, that is, despite predictions of imminent or near-future collapse of its economy, it has still attracted massive FDI. We then, in Section 2.4, identify the major investors in China and examine their country or ethnic characteristics in Section 2.5. Based on these findings, in Section 2.6, after a brief review of the current literature on the determinants of FDI, we propose a panel data analysis. Section 2.7 concludes.

2.2   The World Trend of FDI — China as an Attractor

China opened her 14 coastal cities (Dalien, Qingdao, Shanghai, etc.) only in early 1985 and published the "Regulation on Encouraging

Investment by Foreign Firms" in late 1986 (CPCB, 2002, p. 67). But the economic reform and FDI intensified only after Deng Xiaoping's southern tour in early 1992. Thus, FDI in China is a recent phenomenon (see the columns of Figures 2.1 and 2.2).

Table 2.1 shows the amount, growth rates, and world share of FDI in major regions and countries[2] from 1991 to 2002. Levels are shown in bold face and in USD billion. The first three rows (Part A) show that the FDI inflow average during the recent period (1997–2002) was US $853 billion per year, which is a 235% (or 3.35 times) increase over the annual average of US $254 billion of the earlier period (1991–1996). Thus, the world FDI increased rapidly. However, it also fluctuated abruptly. It almost tripled from US $482 billion in 1997 to US $1,400 billion in 2000, but fell more than 50% to a mere US $651 billion in 2002. The coefficient of variation[3] is 39%. Thus, the world capital inflows have been volatile in almost all regions and countries. Table 2.1 shows that volatility has been higher among the developed economies (Part B), which have accounted for, on average, 73% of the world FDI inflows (in smaller italic fonts). The United States (62% CV) experienced the greatest fluctuation, then Japan (52%), followed by the European Union (50% CV).

By comparison, the volatility in developing economies (Part C) is subdued (15% CV), although their aggregate world share of FDI inflows has averaged only 24% in the recent period. The ASEAN5 countries (Indonesia, Malaysia, the Philippines, Thailand, and Vietnam) as a whole (Part D) have consistently lost FDI inflow since 1997, except in 2002, and have fluctuated substantially (63% CV), although their world share has been a mere 1.1% in the recent period.

•

---

[2]The data are taken from the data annexes of UNCTAD (2003). Note that the FDI inflow amounts of developed economies and developing economies somehow do not sum to the world total, apparently FDI from free ports (see Table 4.3) are not included.

[3]The coefficient of variation here is defined as the ratio of unbiased (or sample) standard deviation divided by the mean and then multiplied by 100. The last column (CV) of the table is calculated for 1997–2002.

Table 2.1: World Distribution of FDI Inflows

By Host Country and Region, 1991–2002, % and USD Billion

	Avg/yr 91-96	1997	1998	1999	2000	2001	2002	Avg/yr 97-02	CV %
(A) World	**254.3**	**481.9**	**686.0**	**1079.1**	**1393.0**	**823.8**	**651.2**	**852.5**	**39**
Growth rate(%)		89.5	42.4	57.3	29.1	-40.9	-21.0	235.2	
World share(%)	*100.0*	*100.0*	*100.0*	*100.0*	*100.0*	*100.0*	*100.0*	*100.0*	
(B) Developed econ	**154.6**	**269.7**	**472.3**	**824.6**	**1120.5**	**589.4**	**460.3**	**622.8**	**49**
Growth rate(%)		74.4	75.1	74.6	35.9	-47.4	-21.9	302.7	
World share(%)	*60.8*	*56.0*	*68.8*	*76.4*	*80.4*	*71.5*	*70.7*	*73.1*	
European Union	**87.6**	**127.9**	**249.9**	**475.5**	**683.9**	**389.4**	**374.4**	**383.5**	**50**
Growth rate(%)		46.0	95.4	90.3	43.8	-43.1	-3.9	337.9	
World share(%)	*34.4*	*26.5*	*36.4*	*44.1*	*49.1*	*47.3*	*57.5*	*45.0*	
USA	**46.8**	**103.4**	**174.4**	**283.4**	**314.0**	**144.0**	**30.0**	**174.9**	**62**
Growth rate(%)		120.8	68.7	62.5	10.8	-54.1	-79.1	273.4	
World share(%)	*18.4*	*21.5*	*25.4*	*26.3*	*22.5*	*17.5*	*4.6*	*20.5*	
Japan	**0.9**	**3.2**	**3.2**	**12.7**	**8.3**	**6.2**	**9.3**	**7.2**	**52**
Growth rate(%)		262.4	-1.0	299.2	-34.7	-25.0	49.4	706.2	
World share(%)	*0.3*	*0.7*	*0.5*	*1.2*	*0.6*	*0.8*	*1.4*	*0.8*	
(C) Developing eco	**91.5**	**193.2**	**191.3**	**229.3**	**246.1**	**209.4**	**162.1**	**205.2**	**15**
Growth rate(%)		111.2	-1.0	19.9	7.3	-14.9	-22.6	124.3	
World share(%)	*36.0*	*40.1*	*27.9*	*21.2*	*17.7*	*25.4*	*24.9*	*24.1*	
Africa	**4.6**	**10.7**	**8.9**	**12.2**	**8.5**	**18.8**	**11.0**	**11.7**	**32**
Growth rate(%)		131.6	-16.3	37.0	-30.6	121.1	-41.4	153.6	
World share(%)	*1.8*	*2.2*	*1.3*	*1.1*	*0.6*	*2.3*	*1.7*	*1.4*	
South America	**15.0**	**48.2**	**52.4**	**70.3**	**57.2**	**39.7**	**25.8**	**49.0**	**31**
Growth rate(%)		221.9	8.7	34.2	-18.6	-30.7	-34.9	226.8	
World share(%)	*5.9*	*10.0*	*7.6*	*6.5*	*4.1*	*4.8*	*4.0*	*5.7*	
Asia	**59.4**	**109.1**	**100.0**	**108.5**	**142.1**	**106.8**	**95.0**	**110.2**	**15**
Growth rate(%)		83.6	-8.3	8.5	30.9	-24.9	-11.0	85.6	
World share(%)	*23.4*	*22.6*	*14.6*	*10.1*	*10.2*	*13.0*	*14.6*	*12.9*	

(Continued)

Table 2.1: (*Continued*)

	Avg/yr 91-96	1997	1998	1999	2000	2001	2002	Avg/yr 97-02	CV %
(D) East & SE Asia	**56.1**	**100.1**	**90.1**	**105.3**	**138.7**	**97.6**	**88.6**	**103.39**	**18**
Growth rate(%)		78.2	-10.0	16.9	31.7	-29.6	-9.2	84.2	
World share(%)	*22.1*	*20.8*	*13.1*	*9.8*	*10.0*	*11.8*	*13.6*	*12.1*	
(E) NIEs total	**15.5**	**30.0**	**28.0**	**50.1**	**88.6**	**42.4**	**24.8**	**44.0**	**54**
Growth rate(%)		94.0	-6.7	78.9	76.9	-52.2	-41.5	184.5	
World share(%)	*6.1*	*6.2*	*4.1*	*4.6*	*6.4*	*5.1*	*3.8*	*5.2*	
1 **Korea**	**1.2**	**2.8**	**5.4**	**9.3**	**9.3**	**3.5**	**2.0**	**5.4**	**60**
Growth rate(%)		130.5	90.3	72.5	-0.5	-62.0	-44.1	337.2	
World share(%)	*0.5*	*0.6*	*0.8*	*0.9*	*0.7*	*0.4*	*0.3*	*0.6*	
2 **Taiwan**	**1.3**	**2.2**	**0.2**	**2.9**	**4.9**	**4.1**	**1.4**	**2.6**	**65**
Growth rate(%)		71.5	-90.1	1218	68.4	-16.6	-64.8	101.9	
World share(%)	*0.5*	*0.5*	*0.0*	*0.3*	*0.4*	*0.5*	*0.2*	*0.3*	
3 **Singapore**	**6.9**	**13.5**	**7.6**	**13.2**	**12.5**	**10.9**	**7.7**	**10.9**	**25**
Growth rate(%)		97.4	-43.9	74.4	-5.9	-12.2	-30.1	59.1	
World share(%)	*2.7*	*2.8*	*1.1*	*1.2*	*0.9*	*1.3*	*1.2*	*1.3*	
4 **Hong Kong**	**6.1**	**11.4**	**14.8**	**24.6**	**61.9**	**23.8**	**13.7**	**25.0**	**75**
Growth rate(%)		87.7	29.9	66.5	152.0	-61.6	-42.3	313.1	
World share(%)	*2.4*	*2.4*	*2.2*	*2.3*	*4.4*	*2.9*	*2.1*	*2.9*	
(F) ASEAN5 total	**12.8**	**18.7**	**13.3**	**10.5**	**5.2**	**3.4**	**5.1**	**9.3**	**63**
Growth rate(%)		37.9	-34.5	-23.9	-69.4	-43.8	40.6	-27.1	
World share(%)	*5.0*	*3.9*	*1.9*	*1.0*	*0.4*	*0.4*	*0.8*	*1.1*	
5 **Indonesia**	**3.0**	**4.7**	**-0.4**	**-2.7**	**-4.6**	**-3.3**	**-1.5**		
6 **Malaysia**	**5.4**	**6.3**	**2.7**	**3.9**	**3.8**	**0.6**	**3**		
7 **Philippines**	**1.2**	**1.3**	**1.7**	**1.7**	**1.3**	**1.0**	**1.1**		
8 **Thailand**	**2.0**	**3.9**	**7.5**	**6.1**	**3.4**	**3.8**	**1.1**		
9 **VietNam**	**1.2**	**2.6**	**1.7**	**1.5**	**1.3**	**1.3**	**1.2**		
10 **China**	**25.5**	**44.2**	**43.8**	**40.3**	**40.8**	**46.8**	**52.7**	**44.8**	**10**
Growth rate(%)		73.6	-1.1	-7.8	1.1	14.9	12.5	75.7	
World share(%)	*10.0*	*9.2*	*6.4*	*3.7*	*2.9*	*5.7*	*8.1*	*5.3*	
11 **India**	**1.1**	**3.6**	**2.6**	**2.2**	**2.3**	**3.4**	**3.4**	**2.9**	**22**
Growth rate(%)		233.5	-27.2	-17.7	7.0	46.7	1.4	170.2	
World share(%)	*0.4*	*0.8*	*0.4*	*0.2*	*0.2*	*0.4*	*0.5*	*0.3*	

Notes: CV = coefficient of variation. The data are from balance-of-payments statistics. 1997 growth rate is taken as 1997 FDI over the average 1991–1996 FDI.

Source: UNCTAD (2003, Annex Table B1).

The FDI inflows to the NIEs (Part E, Asian Newly Industrializing Economies: South Korea, Taiwan, Singapore, and Hong Kong) have increased considerably between the two periods, except for Singapore, but they also have had a higher degree of fluctuation, especially Hong Kong and Taiwan. Their fluctuation has even exceeded that of the developed economies. The sudden increase in FDI in Hong Kong and Taiwan in 2000 might be due to foreign firms' anticipation of emerging opportunities in China after China's accession to WTO, and their desire to "park funds" in Hong Kong and Taiwan.[4] After 2001, these funds have gone directly into China rather than "routing" through Hong Kong and Taiwan, explaining the drastic decrease in FDI in these two economies in the subsequent two years. A similar explanation may be applied to the decrease in FDI in Korea and Singapore in 2001 and 2002, after their FDIs relocated to China.

China and India are two major exceptions in the world (see the last part of Table 2.1). FDI inflows in both countries have increased steadily since 1997, except for a slight decrease in 1998 and 1999, and both countries showed an increase in FDI inflows even during 2001 and 2002. Comparing the two periods, Chinese FDI increased only 76%, and Indian FDI, 170%, and China had the smallest volatility (10% CV) among the regions and countries listed in Table 2.1 during this period. However, in terms of world shares, India had consistently less than 1%, while China attracted 3–10% of world FDI. In 2002, Chinese FDI inflow was US $52.7 billion, 8.1% of the world share, greatly exceeding the FDI inflow to the United States, US $30 billion, which was 4.6% of the world share. In other words, when the developing countries, especially the governments in the Asia-Pacific regions, were starving for FDI during 2001 and 2002, China alone attracted as much as a quarter to a third of the foreign capital flowing into developing economies.

---

[4]In the 2001 survey of over 3,000 foreign transnational corporations (TNC) in Hong Kong, 45% planned to increase investment in China, while 93% considered the investment climate in China to be favorable or very favorable in the next five years (UNCTAD, 2001, p. 25).

2.3   The Strange Attractor

What makes China so attractive for FDI, and who are the major investors in China? It is certainly not attractive because of the high rate of return on FDI. Table 2.2 shows the rates of return based on FDI income divided by the average FDI stock between the beginning and the end of the year (UNCTAD, 2003, Annex). For individual investment projects, the average return on FDI in China from 1999 to 2001 was 5.9%, lower than the world average of 6.5% as well as the developed countries' average of 6.7%, and only about 1.5% higher than the developing economies' average of 4.4%. Among the 10 Asian countries listed in Table 2.2, the return from FDI in China[5] (5.9%) was much less than the average returns of these 10 countries (7.7%) and less than 50% of that in Hong Kong (12.5%), Malaysia (12.3%), Papua New Guinea (11.3%), and the Philippines (7.3%)

More generally, to see the low rates of return on investment in China from another angle, Gugler, Mueller, and Yurtoglu (2003) calculated the returns (q_m) on corporate investment (not necessarily FDI) as a fraction of the costs of capital[6] in 47 countries. China's five-year return on corporate investment was a mere 45% of its cost of capital, ranked 43rd, much lower than those of ASEAN4 and most of the South American countries, and only about one-half of that of India. Despite the low rates of return on investment, China has attracted a great deal of FDI, as we have seen in Table 2.1, while all

---

[5]Michel Plummer commented on the original paper that "Firms don't immediately expect a return from their investments, gives one explanation of China's low return. They often take quite a while before they generate income that would show up in the BOP. Given that FDI inflows in China are relatively NEW, perhaps this could explain why rates of return are low ... the return on the huge increase in the denominator will only show up in the numerator after a while." However, China's rates of return on investment are still very low even if we consider the period from 1994 to 1999 (Gugler *et al.*, 2003, p. 3, 9).

[6]$q_m = r/i$, where r is the return on a firm's investment, and i is its cost of capital, and is the marginal Tobin's q, that is, "the change in the market value of a firm divided by the change in its capital stock (investment) that caused it" (Gugler *et al.*, 2003, p. 3, 9). It is an ordinary least-squares estimate for each country. Note that, conceivably, the rates of return on FDI investment should be higher than the general corporate investment in order to attract FDI.

Table 2.2: Rates of Return on FDI, Selected Countries

In Percent

	1999	rkg	2000	rkg	2001	rkg	Avg	rkg
	1999		2000		2001		1999-2001	
World average	**7.1**		**6.8**		**5.5**		**6.5**	
Developed countries avg	7.4		7.1		5.7		6.7	
Developing economies avg	4.6		4.3		4.2		4.4	
Hong Kong	13.6	1	12.5	2	11.5	1	12.5	1
Malaysia	11.5	3	14.1	1	11.2	2	12.3	2
Papua New Guinea	13.6	2	10.1	3	10.1	3	11.3	3
Philippines	3.6	6	9.5	5	8.8	5	7.3	4
Kazakhstan	3.2	8	9.6	4	9	4	7.3	5
Azerbaijan	0.1	10	9.3	6	8.6	6	6.0	6
China	**5.6**	**4**	**6.2**	**7**	**5.8**	**8**	**5.9**	**7**
Indonesia	5.5	5	5.7	9	5.4	9	5.5	8
Pakistan	3.4	7	6.1	8	7	7	5.5	9
Korea	3.0	9	3.1	10	3.3	10	3.1	10
Average returns/10 countries	6.31		8.62		8.07		7.7	

Source: UNCTAD (2003, Annex Table A.II.2). The data are from balance-of-payments statistics.

other countries were not attracting, or even losing, foreign capital. Apparently, the law of supply and demand of foreign capital has not been working in the Chinese case.

Praise of the achievement of China's economic reform and development, and its accession to WTO in December 2001, have undoubtedly fostered the expectation of a "1.3 billion consumer market" (Studwell, 2002). However, massive official corruption[7] and governance deficits (Pei, 2002), weak infrastructure, high urban unemployment (15%) (BW, 2004; Formey, 2003), a huge

---

[7] According to the Corruption Perception Index (CPI) of Transparency International, in 2003, China ranked 66th out of 133 countries, and 2002 score of the bribe payer's index was 20th out of 21 countries. Its CPI average from 1995 to 2001 was 3.0, lower than Japan (6.5), Korea (4.3), Taiwan (5.3), Singapore (9.0), Malaysia (5.1), Thailand (3.1), the same as that of the Philippines, but higher than that of Indonesia (2.1). The general theory is that corruption is detrimental to FDI inflows.

national debt (176% of GDP) (Business Week, 2004), enormous non-performing bank loans (45% of outstanding loans) (Business Week, 2004; Lague, 2002), a fragile banking system (Business Week, 2004; Lague, 2002), an agricultural crisis (Wolf *et al.*, 2003), etc., in China are often given as reasons of possible future economic crisis and even collapse in China. In addition to anecdotal horror stories in Chang (2001), Studwell (2002), and Chan (2004), Wolf *et al.* (2003) recently have examined nine potential adversities that China will face over the next decade. Their separate effects of diminishing China's economic growth rates are (% in parentheses): HIV/AIDS and epidemic diseases (1.8–2.2); water shortage and pollution (1.5–1.9); energy shortage (1.2–1.4); Taiwan and other potential crises (1.0–1.3); possible shrinkage of FDI (0.6–1.6); fragility of the financial system and state-owned enterprises (0.5–1.0); corruption (0.5); and unemployment, poverty, and social unrest (0.3–0.8).

Furthermore, a recent Global Competitiveness Report by World Economic Forum (WEF, 2003) ranked China's economic prospects over the next few years as 44th out of 82 countries in the world, due to its deteriorating public infrastructure, severe political corruption, and underdeveloped legal system, etc. China ranked[8] far below Taiwan (5th), Singapore (6th), Korea (18th), Hong Kong (24th), Malaysia (29th), and Thailand (32nd). With these potential economic, social, and political problems or disasters, it is indeed "strange" that China still can attract so much FDI.

2.4 The Major Players

Who are the players in China's capital market, and what are their motives? Table 2.3 shows the major players in China's actual (instead

---

[8]China consistently ranked slightly below the 50 percentile among the countries surveyed in WEF. In 1999, it ranked 32nd out of 59 countries, far below Singapore (1st), HK (2nd), Taiwan (4th), Korea (22nd), but one rank above the Philippines (33rd), Indonesia (37th), and India (52nd). Its growth projections for 2000–2008 in 1999 ranked 17th out of 59 countries, below Singapore (1st), Taiwan (2nd), HK (4th), Indonesia (11th), the Philippines (14th), but above Korea (21st) and Thailand (23rd). Also see Hsiao and Hsiao (2002, pp. 200–203).

of approved) FDI market.[9] The data consist of cases in 1,000, amount in USD million (m) or USD billion (b), and the size (amount per case) in USD million. Levels are in bold face fonts. They are divided into the cumulative FDI up to 1999, and the FDI in 2002. The data are then grouped into six regions. We define the Asian developed countries (ADCs), consisting of Japan, Taiwan, Singapore, and Korea. As usual, if Hong Kong is added, we denote it as ADCs+ in Part A of the table. The cases and amount of FDI from Macao are very small compared with those from Hong Kong; nevertheless, we have listed Macao in the ADCs+ group for reference. Part B: North America consists of the United States and Canada; Part C: ASEAN4, consists of Malaysia, Thailand, the Philippines, and Indonesia; the Part D: European Union, including UK, Germany, France, Netherlands, and 11 others[10]; Part E: Free Ports include Virgin Islands, Cayman Islands, and Western Samoa; and lastly, Part F: "Others" include all other countries. For each category, the total ranking (rkg) of 31 economies (including separate Hong Kong and Macao) is given at the right-hand side of each number. Inside each region, the countries are ranked according to the descending order of the up-to-1999 amount.

Up to 1999, about 342,000 cases and US $308 billion were invested in China (Columns (1) and (3)). Most of them were of very small size, on average US $0.9 million per case, or no more than US $2 million per case.[11] In 2002 alone, 34,000 cases and US $53 billion were invested, and the average size of the investment increased to

---

[9]The Chinese data show the approved and actual amounts of FDI. The approved amount is, on average, twice larger than the actual amount. There is no distinction between approved and actual cases. Here, we consider the cases to be actual cases. For earlier FDI data in Table 4.3, see La Croix *et al.* (1995, p. 16).

[10]They are Italy, Sweden, Belgium, Denmark, Austria, Spain, Finland, Luxembourg, Ireland, Portugal, and Greece. Except Italy (a total of US $0.5 billion) and Sweden (US $0.2 billion), all others had mere 0.1 billion or smaller investment, although their size is larger than Taiwan's US $0.5 million.

[11]If the cases in Table 2.3 are on the approval basis, and if the approval cases are, like the amount, twice larger than the actual cases, then the actual size will be about US $1.8 million, still a very small amount.

US \$1.5 million, an increase of 50%, but still a very small amount indeed.[12]

At a disaggregate level, Table 2.3 shows that, up to 1999, 86% of the cases and 75% of the total amount came from the ADCs+ (see the bordered cells), and Hong Kong alone contributed about half of the total cases (54%) and amount[13] (50%). This predominance has decreased recently, but Hong Kong still had 31% of total cases and 34% of total FDI in China in 2002. The size of the Hong Kong investment doubled in 2002, to US \$1.6 million, indicating a closer tie between China and Hong Kong, but, due to a general increase in the size of investments from other countries, its ranking improved only from 18th to 14th.

The Japanese and Taiwanese investments were a distant second, slightly less than 8% of the total amount for each country up to 1999 and also in 2002, but the number of Taiwanese cases (13–14%) was consistently twice as large as the number of Japanese cases (6–8%), implying that the Taiwanese investment was much smaller per case. In fact, the size of the average Taiwanese investment was the smallest among the countries, a mere US \$0.5–0.8 million, ranking at the bottom 27th or 30th among the 31 countries in Table 2.3, reflecting, perhaps, the political risk and instability between Taiwan and China across the Taiwan Strait.

The other members of ADCs+, Singapore and Korea, played relatively minor roles, but their rankings were still high among the major investors. The average size of a Singapore investment (US \$1.7–2.5 million) was the largest among the ADCs+, larger than that of Japan (US \$1.3–1.5 million), but not as high as investments from

---

[12]Note that the average is misleading. The outliers are Coca Cola which invested \$1.1 billion (in USD, same below), Kodak, \$1.2 billion, Motorola, \$3.4 billion, Proctor and Gamble, \$1 billion, Siemens, \$610 million, and Yum Brands (KFC and Pizza Hut) over \$400 million. They are reported to be profitable (Chang and Wonnacott, 2003).

[13]Part of the Hong Kong investment is actually either Taiwanese investment or Chinese capital from China in disguise, or round-tripping (UNCTAD, 2001, p. 25).

Table 2.3: Cumulative FDI and 2002 FDI into China

1979–1999, and 2002

(in percent and US$)

Country	1979-1999						2002					
	Case		Amount		Size		Case		Amount		Size	
unit	%	Rk	%	Rk	m	Rk	%	Rk	%	Rk	m	Rk
	(1)	(2)	(3)	(4)	(5)	(6)	(7)	(8)	(9)	(10)	(11)	(12)
Grand Total $	**342** *(t)*		**307.6** *(b)*		**0.9**		**34.2** *(t)*		**52.7** *(b)*		**1.5**	
Grand Total %	100		100				100		100			
(A) ADC+ ($)	**274.8** *(t)*		**230.8** *(b)*		**0.8**		**23.9** *(t)*		**31.5** *(b)*		**1.3**	
HK	54.1	*1*	50.3	*1*	**0.8**	*18*	31.1	*1*	33.9	*1*	**1.6**	*14*
Macao	1.9	*8*	1.2	*11*	**0.6**	*26*	1.5	*11*	0.9	*16*	**0.9**	*27*
Taiwan	12.7	*2*	7.8	*4*	**0.5**	*27*	13.9	*2*	7.5	*5*	**0.8**	*30*
Japan	5.5	*4*	8.1	*3*	**1.3**	*11*	7.9	*5*	7.9	*4*	**1.5**	*17*
Korea	3.7	*6*	2.9	*8*	**0.7**	*23*	11.5	*3*	5.2	*6*	**0.7**	*31*
Singapore	2.5	*7*	4.8	*5.0*	**1.7**	*9*	2.7	*8*	4.4	*8*	**2.5**	*10*
Total % of (A)	80.5		75.0				68.6		59.8			
(B) NorthAm ($)	**33.1** *(t)*		**27.7** *(b)*		**0.8**		**4.1** *(t)*		**6.0** *(b)*		**1.5**	
USA	8.4	*3*	8.3	*2*	**0.9**	*17*	9.7	*4*	10.3	*3*	**1.6**	*15*
Canada	1.3	*9*	0.7	*14*	**0.5**	*29*	2.0	*9*	1.1	*13*	**0.8**	*29*
Total % of (B)	9.7	*12*	9.0	*16*			11.7		11.4			
(C) ASEAN4 ($)	**6.6** *(t)*		**5.4** *(b)*		**0.8**		**0.7** *(t)*		**0.9** *(b)*		**1.2**	
Thailand	0.8	*10*	0.6	*16*	**0.7**	*24*	0.5	*18*	0.4	*18*	**1.2**	*23*
Malaysia	0.6	*14*	0.7	*15*	**1.0**	*15*	0.9	*14*	0.7	*17*	**1.2**	*24*
Philippines	0.4	*17*	0.3	*19*	**0.7**	*21*	0.4	*19*	0.4	*19*	**1.2**	*21*
Indonesia	0.2	*19*	0.2	*20*	**1.0**	*16*	0.3	*22*	0.2	*22*	**1.3**	*19*
Total % of (C)	1.9		1.8				2.1		1.6			
(D) EU ($)	**10.3** *(t)*		**21.6** *(b)*		**2.1**		**1.5** *(t)*		**3.7** *(b)*		**2.5**	
UK	0.8	*11*	2.5	*9*	**3.0**	*5*	1.0	*13*	1.7	*11*	**2.7**	*7*
Germany	0.6	*12*	1.6	*10*	**2.3**	*7*	1.0	*12*	1.8	*10*	**2.6**	*8*
France	0.5	*15*	1.2	*12*	**2.3**	*6*	0.5	*17*	1.1	*14*	**3.6**	*4*
Netherlands	0.2	*18*	0.7	*13*	**3.0**	*4*	0.4	*20*	1.1	*15*	**4.5**	*2*
Other EU	1.0		1.1		**1.0**		1.5		1.4		**1.5**	
Total % of (D)	3.0		7.0				4.3		7.0			
(E) Free Ports ($)	**2.4** *(t)*		**11.0** *(b)*		**4.6**		**2.7** *(t)*		**8.2** *(b)*		**3.0**	
Virgin islands	0.6	*13*	3.1	*7*	**4.6**	*2*	5.6	*7*	11.6	*2*	**3.1**	*6*
Western Samoa	0.1	*24*	0.2	*21*	**3.5**	*3*	1.5	*10*	1.7	*12*	**1.7**	*13*
Cayman islands	0.0	*26*	0.3	*18*	**6.3**	*1*	0.6	*16*	2.2	*9*	**5.9**	*1*
Total % of (E)	0.7		3.6				7.7		15.5			
(F) Others ($)	**14.5** *(t)*		**11.1** *(b)*		**0.8**		**2.0** *(t)*		**2.4** *(b)*		**1.2**	
Total % of (F)	4.2	*5*	3.6	*6*			5.6	*6*	4.6	*7*		*20*

Notes: Levels are in bold face, all others are in %. Grand Total % is the sum of Total % of (A) to (F). Note that the number in bold face is the amount or value in *t* (thousands); *b*, in USD billion; and *m*, in USD million. Size is calculated separately by dividing amount by case, and in USD million.

Sources: National Committee of Foreign Economy and Trade; China Statistical Yearbook, various years.

major EU countries, and the size of an average Korean investment was consistently smaller (US \$0.7 million), closer to that of Taiwan.

Beside the ADCs+, the major sources of FDI were from (B) North America, namely, the USA (about 10% in cases and amount), (D) EU (about 3–4% in cases and 7% in amount), (E) Free Ports and "(F) Others." The average size of an EU investment was almost twice that of a USA investment. As expected, investment from (C) ASEAN4 was negligible, less than 2% of total cases and amount. In terms of size, investment from the (E) Free Ports was the largest, ranging from US \$3 million to US \$6.3 million, exceeding the sizes from other areas or countries. In 2002, FDI from the Free Ports was as high as 15.5% of the FDI in China. These free ports are tax-free refuges for foreign funds and their FDI may have consisted of private "returned" funds from anonymous sources in China, Hong Kong, or Taiwan (UNCTAD, 2001, p. 25). Note that the size of the (D) EU investment was also relatively large, larger than that of the USA. However, four countries, UK, Germany, France, and the Netherlands, dominated the EU investment. Investment by other EU members was generally small in amount and size, roughly comparable with that of ASEAN4.

In general, Table 2.3 shows that the predominant players in the FDI inflows to China have been the ADCs+, especially Hong Kong and Taiwan, and the others have been the United States and the EU as a whole. Figure 2.1 shows the time-series trend of the cases, and Figure 2.2 shows the amount of FDI inflows to China, from Hong Kong and Macao (shown by a solid light line, which includes the data on Macao), Taiwan (a solid line with triangle), Japan (a solid line with circle markers), the United States (a dotted line), and EU (a heavy dash line), all measured from the left-hand side axis, and also the total cases of FDI inflows to China in columns, measured from the right Y-axis with Italic axis labels. As expected, since Hong Kong's investment consisted of more than 50% of the total FDI, the shape of the total FDI columns in both figures roughly follows the shape of the Hong Kong FDI. The earlier the data, the stronger this coincidence, especially before 1991, indicating the exclusive contribution to the Chinese economy of Hong Kong investment. After 1992, investment

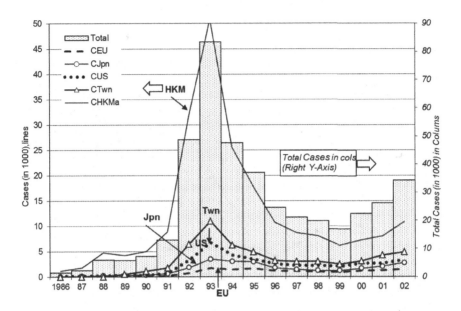

Figure 2.1: Foreign Direct Investment in China
Cases

from Taiwan, Japan, and the USA increased up to 1993, and the Taiwanese investment was next to that of Hong Kong but higher than any of these countries throughout 1986–2002, followed by Japan and the EU. Note that in Figure 2.1, the order of the cases did not change throughout this period.

Figure 2.2 shows the amount of the investment by some major economies. The total amount of inward investment (the columns, measured from the right Y-axis) accelerated from 1992 to 1998 and then decreased somewhat and reached the highest amount in 2002. Taiwanese investment in China (the solid line with triangle markers) was the distant second until 1996, but caught up by Japan in 1996, and by the US and the EU in 1997, and tended to become the lowest among these countries in the early 2000s. Meanwhile, investment from Hong Kong started decreasing after 1997 when Hong Kong was returned to China.

The dotted line with black square markers in Figure 2.2 shows the size (= amount/case) of overall FDI in units of US \$100,000 measured

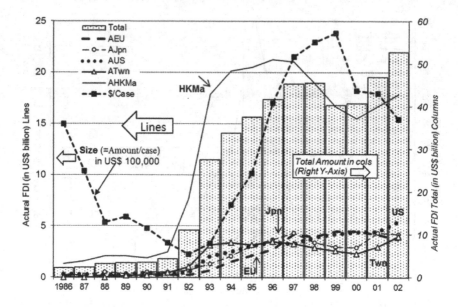

Figure 2.2: Actual Foreign Direct Investment in China
Total Amount and Amount per Case

from the left Y-axis. The overall size was US $1.5 million in 1986, but it steadily decreased to about US $0.2 million in 1992, showing the influx of a great number of small and medium enterprises (SMEs) from Hong Kong (Figure 2.1). The size then increased steadily until 1999 to about US $2.3 million, due to a faster increase in the amount of total investment, then decreased again to US $1.5 million in 2002, due again to influx of mostly SMEs from Hong Kong and Taiwan.

Figures 2.3 and 2.4 show the proportion of the five leading investors in the total FDI from 1986 to 2002. It is clear that before 1992, the five investors dominated the scene, and the proportions of cases (Figure 2.3) and amounts (Figure 2.4) were maintained rather steadily. After 1992, the contribution from other countries and regions increased. However, the three leading investing countries, Taiwan, Japan, and the USA, maintained more or less the same proportions throughout the years. Apparently, EU and other investors expanded in the Chinese capital market at the expense of

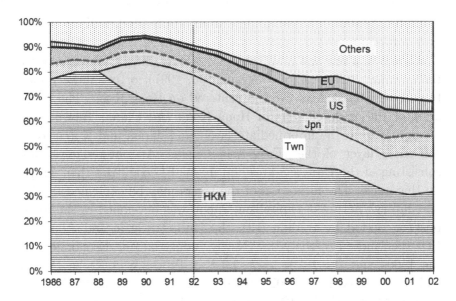

Figure 2.3: Foreign Direct Investment in China

Cases, in % of total, 1986–2002

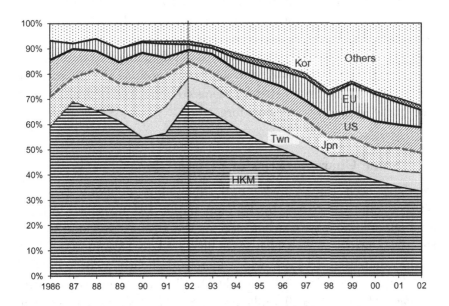

Figure 2.4: Actual Foreign Direct Investment in China

Amount, in % of total, 1986–2002

Hong Kong/Macao investors. The trend appears to continue in the near future.

Figures 2.3 and 2.4 and Table 2.3 vividly show the existence of the so-called "China Circle" (Naughton, 1997), or, what we prefer to call, the "East Asia Circle," centered on Hong Kong. The inner layer of the circle consists of Hong Kong and China. Taiwan and Singapore form the intermediate layer, and Japan and Korea form the outer layer of the "East Asia Circle." An outer–outer layer consisting of the United States and major EU countries then wraps up this circle. The formation of the layers may be explained by the "predatory" nature of capitalism: Japan was developed in the early postwar period by trading with the United States, and Japanese FDI then moved to the NIEs (Newly Industrializing Economies) in the 1960s and the 1970s, especially to Taiwan and Korea (Hsiao and Hsiao, 1989, 1996, 2002, 2003). After the NIEs grew to ADCs+ in the 1980s and the 1990s, they found opportunities in nearby China. All these developed countries are now flocking to China, or have started "exploiting" China. In fact, this phenomenon is nothing new. It happened to Taiwan and Korea from the 1970s to the 1990s (Hsiao and Hsiao, 1996, 2003), while the Chinese, Indian, and Latin American economists were condemning "American and Japanese imperialism" and FDI, which was seen as the vanguard of "imperialist capitalism." History seems to be repeating itself, except that those economists are now forgotten.

2.5   Some Characteristics of FDI to China

We have seen that Chinese FDI inflows are dominated by the ADCs+, and much less by US and major EU investors. Almost all FDI inflows were concentrated in the Eastern Region: 80% of the cases up to 1999, which even increased to 85% in 2002; 86% of the amount up to 1999, which increased slightly to 87% in 2002 (see Hsiao and Hsiao, 2004, Table 5). The size of investment also increased from US $1.0 million to US $1.6 million. The Central Region (12%), and then the Western Region (7%), followed the Eastern Region in ranking. In the Eastern Region, the investment was further concentrated in Guangdong, Jiangsu, Fujian, and Shanghai Municipality. These four locations alone consisted of 50–60% of cases and amount, and they are geographically close to the two major investors: Hong Kong and Taiwan. They, in general, had a larger size per case than the average size of the whole Eastern Region.

The investments in the Eastern Region were further concentrated in five major cities within these provinces: Shenzhen in Guangdong,[14] Xiamen in Fujian, Qingdao in Shandong, Dalian in Liaoning, and Ninpo in Zhejiang. The concentration of FDI in these five cities even exceeded some of the provinces as a whole in the Eastern Region. Combined with the data for the ADCs+ in Table 2.3, it appears that Guangdong, especially Shenzhen, served as the natural hinterland for Hong Kong Chinese, who speak Cantonese, and Fujian, especially Xiamen, served as the natural hinterland for the Taiwanese, who speak South Fujianese. The Japanese and Koreans favored the Northern coastal provinces and cities, such as Shandong and Liaoning.[15] The American and EU investors favored modern political and economic centers like Shanghai, Beijing, or Tianjin, in addition to Guangdong, which is closer to branches in Hong Kong. Thus, because of these unique geographical proximities and language and cultural similarities with neighboring investors,[16] which have lowered the transaction cost of investment, as well as other factors

---

[14] "With the help of capital from Taiwan, the industrial belt stretching from Shenzhen to Dongguan has emerged as the world's largest supplier of information equipment. More than half of the roughly 13,000 foreign companies in Dongguan were ... from Hong Kong, but Taiwan ... has ... 4000 firms (... Japanese companies 300) ... , some 80–90 percent of the parts for such devices can be procured in an area within one-hour distance. The Zhujiang Delta has turned into a veritable battlefield ... It is said that for every firm that successfully moves into China, there is another firm that fails" (Seki, 2003).

[15] For the details of FDI from Hong Kong, Taiwan, and Korea in China, see various chapters in La Croix et al. (1995) and Lee (1996).

[16] The primitive and imperfect legal regime in China made Western MNC wary about security and stability, but benefit overseas Chinese (especially those from Hong Kong) because of cultural and linguistic links (Wei, 1998, p. 336), perhaps through "Guanxi" and corruption.

proposed by neoclassical theory, China has been able to attract various investors.[17]

These various investors also found division of labor in China. Table 2.4 shows China's approved (not actual) FDI by industry and the size per case using the Chinese sources. The actual investment by industry is available only for 2002, and only the approved amount of 2002 is available. Table 2.4 shows again that the actual FDI was only about a half of the approved FDI in 2002. Note that percentage distribution has much smaller differences.

In Table 2.4, from 1979 to 2002, the total approved cases were about 424,000, and the amount was US $828 billion, while in 2002 alone there were about 34,000 cases and US $53 billion. The average size in 2002 was US $2.0 million, more than double the average actual investment size (US $0.9 million) from 1979 to 1999, shown in Table 2.3, although the actual size in 2002 remained the same (US $1.5 million). Despite the difference between approved and actual FDI, the FDI projects are apparently becoming larger and larger recently. The accumulated investment in approved amount, 1979–2002, was 2% into primary industry; 68% into secondary industry, of which 63% went to manufacturing; and 30% into tertiary industry, of which real estate and public service received the lion's share (22%).

The size of the investment also varied. The investment in "health, sports, and social welfare" (US $4.6 million) was the largest, although the total amount in this category was negligible (1%), followed by "real estate and public services" (US $4.0 million) and "transportation and communication" (US $4.0 million). On the other hand, the size of investments in "trading and restaurants" (US $1.2 million) and "manufacturing" (US $1.7 million) were the smallest, along with "science and technology" (US $1.1 million) and "education, culture,

---

[17]In Hsiao and Hsiao (1996, p. 272), we have pointed out that "So far as Japanese investment (in Taiwan) is concerned, geographic proximity, historic ties, and socio-linguistic similarity might have played a more important role than the political stability." Similar statements can be applied to the case in South Korea. Most Taiwanese and Koreans spoke Japanese after World War II (Hsiao and Hsiao, 2003). The Chinese case today is merely a repetition of history, with stronger ties on ethnicity and cultural similarity.

Table 2.4: China's Approved FDI by Industry

1979–2002, 2002

Item	Unit	Approved 1979-2002					Appr'd 2002 Actual 2002						
		Cases		Amount US$		Size US$	Amount US$		Cases		Amount US$		Size US$
		1000	%	b	%	m	b	%	1000	%	b	%	m
Total		**424**	*100*	**828**	*100*	**2.0**	**83**	*100*	**34**	*100*	**53**	*100*	**1.5**
Primary industry		**12**	*3*	**16**	*2*	**1.3**	**2**	*2*	**1**	*3*	**1**	*2*	**1.1**
Secondary Industry		**325**	*77*	**566**	*68*	**1.7**	**61**	*74*	**25**	*74*	**39**	*73*	**1.5**
Manufacturing		**310**	*73*	**524**	*63*	**1.7**							
Construction		**10**	*2*	**23**	*3*	**2.3**							
Transp and commun.		**5**	*1*	**19**	*2*	**4.0**							
Tertiary Industry		**87**	*21*	**247**	*30*	**2.8**	**20**	*24*	**8**	*23*	**13**	*25*	**1.6**
Real est & pub services		**45**	*11*	**181**	22	**4.0**							
Trading and restnts		**21**	*5*	**26**	*3*	**1.2**							
Health, sprts, soc welf		**1**	*0*	**5**	*1*	**4.6**							
Edu, cult, and arts		**1**	*0*	**2**	*0*	**1.6**							
Science & technology		**3**	*1*	**3**	*0*	**1.1**							
Others		**15**	*4*	**28**	*3*	**1.9**							

Notes: m = USD million, b = USD billion. The enclosed cells add to 100% as shown in the Total row.
Sources: National Committee of Foreign Economy and Trade; China Statistical Yearbook, various years.

and arts" (US $1.6 million), and the total amount of the last two categories were also very small (both are less than 0.5%).

Comparing these sizes with the sizes of country investments in China in Table 2.3, a clear picture appears: The EU and Free Ports, and to a lesser degree Japanese, investments were most likely to be in "real estate and public services," followed by "transportation and communication," and a negligible amount went in "health, sports, and social welfare." On the other hand, the Hong Kong, Taiwanese, and Korean investments went into trading and restaurants and small-scale manufacturing, or into small research facilities in science and technology. Thus, each layer of the Asian circle found its niche in Chinese markets.

Table 2.5: FDI Firms in China with US $20 Million or More Exports, 1999

Unit: US$ million (m) or billion (b)

Exports US$ m	No. firms 1999	% chg over 1998	Expts US$ b 1999	% chg over 1998	size US$ m 1998 1999	% of China's total FDI expts
10-30	**1049**	11	**17.1**	11	**16 16**	19 9
30-50	**175**	11	**6.6**	12	**38 38**	7 3
50-100	**134**	12	**9.2**	8	**71 68**	10 5
above 100	**83**	38	**17.6**	37	**214 212**	20 9
Sum	**1441**	13	**50.5**	15	**33 35**	57 26

Note: Unit: USD million (m) or billion (b).
Sources: National Committee of Foreign Economy and Trade; China Statistical Yearbook, various years.

Another characteristic of FDI in China was that exports by the FDI firms that exported US $10 million or more comprised about 57% of total FDI exports, or 26% of China's total exports in 1999 (the last two columns of Table 2.5). In other words, Table 2.5 also implies that the smaller foreign firms (including joint venture) that exported US $10 million or less altogether made 43% of the total FDI exports! Thus, if we include the smaller exporters, it is clear that China's vigorous export activities were indeed supported by FDI: About half of China's total exports were made by FDI (CPCB, 2002, p. 6). Furthermore, from Table 2.5, among the FDI firms that exported US $10 million or more, firms that had annual exports of US $10–30 million and those above 100 million did most exporting. Hence, both small and large firms have exported the same percentage of total FDI exports (19–20%) or total national exports (9%). Thus, small firms also engaged vigorously in export activities.

The firms with annual exports above 100 million grew very fast, 37% from 1998 to 1999, and they had much larger export capability per firm: US $212 million as compared with a mere US $16 million for those firms which exported between US $10 million and US $30 million in 1999. This shows that in recent years the larger FDI firms, in addition to aiming at the domestic markets, have also been taking advantages of lower cost of labor and land, and engage in export activities.

The uniqueness of the Chinese FDI policy is that it has allowed FDI flows into the business of trading and restaurants, real estate, and small-scale manufacturing, which compete directly with local business,[18] and are generally frowned upon by other countries. This policy has resulted in massive inflows of small capital from Hong Kong and Taiwan. There may have been political motives[19] on the part of China to lure the Hong Kong Chinese and the Taiwanese into the "China Circle" for future "unification," but, in any case, we have to take into account this unique FDI policy that is not seen in other countries.

We submit that the smallest size of investment by Taiwan and Korea (merely from US $0.5 million to US $0.8 million) among the various countries (Table 2.3) reflects a rational behavior, especially by the Taiwanese.[20] They internalized political risk and invested only a small amount.[21] From the Taiwanese point of view, the main purpose was to take advantage of lower transaction costs (in terms of geographic proximity and language and cultural similarity) and much lower wage rates (about one-tenth of the Taiwanese rates in early years), which enable them to earn quick profits from exports within a year or so.[22] Our findings for Hong Kong and Taiwan are consistent

---

[18] "In the 1980s and the early 1990s ... Chinese government ... systematically suppressed local entrepreneurs" for the sake of FDI, local "silk manufacturing, ivory sculptures, herbal medicine, ... are populated by foreign firms" (IMF, 2002). Also see Huang (2003).

[19] To attract Taiwanese investment in the Xiamen Special Economic Zone, "The first goal was to promote détente between the two sides of the straits and to increase unification prospects ... The "hot tide" of Taiwan investment ... obliged the Taiwan authorities to retreat, ... induced large changes in Taiwan's policies *vis-à-vis* the mainland" (Wei and Zhu, 1995, p. 119).

[20] Almost 500 Chinese missiles are aiming at Taiwan along the Eastern coast of China. The Taiwan Strait is one of the most insecure areas in the world.

[21] Note also that the scale of Taiwanese FDI in China is also "substantially smaller than Taiwanese FDI in other low wage countries," such as Malaysia and Thailand (Chung, 1997, p. 168).

[22] In Xiamen in the early 1990s, Taiwanese "Small-to-medium-size projects (less than US $1 million) accounted for about 65 percent of all projects. ... and returned

with the current literature, theorized in the paper by Janeba (2002), that, although for different reasons from ours, political risk plays a lesser role in the determination of FDI. Furthermore, their quick profits could be realized easily if their contractors and subcontractors also moved to China (the agglomeration effect). This explains, despite the political risk, the increase in the size and amount of investment from these two countries in recent years (Table 2.3) and also explains the investment from Hong Kong (Figure 2.2).

These attitudes and calculations are reflected in various surveys of some ADCs companies that invested in China. Table 2.6 shows

Table 2.6: FDI Motives and Problems of Foreign Firms in China

Survey, Various Years, in %

Country (sources)	K(a)	J(b)	J(c)	T(d)	Problem faced by	J(c)	T(d)
Year	2002	2001	1986	1998	FDI firms in China	1986	1998
Sample size		131		22		141	22
1 New market opportunity	36.2	55	82	64	Confusing legal system	53	68
2 Lower production cost	42.8	78	23	86	Exchange rate/finance	47	50
3 Easier access to resources	5.6	21	18	64	Exports requirements	32	
4 Follow own and other industries		20	36	73	Lack of infrastructure	31	32
5 To increase exports	4.9				Corruption		45
6 Technology transfer	0.9				Admin inefficiency	14	64
7 Countering trade block	3.1				Quality of workers	12	
8 FDI policy	3.8			14			
9 Others	2.7						
Sum	100.0						

Notes: Automobile parts industry survey in Taiwan. Sample size 22. In (b), (c), (d) multiple answers were allowed.
Sources: (a) Lee (2003); (b) CPCB (2002) JETRO survey; (c) Uehara (1987); (d) Hsiao (1998).

profits almost immediately. ... projects are labor intensive. Nevertheless, ... technology and management were more advanced than Chinese firms, most of the Taiwan firms' products were exported overseas. ... Europe and American (75%), Japan (10%), ..." (Wei and Zhu, 1995, p. 117–118). Chung (1997, p. 187–188) noted that, as Taiwanese exporters face harsh international competition, "even savings of 8 percent ... by producing in China, as compared with 5 percent in ASEAN, are enough to attract FDI into China at the expense of the ASEAN countries."

that, in Taiwan's 1998 survey (Column T(d)) of the automobile parts industry invested in China, as much as 86% and 64% of the firms, respectively, wanted to take advantages of lower production cost and easier access to the resources, while 64% was attracted by new market opportunities as the predominant reasons for investment. Similar results were obtained in Japan's 2001 survey (78%, Column J(b)) and Korea's survey (42.8%, Column K(a)). For these firms, the new market opportunity was not as important, as shown by a comparison of Taiwan (64%), Japan 2001 (55%), and Korea (36%). Only in the 1986 survey of Japan it was indicated that new market opportunities played a predominant role (82% versus 23%). This was because, in the early years, only the larger Japanese MNCs invested in China. Other reasons such as following own and other industries (the agglomeration effects) appear to be recent phenomena and of secondary importance for the Japanese FDI, while increasing exports and China's FDI policy (tax holidays, etc.) were not important for the Korean FDI. Thus, the survey results show that the major variables in conventional theory of FDI, namely, low labor cost and market opportunity, have still held in the case of China with different degrees of emphasis. In the same survey of the Taiwanese and the Japanese firms (the right-hand side of Table 2.6), the most common complaints were confusing legal system, followed by exchange rate/financial uncertainty. For the Taiwanese firms, administrative inefficiency and corruption are also major complaints.

2.6 Panel Data Analysis

Conventional analysis of FDI has been based on FDI among the developed economies, or from developed countries to developing countries. There are two types of multinational corporations (MNCs): Vertical MNC locates production units in different countries to take advantage of lower factor prices, especially wage rates, at a certain stage of production (assembly and packaging, Helpman and Krugman, 1985), while horizontal MNC locates the production of similar products and firms in other countries to avoid trade restriction and expand the market (Horstmann and Markusen, 1992). To

consider special features of FDI inflows to China, such as geographic
proximity and cultural/ethnic similarity (as examined in Sections 2.4
and 2.5), Rauch and Trindade (2002) and Gao (2003) have recently
incorporated ethnic Chinese networks into their FDI inflow models of
China. In their cross-section analysis, a variable is the geographical
distribution of ethnic Chinese in about 70 countries. In our view,
however, as Table 2.3 shows, this is quite irrelevant, as only the
ADCs+, predominantly Hong Kong and Taiwan, and to a lesser
degree Singapore, are the almost exclusive investors. Furthermore,
their analyses did not take time variation and interaction between
the countries into consideration, as shown in Figure 2.2, resulting in
a great loss of information.

In a recent conference paper, Kerr and Peter (2001) have proposed
a time-series analysis of the determinants of FDI in China. Using
the Chinese data alone, they find that the coefficients of wage level,
exchange rates, interest rates, tax regime, and the degree of openness
have "expected signs" and are significant. But their model does not
consider the size of the market, geographical proximity, or cultural
similarity and ethnicity, although these factors play important roles
in the cross-sectional analysis.

In this chapter, we propose a panel data analysis, which has the
merit of using information concerning cross-section and time-series
analyses. It can also take heterogeneity of cross-section data explicitly
into account by allowing for individual-specific effects (Davidson and
MacKinnon, 2004), and give "more variability, less collinearity among
variables, more degrees of freedom, and more efficiency" (Baltagi,
2001). Furthermore, the repeated cross-section of observations over
time is better suited to study the dynamics of changes like FDI
inflows.

In recent years, there are several papers on FDI inflows to
China using panel data analysis. These are ably reviewed and
expanded in the book by Wei and Liu (2001). Their panel data for
realized FDI consist of 29 countries (not including Taiwan), which
comprise 88% of total FDI into China from 1984 to 1998, with
nine independent variables in logarithms, all of which, except the
relative exchange rates, are found to be panel stationary at levels.
Since their independent variables include time-invariant variables like

geographic distance and "total cultural distance" (inappropriately using Taiwan as proxy for China), to avoid multicollinearity, the regression coefficients are estimated by using OLS and the random effects models. They find that relative wage rates, relative market size, exports, imports, country risk, and cultural differences are highly significant in determining FDI inflows to China. However, relative real exchange rate and geographic distance are not significant.

In our panel data analysis, based on Table 2.3, we concentrate our analysis on only five major investors from Hong Kong, Japan, Taiwan, Korea, and the United States, which together comprise 84% of FDI cases and 77% of FDI amount before 1999, and 74% of total FDI cases and 65% of FDI amount in 2002. Our purpose is to find the determinants of FDI in China by the major investing countries by grouping cultural factors and political and economic risk together in the fixed effects model of the panel data analysis, using unbalanced panel data[23] from 1986 to 2002. Based on the theory of MNC, as explained above, and recent study of FDI in general, our dependent variable is the log-value of FDI to China (FDI), which is deflated by China's GDP deflator. We have chosen four independent variables, which are explained briefly in the following.

First, we have the two economies' interaction variable, GDPX (in log-value), which is the product of the ith economy's real GDP and China's real GDP, each being deflated by its own GDP deflator. This variable measures the size of markets as envisioned by the horizontal MNC model and has been used in Rauch and Trindade (2002), although they appear to have a hard time rationalizing its use. Our assumption here is that, after taking the logarithm of the product, 1% increase in China's real GDP and 1% increase in the home country's real GDP have the same percentage impact on FDI flows to China. We may think of a kind of equilibrium situation in which, since the products of FDI in China can be sold either in Chinese markets (horizontal MNC) or exported to the home country (vertical MNC), the effect of percentage change in market size, whether it is of the

---

[23]Taiwan's FDI data are available only from 1989 to 2002, and Korea's data from 1990 to 2002.

host country or of the home country, on the percentage change in FDI is the same.

Second, we have the logarithm of the ratio, WRATIO, of the real annual wage of the home country over that of China, the annual wages being deflated by the consumer price indexes of each country. This ratio captures the advantage of factor differentials as emphasized by the vertical MNC model. Rauch and Trindade (2002) and Gao (2003) use the logarithm of GDP per capita between the ith economy and China as the proxy for the wage/technology differential. However, since this proxy can be interpreted in many ways, and since real wage statistics are available, this chapter does not use the proxy.

Third, we have the variable of openness (OPEN). This is measured by the logarithm of the ratio of the sum of China's imports from the ith economy and China's exports to the same economy divided by China's GDP. This variable measures the perceived openness of the individual country regarding the Chinese market. It is found to have the strongest influence on general FDI inflows by Lipsey (2000).

The last variable is the logarithm of the real exchange rate, EXRATE, which is the nominal RMB per unit of the ith economy's nominal currency multiplied by the ratio of the ith country's consumer price index over China's consumer price index. Theoretically, this variable is an important determinant of international capital flows in the financial market (Hsiao and Hsiao, 2001), although its effects on FDI are complicated and the direction of influence on FDI is not well established.

In the dynamic analysis, we include a one-period lagged dependent variable, FDIP, to account for the effect of agglomeration of FDI, that is, the flows of FDI depend on the amount of existing FDI in the previous period. This is indicated as the fourth FDI motives in the survey of firms presented in Table 2.6.

2.6.1 *Panel Unit Root and Cointegration Tests*

Before we make an estimation, we have to test the unit root for the panel data of six variables. There are several methods of testing unit root under panel data setting. We have chosen three common procedures: Levin, Lin, and Chu (2002) t^* panel unit root test (LLC);

Table 2.7: Panel Unit-Root Tests of the Variables

Variables	Levels			First difference		
	LLC	IPS	ADF-Fisher	LLC	IPS	ADF-Fisher
FDI	-2.933	-1.472	16.728	-5.461	-4.112	35.313
	(0.002)***	(0.071)*	(0.081)*	(0.000)***	(0.000)***	(0.000)***
FDIP	-2.052	-1.748	19.627	-1.746	-2.550	24.171
	(0.020)**	(0.040)**	(0.033)**	(0.040)**	(0.005)***	(0.007)***
GDPX	3.585	3.529	2.184	-4.478	-3.955	35.899
	(0.999)	(0.999)	(0.995)	(0.000)***	(0.000)***	(0.000)***
WRATIO	0.323	0.951	4.510	-5.657	-2.991	25.261
	(0.627)	(0.829)	(0.921)	(0.000)***	(0.001)***	(0.005)***
OPEN	-3.126	-1.261	15.174	-7.280	-3.415	33.671
	(0.001)***	(0.104)*	(0.126)	(0.000)***	(0.000)***	(0.000)***
EXRATE	-1.745	-0.335	9.207	-7.276	-4.942	42.996
	(0.041)**	(0.369)	(0.513)	(0.000)***	(0.000)***	(0.000)***

Notes: Test equation includes individual effects, automatic selection of lags based on AIC: 0 to 2, and the p-values are in the parentheses. *** (**, *) denotes rejection of null hypothesis: unit root at the 1% (5%, 10%) level of significance.

Im, Pesaran, and Shin (2003) IPS-W test; and ADF-Fisher Chi-square panel unit root test (ADF-Fisher) by Maddala and Wu (1999). In all these tests, the null hypothesis is that of a unit root. The test results on the six series are mixed and are reported on the left-hand side of Table 2.7. All these tests show clearly that FDI and FDIP are stationary (no unit roots) at least at the 10% level of significance, but GDPX and WRATIO are non-stationary. The variables OPEN and EXRATE have mixed results. Since two of the tests indicate that OPEN is stationary at least at the 10% level of significance and the p-value of the ADF-Fisher test is only 13%, which means it is very close to the 10% level of significance, we may consider OPEN stationary. This is not the case for EXRATE, as two of the tests indicate unit roots with very high p-values. Thus, we may consider it a non-stationary series.

In short, we have three non-stationary level series: GDPX, WRATIO, and EXRATE. The right-hand side of Table 2.7 then presents the tests of the unit root of the six first-difference series. All

Table 2.8: Johansen Cointegration Tests

GDPX, WRATIO, and EXRATE

Country	Max eigenvalue statistic Null hypothesis: rank = r			k
	$r = 0$	$r < 1$	$r < 2$	
Hong Kong	50.664 *(0.000)****	23.027 *(0.002)****	2.000 *(0.157)*	2
Taiwan	34.973 *(0.000)****	10.037 *(0.210)*	4.561 *(0.033)***	1
Korea	57.850 *(0.000)****	8.711 *(0.311)*	1.135 *(0.287)*	1
Japan	52.562 *(0.000)****	12.367 *(0.100)**	5.603 *(0.018)***	2
USA	49.917 *(0.000)****	24.760 *(0.001)****	18.543 *(0.000)****	2
Fisher Chi-sq. *panel co-integ.*	89.906 *(0.00000)****	37.253 *(0.00005)****	39.505 *(0.00002)****	

Notes: Test equation includes constant and linear deterministic trend, and the p-values are in parentheses. *** (**, *) denote rejection of the null hypothesis at the 1% (5%, 10%) level.

three tests indicate that all the first-difference series are stationary, that is, they are all integrated of order zero, $I(0)$, and so, all the non-stationary level series, GDPX, WRATIO, and EXRATE, are integrated of order one, $I(1)$. This result enables us to go a step further to test panel cointegration of these three-level series.

The upper part of Table 2.8 shows the conventional Johansen cointegration tests for these three variables for individual country. The test results indicate that the three variables are cointegrated in all cases. The last two rows show the Fisher Chi-square test, which aggregates the p-values of individual Johansen cointegration test statistics into the panel cointegration test (Christopoulos and Tsionas, 2003). The Fisher test results clearly show that all three variables are strongly panel cointegrated at the 1% level of significance. The evidence for cointegration is sufficiently strong that we do not have a spurious regression problem. This justifies our use of the six-level series in the following panel regression analysis.

2.6.2 *The Fixed Effects Regression Model*

The fixed effects model (FEM) with the dependent variable FDI and the four observed regressors, GDPX, WRATIO, OPEN, and EXRATE, is specified in Eq. (2.1):

$$\text{FDI}_{it} = \alpha_i + \beta_1 \text{GDPX}_{it} + \beta_2 \text{WRATIO}_{it} + \beta_3 \text{OPEN}_{it}$$
$$+ \beta_4 \text{EXRATE}_{it} + \epsilon_{it}, \tag{2.1}$$

where t denotes the time-series in the ith economy's cross-section unit. The FEM assumes that each intercept, α_i, takes into account the influence from unobserved variables, which may differ across the individual cross-section units. α_i does not vary over time. In addition, the FEM assumes that there are common slope coefficients, β_1 to β_4, in Eq. (2.1) for the five cross-section units as a whole.

The left-hand side of Table 2.9 presents the estimated results from the FEM using all 73 unbalanced observations[24] (1987–2002 for Hong Kong, Japan, and the US; 1990–2002 for Taiwan; and 1991–2002 for Korea) from the five cross-section units. We find that all four common slope coefficients are positive. The first three coefficients are highly significant at the 1% level. However, the coefficient of the exchange rate (EXRATE) is significant at the weak 17% level. For example, β_1 is the estimate of the GDPX elasticity of FDI. This means that when the GDPX increases by 1%, the FDI to China from each country increases by 1.4%, that is, the larger the economy and the market interactions, the higher the FDI inflows to China, and the elasticity is greater than 1. The coefficient β_2 (0.779) of WRATIO means that the wage differential between the ith economy and China has a strong influence in attracting more FDI to China. The coefficient β_3 (0.75) for OPEN is positive and significant at the 1% level. Thus, the higher the openness ratio in China, the more FDI inflows, with the elasticity being less than 1. It also indicates that FDI and trade are complementary, rather than substitute, in China, as can be seen partly from Table 2.5. Lastly, the coefficient β_4

---

[24]In the dynamic model, the lagged variable FDIP starts from 1987. To make static and dynamic models to have the same periods of time-series, all the time-series lost one year in the static model.

Development Strategies of Open Economies

Table 2.9: Panel Data Regression
Unbalanced Fixed Effect Model

Dependent variable: FDI		Sample Size 73				
	Static Model			**Dynamic Model**		
	Coef	t-value	p-value	Coef	t-value	p-value
Intercept						
HKM-C	-14.056	-4.59	0.00 ***	-2.811	-1.09	0.28
TWN-C	-15.083	-4.07	0.00 ***	-2.223	-0.73	0.47
KOR-C	-15.392	-3.23	0.00 ***	-0.454	-0.12	0.91
JPN-C	-19.725	-4.20	0.00 ***	-2.671	-0.68	0.50
USA-C	-23.123	-6.27	0.00 ***	-6.614	-2.00	0.05 **
Slope						
FDIP				0.585	8.10	0.00 ***
GDPX	1.409	6.88	0.00 ***	0.409	2.15	0.04 **
WRATIO	0.779	2.87	0.01 ***	0.063	0.30	0.77
OPEN	0.750	4.91	0.00 ***	0.308	2.55	0.01 ***
EXRATE	0.576	1.40	0.17 *	0.776	2.67	0.01 ***
Adjusted R^2	0.886			0.943		
d.w. (d)	1.339					

Note: Asterisks denote significance at the 1% (***), 5% (**), and 20% (*) levels, respectively.

(0.576) for EXRATE is significant at the weak 17% level. This result is expected because China's RMB is pegged with the US dollar and has very few variations in the exchange rate data during the past few years, and thus, it has had little effect on FDI to China.

We also find that the estimate for each intercept α_i, the fixed effect for each country, is significant at the 1% level. This means that there are some qualitative unobservable variables, such as cultural similarity and ethnicity, economic policy, political factors, potential crises, etc., as we have explained in Sections 2.3 and 2.4, which play very prominent roles in determining FDI to China. Conceivably, cultural similarity and ethnicity have a positive effect on FDI inflows from Hong Kong and Taiwan, and to a lesser degree from Korea and Japan, and favorable economic policy and political measures encourage FDI inflows for all home countries. Detractive factors such as massive corruption, huge national debt, the fragile banking system, etc., have negative effects on FDI inflows. The significant negative intercepts for all countries in Table 2.9 indicate that these negative factors override the positive factors decisively and that there are lower limits (or thresholds) of market size, low wage, and openness before positive FDI inflows can take place. This seems to be reasonable interpretation. Note that Hong Kong, Taiwan, Korea, and Japan, in that order, have smaller negative fixed effects than the United States. This would be because the United States and to a lesser degree Japan are unable to take full advantage of cultural similarity and ethnicity.

We have also estimated the FEM in Eq. (2.1) using 60 balanced observations: 12 observations from 1991 to 2002 each from the five cross-section units. We find that the estimation results are very similar to the results in Table 2.9 using the unbalanced datasets. To save space, we do not present the results here. In addition to running the fixed effects model, we have also considered the random effects model. However, since our countries consist of ADCs+ and the United States chosen from Table 2.3, not selected by random sampling from the population, it is not appropriate to estimate the panel regression using the random effects method.[25]

In general, our empirical findings support the theory that market size, wage differential, openness, and country characteristics, except for exchange rate, are the most important factors in attracting FDI in China for these five economies.[26]

2.6.3 *A Dynamic Panel Model*

The dynamic model at the right-hand side of Table 2.9 considers the agglomeration effect explicitly by including FDIP, the one-period

---

[25]Furthermore, since the number of cross-section units ($N = 5$) is smaller than the number of years ($t = fd12$ or more), the random effects model cannot be used.
[26]In the earlier version of this paper, in which we used nominal variables of GDPX, YDIFF, OPEN, and EXRATE, where YDIF is the difference of per capita GDP between the home country and China as a proxy for wage differential, we estimated the cross-section-specific intercepts and slope coefficients for each country and found that, as the conventional theory predicts, the wage differential was significant for Hong Kong and Taiwan, but not for Korea, Japan, and the United States, and the market size is significant for Korea, Japan, and the United States, but not for Hong Kong and Taiwan.

lagged dependent variable as an independent variable in Eq. (2.1), that is,

$$\text{FDI}_{it} = \alpha_i + \beta_1 \text{FDIP}_{it} + \beta_2 \text{GDPX}_{it} + \beta_3 \text{WRATIO}_{it}$$
$$+ \beta_4 \text{OPEN}_{it} + \beta_5 \text{EXRATE}_{it} + \epsilon_{it}, \tag{2.2}$$

where FDIP is the past FDI which captures the motive for FDI firms which follow the investment of its own or other industry to invest in China. The estimation results show that the coefficient of WRATIO becomes insignificant and that of EXRATE becomes highly significant at the 1% level. The interpretation here is that if a firm follows its own and other industries in investing in China, the group externality accrued to the firm, such as convenience in acquiring intermediate materials, information exchange, and increase in the firm's competition and bargaining power against the local labor, etc., may render low wage rates unimportant. On the other hand, increase in investment projects after the firms follow each other in investing in China increases the export activities and competition, making the exchange rates important in determining FDI inflows.

The dynamic model also makes country characteristics, as indicated by the fixed effects, insignificant for the ADCs+, but not for the United States. The intercept of the USA is a negative large value and significant at the 5% level. This means that under the group effect, the negative factors still affect FDI inflows, but the impact on the ADCs+ becomes less important and not significant. For the United States, cultural similarity, ethnicity, geographic distance, potential crisis in Chinese economy and society, etc., still work heavily against US FDI inflows to China.

Furthermore, we have also tried to estimate the autoregressive distributed lag model (ARDL) by extending the lag length of FDI to two and three as the independent variables in Eq. (2.2). The estimates are not much influenced by the additional lags of FDI.[27]

---

[27]In the ARDL models, the coefficients of FDIP, GDPX, and OPEN are always positive and significant at the 10% level. The coefficient of WRATIO is always insignificant. The coefficient of EXRATE is positive and significant for the models with the lag length at one and two, and it is positive but insignificant for the model with the lag length at three.

2.7 Conclusions

This chapter examines why China has attracted so much FDI in recent years while the world FDI inflows to other countries have been decreasing considerably, and many developing countries have been starving for FDI. In fact, available funds for fast-developing countries have apparently been redirected and reallocated to China. The attraction is not that China has higher rates of return from investment, nor that it is an economically, politically, or socially stable and competitive country. On the contrary, the predictions of its collapse, if not imminent, are abundant. Our statistics show clearly that over one-third to one-half of FDI has been from Hong Kong, the core of the "China Circle," followed by Taiwan and other ADCs, that is, the "East Asia Circle," which was responsible for over 75% of the total FDI in China from 1979 to 1999. Even in 2002, the total investment from ADCs+ was 60%.

However, the existence of the "East Asia Circle" is not new, nor "strange"; it happened to Taiwan and Korea during the "Miracle Growth in East Asia" decades ago (Hsiao and Hsiao, 2003). Thus, as before, the "attraction" has been due merely to language and cultural similarity, geographic proximity, and historical ties. In fact, it is often asserted that the US and European investments in China have been "surprisingly small" (Zhang, 2000; Wei, 1998).

We also find that, while the amount of foreign investment in China has been large, the size of investment per case has been quite small, merely US $1–2 million, internalizing the political and social risk in China. Another evidence of uniqueness is that the ethnic investments have been concentrated in China's Eastern coastal cities and region, roughly distributed along the line of linguistic similarity and geographic proximity, and FDI inflows have shown a division of labor among themselves: The Hong Kong and Taiwanese firms find niches in trading and restaurants and small-scale manufacturing, and the American and EU firms in large-scale real estate, public services, transportation, and communication.

To evaluate the determinants of FDI in China, we propose a panel data analysis. After testing panel unit roots and cointegration to avoid spurious regressions, the estimation results show that the fixed effects are negative and highly significant for each and every country, implying that although China appears to be the "chaotic" or "strange" attractor of FDI, the investors from foreign countries are not "strange," rather, they are, after all, rational, as they apparently have taken into account the dire predictions of possible crisis in the Chinese economy. The estimation results also show how the dire predictions could take place: there is a possibility of sudden stop of capital inflows (Calvo, 1998) to China when real income, wage differential, or the degree of openness falls below certain threshold levels. Furthermore, if some of the potential adversities that China will face (Wolf *et al.*, 2003) come true, or the investors were indeed allured to the expectation of "1.3 billion consumers' market" and the boom in FDI turns out to be a bubble, then considering the extreme volatility of FDI inflows, as shown in Table 2.1, future FDI inflows to China indeed cannot be predicted (chaotic).

The dire prediction notwithstanding, we found that, for the five countries as a whole, real market size and real wage differential affect FDI to China positively, consistent with the theory of horizontal as well as vertical models of MNC. The implication is that, admittedly, for the investors from the United States[28] and Japan, market size plays a more important role in investment decision, and for those from Hong Kong, Taiwan, and Korea, wage differential is a more important factor in deciding investment in China.

When the data are aggregated, both variables have a positive effect on FDI inflows to China in the static model, allowing the possibility of both vertical and horizontal MNC models. After all, the survey results of Table 2.6 also indicate both variables are important, although the importance of wage differential is substituted by the agglomeration effect and exchange rate in the dynamic model. The positive effect of openness on FDI inflows indicates that FDI and trade are complementary. They grow together in the case of China, like the cases of Japan, Taiwan, and Korea a decade or two ago.

---

[28]In an earlier study from 1979 to 1997, Zhang (2000) explained that US FDI was small mainly due to small domestic market size, troubled Sino–US relation, and political instability in China.

The effect of change in exchange rate on FDI is positive, indicating Yuan depreciation will make labor and assets in China cheaper and increase the FDI. The effect is weakly significant in the static model but highly significant in the dynamic model.

In general, while the conclusions of this chapter must be qualified by the data and short time-series, it appears that our fixed effects model can explain why China has been a "strange attractor of FDI," and why it is "chaotic": the future of FDI inflows to China cannot be predicted. The estimation results explain our observations quite satisfactorily.

Appendix 2A: Data Sources

Hong Kong, including Macao, (HKM), Japan (JPN), and the United States (USA) have annual FDI data from 1986 to 2002, and Taiwan (TWN) has annual FDI data from 1989 to 2002, all in US dollars, from China Statistical Yearbook and various official websites, in particular, http://www.mofcom.gov.cn (downloaded in December 2003, in Chinese). Korea's annual data (KOR) from 1990 to 2002 are taken from Lee (2003). US GDP in USD billion is from WDI (2003). GDP in USD billion for other countries, China's imports from the home country, and China's exports to the home country, in USD billion, are taken from ICSEAD (2003).

The GDP deflator and exchange rates (annual average rates) are from IMF (2003), except that Taiwan's data are taken from ICSEAD (2003). Wages in manufacturing (for both men and women) and consumer price general indexes (1990 = 100) are taken from Labor Statistics (LABORSTA), the International Labor Office database website (http//laborsta.ilo.org/). Nonlinear interpolation has been applied to the wage series of Japan and Korea.

Acknowledgments

We are grateful to ICSEAD and Professor Eric Ramstetter for making data available to the authors. We thank Professors Doowon Lee, Keith Maskus, Jaw-Yann Twu, Akio Yamashita, and Kevin H. Zhang who helped us in search of references. We are also thankful for the comments by the following people: professors Michael Plummer, T. N. Srinivasan, Manoranjan Dutta, Richard Hooley, Naci Mocan, Steve Beckman, and Shawn Knabb and the participants of the American Economic Association/American Committee of East Asian Studies Joint Session (AEA/ACAES) on China's economic presence: Implications for the Asia-Pacific region at the 2004 Annual Allied Social Sciences Association (ASSA) Meetings, January, San Diego, CA.

This chapter was originally published as a Discussion Paper in Economics, No. 04-06, Department of Economics, University of Colorado, Boulder, and presented at an Economics Seminar at the University of Colorado at Denver. We are also indebted to Professor Robert McNown and Mr. Kyoo-Hong Cho for their valuable suggestions on econometric analysis. As usual, all errors of omission and commission are the authors. Comments and suggestions on this chapter by Professors Michael G. Plummer of Johns Hopkins University at Bologna, Italy, and T. N. Srinivasan of Yale University when the paper was presented at the above 2004 ASSA meetings, were published in the *Journal of Asian Economics*, 15, 2004, 713–717, 671–672.

References

Baltagi, B. H. (2001). *Econometric Analysis of Panel Data* (2nd edn.). New York: Wiley.

Business Week (2004). *Worrying about China*, 19 January, pp. 28–31.

Cabinet Policy Consolidation Bureau (CPCB, Naikakufu Seisaku Tokatsu Kan) (2002). The Main Courses of China's High Growth and Future Perspective, in *The Trend of the World Economy* (Sekai Keizai no Choryu). Fall. Tokyo: Ministry of Finance Press.

Calvo, G. (1998). Capital flows and capital-market crises: The simple economics of sudden stops. *Journal of Applied Economics* 1 (1), 35–54.

Chan, J. (2004). Analysts Warn China on Verge of Economic Crisis [On-Line]. Available at: World Socialist web site, www.wsws.org/Articles/2004/Feb20 04/Chin-F18_Prn.Shtml. Downloaded February 2004.

Chang, G. G. (2001). *The Coming Collapse of China*. New York: Random House.

Chang, L. and P. Wonnacott (2003). Adapting to Chinese customs, cultural changes: Companies from U.S., Europe find profit. *Wall Street Journal*.

Christopoulos, D. K. and E. G. Tsionas (2003). A reassessment of balance of payments constrained growth: Results from panel unit root and panel cointegration tests. *International Economic Journal* 17 (3), 39–54.

Chung, C. (1997). Division of labor across the Taiwan strait: Macro overview and analysis of the electronic industry. In *The China Circle, Economics and Electronics in the PRC, Taiwan, and Hong Kong* [Chapter 6], B. J. Naughton (Ed.). Washington, DC: Brookings Institution Press.

Davidson, R. and J. G. Mackinnon (2004). *Econometrics Theory and Methods.* New York: Oxford University Press.

Formey, M. (2003). Workers' Wasteland, Cover Story. *Time Asia.* Available at: http://www.time.com/Time/Asia/Covers/1101020617/Cover.Html. Relocated to http://content.time.com/time/world/article/0,8599,2054705,00.html (January, 2020).

Gabisch, G. and H. W. Lorenz (1989). *Business Cycle Theory: A Survey of Methods and Concepts.* Berlin: Springer-Verlag.

Gao, T. (2003). Ethnic Chinese networks and international investment: Evidence from inward FDI in China. *Journal of Asian Economics* **14**, 611–629.

Gugler, K., D. C. Mueller and B. B. Yurtoglu (2003). Corporate Governance and the Returns on Investment (Finance WP No. 06/2003). European Corporate Governance Institute, University of Vienna.

Helpman, E. and P. Krugman (1985). *Market Structure and Foreign Trade.* Cambridge: MIT Press.

Horstmann, I. J. and J. R. Markusen (1992). Endogenous market structures in international trade. *Journal of International Economics* **32**, 109–129.

Hsiao, F. S. T. and M. C. W. Hsiao (1989). Japanese experience of industrialization and economic performance of Korea and Taiwan–Tests of similarity. In *Advances in Financial Planning and Forecasting: Supplement 1, Taiwan's Foreign Investment, Exports, and Financial Analysis,* S. C. Hu and C. F. Lee (Eds.). JAI Press, pp. 157–190.

Hsiao, F. S. T. and M. C. W. Hsiao (1996). Taiwanese economic development and foreign trade. In *Harvard Studies on Taiwan: Papers of the Taiwan Studies Workshop: I,* pp. 199–270. The John K. Fairbank Center for East Asian Research, Harvard University. Also in J. Y. T. Kuark (Ed.), *Comparative Asian Economies, Contemporary Studies in Economic and Financial Analysis* 77 (Part B), 211–302. An International Series of Monographs. Greenwich, CT: JAI Press.

Hsiao, F. S. T. and M. C. W. Hsiao (2001). Capital flows and exchange rates: Recent Korean and Taiwanese experiences and challenges. *Journal of Asian Economics* **12** (3), 353–381.

Hsiao, F. S. T. and M. C. W. Hsiao (2002). Taiwan in the Global Economy — Past, Present, and Future. In Peter C. Y. Chow (Ed.), *Taiwan in the Global Economy, From an Agrarian Economy to an Exporter of High-Tech Products.* 161–222. Westport, MA: Praeger.

Hsiao, F. S. T. and M. C. W. Hsiao (2003). 'Miracle Growth' in the twentieth century — International comparisons of East Asian development. *World Development* **31** (2), 227–257.

Hsiao, F. S. T. and M. C. W. Hsiao (2004). The chaotic attractor of foreign direct investment — Why China? Paper presented at *The AEA/ACEAS Joint Session of the 2004 ASSA Annual Meeting,* January, San Diego,

CA. Discussion Paper in Economics, No. 04-06. Department of Economics, University of Colorado, Boulder.

Hsiao, F. S. T. and M. C. W. Hsiao (2015). *Economic Development of Taiwan — Early Experiences and the Pacific Trade Triangle*. Singapore: World Scientific Publishing.

Hsiao, F. S. T. and M. C. W. Hsiao (2016). *Economic Development of Emerging East Asia–Catching Up and Convergence*. London: Anthem Press.

Hsiao, T. T. (1998). A study of comparison, division of labor, and interaction of the automobile industry on both sides of the straits (in Chinese). *The Quarterly Journal of the Bank of Taiwan* **49** (3), 89–123.

Huang, Y. (2003). *Selling China*. UK: Cambridge University Press.

Im, K. S., M. H. Pesaran and Y. Shin (2003). Testing for unit roots in heterogeneous panels. *Journal of Econometrics* **115**, 53–74.

International Centre for the Study of East Asian Development (ICSEAD) (2003). *East Asian Economic Perspectives, Special Issue*. February. Japan: Kitakyushu.

International Monetary Fund (IMF) (2002). Foreign Direct Investment in China: What Do We Need to Know? *Transcript of an Economic Forum*, 2 May.

International Monetary Fund (IMF) (2003). *International Financial Statistics* (IFS). CD-ROM. January.

Janeba, E. (2002). Attracting FDI in a politically risky world. *International Economic Review* **43** (4), 1127–1155.

Kerr, I. A. and V. M. Peter (2001). The Determinants of Foreign Direct Investment in China. Paper Presented at *The 30th Annual Conference of Economists*, University of Western Australia, September.

La Croix, J. S., M. Plummer and K. Lee (Eds.) (1995). *Emerging Patterns of East Asian Investment in China from Korea, Taiwan, and Hong Kong*. New York: M.E. Sharp.

Lague, D. (2002). On the Road to Ruin. *Far Eastern Economic Review*, **14** November, 32–35.

Lee, D. (2003). Trade Balance Effects of Korea's Foreign Direct Investment into China. Paper Presented at The *Conference on Korea and the World Economy, II*. University of Washington, Seattle, 1–2 August.

Lee, J. S. (Ed.) (1996). *The Emergence of the South China Growth Triangle*. Taiwan: Chung-Hua Institution for Economic Research.

Levin, A., C. F. Lin and C. Chu (2002). Unit root tests in panel data: Asymptotic and finite-sample properties. *Journal of Econometrics* **108**, 1–24.

Lipsey, R. E. (2000). Inward FDI and economic growth in developing countries. *Transnational Corporations* **9** (1), 67–95.

Maddala, G. S. and S. Wu (1999). A comparative study of unit root tests with panel data and a new simple test. *Oxford Bulletin of Economics and Statistics* **61**, 631–652.

Naughton, B. (Ed.) (1997). *The China Circle, Economics and Electronics in the PRC, Taiwan, and Hong Kong*. Washington, DC: Brookings Institution Press.

Pei, M. (2002). China's governance crisis. More than musical chairs. *Foreign Affairs* **81** (5), 96–109.

Rauch, J. and V. Trindade (2002). Ethnic Chinese networks and international trade. *Review of Economics and Statistics* **84**, 116–130.

Seki, M. (2003). A shenzhen incubator for Small Japanese firms. *Focus Japan (JETRO)* **30** (3), 10–11.

Studwell, J. (2002). The China Dream: The Quest for the Last Great Untapped Market on Earth. *Grove/Atlantic Monthly*.

Uehara, K. (1987). *Economic Reform and Openness Policy in China: Socialism under Open System* (in Japanese). Tokyo: Aoki Shoten.

UNCTAD (United Nations Conference on Trade and Development) (2001). *World Investment Report 2001: Promoting Linkages*. New York and Geneva: United Nations.

UNCTAD (2003). *World Investment Report 2003, FDI Policies for Development: National and International Perspectives*. New York and Geneva: United Nations.

Wei, S. J. (1998). China's Absorption of Foreign Direct Investment. In H. Lee and D. W. Roland-Holst (Eds.), *Economic Development and Cooperation in the Pacific Basin: Trade, Investment, and Environmental Issues* [Chapter 10], H. Lee and D. W. Roland-Holst (Eds.). Cambridge, UK: Cambridge University Press.

Wei, S. S. and L. Zhu (1995). The Growth of Foreign and Taiwan Investment in the Xiamen Special Economic Zone. In *Emerging Patterns of East Asian Investment in China from Korea, Taiwan, and Hong Kong*. [Chapter 7], Croix et al. (Eds.). NY: M.E. Sharp.

Wei, Y. and X. Liu (2001). *Foreign Direct Investment in China–Determinants and Impact*. UK: Edward Elgar Publishing Limited.

Wolf, C., Jr., K. C. Yeh, B. Zycher, N. Eberstadt and S. H. Lee (2003). *Fault Lines in China's Economic Terrain*. CA: Rand.

World Bank (2003). *World Development Indicators* (WDI). CD-ROM. Washington, D.C.: World Bank.

World Economic Forum (WEF) (2003). *The Global Competitiveness Report*. Cambridge, MA: WEF.

Zhang, K. H. (2000). Why is U.S. direct investment in China so small? *Contemporary Economic Policy* **18** (1), 82–94.

Chapter 3

FDI, Exports, and GDP in East and Southeast Asia — Panel Data versus Time-Series Causality Analyses

Abstract

Foreign direct investment (FDI) discussed in Chapter 2 is only one of the growth factors in economic development. Other major factors are exports and gross domestic product (GDP). What are the causal relations among these three factors? Economists often take two of the three variables at once and find the effects of one variable on the other using time-series analysis, presumably because that simplifies the analysis. Thus, each country has different relations and no unified theory emerges. In this chapter, we consider all three factors simultaneously and compare the results from time-series analysis and panel data analysis. For the first time in the literature, we present the theoretical framework of the vector autoregression (VAR) form for the Granger causality tests. We then use time-series and panel data from 1986 to 2004 to examine the Granger causality relations between GDP, exports, and FDI among China, Korea, Taiwan, Hong Kong, Singapore, Malaysia, the Philippines, and Thailand and the eight rapidly developing East and Southeast Asian economies. After reviewing the current literature and testing the properties of individual time-series data, we estimate the VAR of the three variables to find various Granger causal relations for each of the eight economies. We find that each country has different causality relations and, therefore, the analysis does not yield general rules. We then construct the panel data of the three variables for the eight economies as a group, and we use the fixed effects and random effects methods to estimate the panel data VAR equations for Granger causality tests. The panel data causality results reveal that FDI has unidirectional effects on GDP directly and indirectly through exports, and there also exists bidirectional causality between exports and GDP for the group. Our results indicate that the panel data causality analysis has superior results over the time-series causality analysis. Economic and policy implications of our analyses are then explored in the conclusions.

Keywords: FDI, exports, and GDP; panel data causality analysis; Granger causality analysis; economic development; East and Southeast Asia

3.1 Introduction

In the neoclassical growth model, technological progress and labor growth are exogenous, inward foreign direct investment (FDI) merely increases the investment rate, leading to a transitional increase in per capita income growth but has no long-run growth effect. The new growth theory in the 1980s endogenizes technological progress and FDI has been considered to have permanent growth effect in the host country through technology transfer and spillover. As the world FDI inflows increased steadily and tremendously from US $208 billion in 1990 to almost US $1397 billion in 2000, although it decreased to US $648 billion in 2004 (Hsiao and Hsiao, 2004; UNCTAD, 2006), there is ongoing discussion on the impact of FDI on a host country economy, as can be seen from recent surveys of the literature (de Mello, 1997, 1999; Fan, 2002; Lim, 2001). Most of the studies find positive effects of FDI on transitional and long-run economic growth through capital accumulation and technical or knowledge transfers, especially under an open trade regime (e.g. Basu *et al.*, 2003; Neuhaus, 2006).

However, some studies show that these positive effects may be insignificant, or the effects may even be negative (Carkovic and Levine, 2005), possibly due to crowding out of domestic capital or development of enclave economies. Some also point out that the multinational corporations (MNCs) tend to locate in more productive, fast-growing countries or regions; thus, FDI inflows could be attracted to the growing economies and markets. In short, the causality of FDI and economic growth can run bidirectionally and may pose simultaneity problems to single-equation regression analysis.

In an open economy, technology and knowledge may also be transferred through exports and imports, and thus promote economic growth.[1] However, growth also has effects on trade (Rodriguez and Rodrik, 2000). In the development literature, this is known as the relation between trade regime/outward orientation and growth (Edwards, 1993). In empirical analysis, the policy of outward orientation is generally measured by exports (Greenaway and Morgan, 1998). As such, the topic of exports-growth nexus has been a subject of extensive debate since the 1960s, as can be seen from a recent comprehensive survey of more than 150 papers by Giles and Williams (2000). They found, surprisingly, that there is no obvious agreement to whether the causality dictates export-led growth or growth-led exports, although the early cross-section studies favor the former.[2]

The observations on the FDI-growth nexus and the exports-growth nexus lead us to examine the closely related third side of a triangular relation: the FDI–exports nexus. Perhaps, because the FDI–exports relation affects economic growth indirectly, the FDI–exports nexus has received less attention in academic discussions, and a comprehensive survey of the topic does not seem to exist. Like the other nexuses, the direction whether "FDI causes exports" or "exports cause FDI" is also a matter of dispute (Petri and Plummer,

---

[1]See Frankel and Romer (1999); Frankel *et al.* (1996); Grossman and Helpman (1997, Chapter 9).

[2]Using cointegration and causality tests, Wernerheim (2000) found bidirectional causality between exports and growth.

1998). Trade and FDI are related positively (complement) between asymmetric countries and negatively (substitute) between symmetric countries (Markusen and Venables, 1998).

They also depend on whether FDI is market-seeking (substitutes) or efficiency-seeking (complements) (Gray, 1998), "trade-oriented" or "anti-trade-oriented" (Kojima, 1973), or at the early product life-cycle stage (substitute) or at the mature stage (complement) (Vernon, 1966). Thus, the relation may be positive or negative, if there is a relation at all. On the other hand, exports increase FDI by paving the way for FDI by reducing the investors' transaction costs through the knowledge of the host country's market structure. FDI may also reduce exports by manufacturing goods directly in the host countries to save transportation costs.

The above three kinds of nexus have been studied separately using methods of correlation, regression, or Granger's bivariate causality tests. Very few studies have taken all three variables together or have used panel data causality analysis. The purpose of this chapter is to find the causality relations between FDI, exports, and gross domestic product (GDP) (a proxy for economic growth) among the rapidly growing eight economies in Asia: four East Asian economies: China, Korea, Taiwan, and Hong Kong, and four Southeast Asian countries: Singapore, Malaysia, the Philippines, and Thailand. In addition to time-series analysis for individual economy, we propose to use panel data causality analysis, available only in recent years, for group causality test.

In what follows, in Section 3.2, we present briefly the analytical framework of the interdependence of the three variables in an economy using the mini-general equilibrium Keynesian-type demand-oriented open economy model. This is the basis of the vector autoregression (VAR) analysis in Sections 3.6 and 3.7. In Section 3.3, we explain and justify the choice of the eight economies by examining their historical performance of real GDP per capita from the global economic perspectives. The eight economies are known for their rapid growth through the promotion of exports and encouragement of FDI inflows. We could expect some kinds of causality relations among these three variables in these economies.

Section 3.4 examines the statistical characteristics of the data in each economy and also among the eight economies. In Section 3.5, we review some recent empirical literature on the causality relations among the three variables in a country or a group of countries. In Section 3.6, we first assess the Granger causality relations of each economy using time-series data from 1986 to 2004. In Section 3.7, we construct the panel data from all eight economies and then apply the fixed effects model (FEM) and the random effects model (REM) to estimate the panel data VAR and perform the Granger causality test. The last section concludes by summarizing our findings and discusses the policy implications.

3.2 The Analytical Framework

While it is rather intuitively clear that FDI and exports may promote growth of GDP and that exports and FDI are somehow related, when all three variables are combined, it is rather obscure how they are related in the context of an economic model. The general practice in the literature routinely takes the relations as given in an *ad hoc* manner[3] or expands a production function linearly to make connections. However, here we show that the theoretical underpinning of the econometric model can be derived from the national income model.

For simplicity, we assume equilibrium in the money sector and the government sector. Then, the equilibrium condition[4] of the Keynesian model of aggregate demand and aggregate supply is

$$Y = C(Y) + I(Y, r) + F + X - M(Y, e), \qquad (3.1)$$

where Y, C, I, F, X, M, r, and e are the real GDP, real consumption, real domestic investment, real FDI inflows, real exports, real imports, interest rate, and exchange rate of foreign currency in terms of the

---

[3] An *ad hoc* argument is that when testing the effects of "openness" on growth, both exports (or trade) and FDI should be considered in the true sense of "openness." Omitting one will commit the omission of variable error, rendering the causality relations ambiguous. See Ahmad *et al.* (2004) and Cuadros *et al.* (2004).

[4] Note that (3.1) is an equilibrium condition, not an identity.

domestic currency, respectively. $X - M(Y, e)$, is the current account surplus in domestic currency of the host country.

Since we are interested in the real aspect of the economy, ignoring the financial variables, and writing in more general implicit function form,[5] we have

$$H(Y, X, F) = 0. \qquad (3.2)$$

Thus, we examine the causality relations among the real variables Y, X, and F. If certain regularity conditions are satisfied, the nonlinear functions $C(Y)$, $I(Y, r)$, and $M(Y, e)$, or more directly, Eq. (3.2) can be expanded logarithmically around the origin $(1, 1)$ by the Taylor expansion. Taking the linear part of the variables, regressing each of the three variables on the other two variables, and taking the lags of each variable for the purpose of econometric analysis, we have the prototype of a VAR form for the Granger causality test. Equation (3.3) in Section 3.6.2 shows the final form of the VAR model, which may be written either in levels or in differenced series (see Appendix 3C for details).

3.3   East and Southeast Asia in the World Economy

Instead of lumping many countries in different parts of the world with different backgrounds and stages of development in cross-section analysis, this chapter deals only with eight Asian economies. To show the unique development position of the eight economies in the world economy, Figure 3.1 presents real GDP per capita of the eight economies and other world geographic regions[6] compiled

---

[5] Our theoretical underpinning points out that interest rates and exchange rates are not controlled in the VAR model, and thus points to a shortcoming of this VAR analysis in the literature as a whole. Note that, to be consistent in this linear formulation, there is no room for product terms and other physical variables. This national income model is also elaborated in Chapter 4.

[6] All the data are taken directly from Maddison (2003), measured in internationally comparable 1990 Geary–Khamis dollars (also see Hsiao and Hsiao, 2003a). 8LA consists of Argentina, Brazil, Chile, Colombia, Mexico, Peru, Uruguay, and Venezuela; 7EEC are Albania, Bulgaria, Czechoslovakia, Hungary, Poland, Romania, and Yugoslavia; the 12WECs are Austria, Belgium, Denmark, Finland,

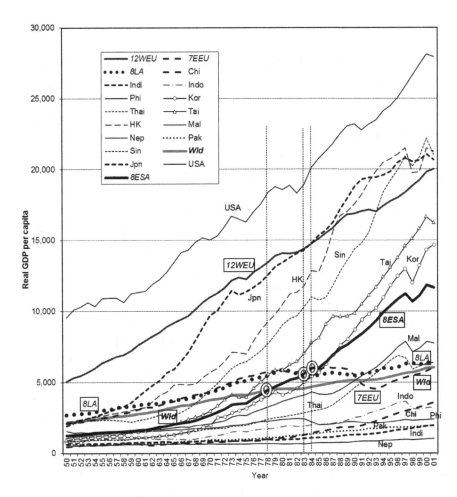

Figure 3.1: Real GDP Per Capita
East and Southeast Asia and the World

by Maddison (2003). The lines are rather cluttered and hard to distinguish. However, our purpose here is only to show how rapidly the real GDP per capita levels of the eight Asian economies have grown and stand out in the world economy during the postwar

France, Germany, Italy, The Netherlands, Norway, Sweden, Switzerland, and the UK.

period. Japan and the USA are included in the figure just for comparison.

Indeed, the diagram shows vividly that the growth of the so-called Asian Newly Industrializing Economies (NIEs), Taiwan (Tai), Korea (Kor), Singapore (Sin), and Hong Kong (HK), are conspicuous, especially compared with other Asian countries such as Nepal (Nep), India (Indi), Pakistan (Pak), China (Chi), Malaysia (Mal), Thailand (Thai), etc., the average of the eight Latin American countries (8LA, the heavy dotted line), the seven East European countries (7EEC, the lower dashed line), or the world average (Wld). While the two small city-state economies, Singapore and Hong Kong, had already caught up with the average of the 12 Western European countries (12WEU, the upper heavy dark line), Taiwan (Tai, the line with triangle markers) and Korea (Kor, the line with circle markers) are growing closer to each other and are also poised to catch up with the average real GDP per capita levels of the 12WEU (also see Hsiao and Hsiao, 2004).

It is interesting to see that in 1950, the levels of real GDP per capita of Japan (Jpn, the heavy dashed line), Singapore (Sin, the dotted line), and Hong Kong (HK, the gray dashed line) were almost the same as that of the world. However, after 50 years of development, they exceeded the average of the 12WEU between the late 1980s and the early 1990s. Taiwan and Korea started well below the world average in 1950, grew side-by-side (Hsiao and Hsiao, 2003a), and accelerated considerably in the 1980s. Malaysia (Mal, the light grey line), Thailand (Thai, light dotted line), the Philippines (Phi, the lower light grey line), and China (Chi, the lower heavy dashed line) also grew after mid-1980s. However, Malaysia and Thailand are only slightly above the world average, but China and the Philippines are still well below the world average.

In general, in 1950, the average real GDP per capita of the eight East and Southeast Asian economies (8ESA, the heavy dark line) was only about 60% of the world average or only 50% of the average of the 8LA economies, but it surpassed the world average by 1978 (the first double circle), and the Latin American average by 1983 (the second double circle). In 1984, it surpassed the average of the 7EEC (the third double circle) and has been growing continuously.

Figure 3.1 also shows that the 8ESA economies as a whole really took off relative to other world regions after the mid-1980s. Clearly, the period of the mid-1980s is the bifurcation point that the eight Asian economies forked out from the other regions, like an open pair of scissors, and has become the most dynamic region in the world. In view of their success, it is of great interest to find the sources of the rapid growth of these eight economies. By examining their dynamic phase, instead of prolonged period, we wish to reduce the possible heterogeneity problem among the countries in the process of estimation: this heterogeneity problem in studying the causality has been pointed out by Nair-Reichert and Weinhold (2000). Thus, we have chosen the data from 1986 to 2004 for our study.

Elsewhere, Hsiao and Hsiao (2003b) examined how the recent information technology (IT) revolution has increased interdependence in terms of the real linkage through trade and investment, and the financial linkage through stock markets, among these eight economies along with the United States and Japan. Recently, applying a gravity-coefficient index to East Asia and Southeast Asia, Petri (2006) shows that the regional interdependence of these eight Asian economies has increased since the mid-1980s, as compared with other periods. These works justify our choice of the countries and the time period for our analysis.

Furthermore, during the dynamic development phase of these eight economies, they alone were the largest recipients of inward FDI among the developing countries; in fact, in recent years, about 50% of the total inward FDI which went to the developing countries in the world (Hsiao and Hsiao, 2004) went to these eight economies. As the inward FDI increases, their intraregional exports and interregional exports to other regions also grew considerably (Hsiao and Hsiao, 2003b). Thus, it is also of great interest theoretically and empirically to examine the interdependence and the role of the three important variables, FDI, exports, and GDP, in the development process of these eight economies during the period from 1986 to 2004.[7]

3.4   Characteristics of the Country Data

Since Maddison's data consist of only GDP per capita, for our purposes, we use the data from the ICSEAD (2006), as explained in the Appendix 3A on the data sources. To examine the data, we graphed (but did not show here). The extended graphs for 1981 to 2005 are given in Figure 4.1 of Chapter 4, and include the time-series of real GDP, real merchandize exports, and real inward FDI for each of the eight Asian economies from 1986 to 2004 (see the explanation of construction of real variables in Appendix 3A). We found some interesting characteristics from the country data.

Except the Philippines, the real GDP levels of all other economies increase over time, and except China, all other economies were affected by the Asian financial crisis of 1997, and the real GDP levels have become more fluctuating after 1997, although less so in Taiwan, Hong Kong, and Singapore. Exports play a vitally important role in all eight economies. By 1997, the real exports have exceeded real GDP in Hong Kong and Singapore, almost the same in Malaysia. In other countries, the amount of real exports ranges from about 30% of the GDP level in China and Korea to about 50% in Taiwan, the Philippines, and Thailand, indicating the possible impact of export activities on real GDP, or vice versa, in all these economies. The Asian financial crisis of 1997 also had some impact on export activities, and exports became more volatile afterward. However, real GDP and real exports of all economies recovered quickly and kept increasing and even surpassed those of the pre-1997 levels. In general, a comparison of the trend of real GDP and real exports shows that they are strongly correlated.[8]

---

[7]Note that including other countries, especially, stagnant, non-export-promoting, low-growth, or low-FDI countries, in our sample will worsen the heterogeneity problems.

[8]The simple correlation coefficients between these two variables for the seven economies (except Philippines) for 1986–2004 range from 0.69 (for Korea) to 0.99 (for Hong Kong). The correlation coefficient for The Philippines is −0.29.

Compared with real GDP and real export activities, real FDI in each economy has much less weight, almost negligible, in terms of its amount, except in China and Hong Kong, and possibly in Singapore. Thus, one may doubt the importance of FDI on an economy. Furthermore, except China and, to a lesser degree, Hong Kong, real FDI tends to decrease after the 1997 Asian financial crisis, prompting one to wonder whether inward FDI in these other countries was redirected to China, and thus reducing the influence of FDI on GDP.

It should be pointed out, however, that while the size of FDI may be very small compared with the level of GDP and even exports,[9] and for this reason, some economists dismissed the importance of FDI in the process of economic development. However, size alone does not matter. It has been observed that FDI generally goes to the key industries such as electric and electronic and high-tech manufacturing sectors of these economies and plays a crucial role in promoting technology transfer and exports in these sectors. Thus, FDI may also have a strong influence on the growth of GDP in a country.

We have seen that the 1997 Asian financial crisis exerts influence on the time-series of real GDP, real FDI, and real exports. All these three variables, except those in China, had decreased significantly in 1998, although most of these economies recovered very quickly. After the 1997 financial crisis, these economies have gone through economic reforms and structural changes. To take into account the effects of 1997 Asian financial crisis, we introduce a dummy variable with the value equal to zero for 1986–1997 and the value equals to one for 1998–2004 in Granger causality test equations in Sections 3.6 and 3.7.

3.5   A Review of Recent Empirical Literature

In the current literature, most of the published works examine bivariate relations, either theoretically or empirically, between the

---

[9]Statistically, this size problem is mitigated by taking the variables in logarithmic form, as we do in later sections.

pairs of GDP and exports, GDP and FDI, or exports and FDI, as we have reviewed in Section 3.1. Despite their interrelationships, as we will see in the literature review that follows, relatively few published works deal with the causality relations among these three variables simultaneously in a group of countries, and fewer papers use panel data VAR causality analysis.

There are several papers on individual country study examining Granger causality of these three variables. Liu *et al.* (2002) found bidirectional causality[10] between each pair of real GDP, real exports, and real FDI for China using seasonally adjusted quarterly data from January 1981 to December 1997; Kohpaiboon (2003) found that, under export promotion (EP) regime, there is a unidirectional causality from FDI to GDP for Thailand using annual data[11] from 1970 to 1999; Alici and Ucal (2003) found only unidirectional causality from exports to output[12] for Turkey using seasonally unadjusted quarterly data from January 1987 to December 2002; Dritsaki *et al.* (2004) found a bidirectional causality between real GDP and real exports, unidirectional causalities from[13] FDI to real exports, and FDI to real GDP for Greece, using annual IMF data from 1960 to 2002.

In addition, Ahmad *et al.* (2004) found unidirectional causalities from exports to GDP and FDI to GDP for Pakistan using undeflated annual data from 1972 to 2001. Cuadros *et al.* (2004) found unidirectional causalities from real FDI and real exports to real GDP in Mexico and Argentina, and unidirectional causality from real GDP to real exports in Brazil using seasonally adjusted quarterly data of Mexico, Brazil, and Argentina from late 1970 to 2000; Chowdhury and Mavrotas (2006) found unidirectional causality from GDP to

---

[10]In their paper, China's quarterly inward FDI and exports were deflated by the GDP deflator (1990 = 1). Quarterly GDP was approximated by monthly gross industrial output, and quarterly exports are taken from IMF.

[11]There is no indication that the data were deflated.

[12]They use Turkish industrial production index as our GDP, export price index as our exports, along with real FDI.

[13]There is no indication that FDI data were deflated in their paper.

FDI for Chile, and bidirectional causality between GDP and FDI in the case of Malaysia and Thailand using data from 1969 to 2000.

For studies of a group of countries, Makki and Somwaru (2004) found a positive impact of exports and FDI on GDP using 66 developing countries' data averaged over 10-year periods, 1971–1980, 1981–1990, and 1991–2000, and the instrumental variable method; Wang *et al.* (2004) used panel data analysis on 79 countries from 1970 to 1998 and found that "FDI is relatively more beneficial to high-income countries, while international trade is more important for low-income countries." But they did not examine the stationarity of the variables to avoid a spurious conclusion and did not apply the panel data causality analysis.

Note that, as Basu *et al.* (2003) have pointed out, the above-mentioned two papers, and like some other papers not included here, only look at the one-way determinants of FDI in regression analyses rather than at the two-way causality linkages between GDP, exports, and FDI, and so they are not strictly comparable with the causality analysis in this chapter.

There are a few examples using causality analysis. Nair-Reichert and Weinhold (2000) found that the Holtz-Eakin causality tests show FDI, not exports, causes GDP using data[14] from 24 developing countries from 1971 to 1995 applying mixed fixed and random (MFR) effects model; Hansen and Rand (2006), using data for 31 countries from 1970 to 2000 and the neoclassical growth model, found that there is a strong bidirectional causality between FDI ratio (FDI/GDP) and GDP. However, they did not take exports into account. Cho (2005) applied the panel data causality analysis and found only a strong unidirectional causality from FDI to exports among the three variables, using annual data of nine economies (the same economies as in this chapter plus Indonesia) from 1970 to 2001. In Cho's model, however, GDP growth is taken as the Malmquist productivity index.

---

[14]The paper does not specify the sources of data, whether the data were deflated, and does not check stationarity.

In general, our survey of recent empirical literature shows that the causality relations vary with the period studied, the econometric methods used, treatment of variables (nominal or real), one-way regression or two-way causality, and the presence of other related variables or inclusion of interaction variables in the estimation equation. The results may be bidirectional, unidirectional, or no-causality relations. Thus, it is very important that the assumptions, the treatment of variables, the sample period, estimation models, and methods should be clearly indicated in the analysis. In any case, the general results appear to show the positive relation from FDI and exports (or trade) to GDP and that the above brief survey also seems to indicate that there may be some interesting causality relations among exports, FDI, and GDP in the process of economic development. Our study follows.

3.6   Individual Economy's Granger Causality Test

The econometric technique requires transforming the values of all real variables into their logarithmic values. The transformed level series are denoted by the lower-case letters, gdp, ex, and fdi. Thus, fluctuations of the variables are considerably mitigated. The econometric technique also calls for taking the first difference (denoted by d) between consecutive logarithmic values, which are the same as the continuous growth rates of the variables, and are denoted by dgdp, dex, and dfdi in this chapter.

In this section, we explain the procedures of Granger causality relations between exports, FDI, and GDP for each economy using its time-series data. Before analyzing the causality relations, we first employ the unit root test to check the stationarity of each series, and if needed, we then use the cointegration test among the three series. Based on the characteristics of the time-series data for each economy, we select either the level series or the first-difference series in the estimation of a VAR model for Granger causality test.

3.6.1   *The Unit Root and Cointegration Tests*

The most commonly used tests of the unit root in time-series are the Dickey–Fuller (DF) test and the augmented Dickey–Fuller

(ADF) test (Dickey and Fuller, 1979, 1981; Said and Dickey, 1984). However, their test critical values (or p-values) for different small sample sizes have to be approximated asymptotically by simulation methods. MacKinnon (1996), applying response surface analysis to annual data, calculated the test p-values (and critical values) for 20 observations, which are available in an econometric software package.[15] Since our sample has 19 observations for each country, it is close enough to 20 observations. Thus, this chapter uses MacKinnon's p-values (or critical values) in the DF or ADF unit root test.[16]

While the DF or ADF unit root test has been the most commonly used test, there are some other tests which have higher power in the sense that the tests are more likely to reject the null hypothesis H_0 of a unit root and accept the alternate Hypothesis H_1 of no unit root. Following the suggestions of Maddala and Kim (1998) and Stock and Watson (2003), we also apply another unit root test called the DF-GLS test (Elliott *et al.*, 1996) for comparison. However, the test critical values available for application are calculated for 50 observations. Therefore, we need to be cautious when we interpret the test results using the DF-GLS test.

Tables 3.1 and 3.2 present the results from the ADF and DF-GLS unit root tests for the level series and the first-difference series, respectively, for each country. In Table 3.1, for the level series, the two tests yield very similar results for China, Korea, and Taiwan. China's ex is a stationary series, but fdi and gdp are not stationary series. Korea's ex is a stationary series, gdp is not a stationary series, but fdi has mixed results. Taiwan's ex and fdi are both stationary series, but gdp is not a stationary series. Therefore, for these three countries, we cannot use the level series in the estimation of regressions for causality analysis. In Table 3.2, for these three countries, the ADF and DF-GLS tests show that all the first-difference series are stationary series.[17] Based on these results, we have chosen to use the

---

[15] See EViews 5.1 (2005).

[16] MacKinnon (1996, p. 613, 615) pointed out the advantage of using annual data versus quarterly or monthly data under i.i.d. error terms. We use annual data, because quarterly or monthly data are not available for FDI.

[17] China's dex and Korea's dfdi (in ADF test) and Taiwan's dgdp (in DF-GLS test) reject the null hypothesis of a unit root at a weak 15% significant level.

Table 3.1: ADF and DF-GLS Unit Root Tests on the Level Series
Eight Individual Economies

Country	ADF test Test-statistic (p-value) k		DF-GLS test k (2)		Country	ADF test Test-statistic, (p-value) k		DF-GLS test k (2)	
1 China					**5 Singapore**				
ex	3	-4.097 **	3	-4.237 ***	ex	1	-2.213	1	-2.111
		(0.03)					(0.45)		
fdi	3	-2.298	3	-2.681	fdi	0	-3.099	0	-3.245 **
		(0.41)					(0.14)		
gdp	3	-1.130	0	-1.428	gdp	0	-1.137	1	-1.708
		(0.89)					(0.89)		
2 Korea					**6 Malaysia**				
ex	1	-3.467 *	1	-3.399 **	ex	0	-1.455	0	-1.495
		(0.08)					(0.81)		
fdi	1	-2.982	1	-3.116 *	fdi	0	-2.240	0	-2.275
		(0.16)					(0.44)		
gdp	0	-2.694	0	-2.502	gdp	0	-1.630	0	-1.682
		(0.25)					(0.74)		
3 Taiwan					**7 Philippines**				
ex	0	-3.742 **	0	-3.281 **	ex	0	-1.912	0	-2.020
		(0.05)					(0.61)		
fdi	3	-4.605 ***	2	-4.330 ***	fdi	3	0.956	0	-2.684
		(0.01)					(0.99)		
gdp	3	-2.622	0	-2.720	gdp	0	-2.285	0	-2.337
		(0.28)					(0.42)		
4 Hong Kong					**8 Thailand**				
ex	0	-3.188	0	-2.341	ex	0	-2.115	1	-1.924
		(0.12)					(0.50)		
fdi	0	-2.747	0	-2.928 *	fdi	2	-2.522	2	-2.663
		(0.23)					(0.31)		
gdp	0	-3.057	0	-2.640	gdp	1	-2.169	1	-2.027
		(0.15)					(0.48)		

Notes: (1) The test equations include constant and linear trend. Null hypothesis: Series has a unit root.
(2) In DF-GLS test, the critical values are -3.77, -3.19, and -2.89 for the 1%, 5%, and 10% levels, respectively.
(3) The lag length (k) is selected by the minimum AIC with maximum lag = 3.
(4) *** (**, *) denotes rejection of null hypothesis at the 1% (5%, 10%) level of significance, respectively.

According to Maddala and Kim (1998), it is acceptable to set the level of significance around the 20% level in a unit root test.

Table 3.2: ADF and DF-GLS Unit Root Tests on the First-Difference Series

Eight Individual Economies

	ADF test		DF-GLS test			ADF test		DF-GLS test	
Country	Test-statistic (p-value)				Country	Test-statistic, (p-value)			
	k		k	(2)		k		k	(2)
1 China						**5 Singapore**			
dex	3	-2.495 w (0.14)	3	-2.898 ***	dex	0	-2.274 w2 (0.19)	0	-2.289 **
dfdi	1	-3.124 ** (0.05)	1	-3.237 ***	dfdi	2	-3.469 ** (0.02)	0	-4.706 ***
dgdp	0	-4.004 *** (0.01)	0	-4.136 ***	dgdp	0	-2.281 w2 (0.19)	0	-2.314 **
2 Korea						**6 Malaysia**			
dex	1	-4.209 *** (0.01)	0	-3.719 ***	dex	0	-3.148 ** (0.04)	0	-3.229 ***
dfdi	0	-2.599 w (0.11)	0	-2.657 **	dfdi	0	-5.670 *** (0.00)	0	-5.853 ***
dgdp	0	-3.727 *** (0.01)	0	-3.709 ***	dgdp	0	-3.411 ** (0.03)	0	-3.505 ***
3 Taiwan						**7 Philippines**			
dex	1	-3.872 *** (0.01)	0	-3.726 ***	dex	0	-3.787 *** (0.01)	0	-3.775 ***
dfdi	3	-4.942 *** (0.00)	0	-4.831 ***	dfdi	0	-5.094 *** (0.00)	1	-2.395 **
dgdp	0	-3.765 *** (0.01)	2	-1.220 w	dgdp	0	-4.189 *** (0.01)	0	-4.229 ***
4 Hong Kong						**8 Thailand**			
dex	0	-3.216 ** (0.04)	0	-2.649 **	dex	0	-2.795 * (0.07)	0	-2.779 ***
dfdi	0	-4.654 *** (0.00)	0	-4.129 ***	dfdi	3	-3.072 ** (0.05)	3	-3.220 ***
dgdp	1	-4.082 *** (0.00)	0	-3.253 ***	dgdp	0	-2.774 * (0.08)	0	-2.811 ***

Notes: (1) The test equations include constant. Null hypothesis: Series has a unit root. (2) In the DF-GLS test, for $k = 0$, the critical values are -2.708, -1.963, and -1.606 for 1%, 5%, and 10% levels, respectively. Other critical values are -2.74 ($k = 3$, 1% level), -2.72 ($k = 1$, 1% level), -1.61 ($k = 2$, 10% level), and -1.96 ($k = 1$, 5% level). (3) The lag length (k) is selected by the minimum AIC with maximum lag = 3. (4) ***, **, *, w, w2 denote rejection of null hypothesis at the 1%, 5%, 10%, 15%, 20% levels of significance, respectively.

first-difference series, dex, dfdi, and dgdp, in the estimation of the VAR model for causality test for China, Korea, and Taiwan.

For Hong Kong, Singapore, Malaysia, the Philippines, and Thailand, the ADF and DF-GLS test results in Table 3.1 show that all the level series are not stationary, except that Hong Kong and Singapore's fdi are stationary at the 10% and 5% levels, respectively, in the DF-GLS test. In addition, in Table 3.2, the ADF and DF-GLS tests show that the first-difference series are all stationary series for these five economies. Therefore, we may consider that all the level series are $I(1)$ and we continue to test the cointegration among the three-level series for each of these five economies using the Johansen cointegration test[18] (Johansen, 1991; Greene, 2003).

Table 3.3 summarizes the results from the Johansen cointegration test. Both the trace test and the maximum-eigenvalue test indicate that the level series, ex, fdi, and gdp, are cointegrated for Hong Kong, Singapore, Malaysia, the Philippines, and Thailand, respectively. Based on the results from unit root tests and cointegration test, we have chosen to use the level series in the estimation of the VAR model for causality test for these five economies.

Table 3.3: Johansen Cointegration Test Summary

Number of Cointegrating Equations in Level Series: ex, fdi, and gdp					
	HK	Sing.	Malaysia	Philip	Thaild
Trace test	2**	1**	2**	1*	2**
Max-eigenvalue test	2*	1**	1*	1*	2**

Notes: (1) The test equations include intercept and linear deterministic trend. (2) **, * denote rejection of the hypothesis at the 5% and 10% levels, respectively.

---

[18]It should be noted that Toda (1994) has shown that the LR tests need a very large sample size, 300 or more observations, to ensure good performance and to detect the true cointegrating rank. In applications, we seldom have such large sample size.

3.6.2   The VAR Model and the Granger Causality Test

We have multivariables, dex, dfdi, and dgdp (or ex, fdi, and gdp), in the VAR(p) model to consider the interactions among their p-lag variables in testing the Granger causality relations. The VAR(p) model involves the estimation of the following system of equations (Greene, 2003; Hsiao and Hsiao, 2001; also, see (3C.16) in Appendix 3C):

$$y_t = \mu + \Gamma_1 y_{t-1} + \Gamma_2 y_{t-2} + \cdots + \Gamma_p y_{t-p} + \varepsilon_t, \qquad (3.3)$$

where y_t is a (3×1) column vector of the endogenous variables, i.e., $y_t = $(dex$_t$ dfdi$_t$ dgdp$_t$)$'$ or (ex$_t$ fdi$_t$ gdp$_t$)$'$ (prime indicates the transpose of a row vector), μ is a (3×1) constant vector, p, the order of lags, each of $\Gamma_1, \Gamma_2, \ldots, \Gamma_p$ is a (3×3) coefficient matrix, each of $y_{t-1}, y_{t-2}, \ldots, y_{t-p}$, is a (3×1) vector of the lagged endogenous variables, and ϵ_t is a (3×1) vector of the random error terms in the system. The lag length p in VAR is then selected by the minimum Akaike Information Criterion (AIC) with maximum lag equals to three. The results show that the optimal lag length for China, Taiwan, and Thailand is three and that for Korea, Hong Kong, Singapore, Malaysia, and the Philippines is one. Following the suggestion of Toda and Yamamoto (1995), we added an additional one-lag if the optimal lag is one. Since we have limited number of observations, we have not added an extra lag when the optimal lag is three, as lag of three is sufficient and exceeds the order of integration and cointegration noted in Toda and Yamamoto.[19] Our method is similar to Hansen and Rand (2006) and Chowdhury and Mavrotas (2006), but we have applied the new method to three variable-panel data causality analysis.

---

[19]Toda and Yamamoto (1995) proposed a method to over-fit VAR to supplement pretests for a unit root and cointegration, as these pretests may have low power. However, their method does not mean to substitute the pretests. In this paper, we have used the pretests and also integrated their suggestions in selecting the lag length of VARs. In an over-fit VAR model, we may use the modified Wald test for the determination of causality directions. Our causality results in Tables 3.4 and 3.5 with VAR(2) are the same as the results when we used the modified Wald test.

In the estimation process of VAR, we first estimate the regression equation with a dummy variable, as defined in Section 3.4, to take into account the effect of the 1997 Asian financial crisis. If the estimated coefficient for the dummy variable is significant at the 10% level, then we keep the dummy variable in the model and use the estimated results to perform the Wald test of coefficients to determine the causality direction. If the estimated coefficient for the dummy variable is not significant, then we delete the dummy variable from the model specification and reestimate the equation for the Wald test of coefficients to determine the causality direction.

Table 3.4 presents the estimated VAR models and the results of Granger causality test for China, Korea, and Taiwan. Note that the results here are derived from using the first-difference series, dex, dfdi, and dgdp. Only in China's dgdp equation, the coefficient of the dummy variable is positive and significant, which indicates that the 1997 Asian financial crisis had no harmful effect on China. The dummy variable was dropped in other equations because it is not significant in the initial estimations. This may indicate that these three countries have recovered from the 1997 financial crisis in a short time period. The Granger causality relations are examined using the Wald test of coefficients (F-test), and each null hypothesis is indicated in the footnote of the table.

For China, we have found a very strong (at the 1% level of significance) unidirectional causality from GDP to FDI and a unidirectional causality from exports to FDI. The coefficient of the dummy variable is positive and significant at the 1% level in the dgdp equation, which implies that the 1997 Asian Crisis had no effect on China. These unidirectional causalities indicate that, during the past two decades, China attracted a large amount of FDI because of its low wage, the expectation of its high-income growth, and the potentially vast market. To a lesser degree, China's inward FDI has also been attracted by its possibility of exporting commodities to developed countries such as the United States, Japan, and European Union, as China becomes the factory of the world. However, contrary to the general perception, the test results here show that China's inward FDI and exports do not Granger cause GDP and so its growth, the

Table 3.4: The Granger Causality Test
China, Korea, and Taiwan

Vector Autoregressions: Use the first-difference series											Wald test	
Dep.		dex(-2)		dfdi(-1)		dfdi(-3)		dgdp(-2)		dummy	Causality Direction	
var.	Const. dex(-1)		dex(-3)		dfdi(-2)		dgdp(-1)		dgdp(-3)		(1)	(2)
	c1	c2	c3	c4	c5	c6	c7	c8	c9	c10	c11	Ho F-test	Ho F-test
1 China VAR(3)													
dex	0.164	0.381	-0.305	-0.244	-0.047	0.104	0.016	-0.07	0.344	-0.293		B 0.041	C 0.171
	(0.45)	(0.52)	(0.73)	(0.74)	(0.93)	(0.85)	(0.97)	(0.94)	(0.71)	(0.71)		(0.99)	(0.91)
dfdi	0.344	0.585	-0.573	-0.249	0.671	-0.553	-0.100	-1.501	-0.804	-0.991		A 3.683	C 13.561
	(0.01)	(0.07)	(0.20)	(0.48)	(0.04)	(0.08)	(0.63)	(0.01)	(0.11)	(0.03)		(0.10)	(0.01)
												ex→fdi*	gdp→fdi***
dgdp	-0.145	0.206	0.252	0.261	0.025	-0.030	0.032	-1.255	-1.165	-1.265	0.454	A 1.742	B 0.043
	(0.06)	(0.17)	(0.27)	(0.21)	(0.82)	(0.84)	(0.78)	(0.01)	(0.04)	(0.01)	(0.01)	(0.30)	(0.99)
2 Korea VAR(2)													
dex	0.095	-0.103	0.406		0.025	-0.175		0.035	-0.671			B 1.523	C 0.427
	(0.15)	(0.90)	(0.63)		(0.82)	(0.12)		(0.96)	(0.39)			(0.27)	(0.67)
dfdi	0.029	2.196	-0.119		0.350	-0.386		-2.846	0.321			A 0.410	C 0.913
	(0.88)	(0.40)	(0.96)		(0.32)	(0.25)		(0.22)	(0.89)			(0.68)	(0.43)
dgdp	0.058	-0.680	0.527		0.025	-0.137		0.590	-0.711			A 0.310	B 0.595
	(0.46)	(0.51)	(0.62)		(0.86)	(0.30)		(0.51)	(0.46)			(0.74)	(0.57)
3 TaiwanVAR(3)													
dex	0.090	-0.038	-0.228	-0.842	-0.003	-0.072	-0.007	-0.42	0.041	1.021		B 2.867	C 2.271
	(0.06)	(0.93)	(0.60)	(0.05)	(0.89)	(0.04)	(0.87)	(0.48)	(0.94)	(0.07)		(0.14)	(0.20)
												fdi→ex#	
dfdi	0.164	-1.156	2.266	-6.235	-0.305	-0.789	-0.877	-5.837	1.781	7.043		A 0.587	C 0.428
	(0.81)	(0.88)	(0.76)	(0.33)	(0.46)	(0.15)	(0.23)	(0.57)	(0.84)	(0.39)		(0.65)	(0.74)
dgdp	0.039	0.173	-0.247	-0.675	-0.009	-0.040	0.004	-0.402	0.203	0.849		A 3.213	B 2.118
	(0.18)	(0.58)	(0.41)	(0.03)	(0.55)	(0.08)	(0.88)	(0.32)	(0.57)	(0.03)		(0.12)	(0.21)
												ex→gdp#	

Notes: (1) The p-values are in parentheses. (2) In Wald test of coefficients, for VAR(3), the null hypothesis A is $c2 = c3 = c4 = 0$, B is $c5 = c6 = c7 = 0$, and C is $c8 = c9 = c10 = 0$, respectively. For VAR(2), the null hypothesis A is $c2 = c3 = 0$, B is $c5 = c6 = 0$, and C is $c8 = c9 = 0$, respectively. (3). ***, **, *, # denote rejection of null hypothesis at the 1%, 5%, 10%, 15% levels of significance, respectively.

(4) Note that we have made rearrangement on the results of the Wald test for Taiwan and Korea, which was wrongfully arranged in the original paper in Hsiao and Hsiao (2006). After the correction, the description in the text is now consistent with the drawing of Figure 3.2.

export-led growth, and the FDI-led growth hypotheses do not seem to be applicable for China. A further study is called for.

For Taiwan, we have found two unidirectional causalities: FDI causes exports and exports cause GDP at the 5% level of significance. These results indicate that the FDI inflows to Taiwan and its exports are important for Taiwan's GDP growth, although the effects of FDI on GDP work only indirectly through exports. For Korea, to our surprise, we have not found any causality relation even at the 15% level of significance. For our curiosity, we have estimated VAR(1) for Korea but found only a weak unidirectional causality from GDP to FDI at the 15% level of significance. Considering a similar development stage, development policies, open economy regimes, and industrial productivities between Korea and Taiwan (Hsiao and Hsiao, 2003a; Hsiao and Park, 2002, 2005), the different results from causality analysis of the two countries are quite intriguing.

Table 3.5 presents the estimated VAR models and the results of Granger causality test for Hong Kong, Singapore, Malaysia, the Philippines, and Thailand, respectively. Note that the results here are based on the level series, ex, fdi, and gdp, with (or without) including the dummy variable, and are noted in Table 3.5.

For Hong Kong, like Korea, we have not found any causality relation at the 15% level of significance. For Singapore, we have found two unidirectional causalities: FDI causes exports and FDI also causes GDP. These results indicate that the FDI inflows are

Table 3.5: The Granger Causality Test

Hong Kong, Singapore, Malaysia, the Philippines, and Thailand

Vector Autoregressions: Use level series											Wald test			
Dep. var.	Const.	ex(-1) ex(-2)	ex(-3)	fdi(-1) fdi(-2)	fdi(-3)	gdp(-1) gdp(-2)	gdp(-3)	dummy			Causality Direction (1)		(2)	
	$c1$	$c2$	$c3$	$c4$	$c5$	$c6$	$c7$	$c8$	$c9$	$c10$	$c11$	Ho	F-test	Ho	F-test
4 Hong Kong VAR(2)															
ex	-9.263	0.598	-0.260		-0.025	-0.032		0.982	0.514			B	0.772	C	0.611
	(0.33)	(0.41)	(0.59)		(0.45)	(0.44)		(0.48)	(0.63)				(0.49)		(0.56)
fdi	-6.153	3.999	-2.310		0.544	-0.164		-5.240	4.551			A	0.193	C	0.135
	(0.95)	(0.57)	(0.62)		(0.11)	(0.69)		(0.70)	(0.66)				(0.83)		(0.88)
gdp	2.103	0.253	-0.130		0.007	-0.010		0.451	0.253			A	0.243	B	0.160
	(0.67)	(0.51)	(0.61)		(0.68)	(0.67)		(0.54)	(0.65)				(0.79)		(0.85)

Table 3.5: (*Continued*)

Vector Autoregressions: Use level series												Wald test			
Dep.		ex(-2)		fdi(-1)		fdi(-3)		gdp(-2)		dummy		Causality Direction			
var.	Const.	ex(-1)	ex(-3)		fdi(-2)		gdp(-1)		gdp(-3)			(1)		(2)	
	c1	c2	c3	c4	c5	c6	c7	c8	c9	c10	c11	Ho	F-test	Ho	F-test

5 Singapore VAR(2)

var.	c1	c2	c3	c5	c6	c8	c9	c11	Ho (1)	F-test (1)	Ho (2)	F-test (2)
ex	2.265 (0.47)	1.364 (0.01)	-0.048 (0.94)	-0.087 (0.14)	-0.164 (0.02)	-0.624 (0.39)	0.307 (0.71)		B	5.636 (0.02)	C	0.416 (0.67)
										fdi→ex**		
fdi	10.027 (0.56)	1.791 (0.47)	1.321 (0.69)	0.132 (0.67)	-0.441 (0.22)	-2.572 (0.51)	-0.452 (0.92)		A	0.443 (0.65)	C	0.263 (0.77)
gdp	3.408 (0.13)	0.425 (0.18)	0.166 (0.69)	-0.055 (0.17)	-0.073 (0.11)	0.409 (0.41)	-0.212 (0.70)		A	1.271 (0.32)	B	3.144 (0.09)
												fdi→gdp*

6 Malaysia VAR(2)

var.	c1	c2	c3	c5	c6	c8	c9	c11	Ho (1)	F-test (1)	Ho (2)	F-test (2)
ex	5.815 (0.13)	2.039 (0.01)	-0.138 (0.87)	-0.008 (0.90)	-0.025 (0.63)	-1.726 (0.02)	0.368 (0.65)	-0.286 (0.06)	B	0.158 (0.86)	C	4.337 (0.05)
												gdp→ex**
fdi	-9.163 (0.68)	-0.112 (0.98)	-1.785 (0.73)	0.164 (0.70)	0.214 (0.51)	1.345 (0.72)	1.781 (0.73)		A	0.554 (0.59)	C	0.395 (0.68)
gdp	7.475 (0.00)	1.295 (0.01)	0.077 (0.87)	-0.020 (0.58)	-0.030 (0.31)	-1.030 (0.02)	0.076 (0.87)	-0.400 (0.00)	A	22.362 (0.00)	B	0.969 (0.42)
										ex→gdp***		

7 Philippines VAR(2)

var.	c1	c2	c3	c5	c6	c8	c9	c11	Ho (1)	F-test (1)	Ho (2)	F-test (2)
ex	7.496 (0.09)	1.428 (0.08)	-0.314 (0.67)	0.032 (0.63)	-0.028 (0.75)	-0.978 (0.28)	0.229 (0.74)	-0.303 (0.07)	B	0.189 (0.83)	C	2.897 (0.11)
fdi	-9.464 (0.66)	1.472 (0.68)	-1.771 (0.65)	0.236 (0.48)	-0.024 (0.95)	-1.620 (0.68)	3.206 (0.36)		A	0.115 (0.89)	C	1.840 (0.21)
gdp	10.187 (0.01)	0.542 (0.33)	-0.507 (0.35)	0.033 (0.49)	-0.012 (0.85)	-0.422 (0.51)	0.492 (0.33)	-0.319 (0.01)	A	0.529 (0.61)	B	0.286 (0.76)

8 Thailand VAR(3)

var.	c1	c2	c3	c4	c5	c6	c7	c8	c9	c10	c11	Ho (1)	F-test (1)	Ho (2)	F-test (2)
ex	3.997 (0.07)	0.441 (0.39)	0.825 (0.24)	-1.125 (0.10)	-0.287 (0.05)	-0.070 (0.38)	0.192 (0.08)	-0.152 (0.76)	-1.124 (0.08)	1.848 (0.03)		B	3.147 (0.11)	C	2.865 (0.13)
													fdi→ex#, gdp→ex#		
fdi	-5.809 (0.37)	2.753 (0.13)	-3.999 (0.10)	1.835 (0.36)	0.533 (0.21)	0.520 (0.07)	-0.769 (0.04)	-2.239 (0.20)	5.074 (0.03)	-2.413 (0.30)		A	1.622 (0.28)	C	3.101 (0.11)
															gdp→fdi#
gdp	14.002 (0.00)	1.191 (0.01)	-1.062 (0.11)	1.259 (0.13)	0.119 (0.33)	-0.165 (0.02)	0.079 (0.15)	-1.268 (0.02)	0.424 (0.33)	-0.605 (0.39)	-0.844 (0.01)	A	5.981 (0.04)	B	4.764 (0.06)
													ex→gdp**, fdi→gdp*		

Notes: (1) The p-values are in parentheses. (2) In Wald test of coefficients, for VAR(3), the null hypothesis A is $c2 = c3 = c4 = 0$, B is $c5 = c6 = c7 = 0$, and C is $c8 = c9 = c10 = 0$, respectively. For VAR(2), the null hypothesis A is $c2 = c3 = 0$, B is $c5 = c6 = 0$, and C is $c8 = c9 = 0$, respectively. (3) *** (**, *, #) denotes rejection of hull hypothesis at the 1% (5%, 10%, 15%) level of significance, respectively.

Post Script: The Wald test results for Singapore and Malaysia in the published paper were wrongly rearranged. We have corrected them in this book so to conform to the description in the text and the drawings of Figure 3.2.

vital to Singapore's GDP and exports. For Malaysia, we have found bidirectional causality between GDP and exports. This agrees with the fact that Malaysia has promoted the export-led growth policy during the past two decades. In addition, in the ex and gdp equations, the dummy variable has negative coefficient and is significant at the 10% and 1% level, respectively. These results imply that the 1997 Asian financial crisis had serious effects on Malaysia's exports and GDP. Compared with other countries, it will take more time for Malaysia's economy to recover from the Asian financial crisis.

For the Philippines, we have found only a weak (significant at the 15% level) unidirectional causality from GDP to exports. Like Malaysia, in the ex and gdp equations, the dummy variable has negative coefficient and is significant at the 10% and 1% levels, respectively. These results, combined with the continuous decreasing of real GDP since 1998, show that the Asian financial crisis had severe effects on the Philippines' exports and GDP, and the Philippines' economy has not recovered since 1997.

The results for Thailand are more exciting. We have found two bidirectional causality relations: one is exports strongly cause GDP (significant at the 5% level), and GDP also causes exports, although weakly (at the 15% level of significance); GDP in turn weakly causes FDI (at 15%), and FDI also causes GDP (at 10%). In addition, there is a weak (at 15%) unidirectional causality from FDI to exports. Like Taiwan and Malaysia, Thailand is an export-led growth economy, and like Singapore, it is also an FDI-led growth economy, and its GDP expansion induces more FDI inflows to Thailand. In the GDP equation, the dummy variable has a negative coefficient and is significant at the 1% level. This implies that the 1997 Asian financial crisis had a strong negative effect on Thailand's GDP, but it is recovering since 2001.

Our causality findings in Tables 3.4 and 3.5 are summarized in Figure 3.2.

While each country has a different story to tell, there are some reservations in the interpretations of the above causality relations using individual country's time-series data. First, each country has only 19 observations of annual data. As we have mentioned above, the available critical values (or p-values) for the ADF and DF-GLS unit

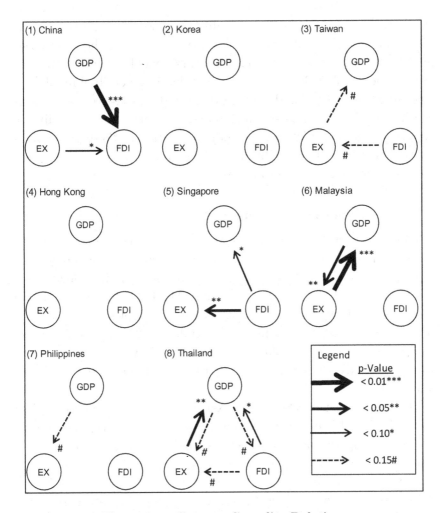

Figure 3.2: Granger Causality Relations
Eight East and Southeast Asian Economies

root tests were calculated for 20 and 50 observations, respectively. Therefore, these critical values (or *p*-values) can only be used as the approximations (or proxies) for our unit root tests in the small sample size. Second, we have not found any causality relations for Korea and Hong Kong. This may be also due to the limited observations in a country's time-series data set. Third, for other countries, except Thailand, we have found only a few causality relations among the three variables, and even the causality directions are not consistent. Since the causality differs from country to country, the time-series analysis based on a single country cannot yield a general rule for development policy. Fourth, the time period is generally limited for a time-series analysis,[20] and, on the other hand, a cross-section analysis is criticized for assuming similar economic structure for vastly diverse countries (Giles and Williams, 2000). A solution to these problems is to pool the data of the eight Asian economies into a panel data set to investigate Granger causality relations for the group.

3.7   The Panel Data Granger Causality Test

A panel data analysis has the merit of using information concerning cross-section and time-series analyses. It can also take heterogeneity of each cross-sectional unit explicitly into account by allowing for individual-specific effects (Davidson and MacKinnon, 2004) and give "more variability, less collinearity among variables, more degrees of freedom, and more efficiency" (Baltagi, 2001). Furthermore, the repeated cross-section of observations over time is better suited to study the dynamic of changes like exports, FDI inflows, and GDP.

The eight East and Southeast Asian economies have more or less similarity in culture and geographical proximity, their rapid economic growth during the past two decades, their openness through trade and inward FDI, especially with the United States and Japan by forming the core of the Pacific trade triangle (Hsiao and Hsiao, 2001, 2003b). Considering the growing interdependence of these eight East and Southeast Asian economies, we propose to pool their eight cross-sectional data over the 19-year period (1986–2004) into a panel data set and then use panel data regressions to examine the causality relations for the group. We then compare the group causality relations with the results from individual economy's study in Section 3.6.

---

[20]In an earlier paper, Hsiao (1987) also found in general the "lack of support for the hypothesis of unidirectional causality from exports to GDP" for the Asian NICs from 1960 to 1982 using the Granger's test and Sims' test.

3.7.1 Panel Data Unit Root Tests

We first test the stationarity of the three panel level series, ex, fdi, and gdp (for simplicity, we use the same notations as used in the study of individual economies). Recent econometric literature has proposed several methods for testing the presence of a unit root under panel data setting. Since different panel data unit root tests may yield different testing results, we have chosen Im, Pesaran, and Shin (2003) IPS-W test and ADF-Fisher Chi-square test (ADF-Fisher) (Maddala and Wu, 1999) to perform the panel data unit root test and compare their results (Christopoulos and Tsionas, 2003). Table 3.6 presents the panel unit root test results of the three-level series and their first-difference series. Both IPS-W and ADF-Fisher tests indicate that the panel level series exports (ex) is a stationary series, gdp is not a stationary series, and fdi has the mixed results. In addition, both tests indicate that the three panel first-difference series dex, dfdi, and dgdp are all stationary series. Therefore, we use the three panel first-difference series in the panel data VAR causality analysis.

3.7.2 Panel Data VAR and Granger Causality Tests

When we estimate panel data regression models, we consider the assumptions about the intercept, the slope coefficients, and the error

Table 3.6: Panel Data Unit Root Tests

Panel Level series			Panel First-difference series		
	IPS W-stat	ADF-Fisher Chi-square		IPS W-stat	ADF-Fisher Chi-square
1 ex	-1.891 **	27.095 **	dex	-4.973 ***	53.456 ***
	(0.03)	(0.04)		(0.00)	(0.00)
2 fdi	-1.035	25.051 *	dfdi	-7.300 ***	78.703 ***
	(0.15)	(0.07)		(0.00)	(0.00)
3 gdp	0.088	13.494	dgdp	-5.981 ***	62.889 ***
	(0.54)	(0.64)		(0.00)	(0.00)

Notes: (1) In level series, the test equations include individual effects and individual linear trends. In the first-difference series, the test equations include individual effects. Automatic selection of lags is based on minimum AIC: 0–3. The p-values are in parentheses. (2) ***, **, * denote rejection of null hypothesis: Panel series has a unit root at the 1%, 5%, 10% levels of significance, respectively.

term. In practice, the estimation procedure is either the FEM or the REM (Greene, 2003). Since the REM requires the number of cross-section units to be greater than the number of coefficients, with our eight cross-section units, we can estimate VAR(p) with lag order $p = 1$ or 2. Since as a general principle, it is desirable to have a longer lag length, we have chosen to estimate the panel data VAR(2) in our causality analysis. We explain briefly the estimation of VAR(2) in the context of the FEM as well as the REM.

3.7.2.1   *The Fixed Effects Approach*

The FEM assumes that the slope coefficients are constant for all cross-section units, and the intercept varies over individual cross-section units but does not vary over time. For our application, the FEM can be written as follows

$$y_{it} = \alpha_i + x_{it}\beta + u_{it}, \tag{3.4}$$

where y_{it} can be one of our three endogenous variables, i is the ith cross-section unit, and t is the time of observation. The intercept α_i takes into account the heterogeneity influence from unobserved variables which may differ across the cross-section units. x_{it} is a row vector of all lag endogenous variables. β is a column vector of the common slope coefficients for the group of eight economies. The error term u_{it} follows the classical assumptions that $u_{it} \sim N(0, \sigma^2)$. In addition, we add an ordinary dummy variable zero for 1986–1997 and one for 1998–2004, into the model to consider the effect of the 1997 Asian financial crisis. The FEM is estimated by the method of the least squares dummy variable (LSDV).

3.7.2.2   *The Random Effects Approach and the Hausman Test*

REM also assumes that the slope coefficients are constant for all cross-section units, but the intercept is a random variable, that is, $\alpha_i = \alpha + \epsilon_i$, where α is the mean value for the intercept of all cross-section units, and ϵ_i is a random error term which reflects the individual differences in the intercept value of each cross-section unit, and $\epsilon_i \sim N(0, \sigma_\epsilon^2)$.

Substituting in Eq. (3.4), we have REM in Eq. (3.5):

$$y_{it} = \alpha + x_{it}\beta + \nu_{it}, \tag{3.5}$$

where $\nu_{it} = \epsilon_i + u_{it}$. It has been shown that ν_{it} and u_{is} (for $t \neq s$) are correlated, so the REM is estimated by the method of generalized least squares.

We use both FEM and REM to estimate the panel data VAR(2) using dex, dfdi, and dgdp for eight Asian economies as a group. We also apply the Hausman test to choose between FEM and REM estimations before implementing the Wald test of coefficients to determine the Granger causality directions. The null hypothesis in the Hausman test is that the correlated REM is appropriate. It is a Chi-square test. If the null hypothesis is rejected, then we use FEM estimation. Our Hausman test results indicate that it is better to use the FEM to estimate the first equation (dex_{it}) and use the REM to estimate the second equation (dfdi_{it}) and the third equation (dgdp_{it}).

3.7.2.3 *The Granger Causality Test*

Table 3.7 presents the estimated panel data VAR(2) with the dummy variable by FEM and REM and the Wald test of coefficients for Granger causality directions (for simplicity, subscripts i and t are omitted, and the cross-section-specific constant terms are not presented in the table). In addition, the coefficients of dummy variable are all negative and significant at the 10% level. This agreed with the fact that the 1997 Asian financial crisis did have some negative and significant impacts on these eight Asian economies as a group. Figure 3.3 summarizes the panel data Granger causality results of Table 3.7.

We have found four very interesting causality relations for the eight Asian economies as a group. They are summarized as follows:

(1) From the first equation (dex_{it}), we have found two unidirectional causalities: GDP causes exports and inward FDI also causes exports. These two causality relations indicate that the growth in domestic products and the large amount of inward FDI are the two vital forces in promoting exports for these eight Asian economies as a group.

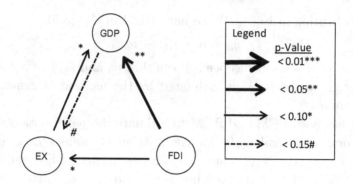

Figure 3.3: Panel Data Granger Causality Relations

Eight Economies

Table 3.7: Panel Data Granger Causality Tests, 1986–2004

UAR - the first-difference series of panel data								Wald test		
Dep.		dex(-2)		dfdi(-2)		dgdp(-2)		Causality Direction		
var. const. dex(-1)			dfdi(-1)		dgdp(-1)		dummy	(1)		(2)
c1	c2	c3	c4	c5	c6	c7	c8	Ho F-test		Ho F-test
1 Fixed effects										
dex	0.116	0.296	-0.095	-0.011	-0.038	-0.250	-0.160	-0.068	B	2.420	C 2.168
	(0.00)	(0.04)	(0.52)	(0.50)	(0.03)	(0.09)	(0.27)	(0.01)		(0.09)	(0.12)
									fdi→ex*,gdp→ex#		
2 Random effects										
dfdi	0.173	1.005	-0.085	-0.283	-0.173	-1.309	-0.111	-0.261	A	0.874	C 1.409
	(0.15)	(0.19)	(0.92)	(0.00)	(0.08)	(0.10)	(0.89)	(0.06)		(0.42)	(0.25)
3 Random effects										
dgdp	0.033	0.271	0.099	-0.018	-0.039	-0.093	-0.164	-0.038	A	2.745	B 3.119
	(0.10)	(0.03)	(0.46)	(0.25)	(0.02)	(0.49)	(0.21)	(0.09)		(0.07)	(0.05)
									ex→gdp*, fdi→gdp**		

Notes: (1) The Hausman test has been used in the selection of the fixed effects or random effects model. (2) The regression equations include the dummy variable because it is significant at the 10% level. Individual cross-sectional constants are not shown here. (3) Notes (1) and (3) in Table 3.4 are also applied here. (4) In Wald test of coefficients, the null hypothesis of A is $c2 = c3 = 0$, of B is $c4 = c5 = 0$, and of C is $c6 = c7 = 0$, respectively.

(2) From the third equation ($dgdp_{it}$), we have also found two unidirectional causalities: exports cause GDP and FDI also causes GDP. These two causality relations indicate that exports and FDI inflows join together to bring up the growth in GDP.

These findings support the export-led growth and the FDI-led growth in these eight Asian economies as a group.

(3) From the first and the third equations together, we have found the bidirectional causality between GDP and exports. In addition, we have found FDI causes exports and GDP. This finding verifies that inward FDI is crucial and significantly benefits the growth of GDP through increased exports, for example, by opening the export-oriented industrial processing zones for inward FDI in these eight Asian economies.

(4) From the second equation (dfdi$_{it}$), we have not found any significant causality relations even at the 15% level. Apparently, the growth of GDP and exports are not the only factors to attract FDI inflows to these eight Asian economies. Other factors, such as the abundant quality labor supply, human capital, low wages, tax holidays, etc., may have to be taken into consideration if we are interested in the determinations of FDI in regression analysis, as we did in Hsiao and Hsiao (2004).

We have found the evidence that, in general, inward FDI has reinforcing effects on GDP: FDI not only has strong direct impact on GDP but also indirectly increases GDP through exports by interactive relations between exports and GDP. Our results not only support the "Bhagwati Hypothesis" (Kohpaiboon, 2003) that "the gain from FDI are likely far more under an export promotion (EP) regime than an import substitution (IS) regime" but also provide the possible theoretical underpinning of the hypothesis: It is because of the FDI's reinforcing effects on GDP through exports.[21]

Due to the reinforcing effects of inward FDI, the economic growth policy priority of a developing country, generally speaking, appears to be to open the economy for inward FDI under the export promotion regime, and then, the interaction between exports and GDP will induce economic development. While this is a general proposition based on the evidence from the eight rapidly growing East and

---

[21] Our finding is also consistent with that found by Neuhaus (2006) for transition economies of Central and Eastern Europe, with added finding of the reinforcing effect of GDP through exports.

Southeast Asian economies as a whole, good examples are given by the development of Singapore, Thailand, and possibly Taiwan, according to our individual country study in Section 3.6.

3.8 Conclusions

The contributions of this chapter appear in several areas:

(1) Instead of the supply-side approach or *ad hoc* relations used in the general literature, we present a Keynesian demand-side model of open economies to explain the interaction between inward FDI, exports, and GDP, and present a model (theoretical underpinning) which is the basis of using VAR procedure.

(2) For empirical studies, we use panel data causality analysis of inward FDI, exports, and GDP (TIG) simultaneously. Our analysis is different from other conventional time-series analysis or cross-section analysis using bivariate models.

(3) There are many theoretical and empirical studies on the bivariate causality between trade (using exports or exports and imports) and growth, openness (as measured by the ratio of exports and imports over GDP) and growth, as well as between trade and FDI, whether FDI is a complementary or a substitute. However, as these three variables are closely related, instead of studying two variables separately at a time, it is natural and worthwhile to examine multivariate causalities among these three variables.

(4) In terms of the data, our analyses are concentrated on the newly developed East Asian economies, Korea, Taiwan, Singapore, Hong Kong, and rapidly developing economies in Asia, China, Malaysia, the Philippines, and Thailand. We have chosen the data period from 1986 to 2004, the most dynamic phase of their development, as compared with other regions of the world, with active exports and inward FDI. Our selection of these eight Asian economies and the period, in addition to panel data analysis, are different from the existing literature, as most of the current publications do the cross-section analysis of a group of either developed countries and/or developing countries, without

due considerations of heterogeneous economic characteristics and different stages of development within the group (see Chapter 4).

(5) Considering the low power in the pretests of a unit root and cointegration in small sample, we also adopted the method suggested by Toda and Yamamoto to over-fit VAR in selecting the lag length for time-series analysis in the country study.

(6) The inter-relations and interactions among real GDP, exports, and inward FDI in Figure 3.3 are illustrated again in the context of the basic macroeconomic model (3.1) in Figure 3B.1 in Appendix 3B.

In general, the most important implication of the econometric results of this chapter for the current literature is our panel data causality findings of the reinforcing effects of inward FDI, and our policy recommendation of attracting inward FDI, in addition to exports, as an important engine of growth. The reinforcing effects are exemplified by the economies of Singapore and Thailand, and possibly, Taiwan.

Another important finding is that, so far as the causality relations between exports, FDI, and GDP are concerned, our illustration in Figure 3.2 shows that the time-series analysis of causality among these three variables for individual country alone may not yield useful information for a general rule for economic policy. Even the widely recognized fast-growing export-oriented countries such as Korea and Hong Kong with relatively large amount of FDI inflows cannot show any causality among the three variables. We submit that some of the inconclusive results of the causality tests between GDP and FDI in the literature surveys in Sections 3.1 and 3.5 are at least due to the shortcoming of time-series analysis.

Only when we pooled the data for the eight similarly developing Asian economies together, and the interaction among countries and heterogeneity are considered in the panel data causality analysis, we found in Figure 3.3 very interesting and meaningful causality relations among FDI, exports, and GDP, with added advantage of being able to ascertain different degrees of importance on the relationships. In conclusion, it appears that the panel data analysis is superior and is the direction of the future: It supplements and enhances the results of the traditional time-series or cross-section analysis.

Lastly, we may point out that recent literature tends to emphasize the contribution of human capital or financial development along with FDI on GDP growth. Human capital, and for that matter, financial development, may be important in a regression estimation or determination of economic growth when the effects of FDI inflows are considered, as shown by Borensztein *et al.* (1998) and Hermes and Lensink (2003). However, the purpose of this chapter is not to estimate such a one-sided effect,[22] which inevitably gives rise to the problem of endogeneity of the variables. Rather, our purpose in this chapter is to test the causality of FDI and GDP, along with exports. All three variables are endogenous variables simultaneously. As such, we may also point out that our panel data analysis does show the expected results that FDI causes GDP either directly, or indirectly, through exports, and thus our analysis may suggest that exports may be a good substitute of, if not complementary to, human capital or financial development in its relation with FDI and GDP.

Appendix 3A:　Data Sources

The inward FDI data from 1986 to 2004 for China, Korea, Taiwan, Hong Kong, Singapore, Malaysia, the Philippines, and Thailand, all in current millions of US dollars, are obtained from the UNCTAD (2006) and the website of the UNCTAD Secretariat (http://stats.unctad.org/fdi/ReportFolders/ReprtFolders.asp x?CS_referer=andCS_ChosenLang=en) as of May 2006. Note that Indonesia is not included in this study due to some negative numbers in FDI data. The data on GDP and total merchandize exports, all in current millions of US dollars, for all eight Asian economies are taken from the ICSEAD (2006) and its website.

The current values of FDI are deflated by the GDP deflators of trade of each country. The current values of GDP have been deflated

---

[22]To control endogeneity of FDI, Borensztein *et al.* (1998) tried several instrumental variables. However, since there is no "ideal" instrument, the endogeneity of FDI and GDP can best be discussed under the causality framework.

by the GDP deflators of each country. The current values of exports are deflated by each economy's export price index. All these deflators are taken from the ICSEAD (2006), and the base year for all deflators has been converted to $2000 = 1$.

Appendix 3B: Expository Notes — Relations in the Macroeconomic Model

In addition to Figure 3.3, the direction and the degree of influence are again shown by the thickness of the arrows in the basic macroeconomic model in Figure 3B.1. Clearly, not all these variables have equal influences. The direction of the arrows suggests again the importance of inward FDI: it not only strongly effects on GDP but also reinforces its effect on GDP through exports (the arrow from F to X).

Note the three domestic demand variables, $C(Y)$, $I(Y,r)$, and $M(Y,e)$ in the equilibrium condition in (3.1). They show clearly that consumption, domestic investment, and imports are a function of income and present very complicated relations among these variables.

On the other hand, the chart also shows the limitations of our policy analysis: we have not only ignored the effects of the domestic

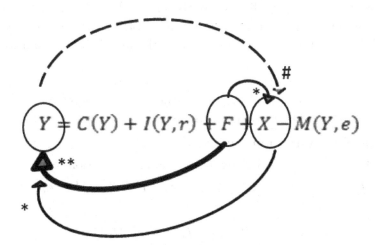

Figure 3B.1: Real GDP, Exports, and Inward FDI in the Basic Macroeconomic Model

demand factors: consumptions $C(Y)$, domestic investment $I(Y,r)$, and imports $M(Y,e)$, we also ignored the financial factors, interest rates, and exchange rates. Here lies the limitation of our analysis and the policy recommendations. Thus, one should be cautious in interpreting our results, and for that matter, any empirical or theoretical analysis.

Note that $C + I$, or $C + I + G$ if government expenditure G is considered, is called domestic absorption. Thus, our analysis considers the development strategies of open economies, namely, the relations of GDP, FDI, and foreign trade, in open macroeconomics.

Appendix 3C: Expository Notes — Theoretical Underpinning of the VAR Model (3.3)

After this chapter was published, we received several requests for explanation and the references on the derivation of the implicit function of Y, X, F in (3.2) from the Keynesian income determination model (3.1), and also derivation of VAR Eq. (3.3) from the implicit function Eq. (3.2). While one of the important features of the VAR model is that "it does not depend on the model, let the data speak itself," this appendix, nevertheless, is added to explain the derivation and justification of the matrix Eq. (3.3) in detail from the macroeconomic theory. The mathematical justification is based on the Implicit Function Theorem and the logarithmic expansion of functions.

More generally, this appendix demonstrates the relationship between a mathematical model (mathematical economics) and statistical method in economics (econometrics).

(1) Implicit Function Theorem

Equation (3.2) can be written as the implicit function form:

$$H(Y, X, F) = Y - C(Y) - I(Y,r) - F - X + M(Y,e) = 0.$$

Hence,

$$H_Y = 1 - C_Y(Y) - I_Y(Y,r) + M_Y(Y,e),$$

where the subscript shows the derivative with respect to the variable Y. C_Y, I_Y, and M_Y are marginal propensity to consume, to invest, and to import. In this general implicit function form, if certain regularity (in this case, derivative) conditions, as shown in the following, are satisfied, any one of the three variables can be solved explicitly as a function of the other two variables.

Each variable is solved explicitly as the function of other two variables as follows. If H_Y is non-zero at an equilibrium point, we can solve (by the Implicit Function Theorem) Y uniquely as, ignoring e and r, function of X and F:

$$Y = L(X, F). \tag{3C.1}$$

Thus, Y is a function of X and F, and a change in X or F will induce a change in Y.

Similarly, since $H_X = -1 \neq 0$ and $H_F = -1 \neq 0$, we can also write X and F explicitly as a function of other two variables:

$$X = M(Y, F), \tag{3C.2}$$

$$F = N(Y, X). \tag{3C.3}$$

(2) Taylor's Expansion

In general, given a function $z = f(x, y)$. If $f(1, 1) \neq 0$, then,

$$f(x, y) \equiv f(\exp(\ln x), \exp(\ln y)) \equiv g(u, v),$$

where we define $u \equiv \ln x$, $v \equiv \ln y$. $f(x, y)$ can be expanded logarithmically by $u = \ln x$ and $v = \ln y$ around $x = y = 1$ as (see Christensen *et al.*, 1973, p. 33):

$$\ln f(x, y) = a_0 + (a_1 \ln x + a_2 \ln y)$$
$$+ \frac{1}{2!}(b_1 \ln^2 x + 2b_2 \ln x \ln y + b_3 \ln^2 y) + \cdots \tag{3C.4}$$

where, by Taylor's expansion, $a_0 \equiv \ln f(1, 1), a_1 \equiv \partial \ln f(1, 1)/\partial \ln x$, $a_2 \equiv \partial \ln f(1, 1)/\partial \ln y$, and $b_1 \equiv \partial^2 \ln f(1, 1)/\partial \ln^2 x$, $b_2 \equiv \partial^2 \ln f(1, 1)/(\partial \ln x \partial \ln y)$, $b_3 \equiv \partial^2 \ln f(1, 1)/\partial \ln^2 y$, etc.

(3) Linear Equations

Applying the above method to Eqs. (3C.1)–(3C.3), taking the linear part of the logarithmic expansion, (3C.1) becomes

$$\ln Y = a_0 + a_1 \ln X + a_2 \ln F \tag{3C.5}$$

or, since $\ln Y = \text{gdp}$ is located at the third equation (row) of (3.3) in the text, we may rewrite (3C.5) as

$$\ln Y = a_{30} + a_{31} \ln X + a_{32} \ln F. \tag{3C.6}$$

Similarly, the logarithmic linear terms of the Taylor's expansion of explicit functions (3C.2) and (3C.3) are

$$\ln X = a_{10} + a_{11} \ln Y + a_{12} \ln F, \tag{3C.7}$$

$$\ln F = a_{20} + a_{21} \ln Y + a_{22} \ln X, \tag{3C.8}$$

respectively, where a_{1j} and $a_{2j}, j = 0, 1$, and 2, are the coefficients of the linear terms of the Taylor expansion similar to (3C.4). In (3C.7) and (3C.8), we add the first subscript 1 and 2 to show the equation number in (3.3).

(4) Change to Simpler Notations

In terms of the notations of using small letters to denote logarithmic variables in the text, we rewrite (3C.6) to (3C.8) in terms of gdp, ex, and fdi, and the a_{ij}'s in terms of μ_i's and γ_{ij}'s as

$$\text{gdp} = \mu_3 + \gamma_{32}\text{ex} + \gamma_{33}\text{fdi}, \tag{3C.9}$$

$$\text{ex} = \mu_1 + \gamma_{12}\text{gdp} + \gamma_{13}\text{fdi}, \tag{3C.10}$$

$$\text{fdi} = \mu_2 + \gamma_{22}\text{gdp} + \gamma_{23}\text{ex}, \tag{3C.11}$$

where the first subscript number denotes the row number in (3.3). Note that in each of the above three equations, the left-hand side is the dependent variable and the right-hand side is the independent variable.

(5) Derivation of the Autoregression Model for Each Variable

To convert the above economic model to an econometric model, that is, the VAR model, and to test the Granger Causality between the three variables, we add the dependent variable to the right-hand side to form an autoregressive model. Thus, each equation of (3C.9)–(3C.11) has the same three variables, ex, fdi, and gdp, on the right-hand side of the equality sign. Fixing the variables in this order and also taking the lag of p periods for each of the variables ex, fdi, and gdp, we have the following econometric model for testing the Granger's causality.

For (3C.9), noting that the variable gdp is listed at the third row in (3.3) and adding the error term, we have the testing equation of causality for gdp for each period:

$$
\begin{aligned}
\text{gdp}_t = {}& \mu_3 + \gamma_{31}^1 \text{ex}_{t-1} + \gamma_{32}^1 \text{fdi}_{t-1} + \gamma_{33}^1 \text{gdp}_{t-1} \quad \text{for period 1} \\
& + \gamma_{31}^2 \text{ex}_{t-2} + \gamma_{32}^2 \text{fdi}_{t-2} + \gamma_{33}^2 \text{gdp}_{t-2} \quad \text{for period 2} \\
& + \cdots \\
& + \gamma_{31}^p \text{ex}_{t-p} + \gamma_{32}^p \text{fdi}_{t-p} + \gamma_{33}^p \text{gdp}_{t-p} \quad \text{for period } p \\
& + \varepsilon_{3t},
\end{aligned}
\tag{3C.12}
$$

where γ_{ij}^k is an element of the coefficients matrix $\Gamma_k = [\gamma_{ij}^k]$ in (3.3) or (3C.16) below, which need to be estimated and tested econometrically, and k is the dummy variable for time lag, $k = 1, 2, \ldots p$, and i is the equation (row) number, $i = 1, 2, 3, j$ is the variable (column) number, $j = 1, 2, 3$, in Γ_k. (3C.12) is the third row, $i = 3$, of Eq. (3.3) or (3C.15).

Similarly, the testing equation for (3C.10) and (3C.11) can be written in terms of time lags like (3C.12). Thus, noting ex is on the first row (or first variable), $i = 1$, of (3.3), for (3C.10), we have

$$
\begin{aligned}
\text{ex}_t = {}& \mu_1 + \gamma_{11}^1 \text{ex}_{t-1} + \gamma_{12}^1 \text{fdi}_{t-1} + \gamma_{13}^1 \text{gdp}_{t-1} \\
& + \cdots + \gamma_{11}^p \text{ex}_{t-p} + \gamma_{12}^p \text{fdi}_{t-p} + \gamma_{13}^p \text{gdp}_{t-p} + \varepsilon_{1t}.
\end{aligned}
\tag{3C.13}
$$

The testing equation for (3C.11) may also be written similar to (3C.12) as, since fdi is the second variable in (3.3), $i = 2$,

$$
\begin{aligned}
\text{fdi}_t = {}& \mu_2 + \gamma_{21}^1 \text{ex}_{t-1} + \gamma_{22}^1 \text{fdi}_{t-1} + \gamma_{23}^1 \text{gdp}_{t-1} \\
& + \cdots + \gamma_{21}^p \text{ex}_{t-p} + \gamma_{22}^p \text{fdi}_{t-p} + \gamma_{23}^p \text{gdp}_{t-p} + \varepsilon_{2t}.
\end{aligned}
\tag{3C.14}
$$

Arranging (3C.12) to (3C.14) in matrix form, we have

$$
\begin{bmatrix} ex_t \\ fdi_t \\ gdp_t \end{bmatrix} = \begin{bmatrix} \mu_1 \\ \mu_2 \\ \mu_3 \end{bmatrix} + \begin{bmatrix} \gamma_{11}^1 & \gamma_{12}^1 & \gamma_{13}^1 \\ \gamma_{21}^1 & \gamma_{22}^1 & \gamma_{23}^1 \\ \gamma_{31}^1 & \gamma_{32}^1 & \gamma_{33}^1 \end{bmatrix} \begin{bmatrix} ex_{t-1} \\ fdi_{t-1} \\ gdp_{t-1} \end{bmatrix}
$$

$$
+ \begin{bmatrix} \gamma_{11}^2 & \gamma_{12}^2 & \gamma_{13}^2 \\ \gamma_{21}^2 & \gamma_{22}^2 & \gamma_{23}^2 \\ \gamma_{31}^2 & \gamma_{32}^2 & \gamma_{33}^2 \end{bmatrix} \begin{bmatrix} ex_{t-2} \\ fdi_{t-2} \\ gdp_{t-2} \end{bmatrix}
$$

$$
+ \cdots + \begin{bmatrix} \gamma_{11}^p & \gamma_{12}^p & \gamma_{13}^p \\ \gamma_{21}^p & \gamma_{22}^p & \gamma_{23}^p \\ \gamma_{31}^p & \gamma_{32}^p & \gamma_{33}^p \end{bmatrix} \begin{bmatrix} ex_{t-p} \\ fdi_{t-p} \\ gdp_{t-p} \end{bmatrix} + \begin{bmatrix} \varepsilon_{1t} \\ \varepsilon_{2t} \\ \varepsilon_{3t} \end{bmatrix} \quad (3C.15)
$$

which is the same as (3.3) and is written as a simultaneous system of difference equations of degree p,

$$
y_t = \mu + \Gamma_1 y_{t-1} + \Gamma_2 y_{t-2} + \cdots + \Gamma_p y_{t-p} + \varepsilon_t, \quad (3C.16)
$$

where y_t and y_{t-i} are 3×1 vectors of three variables at time t and $t - i$, respectively. Subscript i of (3×3) coefficient matrix Γ_i in (3C.16) denotes the i-th time lag for each set of the coefficients of three variables in three equations for $i = 1, 2, \ldots, p$.

(6) Rearrangement of the VAR model

Instead of writing the model in terms of time, we may also rewrite the difference equations (3C.15) or (3C.16) in terms of the three variables as follows. Collecting the same variables of (3C.15), or equivalently, rearranging the order of the variables in (3C.12), and writing in sum form for each variable, we have

$$
gdp_t = \mu_3 + \sum_{i=1}^{p} \gamma_{31}^i ex_{t-i} + \sum_{i=1}^{p} \gamma_{32}^i fdi_{t-i} + \sum_{i=1}^{p} \gamma_{33}^i gdp_{t-i} + \varepsilon_{3t},
$$

$$
(3C.17)
$$

where we summed (3C.12) by a variable (namely, by the three vertical columns of the way Eq. (3C.12) is currently arranged). Note that (3C.17) is the same form as Eqs. (1.1) and (1.2) in Chapter 1 for the two-variable case of gdp and ex, except now that we have a third variable fdi.

Equation (3C.17) may be written in vector form as

$$\text{gdp}_t = \mu_3 + \Gamma_{31}[\text{ex}P] + \Gamma_{32}[\text{fdi}P] + \Gamma_{33}[\text{gdp}P] + \varepsilon_{3t}, \qquad (3C.18)$$

where $[\text{ex}P]$, $[\text{fdi}P]$, and $[\text{gdp}P]$ are $p \times 1$ column vectors of the past P values of variables ex, fdi, and gdp, that is, ex_{t-i}, fdi_{t-i}, and gdp_{t-i}, for $i = 1, \ldots, p$, written as $p \times 1$ column vectors. For example,

$$[\text{ex}P] \equiv (\text{ex}_{t-1}, \text{ex}_{t-2}, \ldots, \text{ex}_{t-p})^T, \qquad (3C.19)$$

where the superscript T shows the transpose of the row vector shown in the parentheses. Similarly, $[\text{fdi}P]$ and $[\text{gdp}P]$ in (3C.18) can be written similar to (3C.19).

$\Gamma_{3j}, j = 1, 2, 3$, in (3C.18) are $1 \times p$ coefficients row vector of the coefficients of the variables ex_{t-i}, fdi_{t-i}, and gdp_{t-i}, respectively. For example, the $1 \times p$ row vector

$$\Gamma_{31} \equiv (\gamma_{31}^1, \gamma_{31}^2, \ldots, \gamma_{31}^p), \qquad (3C.20)$$

is a $1 \times p$ row vector of coefficients of ex_{t-1} in (3C.17). Thus, the scalar product $\Gamma_{31}[\text{ex}P]$ in (3C.18) is the same as the second term $\sum_{i=1}^p \gamma_{31}^i \text{ex}_{t-i}$ in Eq. (3C.17). Similarly, $\Gamma_{3j} = (\gamma_{3j}^1, \gamma_{3j}^2, \ldots, \gamma_{3j}^p)$, for $j = 2$ and 3, are $1 \times p$ row vector of coefficients of $p \times 1$ column vectors of variables $[\text{fdi}P]$ and $[\text{gdp}P]$ in (3C.18).

Using the same method, we may rewrite (3C.13) and (3C.14) as

$$\text{ex}_t = \mu_1 + \sum_{i=1}^p \gamma_{11}^i \text{ex}_{t-i} + \sum_{i=1}^p \gamma_{12}^i \text{fdi}_{t-i} + \sum_{i=1}^p \gamma_{13}^i \text{gdp}_{t-i} + \varepsilon_{1t},$$
$$(3C.21)$$

$$\text{fdi}_t = \mu_2 + \sum_{i=1}^p \gamma_{21}^i \text{ex}_{t-i} + \sum_{i=1}^p \gamma_{22}^i \text{fdi}_{t-i} + \sum_{i=1}^p \gamma_{23}^i \text{gdp}_{t-i} + \varepsilon_{2t}.$$
$$(3C.22)$$

Or, equivalently, following (3C.18), we have

$$\text{ex}_t = \mu_1 + \Gamma_{11}[\text{ex}P] + \Gamma_{12}[\text{fdi}P] + \Gamma_{13}[\text{gdp}P] + \epsilon_{1t}, \qquad (3C.23)$$

$$\text{fdi}_t = \mu_2 + \Gamma_{21}[\text{ex}P] + \Gamma_{22}[\text{fdi}P] + \Gamma_{23}[\text{gdp}P] + \epsilon_{2t}, \qquad (3C.24)$$

where rewriting (3C.18), (3C.23), and (3C.24) in matrix form, we have

$$
\begin{bmatrix} ex_t \\ fdi_t \\ gdp_t \end{bmatrix} = \begin{bmatrix} \mu_1 \\ \mu_2 \\ \mu_3 \end{bmatrix} + \begin{bmatrix} \Gamma_{11} & \Gamma_{12} & \Gamma_{13} \\ \Gamma_{21} & \Gamma_{22} & \Gamma_{23} \\ \Gamma_{31} & \Gamma_{32} & \Gamma_{33} \end{bmatrix} \begin{bmatrix} exP \\ fdiP \\ gdpP \end{bmatrix} + \begin{bmatrix} \epsilon_{1t} \\ \epsilon_{2t} \\ \epsilon_{3t} \end{bmatrix} \quad (3C.25)
$$
$$
3 \times 1 \qquad 3 \times 1 \qquad 3 \times (3 \times p) \qquad (3 \times p) \times 1 \qquad 3 \times 1
$$

In Eqs. (3C.18), (3C.23), and (3C.24), or more directly, (3C.25), the left-hand side is the current variable of the dependent variable, and the right-hand side is the past values of the dependent variable and independent variables for each equation.

Note that the diagonal elements of the coefficient matrix Γ in (3C.25) show the past values of the dependent variable of each equation. Intuitively, we may expect that the past values of the dependent variable, say, $[exP]$ on the right-hand side of (3C.25), will have an impact on the current value of ex on the left-hand side (by the law of continuity). However, the past values of independent variables, say, $[fdiP]$ and $[gdpP]$ in (3C.25), on the right-hand side may or may not have an impact on the current independent variable ex on the left-hand side.

(7) The Causality Tests

Thus, the Granger causality test is intuitively clear (a Nobel Prize winning idea!): We take two equations each time (see Chapter 1 for the special case). For example, in terms of the two Eqs. (3C.23) and (3C.24), we test causality between exports (ex) and FDI (fdi). For simplicity, we use $x => $ (or $\neq>$) y to denote variable x Granger causes (or does not Granger cause) y. There are four possible results of causality testing in this case. It is easier to see the results from (3C.25),

(a) If $\Gamma_{12} = 0$ and $\Gamma_{21} \neq 0$ statistically, then ex $=>$ fdi (unidirectional causality from ex to fdi).
(b) If $\Gamma_{21} = 0$ and $\Gamma_{12} \neq 0$ statistically, then fdi $=>$ ex (unidirectional causality from fdi to ex).
(c) If $\Gamma_{12} \neq 0$ and $\Gamma_{21} \neq 0$ statistically, then fdi $=>$ ex, and ex $=>$ fdi (bidirectional causality between fdi and ex).

(d) If $\Gamma_{12} = 0$ and $\Gamma_{21} = 0$ statistically, then fdi $\neq>$ ex, ex $\neq>$ fdi (no causality between fdi and ex).

The idea is that, in Eq. (3C.23), or equivalently, the first equation of (3C.25), even if we control the past values of the dependent variable [exP] (the first term of (3C.23), not counting the constant), if the coefficients Γ_{12} of the past independent variables [fdiP], taking together, are jointly not statistically significant (based on the F-test, same mentioned later on), and if the past values of the coefficients of the endogenous variable, Γ_{21} of the past dependent variable, exP, taking together, are statistically significant, then we say that ex "causes" fdi, in the sense that the past ex may "forecast" or "explain" the current fdi.

Similarly, four causality tests (a) to (d) hold between ex and gdp for Γ_{13} and Γ_{31}, and for fdi and gdp for Γ_{23} and Γ_{32}. Note that all pairs are symmetric along the diagonal line of the coefficient matrix in (3C.25).

Clearly, the causality defined above is not the same as saying that the flu virus "causes" headache. Thus, more precisely, we should say that "exports Granger causes FDI," and all the assumptions on regression analysis apply.

Appendix 3D: Expository Notes — On the Econometric Procedure

The empirical results of Granger causality tests for levels are shown in Table 3.5.

Note that, taking the difference both sides of Eq. (3C.9), we have

$$dgdp = \gamma_{32}dex + \gamma_{33}dfdi, \qquad (3D.1)$$

where d before the variable shows the differential. For the testing purpose, we may add the constant term, the endogenous variables, and lagged variable as in (3C.12). Similarly, ex in (3C.10) and fdi in (3C.11) can also be written in differential form similar to (3C.13) and (3C.14), or written in matrix form as (3C.15), except now that the constant terms μ_i disappear. Using the same method, we may also construct (3C.25) in terms of differential, in which the constant term disappears. The empirical results of Granger causality tests for difference form are shown in Table 3.4.

Note also that, before discussing the Granger causality using OLS, the econometric procedure requires the determination of the length of the lag P and stationarity of the variables, and also the possibility of cointegration. See Chapter 1.

(1) Lag length: the length should be taken enough to eliminate autocorrelation but as few lags as possible.
(2) Integration of order 0: Test whether the time series of gdp, ex, and fdi are all $I(0)$. If so, apply OLS to the level variables.
(3) Cointegration: If some are $I(1)$ but cointegrated, then we can estimate VAR using cointegrated equations by OLS.
(4) Non-cointegration: If the variables are $I(1)$ but not cointegrated, then we take the difference and estimate the coefficients by OLS, if the differenced variables are $I(0)$.
(5) Continue taking the difference until the series is stationary, and then use the regression analysis.
(6) Perform the Granger causality test.

After Chapter 3 was written, in recent years, the above six econometric procedures are widely available in the textbooks (for example, Gujarati and Porter, 2009 and the references in front matter of this book) and websites (for example, Giles, 2011, which includes using EViews to test Granger causality). We skip the details to save the space.

Acknowledgments

We are grateful to professor Angus Maddison of Groningen Growth and Development Center (GGDC), The Netherlands, and professor Eric Ramstetter of the International Centre for the Study of East Asian Development (ICSEAD), Japan, for introducing the latest data to the authors. We are also grateful to professors Robert McNown, Hiro Lee, Naci Mocan, Steven Beckman, Been-Lon Chen, Masao Oda, Yongkul Won, and Dr. Kyoohong Cho for discussions and suggestions at various stages of writing this chapter. An earlier version of this chapter was presented at the International Conference on "Korea and the World Economy, V," held at Seoul, Korea, July 2006. We also benefited from the discussions with a discussant and the conference participants. Our thanks also go to Professor Hyun-Hoon Lee for the invitation to the conference and hospitality. We also express our appreciation to Professor M. Jan Dutta for his encouragement in completing this chapter. As usual, all errors of omission and commission are ours. Postscript: All the tables and figures have been reformatted, and Appendices 3B–3D, and Figure 3B.1 are added for this chapter. We owe Dr. Soo Khoon Goh for the suggestion of references in Appendix 3D.

References

Ahmad, M. H., S. Alam and M. S. Butt (2004). Foreign Direct Investment, Exports and Domestic Output in Pakistan. Paper Presented at *The 19th Annual General Meeting*, PIDE, Quaid-E-Azam University, Islamabad.

Alici, A. A. and M. S. Ucal (2003). Foreign Direct Investment, Exports and Output Growth of Turkey: Causality Analysis. Paper presented at *The European Trade Study Group (ETSG) Fifth Annual Conference*, Universidad Carlos III De Madrid, Madrid.

Baltagi, B. H. (2001). *Econometric Analysis of Panel Data* (2nd edn.). New York: John Wiley and Sons.

Basu, P., C. Chakraborty and D. Reagle (2003). Liberalization, FDI, and growth in developing countries: A panel cointegration approaches. *Economic Inquiry* **41** (3), 510–516.

Borensztein, E., J. De Gregorio and J.-W. Lee (1998). How does foreign direct investment affect economic growth? *Journal of International Economics* **45**, 115–135.

Carkovic, M. and R. Levine (2005). Does Foreign Direct Investment Accelerate Economic Growth? In *Does Foreign Direct Investment Promote Development?*, T. H. Moran, E. M. Graham and M. Blomstrom (Eds.). Washington, DC: Institute of International Economics, pp. 195–220.

Cho, K. (2005). *Studies on Knowledge Spillovers, Trade, and Foreign Direct Investment — Theory and Empirics*, Ph.D. Thesis. Boulder, CO: Department of Economics, University of Colorado at Boulder.

Chowdhury, A. and G. Mavrotas (2006). FDI and growth: what causes what? *World Economy* **29** (1), 9–19.

Christensen, Laurites, R., Dale W. Jorgenson and Lawrence J. Lau (1973). Transcendental logarithmic production frontier. *Review of Economics and Statistics* **55** (1), 28–45.

Christopoulos, D. K. and E. G. Tsionas (2003). A reassessment of balance of payments constrained growth: Results from panel unit root and panel cointegration tests. *International Economic Journal* **17** (3), 39–54.

Cuadros, A., V. Orts and M. Alguacil (2004). Openness and growth: Re-examining foreign direct investment, trade and output linkages in Latin America. *The Journal of Development Studies* **40** (4), 167–192.

Davidson, R. and J. G. Mackinnon (2004). *Econometrics Theory and Methods.* New York: Oxford University Press.

De Mello, L. R., Jr. (1997). Foreign direct investment in developing countries and growth: A selective survey. *The Journal of Development Studies* **34** (1), 1–34.

De Mello, L. R., Jr. (1999). Foreign direct investment-led growth: Evidence from time series and panel data. *Oxford Economic Papers* **51** (1), 133–151.

Dickey, D. A. and W. A. Fuller (1979). Distribution of the estimators for autoregressive time series with a unit root. *Journal of the American Statistical Association* **74** (366), 427–431.

Dickey, D. A. and W. A. Fuller (1981). Likelihood ratio statistics for autoregressive time series with a unit root. *Econometrica* **49** (4), 1057–1072.

Dritsaki, M., C. Dritsaki and A. Adamopoulos (2004). A causal relationship between trade, foreign direct investment, and economic growth for Greece. *American Journal of Applied Sciences* **1** (3), 230–235.

Edwards, S. (1993). Openness, trade liberalization, and growth in developing countries. *Journal of Economic Literature* **32** (3), 1358–1393.

Elliott, G., T. J. Rothenberg and J. H. Stock (1996). Efficient tests for an autoregressive unit root. *Econometrica* **64** (4), 813–836.

EViews 5.1. (2005). Irvine, CA: Quantitative Micro Software, LLC.

Fan, E. X. (2002). Technological Spillovers from Foreign Direct Investment — A Survey. Asian Development Bank. ERD Working Paper Series No. 33.

Frankel, J. A. and D. Romer (1999). Does trade cause growth? *American Economic Review* **89**, 379–399.

Frankel, J. A., D. Romer and T. Cyrus (1996). Trade and Growth in East Asian Countries: Cause and Effects? NBER Working Paper No. 5732.

Giles, J. A. and C. I. Williams (2000). Export-led growth: A survey of the empirical literature and some non-causality results. Part I. *Journal of International Trade and Economic Development* **9** (3), 261–337.

Giles, Dave (2011), Testing Granger Causality, in *Econometrics Beat: Dave Giles' Block*, A resource for econometrics students and practitioners. Downloaded in September 2018 from https://davegiles.blogspot.com/2011/04/testing-for-granger-causality.html

Gray, H. P. (1998). International Trade and Foreign Direct Investment: The Interface. In *Globalization, Trade and Foreign Direct Investment*, J. H. Dunning (Ed.). Oxford: Elsevier, pp. 19–27.

Greenaway, D. and W. Morgan (1998). Trade Orientation and Economic Development: Theory and Evidence. In *Development Economics and Policy, The Conference Volume to Celebrate the 85th Birthday of Professor Sir Hans Singer* [Chapter 9], D. Sapsford and J. R. Chen (Eds.). New York: St. Martin Press.

Greene, W. H. (2003). *Econometric Analysis* (5th edn.). Upper Saddle River, NJ: Prentice Hall.

Grossman, G. M. and E. Helpman (1997). *Innovation and Growth in the Global Economy*. Cambridge, MA: MIT Press.

Gujarati, D. N. and D. C. Porter (2009). *Basic Econometrics* (5th edn.) New York: McGraw-Hill Irwin.

Hansen, H. and J. Rand (2006). On the causal links between FDI and growth in developing countries. *World Economy* **29** (1), 21–41.

Hermes, N. and R. Lensink (2003). Foreign direct investment, financial development and economic growth. *Journal of Development Studies* **40**, 142–163.

Hsiao, M. C. W. (1987). Tests of causality and exogeneity between exports and economic growth: The case of Asian NICs. *Journal of Economic Development* **12** (2), 143–159.

Hsiao, F. S. T. and M. C. W. Hsiao (2001). Capital flows and exchange rates: Recent Korean and Taiwanese experience and challenges. *Journal of Asian Economics* **12**(3), 353–381.

Hsiao, F. S. T. and M. C. W. Hsiao (2003a). 'Miracle growth' in the twentieth century — international comparisons of East Asian development. *World Development* **31** (2), 227–257.

Hsiao, F. S. T. and M. C. W. Hsiao (2003b). The impact of the US economy on the Asia-Pacific region: Does it matter? *Journal of Asian Economics* **14** (2), 219–241.

Hsiao, F. S. T. and M. C. W. Hsiao (2004). The chaotic attractor of foreign direct investment — Why China? A Panel Data Analysis. *Journal of Asian Economics* **15** (4), 641–670.

Hsiao, F. S. T. and M. C. W. Hsiao (2006). FDI, exports, and GDP in East and Southeast Asia-Panel data versus time-series causality analysis. *Journal of Asian Economics* **17**, 1082–1106.

Hsiao, F. S. T. and C. Park (2002). Productivity growth in newly developed countries — The case of Korea and Taiwan. *The Journal of the Korean Economy* **3** (2), 189–230.

Hsiao, F. S. T. and C. Park (2005). Korean and Taiwanese productivity performance–Comparisons at matched manufacturing levels. *Journal of Productivity Analysis* **23**, 85–107.

Im, K. S., M. H. Pesaran and Y. Shin (2003). Testing for unit roots in heterogeneous panels. *Journal of Econometrics* **115**, 53–74.

International Centre for the Study of East Asian Development (ICSEAD) (2006). *East Asian Economic Perspectives*, Special Issue, February. Kitakyushyu, Japan.

Johansen, S. (1991). Estimation and hypothesis testing of cointegrated vectors in Gaussian VAR models. *Econometrica* **59** (6), 1551–1580.

Kohpaiboon, A. (2003). Foreign trade regimes and FDI-growth nexus: A case study of Thailand. *The Journal of Development Studies* **40** (2), 55–69.

Kojima, K. (1973). A macroeconomic approach to foreign direct investment. *Hitotsubashi Journal of Economics* **14** (1), 1–21.

Lim, E. G. (2001). Determinants of, and the Relation Between, Foreign Direct Investment and Growth: A Summary of the Recent Literature. IMF Working Paper No. WP/01/175.

Liu, X., P. Burridge and P. J. N. Sinclair (2002). Relationships between economic growth, foreign direct investment and trade: Evidence from China. *Applied Economics* **34**, 1433–1440.

Mackinnon, J. G. (1996). Numerical distribution functions for unit root and cointegration tests. *Journal of Applied Econometrics* **11**, 601–618.

Maddala, G. S. and I.-M. Kim (1998). *Unit Roots, Cointegration and Structural Change*. UK: Cambridge University Press.

Maddala, G. S. and S. Wu (1999). A comparative study of unit root tests with panel data and a new simple test. *Oxford Bulletin of Economics and Statistics* **61**, 631–652.

Maddison, A. (2003). *The World Economy: Historical Statistics*. Paris: OECD Development Center.

Makki, S. S. and A. Somwaru (2004). Impact of foreign direct investment and trade on economic growth: Evidence from developing countries. *American Journal of Agricultural Economics* **86** (3), 795–801.

Markusen, J. R. and A. J. Venables (1998). Multinational firms and the new trade theory. *Journal of International Economics* **46**, 183–203.

Nair-Reichert, U. and E. Weinhold (2000). Causality tests for cross-country panels: New look at FDI and economic growth in developing countries. *Oxford Bulletin of Economics and Statistics* **64**, 153–171.

Neuhaus, Marco (2006). *The Impact of FDI on Economic Growth: An Analysis for the Transition Countries of Central and Eastern Europe*. Germany, Heidelberg: Physica-Verlag,

Petri, P. A. (2006). Is East Asia becoming more interdependent? *Journal of Asian Economics* **17**, 381–394.

Petri, P. A. and M. G. Plummer (1998). The Determinants of Foreign Direct Investment: A Survey with Applications to the United States. In *Economic Development and Cooperation in The Pacific Basin: Trade, Investment, and Environmental Issues* [Chapter 7], H. Lee and D. W. Roland-Holst (Eds.). New York: Cambridge University Press.

Said, S. E. and D. A. Dickey (1984). Testing for unit roots in autoregressive-moving average models of unknown order. *Biometrika* **71**, 599–607.

Stock, J. H. and Watson, M. W. (2003). *Introduction to Econometrics*. Boston: Addison Wesley.

Toda, H. Y. (1994). Finite sample performance of likelihood ratio tests for cointegration ranks in vector autoregressions. *Econometric Theory* **11**, 66–79.

Toda, H. Y. and T. Yamamoto (1995). Statistical inference in vector autoregressions with possible integrated processes. *Journal of Econometrics* **66**, 225–250.

Rodriguez, F. and D. Rodrik (2000). Trade Policy and Economic Growth: A Skeptic's Guide to the Cross-National Evidence. In *Macroeconomics Annual 2000*, B. Bernanke and K. Rogoff (Eds.), Cambridge, MA: MIT Press.

United Nation Conference on Trade and Development (UNCTAD) (2006). *World Investment Report*. New York: United Nations.

Vernon, R. (1966). International investment and international trade in the product cycle. *Quarterly Journal of Economics* **80**, 190–207.

Wang, C., S. Liu and Y. Wei (2004). Impact of openness on growth in different country group. *World Economy* **27** (4), 567–585.

Wernerheim, C. M. (2000). Cointegration and causality in the exports-GDP nexus: The postwar evidence for Canada. *Empirical Economics* **25**, 111–125.

Chapter 4

Panel Causality Analysis on FDI–Exports–Economic Growth Nexus in First and Second Generation ANIEs

Abstract

This chapter continues from Chapter 3. Based on the previous results, we explore whether there are different causality relations among the three growth factors due to different stages of economic development. Specifically, using panel data from 1981 to 2005, we examine the Granger causality relations among exports, FDI, and GDP (TIG) in the three first generation Asian newly industrializing economies (ANIEs): Korea, Taiwan, and Singapore, in addition to the four second generation ANIEs: Malaysia, the Philippines, Thailand, and China. After reviewing the current literature, we construct three-variable panel vector autoregression (VAR) models for the first generation ANIEs, the second generation ANIEs, and finally, all seven economies as a group. We then use the fixed effects model to estimate the panel VAR equations for Granger causality tests. The panel data causality results reveal that there are bidirectional causality relations among all three variables for the three first generation ANIEs, but only statistically weak bidirectional causality exists between exports and GDP for the four second generation ANIEs. However, when all seven ANIEs are grouped for panel data analysis, we find that FDI has unidirectional effects on the GDP directly and also indirectly through exports. We also find that exports cause GDP, and there is a bidirectional causality between exports and GDP for the group. Economic and policy implications of our analyses for promoting economic development are then explored in the conclusions.

Keywords: FDI, exports, and GDP; panel data causality analysis; Granger causality; ANIEs

4.1 Introduction

Since World War II, it has been well known that the "economic miracle" took place in Asia (World Bank, 1993), starting from Japan in the 1960s to early 1970s, followed by four Asian Newly Industrializing Economies (ANIEs) — Taiwan, Korea, Singapore, and Hong Kong — in the 1970s and 1980s. In the latter half of the 1980s, while the ANIEs continued to grow, the ASEAN4 — Indonesia, Malaysia, the Philippines, Thailand, along with China — started rapid growth, and the growth fever spread to Vietnam and India in the new millennium. The rapid clustered sequential growth of East Asia is unique in the history of economic development in that it is not shared by other regions of the world (World Bank, 1993; UNCTAD, 1995; Fukasaku *et al.*, 2006). This rapid clustered sequential growth is dubbed as the "flying-geese" model of development (Kojima, 1973, 2000; Ozawa, 2003). While the collapse of the Thai Baht in mid-1997 triggered the Asian financial crisis and consequently the economies of most of the Asian countries suffered — especially Korea, Malaysia, the Philippines, and Thailand — all the Asian economies, nevertheless, successfully resumed their rapid growth after the crises within a few years.

Aside from institutional and organizational factors, the most common economic factor mentioned in these studies is openness of the economy, namely, export promotion policy, and active acceptance of inward FDI (with the exception of Japan). The roles of trade and FDI have been extensively discussed in recent years both in theory and in practice (see Chapter 3). Generally speaking, exports, imports, and inward FDI are sources of new ideas, new goods, new domestic competition, and technology transfer from advanced countries. In addition, to attract FDI, the host governments must maintain stable macroeconomic environment and reduce market distortions. All these enhance economic efficiency and productivity of the economy. The positive relation between openness and economic growth seems overwhelming, at least in theory. However, empirical studies of causalities between openness (trade and FDI) and economic growth are mixed at best. Their relations are not as obvious and straightforward, as shown in the survey of the literature in Chapter 3.

The major purpose of this chapter follows the current literature and investigates the relation between openness (namely, exports and FDI) and economic growth by using panel data analysis, taking the data from seven rapidly developing countries in East Asia (namely, the three first generation ANIEs, consisting of Korea, Taiwan, and Singapore, and the four second generation ANIEs, consisting of Malaysia, the Philippines, Thailand, and China). These seven countries are chosen because of their strong openness policy during the past two decades of rapid development and also due to their clustered sequential growth in East Asia with clearly recognizable different stages of development. This may give us some useful policy implications.

The structure of this chapter is essentially the same as the previous chapter. In Section 3.1 of Chapter 3, we reviewed some recent theoretical and empirical literature on the causality relations among the three variables in a country or a group of countries. Then, in Section 3.2 we briefly presented the analytical framework of the interdependence of the three variables in an economy using the mini-general equilibrium Keynesian-type demand-oriented open economy model. This is the basis of the panel vector autoregression (VAR) analysis in Section 4.3 of this chapter.

In this chapter, after this Introduction (Section 4.1), Section 4.2 reviews some empirical characteristics of exports, FDI and GDP of the nine country data from South Korea, Taiwan, Singapore, Hong Kong, Indonesia, Malaysia, the Philippines, Thailand, and

China, from 1981 to 2005. Section 4.3 presents panel data VAR tests of seven countries (excluding Hong Kong and Indonesia, due to negative FDI for some years), followed by Section 4.4 the Granger causality tests. Section 4.5 discusses the different causality relations when the seven countries are divided into two groups: the first generation Asian Newly Industrializing Economies (ANIEs 1) and the second generation ANIEs (ANIEs 2). Section 4.6 concludes by summarizing our findings and discussing policy implications.

4.2 Some Characteristics of the Country Data

Figure 3.1 of the previous chapter compares the real GDP per capita of East and Southeast Asia to that of the world. To see the characteristics of the individual ANIEs country data, we use the data from the WDI dataset (World Bank, 2007). To examine the data, we graph the time-series of real GDP, real merchandize exports, and real inward foreign direct investment (that is, TIG) for each of the nine Asian economies from 1981 to 2005 in the nine charts of Figure 4.1 (see Appendix 4B for the data sources and the explanation of the construction of real variables in Figure 4.1). Since the magnitude of FDI is generally very small when compared with GDP and exports, we have drawn real FDI on the secondary Y-axis in all the charts in Figure 4.1. From Figure 4.1, we find some interesting characteristics from the country data. Note that we have deleted the chart for Vietnam since we consider Vietnam, along with Cambodia, etc., belongs to the third generation NIEs.

Although we extend the data from 1986–2004 in Chapter 3 to 1981–2005 in this chapter, the basic characteristics of the data of each country do not change. Thus, the description of Section 3.4 in Chapter 3 still applies. In Figure 4.1, except for the Philippines in the early 1980s, the real GDP (rGDP in Figure 4.1) levels of all other economies have increased overtime, and with the exception of China, all economies were affected by the Asian financial crisis of 1997. The real GDP levels become more fluctuating after 1997 (see the dotted straight line). Real exports (rEX in Figure 4.1) increase along with real GDP and appear to play a vital role in all nine economies. By 1997, real exports have exceeded real GDP in Hong Kong (1991),

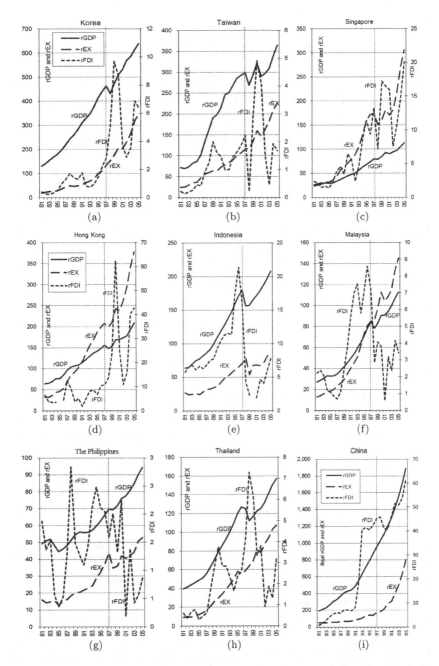

Figure 4.1: rGDP, rEX, and rFDI in Nine East and Southeast Asia Countries

2000 Deflator = 100. In USD billion

Singapore (1985), and Malaysia (1997). In other countries, by the mid-2000s, the amount of real exports ranges from about 30% of the GDP level in China and Korea to about or above 50% in Taiwan, the Philippines, and Thailand, indicating the possible impact of export activities on real GDP, or vice versa, in all these economies.

The Asian financial crisis of 1997 also exerted some impact on export activities, and exports became more volatile afterward. However, the impact appeared to be minimal and short-lived. Real exports and real GDP of all economies recovered quickly and kept increasing, and even surpassed those of the pre-1997 levels. In general, the comparison of the trend of real GDP and real exports shows that real exports and real GDP appear to be strongly correlated. In fact, the simple correlation coefficients between these two variables for the seven economies for 1981–2005 range from 0.17 (for the Philippines) to 0.89 (for Singapore). The correlation coefficients for China, Korea, Taiwan, Malaysia, and Thailand are 0.75, 0.48, 0.61, 0.66, and 0.35, respectively.

Compared to real GDP and real exports activities, real FDI (rFDI in Figure 4.1) in each economy fluctuates considerably, and has much lesser weight, almost negligible, in terms of its amount, as indicated by the large difference in scale of the main (left-hand) Y-axis and that of the secondary (right-hand) Y-axis. China, Hong Kong, and possibly Singapore, are exceptions, as the FDI has relatively large proportion of GDP.

We have seen that the 1997 Asian financial crisis exerted influence on the time-series of real GDP, real FDI, and real exports (namely, real TIG). All three of these variables, with the exception of China, had decreased significantly in 1998, although most of these economies recovered very quickly. After the 1997 financial crisis, these economies go through economic reforms and structural changes. To take into account the effects of the 1997 Asian financial crisis, we introduce a dummy variable which equals zero for 1981–1997 and equals one for 1998–2005, for the Granger causality test equations in Section 4.3. We also note that FDI inflows in Hong Kong in 1985 and in Indonesia around 2000 have negative values (shown by the broken dotted line), thus, they are excluded from our study.

The econometric analysis of this chapter follows closely that of Chapter 3. Thus, we may bypass the review of theoretical and empirical literature and the analytical framework and simply present the results of our panel data analysis in the following sections.

4.3 Panel Data Granger Causality Tests

As we have pointed out in the previous chapter (Section 3.7), a panel data analysis has the merit of using information concerning cross-section and time-series analyses. It is suited to a dataset which has a large sample with a shorter time period like the one we are dealing with. It can allow heterogeneity among different countries and regions, and it can attain a higher power of testing by increasing the degree of freedom, in addition to other advantages (see Baltagi, 2001). In general, the repeated cross-section of observations over time is better suited to study the dynamic of changes of variables like exports, FDI inflows, and GDP.

As we have seen in Figure 4.1, considering the growing inter-dependence of the seven East Asian economies, we construct the seven cross-sectional data over the 25-year period (1981–2005) into a panel dataset. Afterward, we use panel data regressions to examine the causality relation for the whole group, and we divide the seven economies into two groups: the first generation ANIEs (ANIEs 1) and the second generation ANIEs (ANIEs 2). We compare the group Granger causality relations for the three groups.

4.3.1 *Panel Data Unit Root Tests*

We first test the stationarity of the three panel level series: ex, fdi, and gdp (for simplicity, we use these small letters for real exports, real FDI, and real GDP, respectively). As in the previous chapter, we choose Im, Pesaran, and Shin W-test (2003) (IPS-W test) and ADF-Fisher Chi-square test (ADF-Fisher) (Maddala and Wu, 1999) to perform the panel data unit root test and compare their results (Christopoulos and Tsionas, 2003). The results for the three groups are summarized in Table 4.1.

Part (a) of Table 4.1 presents the panel unit root test results of the three-level series and their first-difference series for all seven

Table 4.1: Panel Data Unit Root Tests for ANIEs
Level and First Difference Series

Tests	Effects	Panel Level Series			Panel First Difference Series		
		ex	fdi	gdp	dex	dfdi	dgdp
(a) ANIEs ALL economies							
IPS W-Stat	Indiv	3.741 (0.99)	-1.721** (0.04)	0.565 (0.71)	-4.596*** (0.00)	-9.461*** (0.00)	-5.353*** (0.00)
	Indiv +trend	0.629 (0.74)	-2.155** (0.02)	1.387 (0.92)	-3.140*** (0.00)	-7.311*** (0.00)	-4.464*** (0.00)
ADF-Fisher Chi2	Indiv	4.013 (0.99)	22.582* (0.07)	12.482 (0.57)	53.169*** (0.00)	100.232*** (0.00)	53.002*** (0.00)
	Indiv +trend	13.535 (0.48)	26.201** (0.02)	11.794 (0.62)	36.093*** (0.00)	71.160*** (0.00)	42.257*** (0.00)
(b) ANIEs 1							
IPS W-Stat	Indiv	2.024 (0.98)	-0.793 (0.21)	0.354 (0.64)	-4.427*** (0.00)	-4.461*** (0.00)	-3.718*** (0.00)
	Indiv +trend	-0.917 (0.18)	-2.581*** (0.00)	1.639 (0.95)	-3.348*** (0.00)	-3.943*** (0.00).	-2.984*** (0.00)
ADF-Fisher Chi2	Indiv	0.810 (0.99)	8.103 (0.23)	3.447 (0.75)	30.149*** (0.00)	30.109*** (0.00)	24.121*** (0.00)
	Indiv +trend	8.192 -0.22	16.187** (0.01)	1.306 (0.97)	21.610*** (0.00)	24.747*** (0.00)	18.455*** (0.01)
(c) ANIEs 2							
IPS W-Stat	Indiv	3.202 (0.99)	-1.588* (0.06)	0.441 (0.67)	-2.205** (0.01)	-8.710*** (0.00)	-3.862*** (0.00)
	Indiv +trend	1.675 (0.95)	-0.639 (0.26)	0.420 (0.66)	-1.216# (0.11)	-6.260*** (0.00)	-3.322*** (0.00)
ADF-Fisher Chi2	Indiv	3.202 (0.92)	14.479* (0.07)	9.035 (0.34)	23.020*** (0.00)	70.123*** (0.00)	28.880*** (0.00)
	Indiv +trend	5.343 (0.72)	10.264 (0.26)	10.487 (0.23)	14.484* (0.07)	46.413*** (0.00)	23.803*** (0.00)

Notes: (1) ANIEs 1 includes Taiwan, Korea, and Singapore; ANIEs 2 includes China, Malaysia, Philippines, and Thailand. "All economies" include seven ANIEs 1 and ANIEs 2. (2) The optimal lag length is selected by the minimum AIC with maximum lag 3. (3) The numbers in parentheses denote the *p*-values. (4) *** (**, *, #) denotes rejection of null hypothesis at the 1% (5%, 10%, 15%) level of significance, respectively.

Post Script: This table combines Tables 1 to 3 of the original paper. (see #4 of "Sources of the Chapters" section at the beginning of this book).

countries. Both IPS-W test and ADF-Fisher Chi-square (Chi^2) tests indicate that the panel series FDI (fdi) is likely to be a level stationary series, but ex and gdp are not level stationary series. However, both tests indicate that the three panel first-difference series (denoted by adding d before the variable) dex, dfdi, and dgdp are all stationary series. Therefore, we use the three panel first-difference series in the panel data VAR causality analysis for the group.

In Table 4.1, Parts (b) and (c) show the panel unit root test results for the first and the second generation ANIEs countries, respectively. Both IPS-W and ADF-Fisher tests also indicate that the panel level series of the three variables are not stationary, but the three panel first-difference series are all stationary. Thus, we also use the first-difference series of the three variables panel to study the Granger causalities for the two groups.

4.3.2 *Panel Data VAR and Granger Causality Tests*

When we estimate panel data regression models, we consider the assumptions about the intercept, the slope coefficients, and the error term. In practice, the estimation procedure utilizes either the fixed effects model or the random effects model (Greene, 2003). Since the random effects model requires the number of cross-section units to be greater than the number of coefficients, with our seven cross-section units, we can estimate VAR(p) with lag order $p = 1$ or 2. Otherwise, we would lose too much information if we have more than two lags, for we have data only over 25-year period. The optimal lag lengths are then selected by the minimum AIC method. As will be shown, the random effects model is rejected for all equations, and we explain briefly the estimation of panel VAR in the context of the fixed effects model.

4.3.3 *The Fixed Effects Approach*

As in the previous chapter, the FEM can be written as follows:

$$y_{it} = \alpha_i + x_{it}\beta + u_{it}, \tag{4.1}$$

where y_{it} can be one of our three endogenous variables, i is the ith cross-section unit and t is the time of observation, the intercept, α_i takes into account the heterogeneity influence from unobserved variables which may differ across the cross-section units. The x_{it} is a row vector of all lag endogenous variables.

The β is a column vector of the common slope coefficients for the group of economies. The error term u_{it} follows classical assumption that $u_{it} \sim N(0,\sigma^2)$. In addition, we add an ordinary dummy variable, zero for 1981–1997 and one for 1998–2005, into the model to take into account the effects of the 1997 Asian financial crisis if the dummy is significant at the 10% level. The FEM is estimated by the method of least squares dummy variable (LSDV).

Note that the Hausman test rejects the null hypothesis of random effect model at 5% level in the estimations of the panel VAR for all seven economies as a group.[1] On the other hand, the first and the second generation models have smaller number of cross-section units than the number of the coefficients. Therefore, we cannot use the random effects model. Thus, only the fixed effects model is presented in this chapter.

4.4   The Granger Causality Test

Table 4.2 presents the estimated panel data VAR for all seven economies as a group by FEM, and the Wald test of coefficients for Granger causality directions (for simplicity, subscripts i and t are omitted, and the cross-section specific constant terms are not presented in the table). The coefficients of dummy variable are all negative, but not significant at the 10% level. Thus, the dummy variable was dropped from the regressions. Figures 4.2 to 4.4 summarize the panel data Granger causality results of Table 4.2.

---

[1]For dex, dfdi, and dgdp equations, Hausman test's Chi-square statistics (p-value) are 14.8 (.02), 20.8 (.00), and 14.4 (.03), respectively, all rejecting random effects model at 5% level of significance.

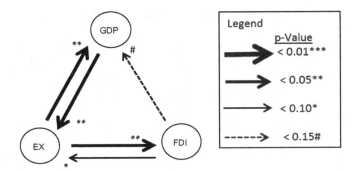

Figure 4.2: Panel Data Granger Causality Relation
All Seven ANIE Countries

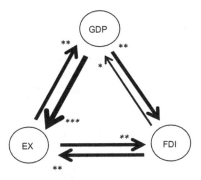

Figure 4.3: Panel Data Granger Causality Relation
ANIEs 1 Countries

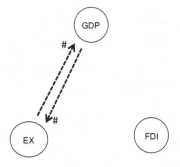

Figure 4.4: Panel Data Granger Causality Relation
ANIEs 2 Countries

Table 4.2: Panel Data Unit Root Tests
First and Second Generation ANIEs

Coeff estimates	(a) ANIEs All (dep var)			(b) ANIEs 1			(c) ANIEs 2		
	dex	dfdi	dgdp	dex	dfdi	dgdp	dex	dfdi	dgdp
1 constant	0.41 (0.01)	0.719 (0)	0.362 (0.03)	0.114 (0.00)	0.307 (0.03)	0.09 (0.00)	0.05 (0.00)	0.049 (0.55)	-0 (0.84)
2 dex(-1)	0.24 (0.03)	0.131 (0.11)	0.151 (0.17)	0.281 (0.09)	2.683 (0.01)	0.325 (0.06)	0.24 (0.09)	0.168 (0.84)	0.127 (0.39)
3 dex(-2)	0.1 (0.34)	0.138 (0.08)	0.255 (0.02)	0.169 (0.32)	0.831 (0.09)	0.401 (0.02)	0.13 (0.34)	0.081 (0.92)	0.227 (0.11)
4 dfdi(-1)	-0.2 (0.15)	0.415 (0)	-0.147 (0.2)	-0.03 (0.21)	-0.43 (0.00)	-0.03 (0.16)	-0 (0.59)	-0.35 (0.00)	-0.01 (0.77)
5 dfdi(-2)	-0 (0.91)	0.236 (0)	-0.021 (0.85)	-0.07 (0.00)	-0.34 (0.02)	-0.05 (0.04)	0 (0.96)	0.098 (0.41)	-0.01 (0.80)
6 dgdp(-1)	0.11 (0.28)	-0.023 (0.77)	0.179 (0.09)	-0.08 (0.65)	-2.52 (0.02)	-0.1 (0.56)	0.17 (0.20)	0.714 (0.338)	0.245 (0.07)
7 dgdp(-2)	-0.3 (0)	-0.144 (0.06)	-0.283 (0.01)	-0.55 (0.00)	-1.99 (0.07)	-0.48 (0.01)	-0.2 (0.08)	-0.69 (0.349)	-0.28 (0.04)
8 dummy				-0.060 (0.04)	-0.42 (0.02)	-0.09 (0.00)			

Wald test of coefficents

HO F-stat	B 2.458 (0.09)	A 3.302 (0.04)	A 4.502 (0.01)	B 4.764 (0.01)	A 4.499 (0.02)	A 4.178 (0.02)	B 0.176 (0.84)	A 0.033 (0.97)	A 2.087 (0.13)

Causality direction:
fdi→ex*   ex→gdp***   ex→fdi**   fdi→ex**   ex→gdp**   ex→fdi**   ex→gdp#

Wald test of coefficents

HO F-stat	C 4.846 (0.01)	C 1.894 (0.15)	B 2.200 (0.11)	C 5.373 (0.01)	C 4.456 (0.02)	B 2.568 (0.09)	C 2.185 (0.12)	C 0.810 (0.45)	B 0.055 (0.95)

Causality direction:
gdp→ex***   fdi→gdp#   gdp→ex***.   fdi→gdp*   gdp→fdi**   gdp→ex#

Notes: (1) The numbers in parentheses denote p-values. (2) *** (**, *, #) denotes rejection of null hypothesis at the 1% (5%, 10%, 15%) level of significance, respectively. (3) Ho=null hypothesis, F-stat=F-statistic. (4) In the Wald test of coefficients, the null hypothesis for A is c2=c3=0, B is c4=c5=0, C is c6=c7=0, respectively.

Post Script: This table combines Tables 4 to 6 of the original paper (see #4 of the "Sources of Collected Papers").

We find five very interesting causality relations for all seven Asian economies as a group. They are summarized as follows:

(1) Similar to the previous chapter, from the first equation (dex) of Table 4.2 (the dex column of Part (a)), we have found that GDP causes exports, and inward FDI also causes exports. On the other hand, from the third equation (the dgdp column of Part (a)), exports and FDI both cause GDP. These four directions of Granger causality are the same as those found in Figure 3.3 of Chapter 3. Although the weight of its importance appears different, the results here generally reinforce the causality relationship. The results show the importance of GDP and FDI in promoting exports, and they also support the existence of export-led growth and the FDI-led growth in these seven Asian economies as a group.

(2) From the second equation (the dfdi column of Part (a)), we find a unidirectional causality from exports to FDI inflows, but not from GDP to FDI inflows. Apparently, the growth of exports is not the only factor that attracts FDI inflows to these seven Asian economies. Other factors, such as the abundant quality labor supply, human capital, low wages, tax holidays, etc. must be taken into consideration if we are interested in the determinations of FDI in regression analysis, as shown in the previous chapter.

(3) From the first and the second equations together, we find bidirectional causality between exports and FDI inflows. This is different from the result in Figure 3.3 of Chapter 3. This shows that exports and FDI inflows have been mutually reinforcing the process of rapid economic growth of the seven Asian economies.

(4) Note the strong bidirectional relations between exports and GDP and also Exports and FDI. This is different from the previous chapter (compare Figure 4.2 and Figure 3.3 of Chapter 3). It shows that, while FDI is important in the process of economic development, the export promotion policy not only promotes FDI, but it will also reinforce the growth of GDP. Thus, the developing countries cannot ignore the importance of export promotion policy.

Like the previous chapter, we find the evidence that, in general, inward FDI has much stronger reinforcing effects on GDP. Namely, FDI not only has a direct impact on the GDP (although not as strong as the previous chapter), but FDI also indirectly increases GDP through exports due to the strong interactive relations between exports and GDP. In fact, these interactive relations are much stronger than those found in the previous chapter. This finding is consistent with, and reinforced with, the findings of the previous chapter supporting the "Bhagwati Hypothesis" (Kohpaiboon, 2003), which states that FDI not only causes the growth of GDP directly, but it also strongly affects the GDP through its effect on exports.

Thus, from our causality analysis in this chapter, we reach the same conclusion as the previous chapter. So far as the Asian first and second generation newly developing economies are concerned, due to the reinforcing effects of inward FDI, the economic growth policy priority of a developing country, generally speaking, appears to open the economy for inward FDI under the export promotion regime, and the interaction between exports and GDP will induce economic development. This is a general proposition based on the evidence from the seven rapidly growing East Asian economies as a whole, which cannot be captured by an individual country study.

4.5   Causality Relations in ANIEs 1 and ANIEs 2

When we divide the seven countries into the first and second generation ANIEs, we find more interesting results. Part (b) of Table 4.2 presents the estimated panel data VAR for the first generation ANIEs as a group by FEM and the Wald test of coefficients for Granger causality directions. The coefficients of dummy variable are all negative and statistically significant at the 5% level. Thus, the dummy variable is included in the regressions. Figure 4.3 summarizes the panel data Granger causality results of Table 4.2 Part (b).

Interestingly enough, we find there exists very strong bidirectional causality relations among GDP, exports, and FDI (namely, TIG) inflows for the first ANIEs as a group. Not only does the causality from GDP to FDI inflows newly emerge, but each causality relations are much more statistically significant than the previous panel VAR results for all seven Asian economies (see Figure 4.2). This indicates that GDP, exports, and FDI inflows are mutually reinforcing each other. Therefore, any policy aiming to stimulate one of the three variables is likely to have positive impact on the other two variables directly and indirectly. This virtuous circle running through the three variables may explain the rapid growth of the first generation ANIEs for the past three decades with prudent government policies attracting FDI and promoting exports. Our results show that, for the semi-mature or mature economy, exports promotion policy appears to be more effective than the FDI promotion policy in enhancing economic growth through strong interaction between the three variables, and so far as FDI is concerned, inward FDI has strong positive effects on GDP; that is, FDI not only has strong direct impact on GDP, but it also indirectly increases GDP through exports by the interactive relations between exports and GDP.

Part (c) of Table 4.2 presents the estimated panel data VAR for the second generation ANIEs as a group, by using FEM and the Wald test of coefficients for Granger causality directions. The coefficients of dummy variable are all negative, but they are not statistically significant at the 10% level. Thus, the dummy variable was dropped from the regressions. Figure 4.4 summarizes the panel data Granger causality results of Table 4.2 Part (c).

Unlike the first generation ANIEs, we do not find many causality relations for the second generation ANIEs. We only find the bidirectional causality between GDP and exports (with a statistically weak 15% level of significance). This, of course, coincides with the fact that the second generation ANIEs have promoted the export-led-growth policy for the past two decades. However, it is striking that FDI inflows have no causal effects on either GDP or exports. This result implies that the second generation ANIEs have not, or could not, fully utilize the beneficial effects of FDI inflows on GDP or exports yet. Therefore, it should be the policy priority for the second generation ANIEs' governments to make sure that FDI inflows exert the reinforcing and beneficial effects on GDP and exports through active acquisition of advanced technology and open trade.

A distinctive pattern emerges from the previous panel VAR analyses for the first and the second generation ANIEs, and for all seven ANIEs. While we cannot find causality relations running from FDI inflows to GDP or exports in the second generation ANIEs as a group, FDI inflows strongly induce GDP and exports in the first generation ANIEs as a group. In addition, GDP, exports, and FDI inflows are mutually reinforcing each other through a strong virtuous circle in the first generation ANIEs, while only statistically weak bidirectional causalities run between GDP and exports in the second generation ANIEs. It appears that large inflow of FDI can occur and exert its impact on the economy only when the economy has advanced to a certain stage of development and proper institutions are put in place.

Furthermore, the comparison of Figures 4.2 and 4.3 seems to suggest an important sequence of development policy. Namely, the second generation ANIEs should start from the export-led economic policy and then follow the FDI-promotion policy to take advantage of the strong interactive relationship between exports and GDP.

4.6   Conclusions

We first recognize that the rapid clustered sequential growth of East and Southeast Asia is unique in the modern world economy, in that it is not shared by other regions or areas. We call these countries, as a whole, the ANIEs. The openness of the economy, as manifested by exports and inward FDI, among others, is the most common economic factor attributed to rapid growth of the ANIEs. Thus, the question how the openness variables, exports, and FDI interacted with GDP — the most important economic growth indicator — within each group and among each of the countries appears to be an important topic of study.

Following the recent study of panel data analysis of Hsiao and Hsiao (2006), we apply panel data analysis to the ANIEs and the two generation groups separately. From this, a very interesting pattern emerges. We find statistically strong bidirectional causality among the three variables in the first generation ANIEs countries, but only a few statistically weak causalities exist in the second generation

ANIEs countries. More specifically, the contributions of this paper appear in several areas:

(1) As in Hsiao and Hsiao (2006), the theoretical underpinning of our analysis is the Keynesian demand-side model of open economies, which is the basis of using VAR procedure.

(2) We use panel data causality analysis for inward FDI, exports, and GDP simultaneously.

(3) As in the previous chapter, individual country analysis of causality between GDP and exports, exports and FDI, and FDI and exports give different causality relations, and consequently does not render a general conclusion. Unless there is a particular reason to study a single country time-series analysis, a multi-country panel data analysis appears to be the best way to study the causal relations.

(4) Since the three variables are closely related, as shown in Eq. (4.1), instead of studying two variables separately at a time, it is natural and worthwhile, as pointed out in the previous chapter (Hsiao and Hsiao, 2006), to examine multivariate causalities among these three TIG variables.

(5) As in Chapter 3, the countries selected for our analysis here are all fast-growing developing countries located in East and Southeast Asia, as compared with other regions of the world, with active exports and inward foreign direct investment promotion policy.

(6) Unlike the previous chapter, we divide the ANIEs in two groups, the first and the second generation countries. We find a prominently distinct pattern of causality for the first generation countries and less incidence of causality among the second generation countries.

(7) As in the previous chapter, we also find the reinforcing effects of inward FDI through exports, and we also corroborate their policy recommendation of attracting inward FDI, in addition to exports, as an important engine of growth. The reinforcing effects are evident in all seven ANIEs as a whole and are exemplified by the first generation ANIEs as a group (Figures 4.2 and 4.3).

(8) More generally, the first generation countries show statistically strong bidirectional causality between FDI and exports, between GDP and exports, and between GDP and FDI. This is compared with the results of the second generation countries, which only have statistically weak bidirectional causality between exports and GDP. We conclude that FDI is generally not effective in promoting economic growth at the lower stage of economic growth, but exports are. It has an important impact and effectiveness only among the newly or already developed countries. This might explain why over 70% of the inward FDI are in the developed countries, and also why most of the inward FDI flowing into developing countries are concentrated on those rapidly growing developing countries.

(9) Another implication of our results is that, at the early stage of development, exports, rather than FDI, appear to be more important in promoting economic growth. This interpretation is consistent with the general fear, or Marxist concern, that FDI is the vanguard of imperialistic capitalism and may compete with, or even destroy, the burgeoning domestic infant industries, including the export industries.

(10) In this connection, considering a statistically weak unidirectional causality from FDI to GDP in the general case (Figure 4.2) and stronger unidirectional causality from GDP to FDI in the first generation case (Figure 4.3), FDI is generally attracted to the high income countries. The implication is that economic policy of low income countries to attract FDI may not be effective or even futile. Rather, low income countries should promote exports at the beginning of its development. After export promotion policy has succeeded in lifting the national income, FDI will come and start to have positive reinforcing interrelated impacts on exports and GDP and enhance further growth.

(11) Another interpretation of our results is that there is a sequence of open economic strategies. The developing countries should start the exports promotion policy first and, afterward, start inward FDI-promotion policy. It appears that, for the low-income low-exports countries, the FDI promotion policy is futile

in promoting economic growth in the sense that FDI will not be attracted. This may be so because the promotion of exports requires a certain domestic economic infrastructure and social environment, which attract foreign investment.

(12) Lastly, our analysis sheds some light on the theoretical and empirical controversies between the export-led growth and the growth-led exports. Our analysis shows that for the fast growing economies in general, the results of Chapters 3 and 4 indicate that the causality between exports and growth is bidirectional: the growth-led exports are as important as exports-led growth, and, contrary to the conventional wisdom, the growth-led exports are more important than the exports-led growth in the first-generation ANIEs.

Appendix 4A: Causality among FDI, Exports, and GDP in the Macroeconomic Model

As in Figure 3.3 of the previous chapter, the interrelations and interaction among the three variables (in Figure 4.2 for all seven ANIEs) in the context of the macroeconomic model is illustrated in Figure 4A.1. When two figures are compared, we find a strong causal

Real GDP, Exports, and Inward FDI
Causality in the Basic Macroeconomic Model

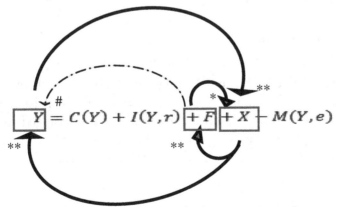

Figure 4A.1: Real GDP, Exports, and Inward FDI
Causality in the Basic Macroeconomic Model

relationship from GDP to exports. Thus, this chapter reconfirms that exports and GDP are very closely related, more so than between FDI and GDP. Its policy implication is that the developing government should emphasize export-promotion policy before it engages in foreign investment promotion policy.

Appendix 4B: Data Sources

The data on GDP and merchandise exports from 1981 to 2005, all in current USD million, for the seven Asian economies, and their GDP deflators (2000 deflator $= 100$), except Taiwan's GDP and exports and Singapore's exports, are taken from the World Bank's *World Development Indicators* (2007) dataset. Taiwan's current GDP, merchandise exports, and GDP deflator ($2000 = 1$) are taken from the *Macroeconomic Database*, National Statistics, Republic of China (http://eng.sta.gov.tw). For Singapore, merchandise exports are taken from ICSEAD dataset. The current values of GDP and merchandise exports are deflated by the GDP deflator of each country in order to convert to the real values. The inward FDI data are obtained from UNCTAD's World Investment Report dataset, and they are deflated by the GDP deflator to attain the real FDI values. Note that all variables are in logarithms, and Indonesia and Hong Kong are not included in the regression analyses due to some negative numbers in the FDI data.

Acknowledgments

We are grateful to Professors Mei-Chu W. Hsiao of the University of Colorado at Denver, and Kyungwook Choi of the University of Seoul for helpful comments and suggestions. For consistency with Chapter 3, Chapter 4 has been rewritten and rearranged from the previous paper originally published in the *Journal of the Korean Economy*, 2008. Appendix 4A was added for this chapter.

References

Baltagi, B. H. (2001). *Econometric Analysis of Panel Data* (2nd edn.). New York: John Wiley and Sons.

Chowdhury, A. and G. Mavrotas (2006). FDI and growth: What causes what? *World Economy* **29** (1), 9–19.

Christopoulos, D. K. and E. G. Tsionas (2003). A reassessment of balance of payments constrained growth: Results from panel unit root and panel cointegration tests. *International Economic Journal* **17** (3), 39–54.

EViews 6.0. (2007). Irvine, CA: Quantitative Micro Software, LLC.

Fukasaku, K., M. Kawai, M. G. Plummer, and A. Trzecial-Duval (Eds.) (2006). *Miracle, Crisis and Beyond: A Synthesis of Policy Coherence Towards East Asia*. Paris: OECD Publishing, p. 88.

Greene, W. H. (2003). *Econometric Analysis* (5th edn.). Upper Saddle River, NJ: Prentice Hall.

Hsiao, F. S. T. and M.-C. W. Hsiao (2006). FDI, exports, and GDP in East and Southeast Asia — Panel data versus time-series causality analysis. *Journal of Asian Economics* **17**, 1082–1106.

Im, K. S., M. H. Pesaran and Y. Shin (2003). Testing for unit roots in heterogeneous panels. *Journal of Econometrics* **115**, 53–74.

International Centre for the Study of East Asian Development (ICSEAD) (2006). *East Asian Economic Perspectives*. Special issue, February.

Kohpaiboon, A. (2003). Foreign trade regimes and FDI-growth nexus: A case study of Thailand. *The Journal of Development Studies* **40** (2), 55–69.

Kojima, K. (1973). A macroeconomic approach to foreign direct investment. *Hitotsubashi Journal of Economics* **14** (1), 1–21.

Kojima, K. (2000). The Flying Geese model of Asian economic development: Origin, theoretical extensions, and regional policy implications. *Journal of Asian Economics* **11** (4), 375–401.

Maddala, G. S. and S. Wu (1999). A comparative study of unit root tests with panel data and a new simple test. *Oxford Bulletin of Economics and Statistics* **61**, 631–652.

Ozawa, T. (2003). Pax Americana-led macro-clustering and flying-geese-style catch-up in East Asia: Mechanisms of regionalized endogenous growth. *Journal of Asian Economics* **13** (6), 699–713.

United Nation Conference on Trade and Development (UNCTAD) (1995). *World Investment Report*. New York and Geneva: United Nations.

United Nation Conference on Trade and Development (UNCTAD) (2006). *World Investment Report*. New York and Geneva: United Nations.

World Bank (1993). *The East Asian Miracle, Economic Growth and Public Policy*. World Bank Policy Research Report. Oxford: Oxford University Press.

World Bank (2007). *World Development Indicators dataset*.

Chapter 5

The IT Revolution and Macroeconomic Volatility in Newly Developed Countries — On the Real and Financial Linkages

Abstract

The emergence of Asia is often credited to the emergence of information technology (IT) revolution. In this chapter, we concentrate on the impact of the IT revolution on the three newly developed countries (NDCs) — South Korea (hereafter Korea), Singapore, and Taiwan — denoted collectively as Asian NDC-3, three Asian Newly Developed Countries. The impact of the IT revolution on these three countries has two routes: one is the impact on GDP growth (the real linkage) through trade and foreign direct investment (FDI), and the other is the impact on stock prices (the financial linkage) through stock markets. The main purpose of this chapter is to use recently developed econometric techniques to find the causal relationship between the volatilities of the financial markets, as represented by the volatility of stock price index, and economic growth, as manifested in the volatility of GDP. Based on the modified Mundell–Fleming–Dornbusch macroeconomic model, we also include five variables — consumer price index, exchange rate, interest rate, narrow money supply (M1), and merchandise exports. This chapter measures volatility by the square roots of conditional variances that are generated by the Generalized Autoregressive Conditional Heteroskedasticity (GARCH) procedure. In terms of methodology, our contributions lie on the time-series and panel data Granger causality analyses of financial markets and economic growth, and on the use of the ARCH or GARCH model to estimate volatilities. In terms of the countries, our analysis is concentrated on the impact of the IT revolution on the NDCs with similar stage of economic development: Korea, Singapore, and Taiwan.

Keywords: Macroeconometric modeling; volatility analysis; GARCH-VAR; Granger causality; financial and real analyses; East Asian development

5.1 Introduction

The past two decades were the era of the New Economy — the era of economic prosperity and new business, social, and economic practices, which were mainly due to the US telecommunications deregulation in 1996. Two trends characterize the New Economy: rapid globalization of the world economy through trade and investment, and the revolution in information and communication technology (ICT or IT). It is an "IT Revolution" because of the fast upgrading of computer hardware, software, and telecommunications equipment and because of the steep decline in their prices (Pohjola, 2002a, 2002b; IMF, 2001). The United States led these trends and other developed countries followed. IT has changed the world in many ways. It increased the interdependence among countries and the fast pace of communication among people and business, which meant that information could travel more quickly and pervasively. These trends make stock markets and financial institutions in the world closely related, but then they become vulnerable and volatile consequently. At the same time, industries become much more competitive and turbulent. Thus, macroeconomic volatility becomes an important subject from the point of view of economic policy, investment decision, and consumer decision (Daly, 1999; Gavin and Hausmann, 1996).

The fast technological progress and turnover, low cost of learning, externality of networking, and the combination of high-tech and labor-intensive manufacturing processes have enabled the vertical division of labor between the producers of information equipment in the United States and the manufacturing firms of parts in the developing countries. Specialization in IT products in Asia-Pacific countries has enhanced the interdependence between these countries and the United States through trade and foreign direct investment (FDI).

Elsewhere, we have shown that the United States, along with Japan, is a significant investor and trading partner in this region (see Chapter 6). The economic relation between Asia-Pacific countries and the world, especially the United States and Japan, becomes much closer than ever in the last two decades, exposing Asia-Pacific countries to international business fluctuations and increasing their macroeconomic volatility (Hsiao *et al.*, 2003).

Thus, when the US stock market burst, and the US economy entered a recession in 2001, the East Asian stock markets and the economies followed suit. The increased international interdependence enhanced by the IT revolution and subsequent globalization movements have made these Asian economies very vulnerable to the world economic conditions.

In this chapter, we concentrate on the impact of the IT revolution on the three newly developed countries (NDCs) — South Korea (hereafter Korea), Singapore, and Taiwan — denoted collectively as Asian NDC-3. Korea and Taiwan have similar economic and production structures, and they possess similar historical backgrounds (Hsiao and Park, 2002, 2005; Hsiao and Hsiao, 2003). Although it is a city-state, Singapore, like Korea and Taiwan, has developed the IT industry, and is one of the most IT-ready countries in the world. Singapore's GDP growth has surpassed all the Asian countries' GDP growth since its independence in 1965. In view of their rapid economic growth, one may expect that there is a similar significant impact of the IT revolution on these three countries. Hence, the comparisons of their macroeconomic volatility may yield useful policy implications for the developing countries.

The impact of the IT revolution on these three countries has two routes: one is the impact on GDP growth (the real linkage) through trade and FDI, and the other is the impact on stock prices (the financial linkage) through stock markets (Hsiao *et al.*, 2003). Thus, unlike the old economy, the stock prices appear to play an important role in a country's macroeconomic activity in the New Economy.

One of the main concerns for economic policy in developed and developing countries in this age of New Economy and globalization is how the volatility of the stock prices is associated with the volatility of GDP growth. In fact, stock prices affect GDP growth through the wealth effect of increased stock ownership on consumption, through the IT industry's equity financing, through the reduction in transaction and information costs, and through the dispersion of economic risk. The GDP growth also influences stock prices through diversification of assets due to increased wealth, through increased consumption on IT products, and through increased government and private investment in R&D and the production of the IT industry.

Thus, the major purpose of this chapter is to use recently developed econometric techniques to find the causal relationship between the volatilities of the financial markets — as represented by the volatility of stock price index — and economic growth, as manifested in the volatility of GDP. Based on the modified Mundell–Fleming–Dornbusch macroeconomic model, we also include five variables, namely, consumer price index, exchange rate, interest rate, narrow money supply (M1), and merchandise exports. They are generally associated with the macroeconomic aspects of economic growth. Thus, in our econometric model, we include the volatilities of these seven variables in the Granger causality analysis.

In studying the interactions among the economic variables, most of the previous studies use the level or the difference series of the variables and find the causality relations. In this chapter, we treat the variability of variables directly by using the concept of volatility from finance literature. Furthermore, the common method of measuring macroeconomic volatility is to use sample standard deviations (Temple, 2002; Ramey and Ramey, 1995), or sample standard deviations after filtering the time-series data (Agenor *et al.*, 1999).

These methods either ignore the random process, which generate the data (Engle, 1982), or distort the data due to smoothing (Bini-Smaghi, 1991). Thus, in this chapter, as the measure of volatility, we use the square roots of conditional variances that are generated by the Generalized Autoregressive Conditional Heteroskedasticity (GARCH) procedure (Engle, 1982; Bollerslev, 1986; Bera and Higgins, 1993).

The structure of the chapter is as follows: In Section 5.2, we find that, by the 2000s, the economies of Korea, Singapore, and Taiwan had built the critical mass of IT activities. We show this from both the supply and demand sides of their IT activities by comparing with IT activities of some other developed and developing countries. In Section 5.3, we discuss increased volatility of the financial market due to the IT revolution. Section 5.4 presents a simple macroeconomic model of GDP and stock price index, along with five other variables, which is used as a theoretical underpinning of the Vector Autoregression model (VAR) for Granger causality analysis. We also explain the sources of data in this section.

In Section 5.5, we present the estimation of the volatility series for each variable. Using individual country's time-series data, we first estimate the mean equation of each variable, and then test the existence of ARCH effects in the squared residuals by performing Ljung–Box Q-test of autocorrelations and the ARCH test of heteroskedasticity. We then apply the ARCH or GARCH models to obtain the estimated conditional variance series. The time-series of volatility is generated by taking the square roots of the estimated conditional variance series. In Section 5.6, we examine the stationarity properties of volatility and the VAR(p) model. In Section 5.7, we present the empirical results of the Granger causality. In Section 5.8, we use the seven-volatility series from the three countries to compile a panel data set, and we use the fixed effects model (FEM) of panel data VAR to find the Granger causality relationships among the volatilities for the three countries as a group. Section 5.9 concludes.

Our contributions to the literature are in two major areas: In terms of methodology, our contributions lie on the time-series and panel data Granger causality analyses of financial markets and economic growth. Our contributions also lie on the use of the ARCH or GARCH model to estimate volatilities. Most current literature conducts cross-section analysis of either developed countries and/or developing countries, which have heterogeneous economic characteristics and different stages of development. Hence, in terms of countries, our analysis is concentrated on the impact of the IT revolution on the NDCs — Korea, Singapore, and Taiwan — which all have similar developing patterns.

5.2 The IT Revolution in Korea, Singapore, and Taiwan

Korea, Taiwan, and Singapore developed their IT industry from the electronics industry[1] in the 1960s. By the end of the 1990s and the beginning of the early 2000s, their IT industry became the powerhouse of the world. Table 5.1 shows the percentage share of the world electronics production (including information products) of the three countries as compared with the other major Asian countries, namely, the ASEAN5+: Indonesia, Malaysia, the Philippines, Thailand, Vietnam, and China. For comparison, we also show the data of Japan and the United States, along with the West Asian countries of India and Sri Lanka.

As shown in Table 5.1, the world electronics share of Korea, Taiwan, and Singapore increased in the 1990s. Although their absolute shares appear to be low when compared with that of Japan, and possibly the United States (the data are missing), in terms of their population size, as shown in the first column, their world production shares are roughly comparable[2] to those of Japan.

---

[1] For Korea and Taiwan, see Sato (1997), for Taiwan, see Hsiao and Hsiao (1996) and Kawakami (1996). Kawakami concluded that "the rise of Taiwan's PC industry was not sudden and unexpected, but rather a natural extension of the preceding development of the electronics industry." This is also true for other NDCs like Singapore (Wong, 2002).

[2] In 1995, Singapore was an exception; its world share (3.8%) was 54 times of its "fair" world population share of 0.07%. Other Asian NDCs were six times for Korea, eight times for Taiwan, and 12 times for Japan.

Table 5.1: The Digital Divide in East and Southeast Asia

Supply Side

	Pop,% of Wld 2002	% share of Wld Electronics Pdct			% of Imports		% of Exports	
		1990	1995	1998	IT Pdct 1999	Wld 1999	IT Pdct 1999	World 1999
ADC+								
Korea	**0.78**	**3.3**	**4.7**	**3.6**	**22.8**	**2.1**	**23.7**	**2.5**
Taiwan	**0.37**	**2.1**	**2.8**	**3.1**	**23.2**	**1.9**	**46.5**	**2.2**
Singapore	0.07	2.1	3.8	3.5	41.9	1.9	53.7	2.0
Japan	2.09	26.4	25.7	18.0	14.9	5.4	23.1	7.4
HK	0.11	1.2	0.9	0.8	24.5	3.1	2.3	3.1
Sum	*3.41*	*35.1*	*38.0*	*29.0*		14.4		17.2
USA	4.72				17.2	18.3	17.2	12.4
ASEAN5+								
Indonesia	3.47	0.2	0.5	0.5	11.5	0.4	5.4	0.9
Malaysia	0.40	1.1	2.7	2.5	43.2	1.1	47.5	1.5
Philippines	1.31	0.3	0.4	0.7	45.2	0.6	61.1	0.6
Thailand	1.01	0.6	1.2	1.3	24.3	0.9	27.7	1.0
Vietnam					5.9	0.2	2.9	0.2
China	21.04	1.7	2.7	4.3	20.2	2.9	15.6	3.5
Sum	*27.23*	*3.8*	*7.5*	*9.3*		6.0		7.7
South Asia and others								
India	17.06	0.7	0.6	0.6	4.5	0.8	1.5	0.6
Sri Lanka	0.31				3.7	0.1	3.1	0.1

Sources: Population data are from International Telecommunication Union (ITU), 003, IT trade data are from Cornelius *et al.* (2002), commodity trade data are from WDI-CD (2002), and world electronics production data are from Wong (2002).

In addition, the world production shares of Korea, Taiwan, and Singapore are much higher than ASEAN5+ and other countries in the table, showing the vitality of the three countries.

In 1999, the share of IT imports and exports in total imports and exports of each country are very high[3]: 23% and 24%, respectively,

---

[3]The value of IT products is the sum of four items: electrical machinery and equipment, electronic equipment and components, office machinery and supplies,

for Korea; 23% and 47%, respectively, for Taiwan; and 42% and 54% for Singapore, respectively, higher than those of Japan (15%, 23%) and the United States (17%, 17%).

In fact, the percentage ratios of the imports and exports of major IT products over GDP range from 7% to 9% for Korea and from 9% to 19% for Taiwan, which are much higher percentage ratios than those of Japan and the United States (not shown in the table).

The vigorous production and trading activities in IT products in NDC-3 also reflect in the structure and productivity of the manufacturing industry in these countries. Figure 5.1 shows the value-added shares of some manufacturing sectors in Korea and Taiwan, respectively. The matched data at the 15 manufacturing sectors for both countries from 1985 to 1996 are taken from Hsiao and Park (2002, 2005). The high-tech industry category consists of four sectors, which are shown in the charts as Elect (electric, electronic machinery products and repairs), Trans (Transportation products and repairs), Mach (Machinery products and repairs), and Misc (Miscellaneous: Precision Instruments and other manufacturing) sectors, all are denoted in bold font with an underline in the charts.

From the mid-1980s to the mid-1990s, the value-added share of the electric and electronic sector in Korea increased from about 7% to 17%, while that of Taiwan increased from about 12% to 22%, becoming the largest manufacturing sector in each country. It eventually replaced the second largest Food (Food, beverage, and tobacco) sector in Korea, and the Chem (Chemical products, rubber, and plastics) sector in Taiwan (other labels are defined in Figure 5.1 notes). The shares of other sectors in both countries, especially the traditionally important textile and apparel sectors, either declined or stayed at the same levels.

Figure 5.2 shows the time-series profile of sequential multiplicative products of the weighted average Malmquist productivity indexes[4]

---

and telecommunication equipment, as listed in Cornelius *et al.* (2002). Also, see Table 5.1.

[4]The Malmquist productivity index (MPI) is the product of the technology change index (TI) and the efficiency change index (EI). TI measures the relative movement of the production possibility curve (PPC) between two periods, and EI

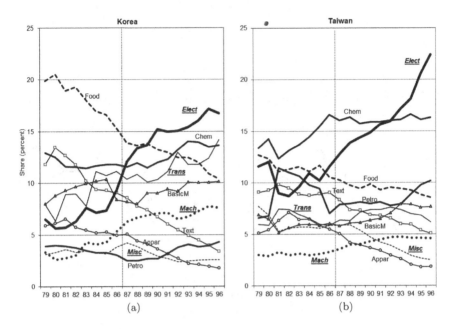

Figure 5.1: Value-Added Shares of Manufacturing Industry

Korea and Taiwan, 1979–96.

Notes: The manufacturing sectors in the "TRADITIONAL" category are (1) **Food**, beverage and tobacco; (2) **Textiles**; (3) Apparel and ornaments or "**Appar**"; (4) Leather; (5) Wood products and non-metallic furniture; (6) Paper and printing. The "BASIC" category includes the following: (7) "**Chem.**" as defined in the text; (8) Petroleum coal and products or "**Petro**"; (9) Non-metallic mineral products; (10) Basic metal products or "**BasicM**"; (11) Fabricated metal products. The "HIGH-TECH" category includes (12) "**Elect**"; (13) "**Trans**"; (14) "**Mach**"; and (15) "**Misc.**" This figure only shows some of the basic products for comparison. The bold faced terms correspond to those sectors in this figure.

from 1985 to 1996 for the traditional, basic, and high-tech categories (Hsiao and Park, 2005). See the definition of these three categories in the Notes to Figure 5.1 of the manufacturing industry. It also shows

---

measures the ratio of the degree of deficiencies of the actual output relative to the corresponding output on the PPC, which, in the case of Figure 5.1, is constructed from a category-wise cross-industry best-practice meta production frontier from the observed outputs each year by linear programs. For details, see Hsiao and Park (2002, 2005). The lines in Figure 5.1 trace the change in productivity index each year (Hsiao and Park, 2005).

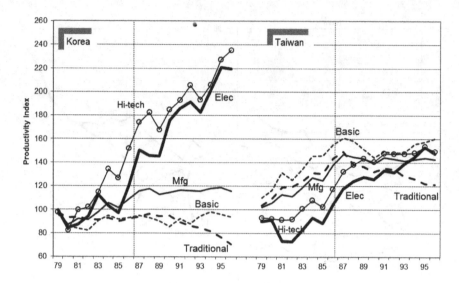

Figure 5.2: Mfg Productivity Change of Three Industrial Categories
Traditional, Basic, and High-tech Industries

the Malmquist productivity index of the electric and electronics sector, as compared with the manufacturing average (denoted as Mfg avg, the light solid line) for Korea and Taiwan. Like the value-added share in Figure 5.1, the high-tech industry, the line with circle markers (along with the electric and electronics sector, the heavy dark line) experiences a massive rise in productivity in both countries from 1985 to 1996. Korea's productivity in the high-tech industry rises about 110% (122% for electric and electronics sector) and that of Taiwan increases about 47% (60% for electric and electronics sector).

Both Figures 5.1 and 5.2 clearly demonstrate the prominent role played by the IT industry in the process of economic development in Korea and Taiwan. The IT industry is the largest, fastest growing, and fastest productivity-improving leading manufacturing sector in both countries. In fact, the governments in the Asia-Pacific region place a top priority on developing the IT industry. Korea has the national initiative for "CYBER KOREA 21", Taiwan for "Green Silicon Island", and Singapore for "Intelligent Island" (Hsiao, Hsiao, and Yamashita, 2003; Liu, 2001). These governments have devoted large resources to R&D in IT development, facilitating technology absorption and adaptation along with induced FDI.

By the early 2000s, Taiwan is the world's third largest producer of IT products, next to the US and Japan. In that same time, Korea is the world's third largest producer of semiconductor chips and is in the forefront of mobile-phone technology (ADB, 2000).

More specifically, the demand-side indicators include three categories: increased telephone network, fast mobile service, and IT. Figures 5.4–5.6 (5.4(a)–5.4(c); 5.6(a) and 5.6(b)) show the recent 10-year IT activities in the Asian NDC-3.

The massive IT production and trading alone cannot qualify Korea and Taiwan as the New Economies. The people must also use IT products in its production, service, and consumption activities (Kapur, 2002). This is indeed the case for Asian NDC-3. According to World Economic Forum (Dutta *et al.*, 2004), the network readiness index is "a nation's or community's degree of preparation to participate in and benefit from information and communication technology (ICT) development."

Figure 5.3 shows the networked readiness index rank for three years, 2001–2002 (upward patterned column on the left), 2002 to 2003 (horizontal patterned column in the middle), and 2003 to 2004 (the black solid column on the right) for each of the three countries. The ranks are Nos. 20, 14, and 20 for Korea; Nos. 8, 3, and 2 for Singapore; and Nos. 15, 9, and 17 for Taiwan, out of 75, 82, and 102 countries, respectively, in the report. As shown in the figure, these rankings are indeed compatible with other developed countries such as Japan, the United Kingdom, and the Netherlands, with the United States as the top leader in the world. To give a global perspective, we also include Japan and the United States for comparison.

Figures 5.4(a)–5.4(c) show a telephone network. Figure 5.4(a) shows the main telephone lines per 100 inhabitants. The Asian NDC-3 (T, the line with triangle markers; K, the line with circle markers; S, the line with square markers) were well below the United States (U, the solid line) and Japan (J, the dashed line) in 1995. The Asian NDC-3 quickly caught up with Japan by 1999, and Taiwan even

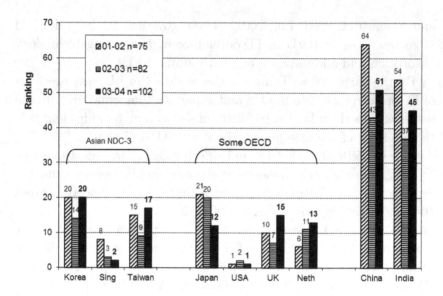

Figure 5.3: Networked Readiness Index Rank

Best = 1 (2001–2004)

caught up with the United States, reached 60 per 100 inhabitants, in 2004.

Figure 5.4(b) exhibits the percentage of household with a telephone. The data are not complete, but it appears that Singapore reached 100% by 2004, and Taiwan reached 98% by 2003, both are higher than the United States (95% in 2003).

Figure 5.4(c) presents the percentage of digital main lines. All Asian NDC-3 reached 100% by 2004, same as Japan, and higher than the United States (98%).

Figure 5.5 displays a major mobile service, with cellular subscribers per 100 inhabitants in the five countries. True to its mobility, all Asian NDC-3 surpassed Japan and the United States in the late 1990s, although they were below Japan and the United States in 1995. By 2004, Taiwan reached 100%, far surpassed Japan (72%) and the United States (62%), followed by Singapore (96%) and Korea (76%).

Figures 5.6(a) and 5.6(b) illustrate the development of IT. Figure 5.6(a) reveals the percentage of the number of computers among

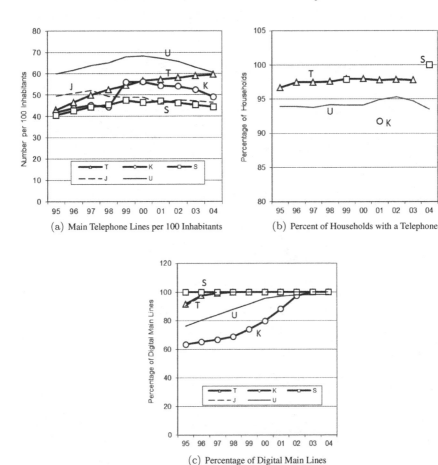

(a) Main Telephone Lines per 100 Inhabitants

(b) Percent of Households with a Telephone

(c) Percentage of Digital Main Lines

Figure 5.4: Telephone Network

population. Here, all three Asian NDC-3 were below the United States in 1995 and still could not catch up with the United States (76%) by 2004. However, by 2004, Singapore (62%) and Korea (54%) already caught up with Japan (54%). Taiwan had only 53% in 2004. All three NDCs still have room to catch up with the United States. Figure 5.6(b) shows Internet users per 100 inhabitants. In 1995, Korea was below other countries, but it surpassed all of them by 2004 (65%), an amazing development. All three NDCs surpassed Japan by 2004.

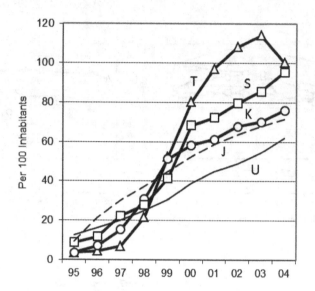

Figure 5.5: Cellular Subscribers

Per 100 Inhabitants

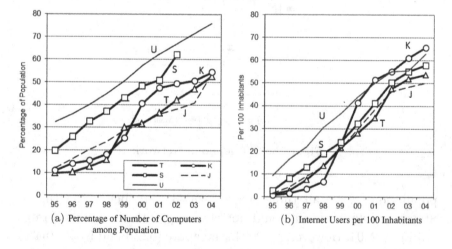

(a) Percentage of Number of Computers among Population

(b) Internet Users per 100 Inhabitants

Figure 5.6: Information Technology

In general, we submit that, while the statistical evidence is mixed, the New Economy has created domestic demand for information products and services in Korea, Singapore, and Taiwan, as much as other advanced countries, and the majority of people in these Asian

NDC-3 start taking advantage of the IT revolution. In fact, they already have accumulated the critical mass of the IT revolution and entered the era of the New Economy.

5.3 Increased Volatility of the Financial Market

The arrival of the New Economy strengthened the financial linkages across the countries (IMF, 2001, p. 121, 128). Since new IT firms tend to be younger, smaller, and riskier, the IT sector relies more on equity financing[5] (IMF, 2001, p. 131). This characteristic has been observed in a variety of economies of developed or developing countries. In Taiwan, for example, the IT industry invested 44% of the total manufacturing capital in 2000 and financed almost 38% of the IT investment through the stock market (Cheng, 2002).

Greater reliance on equity finance and, consequently, the stock markets across the countries, makes the IT sector of Korean and Taiwanese economies, and for that matter the Singaporean economy, vulnerable to the international stock price movements (Hsiao *et al.*, 2003). How does the international linkage of stock markets influence the domestic macroeconomic fluctuations? If only a small number of people hold the IT stock, and the IT stocks have little weight in the national income, then international financial linkages should not have much of an effect on domestic consumption or business cycles. However, this is not the case in the Asian NDC-3.

Many years of booms in the IT industry, before the 2001 slump, boosted the local stock market prices, stimulating stock ownership in these countries. This may be seen from the stock market capitalization relative to GDP. The Asian NDC-3 have a capitalization ratio close to or above 50% of GDP in 2000, with Korea ranked 19th and Taiwan ranked 12th (as compared with Japan 2nd, USA 1st)

---

[5]IMF (2001, p. 131). If a new IT project is promising, "before the dot.com bubble, it usually takes five to seven years for start-up firms to go to the initial public offering (IPO market). During the dot.com boom, this period was shortened, especially for e-commerce business" (Aoki and Takizawa, 2002). The IPO in the stock market has launched a new era for the IT firms.

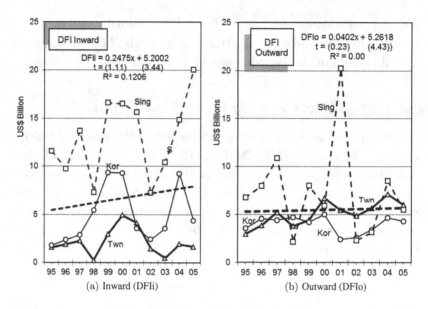

Figure 5.7: Direct Foreign Investment

Korea, Taiwan, and Singapore, 1995–2005

in the world, indicating the predominance of equity assets in the society.[6]

Figure 5.7 presents inward and outward (FDI for the Asian NDC-3 and their annual averages from 1995 to 2005. While both inward and outward investments increased over the 10 years, the coefficient of the time trend (x) of inward investment is 0.25, which is not significant at the 5% level, and that of outward investment is 0.04, which is not significant at the 10% level. This shows that inward and outward investments are almost constant during this period.

However, this is not the case for portfolio investment (mainly in the stock markets). Figure 5.8 shows that the inward and outward portfolio investments increased significantly every year from 1995 to 2005 with increasing fluctuations. The regression coefficient is 1.11 for inward portfolio investment and is significant at the 10% level, while that of the outward investment is 1.53 and is significant at the

---

[6]The world ranking is taken from Kurian (2001), which is also based on Economic Intelligent Unit (EIU) data but does not mark the year the statistics were taken.

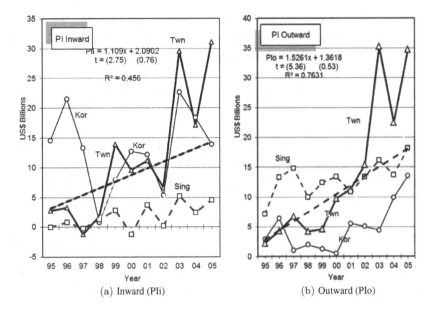

Figure 5.8: Portfolio Investment

Korea, Taiwan, Singapore, 1995–2005

1% level. The figure shows that the activities of portfolio investment increased considerably after 2002, especially for Taiwan and, to a lesser degree, for Korea.

The increase in stock market activities and foreign portfolio investment implies that a sharp change in equity prices will change individuals' wealth (the wealth effects). Since wealth is a key factor for determining consumption, household consumption also changes (Edison and Slok, 2001; Bertaut, 2002), and so does the growth of an economy. Thus, the IT revolution has strengthened the international dependence and financial linkages among countries of new economies (Hsiao, Hsiao, and Yamashita, 2003).

5.4 A Simple Macroeconomic Model and Sources of Data

While the classical economists used to think of money as a veil, the arrival of the New Economy has witnessed the increasing influence of financial markets on the economy. To examine the relationship between GDP and other variables, we adopt the Mundell–Fleming–Dornbusch macroeconomic model, with a modification to include the influence of stock prices as follows:[7]

$$Y = C(Y, s, i, p) + I(Y, i, \alpha) + N(s, i, \alpha) + X(e, T), \quad (5.1)$$

$$M = L(Y, i, \alpha), \quad (5.2)$$

where Y is GDP, C is the consumption which depends on stock price s (the wealth effect), interest rate i (the saving effect), and consumer price p. I is the conventional investment as a function of interest rate i and other factors α, such as risk, institutional structure, etc.; N is IT investment as a function of stock price s, the interest rate i, and other factors α. X is the net export function (net of imports) which is a function of the exchange rate e and the openness T. M is the money supply, which is constant, and L is the liquidity preference (money demand), which depends on Y, interest rate i, and other factors α. Since we are interested in the short-run relationship between the economic variables, the non-price variables are measured in the nominal term. As usual, the partial derivatives have the following sign:

$$C_s > 0, C_Y > 0, C_i < 0, C_p < 0, I_Y > 0, I_i < 0, I_\alpha \neq 0,$$

$$N_s > 0, N_i < 0, N_\alpha \neq 0, X_e < 0, X_T > 0, L_Y > 0, L_i < 0, L_\alpha \neq 0.$$

Thus, under certain mathematical regularity conditions, we may solve for the equilibrium variables Y and i as:

$$Y = Y(s, e, p, M, T, \alpha), \quad (5.3)$$

$$i = i(s, e, p, M, T, \alpha). \quad (5.4)$$

Or, more generally, writing the above two equations in an implicit function form:

$$G(Y, i; s, e, p, M, T, \alpha) = 0, \quad (5.5)$$

$$H(Y, i; s, e, p, M, T, \alpha) = 0. \quad (5.6)$$

---

[7]We used this model extensively in Hsiao and Hsiao (1994, 1995, 2006).

Since the institutional factor α is not readily measurable, we may eliminate α from the two equations and obtain a single equation

$$F(Y, i, s, e, p, M, T) = 0. \tag{5.7}$$

Thus, we have seven macroeconomic variables for our economy. This is the theoretical underpinning of the model that we use in this chapter. For statistical purposes, we take these variables as random. Taking the variance function after linearization, we can find the VAR model and Granger causality relations of volatilities among the seven variables (the process is similar to Appendix 3C in Chapter 3).

The main data source for the seven macroeconomic variables from 1985 to 2006 for Korea, Singapore, and Taiwan are collected directly or calculated from the data in ICSEAD (2003). The data from the ICSEAD 2005–2007 issues published on its website are also utilized.

In our notations,

- cpi is the consumer price index (year 2000 = 100);
- exc is the exchange rate (annual average rate) in national currency (Korean Won, Singapore dollar, and New Taiwan dollar, respectively) per USD;
- gdp is the gross domestic products in current USD billions;
- int is the lending rate in % (note that the data for Taiwan's leading interest rate are collected from TSDB, 2007);
- m1 is the narrow money supply (M1) in USD billions;
- spi is the year-end stock price index (year 2000 = 100, they are Korea's Seoul Composite Indexes, Singapore's Straits Times Indexes, and Taiwan Weighted Indexes);
- xpt is the total merchandise exports in USD billions.

We also introduce a dummy variable, with a value of zero from 1985 to 1997 and a value of one from 1998 to 2006, to take into account the effects of 1997–1998 Asian financial crises in the VAR model for the Granger causality analysis.

5.5   Estimations of ARCH/GARCH and Volatilities

For econometric analysis, all seven time-series of macroeconomic variables are transformed into their natural logarithmic values. In estimating the time-varying conditional variance for each variable, we begin with the estimation of the mean equation

$$y_t = c + \varepsilon_t, \tag{5.8}$$

where y_t is the cpi series (or exc, gdp, int, m1, spi, and xpt, respectively), c is the constant term, and ε_t is the error term. We estimate Eq. (5.8) and obtain the residuals series. We then apply the Ljung–Box Q-test of autocorrelations to test the existence of the ARCH effect in the squared residuals (Engle, 2001). We also use the ARCH(q) heteroskedasticity test (a chi-squared test, by computing T^*R^2 in the regression of estimated ε_t^2 on a constant and q-lagged values, where T is the number of observations).

For all three countries, the results from both tests show that all seven squared residuals series from the estimation of mean equations have significant ARCH effects. Therefore, we proceed to use the standard GARCH (1, 1) model to estimate the time-varying conditional variance (σ_t^2). The model is:

$$\sigma_t^2 = \alpha + \beta \varepsilon_{t-1}^2 + \gamma \sigma_{t-1}^2. \tag{5.9}$$

Equation (5.9) specifies that the conditional variance at time t is a function of three terms: the intercept (α); ARCH(1), the first lag of the squared residual (ε_{t-1}^2) from the mean equation; and GARCH(1), the first lag of the conditional variance (σ_{t-1}^2). To have positive conditional variance, it requires that the coefficients satisfy $\alpha > 0, \beta > 0, \gamma > 0$, and $(\beta + \gamma) < 1$ (Bollerslev, 1986; Engle, 2001; Greene, 2003). In empirical practice, these conditions may not all be satisfied.

In this study, when the estimated coefficient γ for GARCH(1) is negative, we estimate GARCH(2, 1). If the GARCH(1) term has negative coefficient again, then we delete the GARCH(1) term in Eq. (5.9) and estimate the conditional variance using ARCH(1) model, which is:

$$\sigma_t^2 = \alpha + \beta \varepsilon_{t-1}^2, \tag{5.10}$$

where $\alpha > 0$ and $0 < \beta < 1$. If these conditions do not satisfy, then we go to estimate ARCH(2) model, which is:

$$\sigma_t^2 = \alpha + \beta_1 \varepsilon_{t-1}^2 + \beta_2 \varepsilon_{t-2}^2, \tag{5.11}$$

where $\alpha > 0, \beta_1 > 0, \beta_2 > 0$, and $(\beta_1 + \beta_2) < 1$.

After estimating the selected ARCH or GARCH model, we again apply the Ljung–Box Q-test of autocorrelations in the squared standardized residuals and also the heteroskedasticity ARCH test to check that there is no residual ARCH in the model. Based on these criteria, the conditional variance series of Korea's gdp, m1, and spi; Singapore's cpi, exc, gdp, int, and m1; and Taiwan's gdp and xpt are estimated by ARCH(1). The conditional variance series of Korea's cpi, xpt, Singapore's xpt, and Taiwan's cpi, exc are estimated by ARCH(2). The conditional variance series of Singapore's spi and Taiwan's spi are estimated by GARCH(1, 1). The conditional variance series of Korea's exc, int, and Taiwan's int, m1 are estimated by GARCH(2, 1).

Finally, we use the best-fitted ARCH or GARCH model to compute the time-varying conditional variance series (σ_t^2) for each variable. The positive square roots of these estimated time-varying conditional variance series are the measures of the time-varying volatility series (σ_t) for each variable. We denote these seven-volatility series by cpiv, excv, gdpv, intv, m1v, spiv, and xptv, respectively, for each country.

5.6   A Unit Root Test on Volatilities and VAR Model

5.6.1   *A Unit Root Test on Volatilities*

Before analyzing Granger causality directions among the seven volatilities, we employ the Augmented Dickey–Fuller (ADF) test of unit root to check the stationarity of each volatility series (Dickey and Fuller, 1979, 1981; Hsiao and Hsiao, 2006). Table 5A.1 of Appendix 5A presents the ADF unit root test results. For level series of volatilities: Korea's cpiv, gdpv, and m1v are stationary, but excv, intv, spiv, and xptv are not stationary; Singapore's level series of volatilities are stationary, except xptv which is not stationary; and Taiwan's excv, gdpv, and spiv are stationary, but cpiv, intv, m1v, and xptv are not stationary.

These mixed results from the unit root test indicate that we cannot use the level series of volatilities in the regressions for causality analysis. Therefore, we continue to perform the ADF unit root test on the first-difference (d) series of volatilities (i.e. dcpiv, dexcv, dgdpv, dintv, dm1v, dspiv, and dxptv). For all three countries, the ADF test yields similar results that all seven first-difference series of volatilities are stationary. Hence, we choose to use them in the estimation of VAR to find Granger causality relations.

5.6.2 *The VAR Model*

The VAR model in order p involves the estimation of the following equation system (see Hsiao and Hsiao, 2006):

$$y_t = \mu + \Gamma_1 y_{t-1} + \cdots + \Gamma_p y_{t-p} + \varepsilon_t, \qquad (5.12)$$

where

$y_t = a\,(7 \times 1)$ vector of the endogenous variables (i.e. the dcpiv, dexcv, dgdpv, dintv, dm1v, dspiv, and dxptv).

$\mu = a\,(7 \times 1)$constant vector,

$\Gamma_i, i = 1, 2, \ldots, p$ (the order of lags) is a (7×7) coefficient matrix;

$y_{t-i} = a\,(7 \times 1)$ vector of the ith lagged endogenous variables;

$\varepsilon_t = a\,(7 \times 1)$ vector of the error terms.

We also introduce an exogenous dummy variable, as specified previously in the data sources section, into the VAR model to take into account the effect from the Asian financial crisis of 1997–1998. Since our data set for each country has only 22 observations, we estimate the VAR(1) model in this study.

5.7 Individual Country's Granger Causality Test

5.7.1 *The Granger Causality Test for Korea*

Part A of Table 5.2 presents the results of the Granger causality test from the VAR(1) model, using the seven first-difference volatilities for Korea. We have found nine unidirectional causality relationships that are significant at the 10% level or less. Figure 5.9 summarizes the

(a) Korea

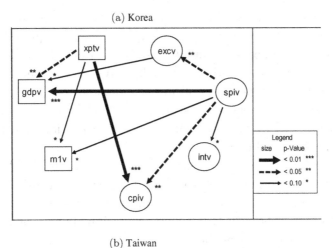

(b) Taiwan

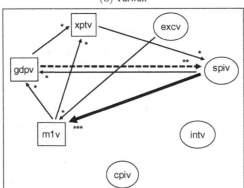

(c) Singapore

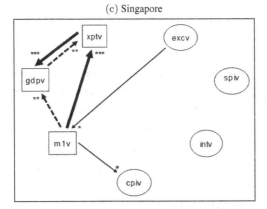

Figure 5.9: Causality Directions

results. To make the contrast between the real sector and the financial sector in the table, we enclose GDP (gdpv) in a heavy square box, and the stock price index (spiv) in a heavy circle. A double-headed arrow line connects the bidirectional causality. We present the economic interpretations and policy implications as follows.

We have found very interesting results. The causality relations are concentrated in the financial sector of stock prices and the real sectors of GDP and exports.

First, Korea's stock markets (spiv, Column 6) unidirectionally causes five other volatilities, namely, consumer prices (cpiv), exchange rates (excv), GDP (gdpv), interest rate (intv), and money supply (m1v). There is no feedback relationship. Therefore, the stock market fluctuation causes the instability of these five macroeconomic variables, except exports, and no feedback to the stock market.

Furthermore, in Eqs. (1)–(5) in Part A (Korea) of Table 5.2, the sign of the coefficients for dspiv(−1) are all significant at the 10% level or less. This implies that there are unidirectional effects (namely, an increase or a decrease in a variable's volatility will cause a similar increase or decrease in another variable's volatility) from stock price volatility to consumer price, GDP, exchange rate, interest rate, and M1 volatilities, with the exception of exports volatility. Note that the effect on GDP volatility is the strongest. Therefore, the economic policies that can maintain the stability of the stock price fluctuations are of great importance for the Korean economy.

Second, we have also found three other unidirectional causality relations from exports (xptv, Column c7) to consumer price index (cpiv), GDP (gdpv), and money supply (m1v). In Eqs. (1), (3), and (5) in Part A, the sign of the coefficients for dxptv(−1) (in Column c7) are all significant at less than the 10% level. This implies that there are unidirectional effects (namely, an increase in a variable's volatility will cause another variable's volatility) between exports volatility and consumer price, GDP, and M1 volatilities.

In Eq. (3) of Part A, there is another unidirectional causality relation from the exchange rate (excv) to GDP (gdpv), with a significant coefficient of the exchange rate (dexcv(−1) Column c2).

Table 5.2: The Granger Causality Test

Individual Country

Vector Autoregression (1, c, dummy): Use first-difference series of volatility

Dep. var.	dcpiv(-1) c1	dexcv(-1) c2	dgdpv(-1) c3	dintv(-1) c4	dm1v(-1) c5	dspiv(-1) c6	dxptv(-1) c7	cons. c8	dummy c9
A. Korea									
1 dcpiv	-0.352	-0.071	0.358	0.011	-0.083	0.179	-0.268	-0.063	0.128
	(0.24)	(0.40)	(0.14)	(0.93)	(0.62)	(0.03)	(0.01)	(0.00)	(0.00)
						spiv→cpiv**	xptv-->cpiv***		
2 dexcv	1.244	-0.287	-0.258	-0.035	-0.422	0.871	-0.509	-0.033	0.095
	(0.44)	(0.53)	(0.84)	(0.96)	(0.64)	(0.05)	(0.31)	(0.61)	(0.45)
						spiv→excv**			
3 dgdpv	-0.466	-0.378	0.726	0.402	-0.263	0.588	-0.518	-0.126	0.207
	(0.49)	(0.07)	(0.19)	(0.20)	(0.49)	(0.00)	(0.03)	(0.00)	(0.00)
		excv→gdpv*				spiv→gdpv***	xptv→gdpv**		
4 dintv	0.524	-0.362	0.000	0.228	-0.198	0.467	-0.375	-0.003	0.093
	(0.56)	(0.17)	(1.00)	(0.57)	(0.69)	(0.06)	(0.19)	(0.94)	(0.20)
						spiv→intv*			
5 dm1v	-0.864	-0.214	-0.175	0.310	0.523	0.385	-0.527	-0.178	0.273
	(0.32)	(0.39)	(0.80)	(0.43)	(0.30)	(0.10)	(0.07)	(0.00)	(0.00)
						spiv→m1v*	xptv→m1v*		
6 dspiv	-0.820	-0.197	0.123	0.355	-0.171	-0.096	0.173	-0.118	0.157
	(0.66)	(0.71)	(0.93)	(0.67)	(0.87)	(0.84)	(0.76)	(0.14)	(0.29)
7 dxptv	0.381	-0.316	-0.020	0.333	-0.119	0.223	-0.264	-0.139	0.223
	(0.81)	(0.50)	(0.99)	(0.65)	(0.90)	(0.58)	(0.59)	(0.05)	(0.10)
B. Taiwan									
1 dcpiv	-0.037	-0.158	-0.111	0.008	0.056	-0.053	-0.008	-0.029	0.029
	(0.92)	(0.43)	(0.62)	(0.72)	(0.46)	(0.47)	(0.94)	(0.08)	(0.10)
2 dexcv	0.319	0.207	-0.053	-0.011	-0.040	0.192	0.041	0.015	-0.026
	(0.61)	(0.54)	(0.89)	(0.78)	(0.76)	(0.14)	(0.83)	(0.57)	(0.37)
3 dgdpv	-0.053	-0.108	-0.649	-0.003	0.244	0.204	0.159	-0.107	0.097
	(0.93)	(0.74)	(0.10)	(0.94)	(0.07)	(0.10)	(0.39)	(0.00)	(0.00)
					m1v→gdpv*	spiv→gdpv*			
4 dintv	0.233	3.531	2.331	-0.172	-0.657	-0.080	-1.347	0.005	0.207
	(0.96)	(0.20)	(0.45)	(0.59)	(0.53)	(0.94)	(0.39)	(0.98)	(0.37)
5 dm1v	-0.783	1.195	-1.006	0.000	0.308	0.956	0.069	-0.152	0.234
	(0.53)	(0.09)	(0.20)	(1.00)	(0.24)	(0.00)	(0.85)	(0.01)	(0.00)
		excv→m1v*				spiv→m1v***			
6 dspiv	-0.395	-0.399	-0.914	0.014	0.014	0.401	0.413	-0.078	0.054
	(0.55)	(0.27)	(0.04)	(0.74)	(0.92)	(0.01)	(0.06)	(0.01)	(0.09)
			gdpv→spiv**				xptv→spiv*		
7 dxptv	0.177	-0.026	-1.194	0.059	0.413	0.233	0.044	-0.128	0.139
	(0.86)	(0.96)	(0.07)	(0.37)	(0.07)	(0.26)	(0.89)	(0.01)	(0.01)
			gdpv→xptv*		m1v→xptv*				

(Continued)

Table 5.2: (*Continued*)

Vector Autoregression (1, c, dummy): Use first-difference series of volatility								
		dexcv(-1)		dintv(-1)		dspiv(-1)	cons.	
Dep.	dcpiv(-1)		dgdpv(-1)		dmlv(-1)		dxptv(-1)		dummy
var.	c1	c2	c3	c4	c5	c6	c7	c8	c9

C. Singapore

Dep. var.	c1	c2	c3	c4	c5	c6	c7	c8	c9
1 dcpiv	0.280	-0.005	-0.013	-0.110	0.078	0.011	0.006	-0.006	0.007
	(0.21)	(0.93)	(0.82)	(0.23)	(0.09)	(0.60)	(0.69)	(0.07)	(0.16)
					m1v→cpiv*				
2 dexcv	0.378	0.599	-0.195	0.267	0.123	-0.040	-0.045	-0.013	0.007
	(0.75)	(0.08)	(0.52)	(0.58)	(0.60)	(0.73)	(0.60)	(0.46)	(0.76)
3 dgdpv	0.542	0.284	-0.443	-0.219	0.431	0.078	0.225	-0.094	0.103
	(0.57)	(0.28)	(0.10)	(0.58)	(0.04)	(0.42)	(0.01)	(0.00)	(0.00)
					m1v→gdpv**		xptv→gdpv***		
4 dintv	-0.175	0.046	-0.073	-0.248	-0.091	0.007	0.018	-0.025	0.032
	(0.84)	(0.85)	(0.75)	(0.50)	(0.61)	(0.94)	(0.78)	(0.08)	(0.10)
5 dmlv	1.063	0.830	-0.101	0.785	-0.225	0.050	0.078	-0.122	0.167
	(0.53)	(0.08)	(0.81)	(0.27)	(0.50)	(0.76)	(0.53)	(0.00)	(0.00)
		excv→m1v*							
6 dspiv	-0.664	0.672	-0.030	0.548	-0.039	-0.580	0.011	-0.110	0.120
	(0.80)	(0.34)	(0.96)	(0.61)	(0.94)	(0.04)	(0.95)	(0.01)	(0.04)
7 dxptv	-3.296	0.289	-2.204	-1.928	2.191	0.310	0.230	-0.167	0.192
	(0.30)	(0.73)	(0.02)	(0.15)	(0.00)	(0.32)	(0.32)	(0.00)	(0.01)
			gdpv→xptv**		m1v→xptv***				

Notes: (1) The *p*-values are in the parentheses. (2) ***, **, * denote rejection of null hypothesis at the 1%, 5%, 10% levels of significance, respectively.
Note also that the circle shows financial links and the square box show the real links. The arrow shows the causality direction.

This implies that there is also a weak causality between exchange rate volatility and GDP volatility.

Figure 5.8(a) illustrates the above interaction among the seven variables. The width of line shows the level of significance, as noted in the legend. The figure shows the financial sector most likely originated the fluctuations of the Korean economy, especially the fluctuation of the stock market prices. An exchange rate variation has slight effect on GDP. The export variations also exert a strong impact on the consumer price index, GDP, and the money supply.

Note that, for the Korean economy, the variability of interest rates (intv), consumer prices (cpiv), money supply (m1v), and even GDP (gdpv) are passively affected by the variability of exchange rates, the variability of exports, and especially the variability of the stock market.

5.7.2   The Granger Causality Test for Taiwan

Part B of Table 5.2 presents the results of the Granger Causality test from the VAR(1) model, using the seven first-difference volatilities for Taiwan. We found eight unidirectional causality relations that are significant at the 10% level or less. Figure 5.8(b) summarizes the results. We present the economic interpretations and policy implications in what follows.

First, we have found bidirectional causality relations between the stock market (spiv) and GDP (gdpv), with an effect from stock price to GDP and a stronger effect from GDP to stock price. They show a strong interaction among the volatilities of the financial sector's stock prices and the real sector's GDP.

Second, we also found four unidirectional causality relations, namely, the stock market variability (piv) strongly Granger causes the money supply variability (m1v) (with an enhancement effect). In turn, money supply variability causes GDP variability, which then cause the export variability, and consequently causes the stock market variability. Together, they form a chain effect from the fluctuation of the financial sector's stock prices (spiv) to the fluctuations of the real sector's M1, GDP, and exports. Then, the exports volatility causes the stock price volatility.

Third, we have found other two unidirectional causality relations, namely, the exchange rate variability (excv) causes money supply variability (m1v). The money supply variability, then, causes the export variability.

Note that, for the Taiwanese case, the exchange rate variability is independently determined from external factors, and its variability causes money supply variability. The interest rate variability (intv) and consumer price variability appear to be independent from each other, and also from the rest of the variables.

5.7.3 *The Granger Causality Test for Singapore*

Part C of Table 5.2 presents the results of Granger causality test from VAR(1) model using the seven first-difference volatilities for Singapore. We have found six causality relationships that are significant at the 10% level or less. Figure 5.9(c) summarizes the results. We present the economic interpretations and policy implications below.

First, we have found quite different causality relations in Singapore compared with those in Korea and Taiwan. The causality relations are concentrated in the real sectors of GDP, exports, and M1, instead of the financial sectors, stock prices, and interest rate. Singapore's export variation (xptv) and GDP variation (gdpv) have bidirectional causalities, and the impact of exports on GDP is stronger than that of GDP on exports.

We see the causality from export variation (xptv) to GDP variation (gdpv), indicating that Singapore's economy strongly depends on exports, and the fluctuations in exports activities will cause the fluctuations in GDP. On the other hand, the GDP variation (gdpv) also causes the export variation (xptv). The effect is clearly bidirectional.

Second, we have found money supply variation (m1v) unidirectionally causes the variations of GDP (gdpv), exports (extv), and consumer prices (cpiv). This indicates that Singapore's stable monetary policy is important to bring the stability of the economy, namely, GDP, exports, and consumer price.

Third, like Taiwan, the exchange rate variation appears to be independent, but there is a unidirectional causality relation from the exchange rate variation (excv) to the money supply variation (m1v) with enhancement effects, but the relation is significant at the 10% level only. Furthermore, the stock market variation and interest variation appear to be independent of each other, and also independent from the rest of the economy.

Note that, in Singapore, the money supply volatility unidirectionally causes exports, GDP, and consumer price index volatilities. Unlike the case of Taiwan, the stock market volatility does not cause the money supply volatility. Therefore, money supply is a destabilizing factor for GDP, exports, and the consumer price, showing the importance of the monetary policy.

In general, while each country has a different story to tell, there are some reservations in the interpretations of the above individual country's causality relations. First, the individual country's time-series analysis is based on a sample of only 22 observations of annual data. Second, since the results of the causality relations differ from country to country, the time-series analysis based on a single country cannot yield a general rule for development policy. Third, the time period is generally limited for a time-series analysis. On the other hand, the cross-section analysis is criticized for assuming a similar economic structure for vastly diverse countries (Giles and Williams, 2000). A solution to these problems is to pool the time-series data of Korea, Taiwan, and Singapore into a panel data set to investigate the Granger causality relations for the group.

5.8   Panel Data VAR and the Granger Causality Test

A panel data analysis has the merit of using information from cross-section and time-series analyses. It can also take heterogeneity of each cross-sectional unit explicitly into account by allowing for individual-specific effects (Davidson and MacKinnon, 2004) and allow for "more variability, less collinearity among variables, more degrees of freedom, and more efficiency" (Baltagi, 2001). Furthermore, the repeated cross-section of observations over time is better suited to study the dynamic of changes, like macroeconomic volatilities in this study (Hsiao and Hsiao, 2006).

The three NDCs — Korea, Taiwan, and Singapore — have similarity with regard to culture and geographical proximity. Their rapid economic growth during the past three decades and their openness through the trade of high-tech products, especially with the United States and Japan, have formed the core of the Pacific trade triangle (Hsiao and Hsiao, 2001, 2003). Considering the growing interdependence of these three Asian NDC-3, we propose to pool their seven first-difference macroeconomic volatilities into a panel data set of 63 observations and use panel data regressions to examine the Granger causality relations for the group. We then compare the group Granger causality relations of the volatilities with the results from individual country's study in Section 5.7.

5.8.1   *Panel Data Unit Root Tests*

We first test the stationarity of the seven panel first-difference series of volatilities, dcpiv, dexcv, dgdpv, dintv, dmlv, dspiv, and dxptv (for simplicity, we use the same notations as used in the study of individual countries). Recent econometric literature has proposed several methods for testing the presence of a unit root under a panel data setting. Since different panel data unit root tests may yield different testing results, we have chosen the IPS-W test (Im, Pesaran, and Shin, 2003) and the ADF-Fisher Chi-square test (Maddala and Kim, 1998) to perform the panel data unit root test and compare their results (Christopoulos and Tsionas, 2003). Table 5.3 presents the panel unit root test results of the seven series. Both the IPS-W and the ADF-Fisher tests indicate that the seven panel first-difference series of volatilities are all stationary series at the 1% level of significance. Therefore, we can use them in the panel data VAR Granger causality analysis.

Table 5.3: Panel Unit Root Tests
Korea, Singapore, and Taiwan

	Panel data: First-difference series of volatilities				
		IPS W-stat		ADF-Fisher Chi-square	
1	dcpiv	-5.705 (0.00)	***	35.524 (0.00)	***
2	dexcv	-2.904 (0.00)	***	18.585 (0.00)	***
3	dgdpv	-10.468 (0.00)	***	63,066 (0.00)	***
4	dintv	-4.279 (0.00)	***	26.941 (0.00)	***
5	dmlv	-7.286 (0.00)	***	43.934 (0.00)	***
6	dspiv	-3.2 (0.00)	***	20.493 (0.00)	***
7	dxptv	-4.668 (0.00)	***	29.699 (0.00)	***

Notes: (1) The test equations include individual effects and individual linear trends. Automatic selection of lags based on minimum AIC: 0 to 4. (2) The p-values are in parentheses. (3) *** denotes rejection of null hypothesis: panel series has unit root (assumes individual unit root process) at the 1% level of significance.

5.8.2   *Panel Data VAR*

When we estimate panel data regression models, we consider the assumptions about the intercept, the slope coefficients, and the error term. In practice, the estimation procedure is either the panel FEM or the panel random effects model (Greene, 2003). Since we particularly select the three Asian NDCs — Korea, Singapore, and Taiwan — in this study, our selection of the cross-section units is not from a random process, so we do not use the random effects model here. The appropriate method is the panel fixed effects model, and we briefly explain it in what follows.

The panel FEM assumes that the slope coefficients are constant for all cross-section units. It also assumes that the intercepts vary over individual cross-section units, but they do not vary over time. For our application, we write the FEM as follows:

$$y_{it} = \alpha_i + x_{it}\beta + u_{it}, \tag{5.13}$$

where y_{it} can be one of our seven first-difference series of volatilities (i.e. the endogenous variables in VAR), i is the ith cross-section unit, and t is the time of observation. The intercept, α_i, takes into account the heterogeneity influence from unobserved variables, which may differ across the cross-section units. The x_{it} is a row vector of all lag endogenous variables. β is a column vector of the common slope coefficients for the group. The error term u_{it} follows the classical assumptions that $u_{it} \sim N(0, \sigma_u^2)$. In addition, as in the individual country study, we add an ordinary dummy variable into the model to take into account the effect of the 1997–1998 Asian financial crisis. For the purpose of comparison with the causality relations from the individual country's study, we also use the VAR(1) model in the panel FEM.

5.8.3   *The Granger Causality Test: Panel Data of Volatilities*

Table 5.4 and Figure 5.10 present the estimated Granger causality directions between the seven macroeconomic volatilities using panel

Table 5.4: The Granger Causality Test

Panel Data from Korea, Singapore, and Taiwan

Panel Fixed Effects (Cross-Section) Model

Vector Autoregression (1, c, dummy): Use first-difference series of volatilities

		dexcv(-1)	dintv(-1)	dspiv(-1)		cons.		fixed effects			
Dep.	dcpiv(-1)	dgdpv(-1)	dmlv(-1)	dxptv(-1)		dummy					
var.	c1	c2	c3	c4	c5	c6	c7	c8	c9	Kor-c	Sin-c	Twn-c

1 dcpiv 0.141 -0.015 -0.013 0.004 0.021 0.019 -0.032 -0.027 0.040 -0.003 0.001 0.002
(0.36) (0.73) (0.89) (0.89) (0.63) (0.55) (0.42) (0.00) (0.00)

2 dexcv 0.381 -0.105 -0.588 -0.067 0.151 0.299 0.033 -0.010 0.001 0.010 -0.013 0.003
(0.47) (0.46) (0.07) (0.43) (0.30) (0.01) (0.81) (0.65) (0.97) gdpv → excv *
spiv → excv ***

3 dgdpv -0.391 -0.016 -0.032 0.011 0.080 0.234 0.060 -0.100 0.119 0.005 -0.006 0.001
(0.20) (0.85) (0.86) (0.82) (0.34) (0.00) (0.45) (0.00) (0.00) spiv → gdpv ***

4 dintv 0.032 -0.026 0.020 -0.184 -0.127 0.112 -0.059 -0.004 0.062 0.019 -0.030 0.010
(0.97) (0.92) (0.97) (0.24) (0.64) (0.58) (0.81) (0.92) (0.30)

5 dmlv -0.624 0.143 -0.618 0.039 0.330 0.436 -0.082 -0.167 0.225 0.003 0.000 -0.003
(0.23) (0.31) (0.06) (0.64) (0.03) (0.00) (0.54) (0.00) (0.00) gdpv → mlv *
spiv → mlv ***

6 dspiv -0.137 0.001 -0.385 0.042 -0.096 -0.035 0.164 -0.109 0.118 0.007 -0.001 -0.005
(0.82) (0.99) (0.30) (0.67) (0.57) (0.78) (0.30) (0.00) (0.00)

7 dxptv -0.067 0.052 -0.774 0.063 0.304 0.170 0.073 -0.142 0.187 0.007 -0.010 0.003
(0.92) (0.76) (0.05) (0.53) (0.09) (0.20) (0.66) (0.00) (0.00) gdpv → xptv **
mlv → xptv *

Notes: (1) The p-values are in parentheses. (2) ***, **, * denote rejection of null hypothesis at the 1%, 5%, 10% levels of significance, respectively. (3) Kor = Korea, Sin = Singapore, and Twn = Taiwan.

FEM. Note that, the coefficients of dummy variable are all positive and five out of the seven of them are significant at the 1% level. This agrees with the fact that the 1997–1998 Asian financial crises did have significant effects on the volatilities of the seven macroeconomic variables in these three countries as a group. Figure 5.9 summarizes the panel data Granger causality directions in Table 5.4.

We have found seven very interesting unidirectional causality relations from the panel data analysis.

First, from the financial sector, due to the IT revolution, the volatility of stock price index (spiv) unidirectionally causes the

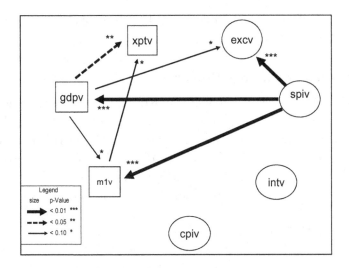

Figure 5.10: Causality Directions, Panel Data
Korea, Taiwan, and Singapore

volatilities of exchange rate (excv), GDP (gdpv), and money supply (m1v). In Eqs. (2), (3), and (5) of Table 5.4, the three coefficients of dspiv(−1) (the Column c6) are all significant at the 1% level (circled in the table). They indicate that the volatility of stock price index has strong effects on the volatilities of exchange rate, GDP, and M1. They also indicate that the economic policies, to decrease the fluctuations in the stock markets, will also promote the stability of exchange rate, GDP, and money supply in these countries.

Second, from the real sector, the volatility of GDP (gdpv) unidirectionally causes the volatilities of exchange rate (excv), money supply (m1v), and exports (xptv). In Eqs. (2), (5), and (7) of Table 5.4 (in square boxes), the three coefficients of dgdpv(−1) (the Column c3) are all significant at the 5% or 10% level. These results indicate that the volatility of GDP has an effect on the volatilities of exchange rate, M1, and exports. They also indicate that the economic policies, to promote the GDP growth, will affect the volatilities of exchange rate, M1, and exports in these three countries. In addition, we have also found that money supply volatility (m1v) unidirectionally causes the exports volatility (xptv) (the last row of Table 5.4).

5.9   Some Concluding Remarks

In this chapter, we have shown that Korea, Taiwan, and Singapore, the three NDCs in Asia, are powerhouses of the IT revolution, when viewed from either the supply side of the world or domestic production and trade, or from the demand side of the world or domestic consumption and services. The New Economy strengthened financial linkages across the countries in the Asia-Pacific region, and their close ties with the international stock markets, especially those of the United States and Japan, become an important route of transmitting international business cycle to these three countries, affecting their macroeconomic stability. From this vantage point of view, this chapter sets up a simple macroeconomic model and examines the causal relations between the volatilities of seven variables: GDP, consumer price index, stock price index, the interest rate, exchange rate, money supply, and exports (openness) of the economy.

The results of our causality test for Korea are especially illuminating.

For Korea, the financial sector, especially the stock market, plays an important role in determining the stability of the real sectors. The findings indicate that the important macroeconomic policy for achieving Korea's economic stability is, at least in the short run, to reduce the volatility of the stock market prices but not the other way around. For the first time, this chapter presents analytically the importance of the stock price volatility in driving the business cycle in Korea, a newly developed county. Since, in our model, the stock price affects output through consumption (the wealth effect) and IT investment, this chapter points to the need of a closer examination of the relationship between stock prices and consumption as well as investment. In this sense, we have brought the financial sector into macroeconomic analysis.

For Taiwan, both the financial sector and the real sector appear to be better integrated. There is a bidirectional causality between the GDP variability and the stock market, and the stock market variability will have an impact on the variability of all the real variables in sequence. Variability of the stock market will have a strong impact on money supply, to GDP, to exports, and back to stock market itself. Our results also show that, in Taiwan, monetary policy, which depends on the foreign exchange variation, plays an important role in changes of GDP and exports. This is not indicated in the Korean case.

Curiously, Singapore presents a case quite different from Korea and Taiwan. In Singapore, we have found that the stock market, as well as the interest rate, is isolated from the other five variables of this study, and the exchange rate is not influenced by the domestic economy. They are only influenced by the factors outside Singapore. There is a close tie between exports and GDP, and like with Taiwan, monetary policy plays an important role in stabilizing the economy.

In all three cases, the variation of the interest rate and the exchange rates either have no effect on the economy or play a rather minor role in the economy.

In the literature, Aghion *et al.* (1999), Acemoglu and Zilibotti (1997), Darrat and Haj (2002), Easterly *et al.* (2000), and Levine and Zervos (1998) have found that the financial development reduces macroeconomic volatility. So far as the stock market is concerned, these findings are also consistent with our results on Korea and Taiwan but not with those of Singapore.

Our panel data results reinforce our results from Korea and Taiwan. When we pool the volatilities of seven macroeconomic variables of the three countries, we found a very clear pattern of causality between financial and real sectors. First, the stock price volatility is clearly a very strong factor affecting volatility of exchange rate, GDP, and money supply. The impact is unidirectional. Our result is consistent with the finding that the stock prices affect GDP through the wealth effect. Second, money supply is also a destabilizing factor of exports. Third, more importantly, GDP is an influencing factor for exports, money supply, and exchange rate, although the effect is rather weak.

From panel data Granger causality analysis, we have found the evidence that, in general, the volatility of stock prices due to the IT revolution has directly and strongly caused the fluctuations of some important macroeconomic variables, such as exchange rate, GDP, and supply of money in the NDCs. The policy implication of these findings is that the government should recognize the international impact of the stock markets and pay more attention to the stock price volatility so that it will not affect GDP, exchange rate, and money supply. On the other hand, our overall results indicate that the volatility in the GDP level is less of concern since its impact on exports, exchange rate, and money supply are generally absent or minor as compared with the stock price volatility.

Appendix 5A: The ADF Unit Root Test on Volatility Series for Korea, Singapore, and Taiwan

Table 5A.1: The ADF Unit Root Test on Volatility Series

Panel Data Korea, Singapore, Taiwan

Level series of volatilities				First-difference series				
	k	Test-statistic	*(p-value)*		k	Test-statistic	*(p-value)*	
Korea								
cpiv	4	-2.887	*0.07*	*	dcpiv	0	-6.523	*0* ***
excv	0	-2.124	*0.24*		dexcv	1	-4.848	*0* ***
gdpv	2	-4.199	*0* ***	dgdpv	0	-7.386	*0* ***
intv	4	3.752	*0.99*		dintv	0	-5.851	*0* ***
mlv	2	-2.759	*0.08*	*	dmlv	1	-1.631	*0.09* *
spiv	0	-2.345	*0.17*		dspiv	1	-4.295	*0.02* **
xptv	2	0.042	*0.99*		dxptv	0	-6.517	*0* ***
Singapore								
cpiv	3	-5.282	*0* ***	dcpiv	3	-4.507	*0.01* ***
excv	1	-3.984	*0.03* **	dexcv	1	-2.985	*0.01* ***
gdpv	1	-5.483	*0* ***	dgdpv	1	-4.005	*0.03* **
intv	0	-3.683	*0.01* ***	dintv	3	-4.851	*0* ***
mlv	1	-4.8	*0* ***	dmlv	0	-7.246	*0* ***
spiv	2	-3.166	*0.04* **	dspiv	1	-4.576	*0.01* ***
xptv	0	-1.59	*0.11*		dxptv	4	-3.599	*0.06* *
Taiwan								
cpiv	2	-2.579	*0.11*		dcpiv	0	-4.587	*0.01* ***
excv	3	-4.321	*0.02* **	dexcv	0	-3.564	*0* ***
gdpv	0	-2.392	*0.02* **	dgdpv	0	-11.323	*0* ***
intv	0	-1.067	*0.25*		dintv	1	-4.157	*0* ***
mlv	4	-0.835	*0.94*		dmlv	3	-8.519	*0* ***
spiv	4	-3.601	*0.02* **	dspiv	4	-2.21	*0.03* **
xptv	0	-1.569	*0.11*		dxptv	2	-3.982	*0.03* **

Notes: (1) The test equations include constant and/or linear trends when they are significant at the 10% level. Null hypothesis: Series has a unit root. (2) The lag length (k) is selected by the minimum AIC with maximum lag = 4. (3) ***, **, or * denotes rejection of the null hypothesis: series has a unit root, at the 1%, 5%, or 10% level of significance, respectively.

Acknowledgments

This chapter was presented at the Seminars of the Department of Economics, University of Colorado, Denver, 2007, of the Midwestern Intercollegiate Conference at the University of Missouri, 2007, and the joint International Conference of American Committee for Asian Economic Studies (ACAES) and the Rimini Centre for Economic Analysis (RCEA), Italy, August 2008. We are grateful for these conference organizers for their invitation and hospitality. As usual, discussions with Professor Robert McNown are most helpful. All errors of commissions and omissions are ours.

References

Acemogu, D. and F. Zilibotti (1997). Was Prometheus unbound by chance? Risk, diversification, and growth. *Journal of Political Economy* **105**, 709–751.

Agenor, Pierre-Richard, C. John McDermott and Eswar S. Prasad (1999). Macroeconomic Fluctuations in Developing Countries: Some Stylized Facts, IMF Working Paper, WP/99/35.

Aghion P, A. Banerjee and T. Piketty (1999). Dualism and macroeconomic volatility. *Quarterly Journal of Economics* **114**, 1359–1397.

Aoki, M. and H. Takizawa (2002). Understanding the Silicon Valley Phenomena, World Institute for Development Economic Research (WIDER), United Nation University (UNU), Discussion Paper No. 2002/11.

Asia Development Bank (ADB) (2000). *Asian Development Outlook 2000 Update*, Manila: Asia Development Bank.

Baltagi, B. H. (2001). *Econometric Analysis of Panel Data* (2nd edn.). New York: John Wiley and Sons.

Bertaut, Carol C. (2002). Equity Prices, Household Wealth, and Consumption Growth in Foreign Industrial Countries: Wealth Effects in the 1990s, International Finance Discussion Papers, No. 724, Board of Governors of the Federal Research System.

Bera, A. K. and M. L. Higgins (1993). ARCH models: Properties, estimation and testing. *Journal of Economic Survey* **7** (4), 305–362.

Bini-Smaghi, L. (1991). Exchange rate variability and trade: Why is it so difficult to find any empirical relationship? *Applied Economics* **23**, 927–936.

Bollerslev, T. (1986). Generalized autoregressive conditional heteroskedasticity. *Journal of Econometrics* **31**, 307–327.

Cheng, Ya-Chi (2002). A study of the IT business cycle and the Taiwanese economy (in Chinese), *Industry of Free China*, 49–73.

Christopoulos, D. K. and E. G. Tsionas, (2003). A reassessment of balance of payments constrained growth: Results from panel unit root and panel cointegration tests. *International Economic Journal* **17** (3), 39–54.

Cornelius, Peter K., Friedrich von Kirchbach, Fiona Paua, Nicolai Semine (2002). Trade in ICT Products: The Global Framework and Empirical Evidence, Chapter 10 of *The Global Information Technology Report, Reading for the Networked World*, Geoffrey S. Kirkman, Peter K. Cornelius, Jeffrey D. Sachs, and Klaus Schwab, World Economic Forum, Center for International Development. NYC: Oxford University Press.

Daly, K. (1999). *Financial Volatility and Real Economic Activity*. Ashgate Publishing Ltd.

Darrat, Ali F. and Mahmoud Haj (2002). Economic Fluctuations in MENA: Does Financial Market Development Matter? Working Paper, presented at *The Economic Research Forum Ninth Annual Conference*, 26–28 October.

Davidson, R, and J. G. MacKinnon, (2004). *Econometrics Theory and Methods*. New York: Oxford University Press.

Dickey, D. and W. Fuller (1979). Distribution of the estimators for autoregressive time series with a unit root. *Journal of the American Statistical Association* **74**, 427–431.

Dickey, D. and W. Fuller (1981). Likelihood ratio tests for autoregressive time series with a unit root. *Econometrica* **49**, 1057–1072.

Dutta, S., B. Lanvin and F. Paua (2004). *The Global Information Technology Report, Towards and Equitable Information Society*. New York: Oxford University Press.

Easterly, W., R. Islam and Joseph E. Stiglitz (2000). Shaken and stirred: Explaining growth and volatility. *World Bank Economic Review*.

Edison, Hali and Torsten Slok (2001). Wealth Effects and the New Economy, IMF Working Paper WP/01/77.

Engle, R. F. (1982). Autoregressive conditional heteroskedasticity with estimates of the variance of United Kingdom inflation. *Econometrica* **50**, 987–1008.

Engle, R. F. (2001). GARCH 101: The use of ARCH/GARCH models in applied econometrics. *Journal of Economic Perspectives* **15** (4), 157–168.

Gavin, Michael and Ricardo Hausmann (1996). Determinants of Macroeconomic Volatility in Developing Countries, Inter-American Development Bank Working Paper.

Giles, J. A. and C. L. Williams, (2000). Export-led growth: A survey of the empirical literature and some non-causality results, Part I. *Journal of International Trade and Economic Development* **9** (3), 261–337.

Greene, William H. (2003), *Econometric Analysis* (5th edn.) New Jersey: Prentice-Hall.

Hsiao, Frank S. T. and Mei-Chu W. Hsiao (1994). Monetary policy coordination between large and small countries: An empirical study *Journal of Economic Development* **19** (2), 7–46.

Hsiao, Frank S. T. and Mei-Chu W. Hsiao (1995). International policy coordination with a dominant player—The case of the United States, Japan, Taiwan, and Korea. *Journal of Asian Economics* **6** (1), 29–51.

Hsiao, Frank S. T. and Mei-Chu W. Hsiao (1996). Taiwanese Economic Development and Foreign Trade, in *Harvard Studies on Taiwan: Papers of the Taiwan Studies Workshop I*. The John K. Fairbank Center for East Asian Research, Harvard University, 199–270. Also in *Comparative Asian Economies*,

J. Y. T. Kuark (Ed.), *Contemporary Studies in Economic and Financial Analysis*, 77 (Part B), An International Series of Monographs. Greenwich, CT: JAI Press, 211–302.

Hsiao, Frank S. T. and Mei-Chu W. Hsiao (2001). Capital flows and exchange rates: Recent Korean and Taiwanese experience and challenges. *Journal of Asian Economics* **12** (3), 353–381.

Hsiao, Frank S. T. and Mei-Chu W. Hsiao (2003). Miracle growth in the twentieth century — International comparisons of East Asian development. *World Development* **31** (2), 227–257.

Hsiao, Frank S. T. and Mei-Chu W. Hsiao (2006). FDI, exports, and GDP in East and Southeast Asia — Panel data versus time-series causality analysis. *Journal of Asian Economics* **17**, 1082–1106.

Hsiao, Frank S. T., Mei-Chu W. Hsiao and Akio Yamashita (2003). The impact of the US economy on the Asia-Pacific region: Does it matter? *Journal of Asian Economics* **14** (2), 219–241.

Hsiao, Frank S. T. and Changsuh Park (2002). Productivity growth in newly developed countries—The case of Korea and Taiwan. *The Journal of the Korean Economy* **3** (2), 189–230.

Hsiao, Frank S. T. and Changsuh Park (2005). Korean and Taiwanese productivity performance—Comparisons at matched manufacturing levels. *Journal of Productivity Analysis* **23**, 85–107.

Im, K. S. Pesaran, M. H. and Y. Shin (2003). Testing for unit roots in heterogeneous panels. *Journal of Econometrics* **115**, 53–74.

International Centre for the Study of East Asian Development (ICSEAD) (2003). Recent Trends and Prospects for Major Asian Economies, *East Asian Economic Perspectives* (EAEP), Special issue, **14** (1).

International Monetary Fund (IMF) (2001). *World Economic Outlook 2001, The Information Technology Revolution*, October.

Kapur, Sandeep (2002). Developing Countries in the New Economy — The Role of Demand-side Initiatives, World Institute for Development Economic Research (WIDER), United Nation University (UNU), Discussion Paper No. 2002/73.

Kawakami, Momoko (1996), Development of the Small- and Medium-Sized Manufacturers in Taiwan's PC Industry, Discussion Paper Series, No. 9606. Chung-hua Institute of Economic Research, Taipei, Taiwan.

Kurian, G. T. (2001). *The Illustrated Book of World Rankings* (5th edn.). New York: M.E. Sharpe.

Levine, R. and S. Zervos (1998). Stock markets, banks, and growth. *American Economic Review* **88**, 537–558.

Liu, Po-Li (2001), A study of national strategy of promoting IT in Japan-Also on Taiwan's knowledge economy development plan (in Chinese). *Industry of Free China* **91** (9), 1–47.

Maddala, G. S. and I-M. Kim (1998). *Unit Roots, Cointegration, and Structural Change*. UK: Cambridge University Press.

Pohjola, Matti (2002a). The new economy in growth and development. *Oxford Review of Economic Policy* **18** (3), 380–396.

Pohjola, Matti (2002b). The new economy: Facts, impacts and policies. *Information Economics and Policy* **14**, 133–144.

Ramey, Garey and Valerie A. Ramey (1995). Cross-country evidence on the link between volatility and growth. *American Economic Review* **85** (5), 1138–1151.

Sato, Yukihito (1997). Diverging development paths of the electronics industry in Korea and Taiwan. *The Developing Economies* **35** (4), 401–421.

Taiwan Statistical Data Book (TSDB) (2007). Council for Economic Planning and Development, Executive Yuan, Taiwan.

Temple, Jonathan (2002). The assessment: The new economy. *Oxford Review of Economic Policy* **18** (3), 241–264.

World Bank (2002). *World Development Indicators WDI-CD*, World Bank.

Wong, Poh Kam (2002). ICT production and diffusion in Asia: Digital dividends or digital divide? *Information Economics and Policy* **14** (2), 167–187.

Part II

The United States and Emerging East and Southeast Asia

Chapter 6

The Impact of the US Economy on the Asia-Pacific Region — Does It Matter?

Abstract

This chapter continues the discussion of real and financial linkages in Chapter 5. From the viewpoint of world political economic development, the United States plays a very important role in the world, especially in the emerging Asia, through its IT industry. We first confirm the interdependence of the United States and the Asia-Pacific region by examining the regional trade and investment relationship between the United States and the Asia-Pacific region. We then explore the real linkage through trade and investment and the financial linkage through stock markets. These linkages are strengthened by the recent information technology (IT) revolution. The pairwise and vector autoregression (VAR) are used to test the Granger causality of real linkage in terms of GDP and the financial linkage in terms of the daily stock price indices among these countries. Impulse response functions and variance decomposition from VAR are illustrated. Our results show that there is no significant unidirectional causality from the US GDP to those of Japan, Taiwan, Korea, and China. But the slump in the US stock price indices will cause the stock market recession in Japan, Korea, and Taiwan, but not in China. Thus, the US financial condition plays an important role in these Asian countries through financial linkages.

Keywords: US and Asia-Pacific region; regional interdependence; IT revolution; VAR; causality

6.1   Introduction

Since the mid-1980s, the United States and the Asia-Pacific countries have increasingly formed a new international division of labor in the new economy of information technology (IT), defined as computer hardware, software, and telecommunication equipment (IMF, 2001, p. 105). The Asia-Pacific countries here include the Asian Developed Countries (ADCs): South Korea (hereafter Korea), Taiwan, Singapore, and Japan; and the ASEAN4+: Indonesia, Malaysia, the Philippines, Thailand, and China. When Hong Kong, which is increasingly integrated with China, is included in the ADCs, we denote them separately as the ADCs+. By 2000, about 30–50% of total exports of these two groups consisted of IT products, or about 10% of their GDP (IMF, 2001, p. 107, 122, 126). As the United States, along with Japan, is a significant investor in this region, and a majority of their products are exported to the United States (see below), the economic relation between these Asian countries and the United States is becoming much closer than ever. This chapter examines the interdependence between the United States and some selected countries in these two groups of Asian countries and assesses the impact of the recent US recession on this regional economy.

After a prolonged prosperity, the recovery of the Asian economies from the 1997 Asian financial crisis (Hsiao and Hsiao, 2001a) was swift, thanks to the booming IT markets in the United States from 1999 to 2000. However, since mid-2000s, a decrease in the demand for IT products and the subsequent worsening of the US economy (IMF, 2001, p. 79), aggravated by the 9/11 terrorist attack and over-investment in the IT sectors in the United States and the Asian countries, led to a sharp decrease in exports and slower GDP growth in these Asian countries (IMF, 2001, p. 33). The slump in the US IT markets transmitted quickly to the Asia-Pacific region through trade and foreign investment as well as stock markets. The transmission has been fast and devastating.

The reason is that the United States is not only the largest economy in the world, it is also an important trading partner and a major supplier of technology and capital. Thus, in Section 6.2, we first discuss the role of the United States as a major trading partner, investor, and capital lender to the countries in the Asia-Pacific region. We also examine the importance of the ADCs as exporters and importers to and from the United States.

In Section 6.3, we discuss the impact of the IT revolution on the United States and these two groups of the Asia-Pacific region, which have successfully specialized in producing and exporting IT products. We explore the real linkage between them through trade and investment and the financial linkage through stock markets. The strengthening of the real and financial linkages arising from the IT revolution and the increased vulnerability of these countries to international macroeconomic fluctuations is noted.

We then, in Section 6.4, select five countries, the United States, Japan, Korea, Taiwan (the major ADCs+), and China (the major ASEAN4+), to test the causality of the GDP series. We first check the pairwise Granger causality for 10 pairs of the countries and then use the vector autoregression (VAR) model to test Granger causality. Impulse response functions and variance decomposition of each variable are derived and illustrated. Similar methods are used in Section 6.5 to test the causality of the stock indices of the five countries. Section 6.6 concludes.

6.2 The Interdependence of the United States and the Asia-Pacific Region

Figure 6.1 shows the share of GDP of the world's 174 countries[1] in year 2000 (WB, 2002). The US GDP alone accounted for almost

---

[1]Taiwan's GDP data in current USD (US $309 billion) is taken from ICSEAD (2002), and added to the world total of US $31.5 trillion to calculate percentage. EMU+ includes 12 countries in the European Monetary Union (Austria, Belgium, Finland, France, Germany, Greece, Ireland, Italy, Luxembourg, the Netherlands, Portugal, and Spain) and United Kingdom (WB, 2002).

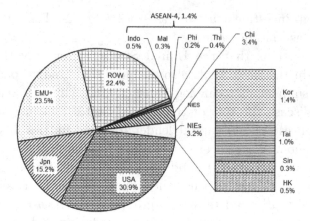

Figure 6.1: World Share of GDP
2000, in current US$

31% of world GDP. Japan at 15.2% was a distant second, followed by China, 3.4%. In contrast, the NIEs (Newly Industrializing Economies, namely, Korea, Taiwan, Singapore, and Hong Kong) had a 3.2% share, and the ASEAN4 had about a 1.4% share. Thus, the difference is so enormous that the US economy could be expected to exert significant influence over the individual countries in the region economically and politically.[2]

In fact, this is the case. Column (a) of Table 6.1 shows the merchandise trade with the United States as a percentage of the total merchandise trade for each country in the region. In 1999, except in Hong Kong, the weight of the US trade is over 10%, and in the Philippines, China, and Japan even as high as 28–30% of their total trade. Generally speaking, the weight of the US decreased in the ADCs+ in the 1990s and increased in ASEAN4+ countries, indicating the success of diversification of the direction of trade in

---

[2]In the original version of this paper, we presented the purchasing power parity share weight of GDP. In that case, the US GDP accounted to 22% of the world GDP; China, 11.5%; Japan, 7.5%; NIEs, 3.4%; and ASEAN4, 3.6%. Since we are interested in the impact (instead of welfare) of the current US GDP on GDPs of the Asia-Pacific countries, we decided to use GDP in current USD.

Table 6.1: Merchandise Trade with the United States and in IT Products

	(a) Trade with USA % of Total Trade			(b) Trade with USA % of GDP			(c) IT Exports % of Total Trade	
	1980	1990	1999	1980	1990	1999	1990	1999
World Avg	12.2	13	15.5	4	4	5.7	8.8	14.1
ADC+								
Korea	23	26	21	15	13	13	22.1	29.7
Taiwan	29	28	22	28	21	18	21.0	37.1
Singapore	12	16	16	43	49	42	36.5	52.8
Japan	21	29	28	2	5	10	23.3	21.8
HK	18	10	7	27	23	15	15.6	22.0
ASEAN-4+								
Indonesia	21	11	14	8	5	9	0.5	6.1
Malaysia	17	16	21	16	20	39	27.9	52.4
Philippines	29	30	30	12	14	26	22.7	63.0
Thailand	14	15	19	7	10	16	15.3	26.1
China	14	22	28	5	5	4	...	15.4
United States							13.1	18.1

Sources: (a), (b) from Arora and Vamvakidis (2001), which is based on IMF Direction of Trade Statistics and World Economic Outlook. Taiwan's data are calculated from TSDB (2002) in nominal USD. (c) WTO (2000, Table IV, p. 57). Exports of office machines and telecom equipment of selected economies, 1990–1999.

the ADCs+ economies. Nevertheless, for all these countries, trade with the US is still predominant.

A more direct impact of trade volume on economic activity may be measured by taking the proportion of US trade as a percentage of GDP in each country, as shown in Column (b) of Table 6.1. The percentage apparently varies inversely with the size of the economy, as indicated in Figure 6.1: only 4% in China and 10% in Japan in 1999. Other countries range from 13% in Korea to a whopping 42% in Singapore. Thus, the transmission of macroeconomic fluctuations from the US to smaller countries through trade relations alone may be expected to be substantial.

Column (c) shows that the IT products hold the bulk of exports: Most are exported to the US and the rest to other inter- or intra-regional countries. Except for Japan, which shows a slight decrease, the proportion of IT products in the total merchandise trade increased considerably from 1990 to 1999, at least 30% for all countries. Among them, the ratio of Indonesia increased almost 13 times and that of the Philippines three times. In 1999, the proportion of IT products in the total trade of the Philippines was 63%, followed by Singapore at 53%. As we will see in the Section 6.3, this increase renders these countries quite vulnerable to the IT-induced business cycle.

As well as by trade, US economic conditions may influence its trading partners through its foreign direct and portfolio investment flows[3] and also through stock markets. Column (a) of Table 6.2 presents the shares of US and Japanese foreign direct investment (FDI) in the Asia-Pacific region. We added the share of Japanese FDI, since Japan is another large investor in the area, competing with the United States. The first row of each country shows the total inward FDI[4] in USD billion, but in some cases in the domestic currency, converted to USD. The percentage shares of US FDI and Japanese FDI are then calculated. Exceptions to the designated year are shown in parentheses.

In general, the grand total of FDI investment in the nine countries increased considerably in the 1990s: 3.7 times in the ADCs+ and 5.1 times in the ASEAN+, 4.6 times overall for all nine countries, indicating the rapidly increasing openness of the Asia-Pacific region. Most of the increased FDI came from the USA, as the proportion

---

[3]In studying the relative impact of the US and Japanese business cycles on the Australian economy in terms of real GDP from 1959:3 to 1996:4, Lee *et al.* (2003) found that the main transmission channel of the US business cycle to the Australian business cycle was FDI (i.e. what they call the financial market), while that of Japan was trade. They also found that the US output had a stronger impact than the Japanese output. They did not consider the stock market linkage.

[4]Each country has a different method of interpreting and collecting FDI data. For example, inward flow data of Indonesia "are based on approvals and exclude foreign direct investment in the oil and gas industry, banking, nonbank financial institution, insurance and leasing. Reported data include cancellations, expansions, mergers, net value of alterations and shifting of projects from foreign to domestic investment or vice versa" (UNCTAD, 2000). Thus, Indonesia's FDI may be underreported.

Table 6.2: Shares of FDI Flow and Stocks of Lending

In US$ Billions, and Percent

Country		(a) FDI 1990	1995	1998 Notes	(b) Lending 1990	1995	2000
1 Korea	Total $	0.8	1.9	8.9 a	28.7	77.5	58.8
	US %	**40**	**33**	**34**	**14**	**10**	**11**
	Japan %	*29*	*22*	*6*	*32*	*28*	*18*
2 Taiwan	Total $	2.3	2.9	3.7 a	10.0	22.5	18.1
	US %	**25**	**45**	**25**	**18**	**12**	**12**
	Japan %	*36*	*20*	*14*	*29*	*14*	*17*
3 Singapore	Total $	2.6	3.1	8.5	140.6	192.5	100.0
	US %	**33**	**41**	**53** (97)	**3**	**3**	**3**
	Japan %	*36*	*38*	*10*	*56*	*40*	*27*
4 Japan*	Total $	2.8	3.9	10.2 a			
	US %	**24**	**48**	**60**			
Total $	ADCs	9	12	31 3.7 b	179	293	177
Avg %	**US**	**30**	**42**	**43**	**12**	**8**	**8**
Avg %	*Japan*	*34*	*26*	*10*	*39*	*27*	*20*
5 Indonesia	Total $	8.8	39.9	33.8 a	24.7	44.5	40.2
	US %	**2**	**7**	**3** (97)	**5**	**6**	**8**
	Japan %	*26*	*9*	*16*	*61*	*47*	*25*
6 Malaysia*	Total $	1.7	2.3	1.5	7.3	16.8	20.8
	US %	**6** (91)	**22**	**15**	**5**	**9**	**5**
	Japan %	*37*	*23*	*18*	*61*	*44*	*27*
7 Philippines	Total $	0.2	0.8	0.9	9.3	8.3	16.5
	US %	**27**	**7**	**28**	**34**	**35**	**11**
	Japan %	*28*	*30*	*17*	*32*	*12*	*18*
8 Thailand*	Total $	2.5	2.0	2.8	13.6	62.8	26.6
	US %	**10**	**13**	**22** (97)	**9**	**7**	**4**
	Japan %	*43*	*28*	*36*	*55*	*59*	*37*
9 China	Total $	3.5	37.5	45.3 13.0 b	22.3	48.4	58.2
	US %	**13**	**8**	**7** (97)	**1**	**4**	**2**
	Japan %	*14*	*8*	*10*	*54*	*36*	*18*
Total	ASEAN4	17	83	84 5.1 b	77	181	162
Avg %	**US**	**11**	**11**	**15**	**11**	**12**	**6**
Avg %	*Japan*	*30*	*20*	*19*	*52*	*40*	*25*
GrdTotal $	9 countries	25	94	116 4.6 b	256	473	339
GrdAvg %	**US**	**20**	**25**	**27**	**11**	**11**	**7**
GrdAvg %	*Japan*	*31*	*22*	*16*	*48*	*35*	*23*

Notes: a = on approval base. b = increase of 1998 FDI over 1990 FDI. (97) = 1997 estimate.

Sources: UNCTAD (2000). (a) Originally given in local currency and converted to USD by average yearly exchange rate from ICSEAD (2002). For Japan, see JSY (1994, 2001).

of US investment in the total FDI in the countries increased in both groups, especially in the ADCs, while that of overall Japanese investment in the eight countries decreased considerably over the decade, the largest decrease occurring in the ADCs.

Compared with 1990, FDI in China increased 13 times in 1998, consisting of almost 54% of FDI in the ASEAN4+ or 40% of FDI in grand total. Interestingly, the proportion of FDI in China from both the USA and Japan decreased 6% and 4%, respectively, indicating the relative increase of FDI in China from Taiwan, Korea, and other countries. China is followed by Korea, which increased 11 times; the Philippines, 4.5 times; Indonesia, 3.8 times; and Singapore, 3.2 times. Malaysia is the only country that shows a slight decrease in FDI. The US proportion of FDI has increased in all the countries, except Korea and China, suggesting the general increase of economic influence of the United States in this region. Note that, although the proportion of US investment in Korea has decreased, the US still contributes 34% of the total FDI in Korea; thus, US economic conditions may still exert considerable impact on the Korean economy.

Column (b) of Table 6.2 shows that the US banks are far smaller lenders to these countries than the Japanese banks (Callen and McKibbin, 2001). The US share of lending to the ADCs remains almost the same and small, less than 10%, while that to the ASEAN4+ tends to be decreasing and also small, also less than 10%. Thus, US monetary policy, especially changes in interest rate, has a limited effect on these Asia-Pacific countries.

We have seen the dominance of the US role in Asian exports and direct investment. On the other hand, the United States also increasingly depends on trade with the Asia-Pacific region, especially with the ADCs. The left-hand side of Figure 6.2 shows that, in 2000, the US exports to the ADCs+ consisted of about 20% of its total exports. In fact, among the 10 leading exporting partners of the United States in 2000, Japan ranked third (following Canada and Mexico), Korea sixth, Taiwan seventh, and Singapore tenth, and the trend in Korea and Taiwan is increasing (SAUS, 2001). At a lesser scale, about 6% of the United States exports went to the ASEAN4+ countries, a total of 25% to both areas.

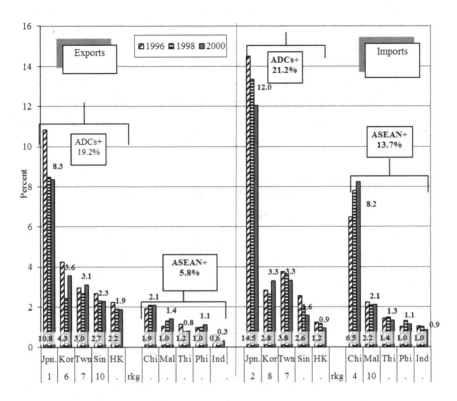

Figure 6.2: US Exports and Imports from the Asia-Pacific Region
Ratios to Total Exports and Imports
Notes: The top (bottom) numbers are 2000 (1996) ratios.

On the import side, the United States also relies more on Asia. It imported 21% from the ADCs+ and 14% from the ASEAN4+, a total of 35%. Among them, Japan ranked second, China fourth, Taiwan seventh, Korea eighth, and Malaysia tenth. Thus, a change in economic conditions in the Asia-Pacific area will have an impact on the US economy.

It may be interesting to point out that among the US patents granted to residents of areas outside the United States and its territories, the three major ADCs alone had 54% of the total patents granted in 1999: Japan, 32,513 patents, ranked first; Taiwan, 4,526, ranked third, only behind Germany; and Korea, 3,679, ranked sixth, after France and the United Kingdom (SAUS, 2001, p. 846). Few people are aware that the vigorous inventive and innovative activities of these three countries, especially Taiwan and Korea, have exceeded most of the OECD countries and are comparable to Germany, France, and the United Kingdom. Thus, the US recession and the subsequent decrease in revenue from the massive use of patented products in the United States also sends a blow to these countries.

6.3 The IT Revolution and the Global Real and Financial Linkages

The recent IT revolution has contributed several new features to the interdependence between the United States and the Asia-Pacific countries.

The core of the IT revolution is semiconductors, the power of which has doubled every 18–24 months (Moor's Law) and the prices of which have decreased steadily and rapidly. The fast technological obsolescence and turnover, low cost of learning, externality of networking, and the combination of high-tech and labor-intensive manufacturing process in this field have enabled a vertical division of labor between computer producers in the United States and developing countries, like the ASEAN4+, for offshore sourcing of IT peripherals (EPA, 2000). Specialization in IT products in the Asia-Pacific countries has enhanced the interdependence between the United States and these countries through trade and FDI. At the same time, this specialization has exposed these countries to the recent IT shock originating from the slump in demand for IT products in the United States.

The governments in this region place a top priority on developing the IT industry. Singapore has a national initiative for an "Intelligent Island," Taiwan for a "Green Silicon Island," and Malaysia for a "Multimedia Super Corridor." Other ASEAN4+ countries are also establishing special IT enclaves (ADB, 2000). As most of the IT products are exported, as shown in Column (c) of Table 6.1, strong international linkages may be expected to continue in the near future.

Furthermore, the governments of the ADCs have devoted large resources to R&D in the development of IT industries, facilitating technology absorption and adaptation, and further technological and managerial innovations, as evidenced by the patents granted in the United States mentioned above. Taiwan is now the world's third largest producer of IT products, next to the US and Japan, and Korea is the world's third largest producer of semiconductor chips and is in the forefront of mobile-phone technology (ADB, 2000). This also implies that IT products in the ADCs are related horizontally to industries in other advanced countries like the United States and the OECD countries in Europe, and thus the ADCs domestic business cycle of boom and bust in the IT industries is inevitably linked to the international business cycle, increasing the vulnerability of their economies (IMF, 2001, p. 123).

In addition to the supply side of production and exports, the rapidly falling prices of IT products and new services have also stimulated domestic demand for the products within these countries. This is shown in Part A of Table 6.3. While there is a very clear "digital divide" among the two groups, the popularity of IT products, such as telephone main lines, mobile telephones, personal computers (PC), and Internet hosts, in the former NIEs (Korea, Taiwan, Singapore, and Hong Kong) is either almost as great or has already exceeded their popularity in Japan, and even the United States, with the notable exception of the IT R&D scientists and engineers in the USA (see Part B of Table 6.3).

According to the IT indices compiled by the Japan's Economic Planning Agency (EPA, 2000), the differences of the IT infrastructure index[5] and the IT knowledge index of the NIEs and ASEAN4+ from those of Japan are much closer than expected. Although the total

---

[5]The output index and the per capita output index include the outputs of data and office machinery, communication and household audio equipment. The infrastructure index includes the first four items in Part A of Table 6.3, and nine other items, like number of cable TV, credit card usage, etc. The knowledge index considers the numbers of IT scientists, patents granted, high school and college enrollments, students studying in the United States, science paper citation index, etc.

Table 6.3: Use of IT Products and Capitalization
The Asia-Pacific Region

Country	Part A				Part B	Part C	
	Telephone main lines	Mobile telephones	Personal computers	Internet hosts	Scientists & Engnrs in R&D	(a) Equity capitalization	(b)
	per 1000 people			per 10000 people	per million people	% of GDP	Wld Rkg
	1998	1998	1998	Jul-99	1987-97	End of 2000	
USA	661	256	458.6	1508.8	3676	114.9 *	1
ADCs+							
Japan	503	374	237.2	163.8	4,909	66.3	2
Korea	433	302	156.8	55.5	2193	34.4 **	19
Taiwan	526	216	–	–	3532	79.9	12
Singapore	562	346	458.4	322.3	2318	168.3	18
HK	558	475	254.2	142.8	–	406.4	7
ASEAN-4+							
Indonesia	27	5	8.2	0.8	182	20.1	25
Malaysia	198	99	58.6	23.5	93	128.1	11
Philippines	37	22	15.1	1.3	157	60.0 **	26
Thailand	84	32	21.6	4.5	103	24.3	24
China	70	19	8.5	0.5	454	50.7	22

Sources: ADB (2000, p. 65). (a) From Economist Intelligent Unit, Country Finance. (b) World Ranking is based on equity capitalization (not on % of GDP) given in Kurian (2001). *NYSE. **End of September 2000.

value of IT outputs of the two groups in terms of USD are still far behind that of Japan and the USA, the per capita output of IT products among the NIEs has already exceeded that of the United States by 1997, indicating the potential of further development in these countries. The expansion of domestic markets for IT products may help to offset the volatility of exports, but at the same time, it makes consumers and investors more vulnerable to changes in international macroeconomic conditions.

The IT revolution strengthened financial linkages across the countries (IMF, 2001, p. 121, 128). Since new IT firms tend to be younger, smaller, and riskier, the IT sector relies more on equity financing (IMF, 2001, p. 131). This characteristic has been observed in a variety of economies, in both developed and developing countries. In Taiwan, for example, 44% of the total manufacturing capital in

2000 was invested by the IT industry, and almost 38% of the IT investment was financed through the stock market (Cheng, 2002).

Greater reliance on equity finance, and so on the stock markets across the countries, makes the IT sector and the economies in the Asia-Pacific region vulnerable to international stock price movements. Parts a and b of Table 6.4 present the correlation coefficients among the US NASDAQ index, Tokyo Nikkei–Dow–Jones average index, Singapore Straight Times Price Index, and Taiwan Weighted Stock Indices (Cheng, 2002). They show clearly that, compared with 1995–1999, the correlation coefficients increased dramatically in 2000–2001, especially the coefficients between the US stock price index and the stock price indices in other countries. Thus, the close ties between the US stock market and other countries caused the slump in the US market to be reflected rapidly in the stock prices of other countries.

How does the international linkage of stock markets influence domestic macroeconomic fluctuations? If the IT stocks are held only by a small number of people and have little weight in the national income, then international financial linkages should not have much effect on domestic consumption or business cycles. However, this is not the case in most of the Asia-Pacific countries. The many boom years in the IT industry in this region, before the recent slump, boosted the local stock market prices, stimulated stock ownership in the IT-producing and IT-exporting countries.

Part C of Table 6.3 shows stock market capitalization relative to GDP as a proxy for the stock ownership in each country. Except for Korea, the ADCs had capitalization ratios above 50% of GDP in 2000. Their equity capitalization ranked from second to nineteenth in the world,[6] indicating the predominance of equity assets in these societies. Except for Malaysia, the ASEAN4+ countries had lower capitalization ratios, ranging from 20% to 60%, but still high in the world rankings, from 22nd to 25th. This implies that sharp changes in equity prices will change individuals' wealth (the wealth effect

---

[6]The world ranking is taken from Kurian (2001), which is also based on EIU (2002) data but does not mark the year the statistics are taken.

Table 6.4: Correlation Coefficients

Stock Price Indexes, GDP, and Growth Rates

a 1995-1999

Countries	USA(Nasdaq)	Japan	Taiwan
Japan	0.200		
Taiwan	0.133	0.438	
Singapore	0.024	0.448	0.098

b 2000-2001

Countries	USA(Nasdaq)	Japan	Taiwan
Japan	0.772		
Taiwan	0.744	0.812	
Singapore	0.717	0.713	0.712

Correlation coefficients among five countries

c GDP 1979 - 2000

	USA	Japan	Korea	Taiwan
Japan	0.92			
Korea	0.92	0.97		
Taiwan	0.98	0.97	0.97	
China	0.95	0.81	0.86	0.91

d Growth rates of GDP 1980 - 2000

	USA	Japan	Korea	Taiwan
Japan	0.04			
Korea	0.01	0.56		
Taiwan	0.31	0.58	0.59	
China	-0.04	-0.32	-0.01	-0.29

e Daily stock indexes 9/18/01 - 12/13/02

	USA(S&P500)	Japan	Korea	Taiwan
Japan	0.72			
Korea	0.19	0.56		
Taiwan	0.43	0.60	0.90	
China	0.21	0.32	-0.18	-0.14

f Growth rates of daily stock indexes 9/19/01 - 12/13/02

	USA	Japan	Korea	Taiwan
Japan	0.23			
Korea	-0.01	0.11		
Taiwan	0.04	0.01	0.25	
China	0.02	0.08	-0.10	0.03

Sources: Parts a and b: Cheng (2002). Parts c–f: Authors' calculations. Parts c and d: WB (2002). Parts e and f: Finance.Yahoo.com
(2002).

in these societies), and since wealth is a key factor determining
consumption, household consumption will also change (Bertaut,
2002; Edison and Slok, 2001), and therefore the growth of the
economies will be affected. Thus, the IT revolution has strengthened
international dependence and the real and financial linkages.

Parts c–f of Table 6.4 present the correlation coefficients of GDP time-series, the growth rates of GDP from 1979 to 2000, 270 recent common transaction days' stock price indices, and their growth rates from 18 September 2001 to 13 December 2002 for the five countries. The correlation coefficients of GDP (Part c) among the five countries are very high (0.81–0.98), but are low for GDP growth rates (Part d, −0.32 to 0.59). In terms of the growth rates, the correlation coefficients between the United States and all other countries are generally low, especially with Korea and China. Korea and Taiwan have higher correlation with Japan (0.56 and 0.58). Korea and Taiwan also have high correlation coefficient (0.59). There is a great deal of similarity among the three countries in terms of the GDP levels and their growth rates (Hsiao and Hsiao, 2003). China's GDP growth rate consistently has negative correlation coefficients with all other countries. This may be due to China's high GDP growth rates during the past two decades and the slowdown of the GDP growth in the United States and ADCs.

Similarly, the correlation coefficients of daily stock indices are generally higher than their growth rates. The stock indices (Part e) of Japan and the USA are highly correlated (0.72). Similar to the GDP levels and growth rates, the stock indices of Korea, Taiwan, and Japan have higher correlation coefficients (0.56 and 0.60) than with other countries, especially between Korea and Taiwan (0.90). Again China is different. The correlation coefficients of stock indices between China, the United States, and Japan, are low (0.21 and 0.32), and China and Korea along with Taiwan even have small negative correlation coefficients. This may be due to the government control of the stock markets in China. In terms of the growth rates of the stock indices (Part f), the movements among countries seem random, and no clear trend seems to exist, except that Japan and the United States (0.23), and Taiwan and Korea (0.25) show some correlations.

6.4   Causality Tests of the GDP Series

There are several methods of testing international interdependence and linkages. Arora and Vamvakidis (2001) apply usual growth regression to study the impact of the US economic growth on the rest of the world, without considering the financial linkages. Callen and McKibbin (2001) use a G-cubed (Asia-Pacific) model to examine the effect of changes in Japanese policy on the Asia-Pacific region. Watanabe (1996) examines the impact of US stock prices and volatility on the Asia-Pacific region, using an exponential autoregressive conditionally heteroskedastic (EGARCH) model, a variety of regression analysis. In view of our empirical observations in the previous sections, however, we submit that in this interdependent world the best order of analysis would be to first test the causality of the linkages, and after we have found that cause and effect, apply impulse response analysis. In this section, therefore, we test the causality and dynamics of the GDP time-series, and in the next section, we test the stock price index time series.

In this chapter, we choose to test the causality of the US and the major ADCs, Japan, Korea, and Taiwan. China is also chosen from the ASEAN+ countries for the size of its economy and its growing importance in the Asia-Pacific regional economy. The annual GDP in current USD for these countries from 1979 to 2000, except for Taiwan, were obtained from the World Bank's World Development Indicators (WB, 2002). Taiwan's data were taken from the ICSEAD (2002). The GDP time-series are chosen to test the real linkage since the rapid economic growth of Japan, Korea, Taiwan, and China are due to their openness through trade and inward FDI, especially with the United States (Coe *et al.*, 1995; Hsiao and Hsiao, 2001b; Sachs and Warner, 1995, 1996).

Before analyzing the causal relations among the five GDP time-series, we have used the Augmented Dickey–Fuller (ADF) unit-root test to examine the stationarity of each GDP series (Greene, 2003). The ADF test results show that all five-level series (in log values) of GDP are non-stationary at the 10% level of significance, and their first-difference series (i.e. the growth rates of GDP) are all stationary at the 5% or 10% level of significance. Hence, we use the GDP growth rate series in the causality analysis. In addition, we have also applied the Johansen test of cointegration to the five GDP level series. The test results indicate no cointegration at the 1% level of significance. Therefore, the VAR model can be used in testing the causality relationship among the five GDP growth rate series.

6.4.1   *Pairwise Granger Causality Tests*

The annual GDP dataset, however, is adequate for examining pairwise Granger causality relationship among the five countries using stationary first-difference series of GDP (Greene, 2003). The test involves estimating the following two equations:

$$\Delta x_t = \alpha + \sum_{i=1}^{m} \beta_i \Delta x_{t-i} + \sum_{j=1}^{m} \gamma_j \Delta y_{t-j} + \mu_t, \qquad (6.1)$$

$$\Delta y_t = \delta + \sum_{i=1}^{m} \lambda_i \Delta x_{t-i} + \sum_{j=1}^{m} \theta_j \Delta y_{t-j} + \nu_t, \qquad (6.2)$$

where Δx_t and Δy_t are the first-difference series of GDP for a pair of countries, respectively, for example, Japan and China, the USA and Japan, etc. From five countries, we have a total of 10 pairs of Granger causality tests. Δx_{t-i} and Δy_{t-j} are lagged dependent variables, μ_t and ν_t are the random error terms in the equations. The causal relationship in Eq. (6.1) is seen from the Wald's coefficient F-test on the joint significance of the coefficients y_j's of Δy_{t-j}'s, and that in Eq. (6.2) is seen from the joint significance of the coefficients λ_i's of Δx_{t-i}'s. In this bivariate case, we do not include the other variables' influence on the pair of variables in the equations. Thus, the causality relationship is due to the direct influence of the two variables.

Since we only have a small sample of annual data, we have tried to estimate the model with the lag length $m = 1$ and 2. In both cases, we obtained the same causality results. Therefore, we choose to present the results from the lag length $m = 2$ in Table 6.5 (also see Figure 6A.1 in Appendix 6A).

Table 6.5: Pairwise Granger Causality Tests

Growth Rates of GDP, 1980–2000, Lags: 2

Pair	Test result			F-stat	p-value	Causality
1	Japan does not cause	China		0.449	0.65	
	China does not cause	Japan		0.493	0.62	
2	Korea does not cause	China		0.150	0.86	
	China does not cause	Korea		1.533	0.25	
3	Taiwan does not cause	China		0.014	0.99	
	China does not cause	Taiwan		0.456	0.64	
4	USA does not cause	China		0.567	0.58	
	China does not cause	USA		1.250	0.32	
5	Korea does not cause	Japan		1.530	0.25	
	Japan does cause Korea			5.369	0.02 **	Unidirectional
6	Taiwan does not cause	Japan		1.092	0.36	
	Japan does cause Taiwan			9.584	0.002 ***	Unidirectional
7	USA does not cause	Japan		1.542	0.25	
	Japan does not cause	USA		0.041	0.96	
8	Taiwan does not cause	Korea		0.929	0.42	
	Korea does not cause	Taiwan		0.024	0.98	
9	USA does not cause	Korea		0.185	0.83	
	Korea does not cause	USA		0.063	0.94	
10	USA does not cause	Taiwan		1.415	0.28	
	Taiwan does not cause	USA		0.257	0.78	

Note: *** (**) denotes significance at the 1% (5%) level.

From the 10 pairwise Granger causality tests, we have found two unidirectional causality relationships: Japan's GDP growth rate causes Korea's GDP growth rate at the 5% level of significance, and Japan's GDP growth rate also causes Taiwan's GDP growth rate at the 1% level of significance. These results show the strong dependency of the growth of Taiwanese and Korean economies on the Japanese economic growth, but not vice versa.

The testing results also show the US's GDP growth rate unidirectionally causes Japan's GDP growth rate at a weak 25% level of significance.

6.4.2   *VAR Granger Causality Tests*

To take into account the interactions among the five countries, we go one step further by formulating the GDP growth rate series into a system of VAR model (Greene, 2003) to examine the Granger causality relationships among the five countries. The VAR(p) model involves the estimation of the following equation system:

$$y_t = \mu + \Gamma_1 y_{t-1} + \cdots + \Gamma_p y_{t-p} + \epsilon_t, \qquad (6.3)$$

where y_t is a (5×1) column vector of the endogenous variables, that is, $y_t = (\text{DLKOR}_t, \text{DLTWN}_t, \text{DLCHN}_t, \text{DLJPN}_t, \text{DLUSA}_t)'$, the GDP growth rate series of Korea, Taiwan, China, Japan, and the USA. The μ is a (5×1) constant vector, $\Gamma_i, i = 1, 2, \ldots, p$, where p is the order of lags, is a (5×5) coefficient matrix, y_{t-i} is a (5×1) vector of the ith lagged endogenous variables, and ϵ_t is a (5×1) vector of the random error terms. In this case, the dataset allows us to estimate the VAR model at $i = 1$ or 2. We then select the optimal lag length at $i = 1$ by the minimum AIC of the VAR system.

Table 6.6 presents the estimations from VAR(1) model. The Granger causality is examined using the Wald's coefficient F-test on each variable in each equation. The last row presents the summary of the testing results. In this VAR model, we include the other country variables to take into account the indirect influence from other countries. We have found three unidirectional causality relations: Japan's GDP growth rate causes Korea's GDP growth rate and also causes Taiwan's GDP growth rate. These results are consistent with the results of the pairwise Granger causality test discussed above. Furthermore, we have also found that Korea's GDP growth rate causes China's GDP growth rate, as evidenced from the recent closer economic relation between the two countries (see Figure 6A.1 in Appendix 6A for illustration).

Figure 6.3 illustrates the combined impulse response functions of each endogenous variable to trace the effects of injecting a shock into the estimated VAR(1) system due to a policy change and/or external stimuli to an economy that is a one-time shock of one standard deviation of the error term. Specifically, we have found that Korea

Table 6.6: Vector Autoregression Estimates — VAR(1)

Growth Rates of GDP, 1980–2000

Country	Eq. Number Country Dep. Var.	1 Korea DLKOR	2 Taiwan DLTWN	3 China DLCHN	4 Japan DLJPN	5 USA DLUSA
Korea	DLKOR(-1)	-0.141 *(0.66)*	-0.169 *(0.22)*	0.367 *(0.07)* *	-0.346 *(0.20)*	-0.039 *(0.42)*
Taiwan	DLTWN(-1)	0.109 *(0.85)*	0.234 *(0.35)*	-0.445 *(0.22)*	0.115 *(0.82)*	0.089 *(0.33)*
China	DLCHN(-1)	-0.101 *(0.82)*	0.085 *(0.64)*	0.044 *(0.86)*	-0.048 *(0.89)*	0.045 *(0.49)*
Japan	DLJPN(-1)	0.661 *(0.10)* *	0.561 *(0.004)* ***	-0.137 *(0.56)*	0.497 *(0.14)*	0.005 *(0.94)*
USA	DLUSA(-1)	-0.668 *(0.71)*	-0.895 *(0.25)*	0.129 *(0.90)*	-1.035 *(0.49)*	0.073 *(0.79)*
	Constant	0.104 *(0.40)*	0.100 *(0.07)* *	0.096 *(0.20)*	0.129 *(0.22)*	0.048 *(0.02)* **
Unidirect. causality:		**JPN -->KOR** **JPN--->TWN**		**KOR--->CHN**		

Note: DLKOR is the first difference of log-values (growth rates) of Korea's GDP used in the analysis, same notations apply to other countries. The *p*-value is in brackets. *** (** or *) denotes the test is significant at the 1% (5% or 10%) level, respectively.

and Taiwan have very strong responses to a change in Japan's GDP growth rate, and China also has response to a change in Korea's GDP growth rate. They peaked in the second periods, and lasted about four periods.

Figure 6.4 depicts the variance decomposition of each endogenous variable in the estimated VAR(1) system. We have found that a change in Japan's GDP growth rate has played a relatively important role in explaining the variance (about 20%) of Korea's GDP growth rate and the variance (about 40%) of Taiwan's GDP growth rate. The changes in the GDP growth rate of Taiwan and Korea have played an important role in explaining the variance of China's GDP growth rate, about 30% and 10%, respectively. In the case of Japan, Taiwan and Korea have played a relatively important role (15% and 20%, respectively) than the United States (about 5%).

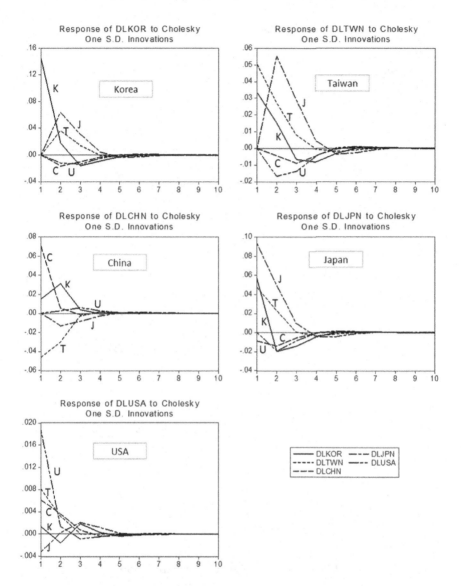

Figure 6.3: Impulse Response Functions-Growth Rates of GDP

DL ≡ Logarithmic Difference of GDP

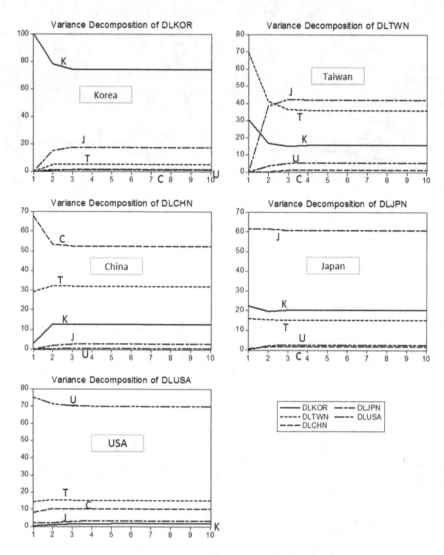

Figure 6.4: Variance Decomposition
Growth Rates of GDP

6.5   Causality Tests of the Stock Price Index Series

The daily stock price indices for China (Shanghai Composite, SSEC), Korea (Seoul Composite, KS11), Japan (Nikkei 225, N225), Taiwan (Taiwan Weighted, TWII), and the USA (S&P 500, GSPC) were retrieved[7] from the Major World Indices (Finance.Yahoo.com, 2002). We have selected 270 recent common transaction days' stock indices at the closing of the market[8] for each of the five countries, from 18 September 2001 to 13 December 2002. The period is chosen to eliminate the immediate effect of the 11 September 2001 tragic event in the New York City.

We apply the same econometric procedures as in analyzing the GDP series above to examine the causality relationships among the stock index series of the five countries. The ADF unit-root tests show that all five-level series (in log-values) of the stock indices are non-stationary at the 10% level of significance, and their first-difference series (i.e. the growth rates of stock indices) are all stationary at the 1% level of significance. In addition, the Johansen test of cointegration for the five stock index series shows that they are not cointegrated. Hence, we use the first-difference series of the stock indices in testing their Granger causality relationships.

6.5.1 *Pairwise Granger Causality Tests*

We apply the pairwise Granger causality tests to the five stationary first-difference series of stock indices. In this case, Δx_t and Δy_t in Eqs. (6.1) and (6.2) are the first-difference series of stock indices for a pair of countries, respectively, and the other notations remain the same. Table 6.7 presents the estimations of the 10 pairwise Granger causality tests, and the last column shows the summary of the test results. We have found the following interesting Granger causality relationships (also see Figure 6A.1 in Appendix 6A):

1. The USA's stock index growth rate unidirectionally causes Japan's stock index growth rate (at the 1% level of significance),

---

[7] We have chosen S&P 500 instead of NASDAQ since the latter consists of 5,000 or so technology stocks, while S&P 500 index consists of major stocks in both technology and non-technology, similar to the stock indexes of other countries.

[8] We first compare the US index and the Japanese index, and choose the stock indexes which have the common transaction days in both countries. We then compare these indexes with those of other three countries, one by one, and select the indexes which have the common transaction days as the US and Japan. Note that, since Cheng (2002) did not specify how the data were selected, the results of Parts (a), (b), (e), and (f) may not be comparable.

Table 6.7: Pairwise Granger Causality Tests–Stock Indexes

Sample: 270, Lags: 2

Pair	Test result			F-stat	p-value	Causality direction
1 Japan	does not cause	China		1.997	0.14	
China	does not cause	Japan		0.943	0.39	
2 Korea	does not cause	China		0.465	0.63	
China	does not cause	Korea		1.337	0.26	
3 Taiwan	does not cause	China		1.596	0.20	
China	does not cause	Taiwan		0.468	0.63	
4 USA	does not cause	China		0.244	0.78	
China	does not cause	USA		2.128	0.12	
5 Korea	does not cause	Japan		0.053	0.95	
Japan	does not cause	Korea		0.242	0.78	
6 Taiwan	does not cause	Japan		0.019	0.98	
Japan	does cause	Taiwan		5.287	0.01 ***	Unidirectional
7 USA	does cause	Japan		20.436	0.00 ***	Unidirectional
Japan	does not cause	USA		1.484	0.23	
8 Taiwan	does cause	Korea		2.915	0.06 *	Bidirectional
Korea	does cause	Taiwan		8.858	0.00 ***	
9 USA	does cause	Korea		2.982	0.05 **	Unidirectional
Korea	does not cause	USA		1.686	0.19	
10 USA	does cause	Taiwan		7.230	0.00 ***	Unidirectional
Taiwan	does not cause	USA		1.141	0.32	

Note: *** (** or *) denotes significance at the 1% (5% or 10%) level.

causes Korea's stock index growth rate (at the 5% level of significance), as well as Taiwan's stock index growth rate (at the 1% level of significance).

2. Japan's stock index growth rate unidirectionally causes Taiwan's stock index growth rate (at the 1% level of significance).
3. There is bidirectional causality between Korea's stock index growth rate and Taiwan's stock index growth rate (at the 1% and 10% levels of significance, respectively).

6.5.2 *VAR Granger Causality Tests*

When we formulate the five stock index growth rate series into a system of VAR to examine the Granger causality relations among the

Table 6.8: Vector Autoregression Estimates–VAR(1)

Growth Rates of Stock Indexes, Sample: 270

		1 Korea	2 Taiwan	3 China	4 Japan	5 USA
Country	Country Dep. variable					
Korea	DLKSID(-1)	-0.001 (0.99)	0.235 (0.00) ***	-0.029 (0.55)	0.002 (0.96)	-0.055 (0.24)
Taiwan	DLTSID(-1)	0.026 (0.71)	0.006 (0.92)	0.005 (0.92)	-0.004 (0.93)	-0.041 (0.43)
China	DLCSID(-1)	0.099 (0.23)	-0.003 (0.97)	-0.033 (0.59)	0.081 (0.17)	0.106 (0.08)*
Japan	DLJSID(-1)	-0.038 (0.64)	0.003 (0.96)	-0.091 (0.14)	-0.137 (0.02)	-0.084 (0.16)
USA	DLUSID(-1)	0.203 (0.02) **	0.112 (0.13)	-0.016 (0.80)	0.393 (0.00) ***	-0.002 (0.98)
	Constant	0.001 (0.31)	0.001 (0.47)	-0.001 (0.29)	-0.001 (0.58)	-0.001 (0.57)
Unidirectional causality		KOR--->TWN		USA--->JPN		
	USA--->KOR					CHN--->USA

Note: DLKSID is the first difference of log-values (growth rates, or percentage change) of Korea's stock index (daily) used in the analysis, same notations apply to other countries. Other notes are the same as Table 6.6.

five countries, the y_t in Eq. (6.3) is a (5×1) vector of the endogenous variables, that is, $y_t =$(DLKSID$_t$, DLTSID$_t$, DLCSID$_t$, DLJSID$_t$, DLUSID$_t$)', the stock index growth rate series of Korea, Taiwan, China, Japan, and the USA. In this case, the optimal lag length $i = 1$ is selected by the minimum AIC of the VAR system.

Table 6.8 presents the estimations from the VAR(1) model on stock index growth rate series for the five countries, and the last row shows the summary of Granger causality test results. We have found the following causality relationships (also see Figure 6A.1 in Appendix 6A):

(1) Like the pairwise Granger causality tests above, the USA's stock index growth rate unidirectionally causes Japan's stock index growth rate (at the 1% level of significance), Korea's stock index growth rate (at the 5% level of significance), as well

as Taiwan's stock index growth rate (at a low, 15% level of significance).

(2) Korea's stock index growth rate unidirectionally causes Taiwan's stock index growth rate (at the 1% level of significance).

(3) Compared with pairwise Granger causality tests, we see two results: One is that Japan's stock index growth rate unidirectionally causes China's stock index growth rate (at a low, 15% level of significance) with a negative coefficient. Another is that China's stock index growth rate unidirectionally causes the USA's stock index growth rate (at the 10% level of significance). It is not clear why this is the case.[9]

Figure 6.5 illustrates the combined impulse response functions of each endogenous variable to trace the effects of injecting a shock into the estimated VAR(1) system due to a policy change and/or external stimuli in a financial market. We have found that the stock index growth rates of Japan, Korea, and Taiwan have relatively strong positive responses to a change in the financial market of the USA, peaked at the second period, and lasted about three to four periods. Furthermore, Taiwan's response to Korea's change is positive and strong.

Figure 6.6 depicts the variance decomposition of each endogenous variable in the estimated VAR(1) system. We have found that a change in the USA's financial market has played a relatively important role in explaining (about 17%) the variance of Japan's stock index growth rate, and a change in Korea's financial market has played a relatively important role in explaining (about 15%) the variance of Taiwan's stock index growth rate. For the case of the USA, only Japan has played some role in explaining the variance of the USA's stock index growth rate. The effects of other countries on Korea and China are almost negligible.

---

[9]There are two groups of stock transactions in China, some are open to foreigners, some are only for local people, and its stock markets are not as free as those in other countries. This may distort the causality relationship with other countries.

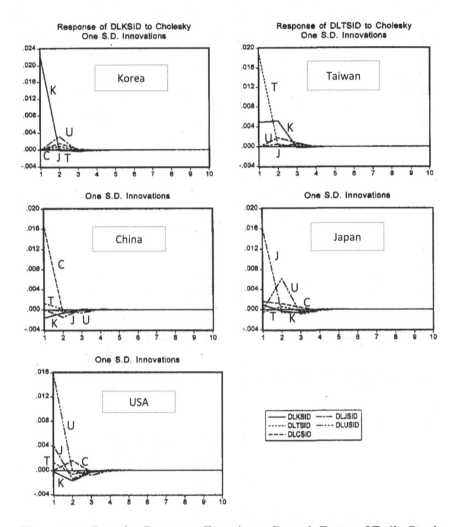

Figure 6.5: Impulse Response Functions -Growth Rates of Daily Stock Indexes Response of DLXSID to Cholesky.

One S.D. Innovation

Note: See Table 6.8 (DLXSID is the first logarithmic difference of country X's daily stock price index).

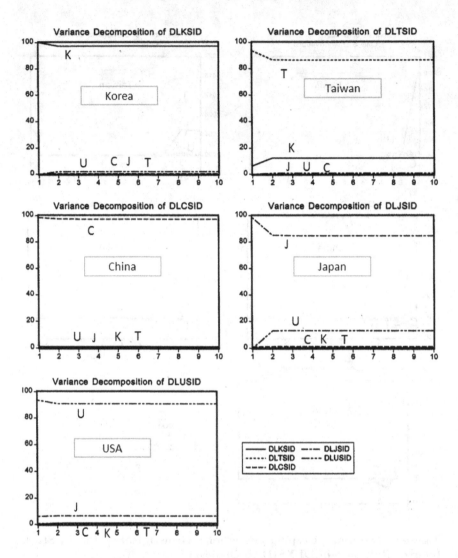

Figure 6.6: Variance Decomposition
Growth Rates of Daily Stock Price Indexes

6.6 Conclusions

Given the size of its economy and resources, one would expect that the United States would exert enormous influence on the stability and growth of closely allied countries in the Asia-Pacific region. This view is popular and intuitive. However, to our knowledge, the literature is still wanting in quantitative assessment of the role of the United States in this region. This paper attempts to fill this gap by first confirming the mutual dependence of the United States and the Asia-Pacific region, which includes the ADCs and the ASEAN4+ countries. We have pointed out that, while the United States is a predominant force in trade and investment in the region, it also relies on the countries in this region for its trade. The IT revolution enhanced the interdependence between the United States and the countries in this region through real and financial linkages.

Our study of linkages also highlights the possible routes of the transmission of the US recession, and more generally, the international business cycle, in the Asia-Pacific region. The impact of the US recession, and for that matter, of Japan and other countries, should be transmitted through trade, FDI, and stock markets. With this understanding, we then performed Granger causality tests on the time-series data of five countries: the United States, Japan, Korea, Taiwan, and China. The results are quite unexpected.

The pairwise Granger causality tests show that the GDP growth rates have unidirectional causality from Japan to Taiwan and Korea. Surprisingly, we did not find significant causality relationships between the United States and any other four countries.

In a larger VAR model in which the influence of other countries is included, the VAR Granger causality tests confirm again the same unidirectional causality of the GDP growth rates from Japan to Taiwan and Korea, and additionally, the unidirectional causality from Korea to China. Apparently, so far as GDP growth is concerned, despite the apparent dominance of the US economy and its increasing interdependence with the Asia-Pacific region, the recent US recession has minimal impact on the GDP growth of the Asia-Pacific region. The recent recession in Taiwan and Korea is more likely influenced by Japan rather than the United States. These results may be due to the fact that the annual GDP time-series data are too short for causality analysis. A further study is called for.

We had no sample problems on the stock price indices, and the results are much more illuminating. The pairwise Granger causality tests of the stock indices show that, other things being equal, there is a very strong unidirectional causality from the United States to Japan, Korea, and Taiwan and also from Japan to Taiwan. In addition, there is bidirectional causality between Korea and Taiwan.

When our analysis is extended to the VAR model, we still obtain the same unidirectional causality from the United States to the three major ADCs, but not to China. Whether the case of China can be found similarly in the ASEAN countries will be our next project of study. We have also found very strong unidirectional causality from Korea to Taiwan and a weak unidirectional causality from Japan to China as well as from China to the United States, a finding that is not intuitive.

In general, based on our dataset, so far as the GDP real linkage is concerned, we have not found the significant unidirectional causality from US GDP growth to the growth of Japan, Korea, and Taiwan, or China. On the other hand, from the financial point of view, the recent US IT recession in the stock market during the past two years has shown a significant unidirectional causality from the United States to Japan, Korea, and Taiwan, but not to China. This shows that the impact of the US recession is transmitted only through the stock markets, or more generally, the financial linkage. In short, the US recession does matter for Japan, Korea, and Taiwan through the financial linkage. Our empirical results seem to confirm the current economic experience between the United States and the Asia-Pacific region.

Appendix 6A: Illustrations of Causality Results of Tables 6.5 to 6.8:

Pairwise and VAR Granger Causality Relations among Five Countries: GDP Growth Rate and Stock Price Change

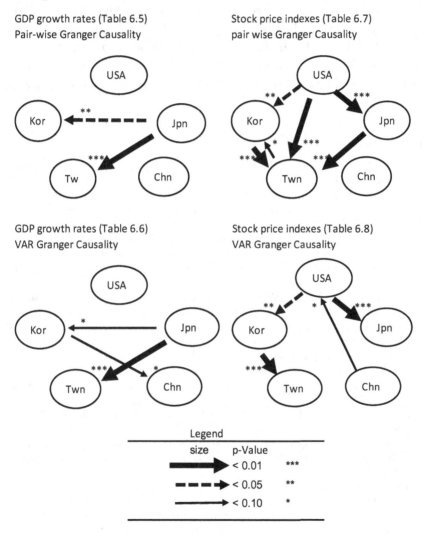

Figure 6A.1: Illustrations of Causality Results of Tables 6.5 to 6.8
Pairwise and VAR Granger Causality

Acknowledgments

The initial research of this chapter was done while the first two authors were visiting researchers at the International Centre for the Study of East Asian Development (ICSEAD), Kitakyushu, Japan, in the summer of 2002. It was presented at the AEA/ACAES Session at the 2003 ASSA Annual Meeting at Washington, DC, January 2003. We are grateful for the hospitality at the ICSEAD and to Professors Steve Beckman, Martin Boileau, Richard Hooley, Hyun-Hoon Lee, Robert McNown, Eric Ramstetter, and James T.H. Tsao for helpful discussions or data collection. All errors of omission and commission are the authors.

References

Asia Development Bank (ADB) (2000). *Asian Development Outlook 2000 Update.* Manila: ADB.

Arora, V. and A. Vamvakidis (2001). The impact of U.S. economic growth on the rest of the world: How much does it matter? IMF Working Paper, WP/01/119.

Bertaut, C. C. (2002). Equity prices, household wealth, and consumption growth in foreign industrial countries: Wealth effects in the 1990s. International Finance Discussion Papers, No. 724. Board of Governors of the Federal Research System.

Callen, T. and W. J. McKibbin (2001). Policies and prospects in Japan and the implications for the Asia-Pacific region. IMF Working Paper, WP/01/131.

Cheng, Y. C. (2002). A study of the IT business cycle and the Taiwanese economy (in Chinese). *Industry of Free China,* 49–73.

Coe, D. T., E. Helpman, and A. W. Hoffmaister (1995). North-South R&D spillovers, NBER Working Paper Series, No. 5048.

Edison, H. and T. Slok, (2001). Wealth effects and the new economy. IMF Working Paper, WP/01/77.

Economic Intelligence Units (EIU) (2002). Downloaded in Summer 2002 from www.viewwire.com/index.asp.

Economic Planning Agency (EPA) (2000). *Asian Economies 2000* (Azia Keizai 2000, in Japanese). Tokyo: Economic Planning Agency, Government of Japan.

Finance.Yahoo.com. (2002). *Major world indices–Daily stock indices,* 15 December 2002.

Greene, W. H. (2003). *Econometric Analysis.* Upper-Saddle River, NJ: Prentice Hall.

Hsiao, F. S. T. and M. C. W. Hsiao (2001a). Capital flows and exchange rates: Recent Korean and Taiwanese experience and challenges. *Journal of Asian Economics* **12**, 353–381.

Hsiao, F. S. T. and M. C. W. Hsiao (2001b). Diminishing returns and Asian NIEs: How they overcome the iron law. In *Proceedings of the Conference on Economic Development in Memory of Professor Mo-Huan Hsing*, Institute of Economics (Ed.), Taipei, Taiwan: Academia Sinica, pp. 239–288.

Hsiao, F. S. T. and M. C. W. Hsiao (2003). 'Miracle growth' in the twentieth century-international comparisons of East Asian development. *World Development* **31** (2), 227–257.

International Centre for the Study of East Asian Development (ICSEAD) (2002). Recent trends and prospects for major Asian economies. *East Asian Economic Perspectives* (EAEP) 13.

International Monetary Fund (IMF) (2001). *World Economic Outlook: The Information Technology Revolution*, October.

Japan Statistical Yearbook (JSY) (1994, 2000). Statistics Bureau, Management and Coordination Agency, Government of Japan.

Kurian, G. T. (2001). *The Illustrated Book of World Rankings* (5th edn.). New York: M.E. Sharpe.

Lee, H. H., H. S. Huh, and D. Harris (2003). The relative impact of the US and Japanese business cycles on the Australian economy. *Japan and the World economy* **15**, 111–129.

Sachs, J. D. and A. Warner (1995). Economic reform and the process of global integration. *Brookings Papers on Economic Analysis, 25th Anniversary Issue*, pp. 1–118.

Sachs, J. D. and A. Warner (1996). *Achieving rapid growth in the transition economies of Central Europe*, Harvard Institute for International Development, Harvard University, January.

Taiwan Statistical Data Book (TSDB) (2002). Council for Economic Planning and Development, Executive Yuan, Taiwan.

United Nations Conference on Trade and Development (UNCTAD) (2000). *World Investment Directory, Foreign Direct Investment, and Corporate Debt. Asia and the Pacific* (Vol. VII). New York: United Nations.

US Census Bureau (2001). *Statistical Abstract of the United States: 2001* (SAUS) (1st edn.). Washington, DC: Economics and Statistics Administration, U.S. Department of Commerce.

Watanabe, T. (1996). Time series analysis of stock prices and international linkages (in Japanese). In *Finance and Capital Markets in Asia* [Chapter 8], M. Kawai, (Ed.). Nihon Keizai Shinbunsha.

World Bank (WB) (2002). *World Development Indicators, 2002*. Washington, DC: The World Bank.

World Trade Organization (WTO) (2000). *International trade statistics*, 2000.

Chapter 7

Gains from Policy Coordination between Taiwan and the United States — On the Games Governments Play

Abstract

As we have seen in Chapters 5 and 6, the US financial conditions influence the emerging economies in Asia, often resulting in economic instability in the region. Thus, in this interdependent and competitive world, one way to prevent external disturbances is to try to coordinate fiscal and monetary policies among the countries. This chapter applies the game-theoretic method to study the nature of potential gains from international monetary policy coordination in a simple two-country model, utilizing Taiwan and the United States. We specify a Mundell–Fleming–Dornbusch type two-country model, in which one country is small and the other is large. We then analytically derive the Nash equilibrium, cooperative equilibrium, and the Stackelberg equilibrium. The second part of the chapter is a simulation study based on the theoretical model of the previous sections. Using the time-series data of Taiwan and the United States, we assume monetary policy as the control variable. We first estimate the parameter of the model through the least squares method from 1976 to 1989 for each country and then use these estimated parameters to simulate the two-country model.

In the case of our two-country model, we find that policy coordination does not pay for the small country, while it is indifferent for the large country. The last section gives explanations, interpretations, and some observations.

Keywords: International policy coordination; game theory; the Mundell–Fleming–Dornbusch two-country model; regression and simulation; Taiwan and the USA

7.1 Introduction

International and interregional economic cooperation requires coordination of economic policies among the participating nations. Since the Plaza Accord in 1985, the subject of international policy coordination has been one of the most debated topics in economics among the developed countries (Branson *et al.*, 1990; Buiter and Marston, 1985; Feldstein, 1988). In the Asia-Pacific region, economic cooperation has also been suggested as early as in the mid-1960s (Oborne and Fourt, 1983; Torii, 1989) and actively advocated in the recent years (Hsiao, 1990; Hsiao and Hsiao, 1989; Shinohara and Lo, 1989). Nevertheless, a rigorous analysis of policy coordination or integration seems never been applied to the Asia-Pacific region. Furthermore, despite its long historical background (see Oborne and Fourt, 1983; Torii, 1989), coordination or integration in the Asia-Pacific region is still at the discussion stage (Shinohara and Lo, 1989). It was reported last year that, to the latest proposal of a yen bloc, "Japanese are supportive, but wary of limelight. ... Tokyo is cool, Taipei and Seoul are wary," and "Southeast Asia keeps distance" (FEER, 1990). It was even observed that "Pacific-Rim nations unlike to form bloc" (JCC, 1990). This is especially conceivable under the circumstance that the gains from policy coordination are uncertain.

In view of this, we apply the game-theoretic method to study the nature of potential gains from international economic policy coordination in a two-country model (McKibbin, 1988; Cooper, 1985) including Taiwan and the United States.

In Section 7.2, we first summarize and compare some basic statistics of Taiwan, South Korea (hereafter Korea), the United

States, and Japan, the four countries which have had very close economic and political relations since World War II. A more detailed exposition of country comparisons may be found in Hsiao and Hsiao (1990, 1983, 1989).

We then specify a Mundell–Fleming–Dornbusch type two-country model (Cooper, 1985; McKibbin, 1988) in Section 7.3, in which one country is small and the other is large. Section 7.4 reviews the properties of this model under the conventionally simplified assumptions of symmetric countries. We then derive the Nash equilibrium, cooperative equilibrium, and the Stackelberg equilibrium analytically. They are illustrated diagrammatically in Figure 7.1.

In Section 7.5, using the time-series data of Taiwan and the United States, we tested the existence of unit roots as well as cointegration. The test results show that we can neither reject the null hypothesis that unit root does exist nor that the variables are not cointegrated. However, we also found that the first-differences of the time-series data are stationary. Hence, in accordance with the current macroeconometric practice, the regression equations of the model are estimated by using the first-differences of the time-series.

The method of derivation expounded in Section 7.4 is then used in the derivation of these equilibria in our general model in Section 7.6. Since fiscal policy, especially the tax system, has not been established in Taiwan, and the foreign exchange rates were fixed before 1980 by the Taiwanese Government, we assume monetary policy as the control variable. Because of the complexity of the model and also to facilitate calculation, the derivations are shown in matrix form in the appendixes. For simplicity, we only compare the cases of Nash equilibrium and the cooperative equilibrium.

We then implement the general model empirically and measure the size of the gains from policy coordination. The literature has suggested that the comparison of a Nash–Cournot and cooperative equilibria shows that the gains may be small (Oudiz and Sachs, 1984; McKibbin, 1988), or coordination may even not pay (Canzoneri and Minford, 1990; Miller and Salmon, 1990). In the case of our two-country model, one small and one large, we have found that policy coordination does not pay for the small country, but is indifferent for the large country. Section 7.7 gives explanations, interpretations, and some observations.

Appendix 7A shows the matrix derivation of Nash and cooperative equilibrium utilities. We have also added two appendixes to help the readers understand this chapter: Appendix 7B Expository Notes: Numerical Derivation of Nash and Cooperative Equilibrium Utilities and Appendix 7C Expository Notes: A Numerical Derivation of Welfare Gain.

7.2 Some Country Statistics

Table 7.1 shows some background information on the four countries. Column (1) shows that in terms of 1988 per capita GNP, the United States, Japan, Korea, and Taiwan ranked 4th, 2nd, 33rd, and 24th among 122 reporting countries and area by the World Bank (Taiwan was added in by the authors).

Columns (4) and (6) show that, except the United States, which is relatively more land abundant (8.67% of the world) than its population (5.20% of the world), the three East Asian countries have very high population density. For example, Taiwan has only 0.03% of the world's land area (Column (6)), but she has 0.42% of the world's population (Column (4), which is about 14 times more than her "fair share" of land. This is compared to 7.4 times for Japan and about 10 times for Korea.

In terms of Gross Domestic Product (GDP) (Column (8)), all four countries enjoy more than their share of population distribution. The GDP share and the population share of the world range from Japan's 6.5 times to Korea's 1.1 times, with Taiwan faring a respectable 1.7 times.

Columns (9)–(13) show that, unlike the United States, the three East Asian countries have achieved rapid growth in per capita GNP during the past three decades. While the United States doubled its per capita GNP from 1978 to 1988, the three others almost tripled their per capita GNP in the same decade! (Column (13)). Like the United States, Japan's growth rate tapered off somewhat during the last two decades, both Korea and Taiwan maintained rapid growth throughout the three decades at average annual rates of 6.8% and 7.3%, respectively (Column (12)).

Table 7.1: Basic Economic Indicators of the Four Countries
The USA, Japan, Korea, and Taiwan

GDPpc Wld ranking Cntry	Pop		Area		GDP		GNPpc						Inflation		Life exp at birth
	Wld share		Wld share	Value	Wld share			Avg annual gr rate	10 yr avg gr rate	incr	Avg annu rate				
	mil	%	1000 km2	%	bil	%	$	%	$	%	(11)/(9)	%	%		
1988	mid-1988		1988		1988		1978	60-78	1988	65-88	78-88	65-80	80-88		1988
(1) (2)	(3)	(4)	(5)	(6)	(7)	(8)	(9)	(10)	(11)	(12)	(13)	(14)	(15)		(16)
4 USA	246.3	5.2	9373	8.67	4847	28.5	9590	2.4	19840	1.6	2.07	6.5	4.0		76
2 Jpn	122.6	2.59	378	0.35	2844	16.7	7280	7.6	21020	4.3	2.89	7.8	1.3		78
33 Kor	42.0	0.89	99	0.09	171	1.01	1160	6.9	3600	6.8	3.10	18.8	5.0		70
24 Twn*	19.9	0.42	36	0.03	124	0.73	2371	7.3	6420	7.3	2.71				74
Total reporting economies/world total/									World average						
			108088		17018				3470						
122	4736	100		100		100				1.5		9.8	14		64

Note: The GDP and per capita GNP at current prices (TSDB, 1990, p. 23, 29) are divided by the year-end selling price of foreign exchange (TSDB, 1990, p. 199). The life expectancy is the average of that of male and female in 1987 (TSDB, 1990, p. 316).

Sources: (1) World Development Report (WDR) (1980, 1990). (2) * The data for Taiwan in this row are calculated from Taiwan Statistical Data Book (TSDB) (1990).

Columns (14) and (15) show that the inflation induced by the high growth rates is stabilized in the recent decade. The last column (Column (16)), life expectancy at birth, is intended to show the standard of living. It ranges from 70 years for Korea to 78 years for Japan.

Tables 7.2 and 7.3 show the external trade relations of the four countries over the past 15 years. Generally speaking, mutual trade of the four countries (exports and imports) measured as the share of GNP, and also of the country's world trade total, show upward trends over time.

Table 7.2 shows the exports and imports dependencies (as percentages of GDP) of the four countries. The table can be divided into four quadrants: trade between USA and Japan (QI), between USA/Japan and Korea/Taiwan (QII), Korea/Taiwan with USA/Japan (QIII), and trade between Korea and Taiwan (QIV).

Table 7.2: Exports and Imports Matrices as Share of Country's GNP

The USA, Japan, Korea, and Taiwan (in %)

ctry\year	75	80	85	89	75	80	85	89	75	80	85	89	75	80	85	89
#		Q1								QII						
USA		USA				Japan				Korea				Taiwan		
1 BOT	—	—	—	—	-0.2	-0.5	-1.2	-1.0	0.0	0.0	-0.1	-0.1	0.0	-0.1	-0.3	-0.3
2 Exp to	—	—	—	—	0.6	0.8	0.6	0.9	0.1	0.2	0.2	0.3	0.1	0.2	0.1	0.2
3 Imp fm	—	—	—	—	0.8	1.3	1.8	1.9	0.1	0.2	0.3	0.4	0.1	0.3	0.4	0.5
Japan																
4 BOT	-0.1	0.6	2.6	1.7	—	—	—	—	0.2	0.2	0.2	0.1	0.2	0.3	0.1	0.2
5 Exp to	2.3	2.8	4.2	3.5	—	—	—	—	0.5	0.5	0.5	0.6	0.4	0.5	0.3	0.6
6 Imp fm	2.4	2.1	1.7	1.8	—	—	—	—	0.3	0.3	0.3	0.5	0.1	0.2	0.2	0.3
Korea		QIII								QIV						
7 BOT	-1.7	-0.5	4.8	2.5	-5.6	-5.4	-3.4	-2.0	—	—	—	—	-0.3	-0.1	-0.2	0.0
8 Exp to	7.6	8.9	12.3	10.1	6.4	5.8	5.2	6.5	—	—	—	—	0.3	0.4	0.2	0.6
9 Imp fm	9.3	9.4	7.5	7.6	12.0	11.3	8.6	8.5	—	—	—	—	0.6	0.5	0.4	0.6
Taiwan																
10 BOT	1.1	5.0	4.9	7.9	-7.2	-7.7	-3.3	-4.6	0.4	0.1	0.1	-0.1	—	—	—	—
11 Exp to	11.8	16.3	12.4	15.8	4.5	5.3	5.5	6.0	0.8	0.6	0.4	0.8	—	—	—	—
12 Imp fm	10.7	11.3	7.5	7.9	11.7	12.9	8.8	10.6	0.4	0.5	0.3	0.8	—	—	—	—

Sources: The calculation of shares is based on the following data sources:
(1) The exports and imports data for the United States, Japan, and Korea
were obtained from *Direction of Trade Statistics* (DOTS) (1982, 1990). (2)
Data of GNP in national currencies and exchange rates for the United States,
Japan, and Korea were obtained from *International Financial Statistics* (IFS),
December (1982, 1990). (3) Data for Taiwan were obtained from TSDB (1990).

In QI, in 1989, the United States' exports to Japan only consisted
of 0.9% of US GNP (see Row 2), but her imports from Japan is 1.9%
of the US GNP (Row 3), resulting in a trade deficit (BOT) of 1%
(Row 1). In contrast, Japan's 1989 export and import dependencies
on the US market is 3.5% and 1.8%, respectively (Rows 5 and 6),
resulting in trade surplus of 1.7% of its GDP (Row 4). In general,
the US consistently had trade deficits with Japan from 1975 to 1989.
The American market is relatively more important for the Japanese
economy than the other way round.

For both countries, trade with Korea and Taiwan constitutes only
a small fraction of their GNP (QII). The same may be said about
the trade between Korea and Taiwan (QIV).

However, this is not the case for trade between Korea and Taiwan on the one hand and United States and Japan on the other (QIII). In 1989, the Taiwanese exports to the United States amounted 15.8% of her GNP (Row 11), and it is 10.1% for Korea (Row 8). Both Korea and Taiwan imported more from Japan (8.5% and 10.6% of the country's GNP, respectively, Rows 9 and 12) than from the United States (7.6% and 7.9% of the country's GNP, respectively). Taiwan consistently had deficits with Japan, and trade surplus with the US. Korea also consistently had trade deficits with Japan, and only in 1980s, it had trade surpluses with the United States.

A greater asymmetry may be observed in the ratios of exports and imports to the country's exports and imports world total, as shown in Table 7.3. In 1989, 34.2% of Japanese exports went to the United States, while only 12.3% of the US exports went to Japan (QI). The ratios in the imports side are more or less similar at 19.7% and 23% of the total world imports of both countries.

Table 7.3: **Exports and Imports Matrices of Country's World Total**

The USA, Japan, Korea, and Taiwan (in %)

Country	USA				Japan				Korea				Taiwan			
	1975	80	85	89	75	80	85	89	75	80	85	89	75	80	85	89
United States					QI								QII			
(E/EWT)*100	—	—	—	—	8.9	9.4	10.6	12.3	1.6	2.1	2.8	3.7	1.5	2.1	2.2	3.1
(I/IWT)*100	—	—	—	—	11.7	12.8	20.0	19.7	1.5	1.7	3.0	4.2	1.7	2.6	4.9	5.2
Japan																
(E/EWT)*100	20.2	24.5	37.6	34.2	—	—	—	—	4.0	4.1	4.0	6.0	3.0	3.6	2.7	4.1
(I/IWT)*100	20.1	17.4	20.0	23.0	—	—	—	—	2.3	2.2	3.2	6.2	1.2	1.5	2.6	4.3
Korea					QIII								QIV			
(E/EWT)*100	30.2	26.4	35.6	33.7	25.5	17.4	15.0	21.6	—	—	—	—	1.2	1.2	0.7	2.1
(I/IWT)*100	25.9	21.9	21.1	25.7	33.5	26.3	24.3	28.6	—	—	—	—	1.7	1.2	1.1	2.2
Taiwan																
(E/EWT)*100	34.3	34.1	48.1	36.3	13.1	11.0	11.3	13.7	2.3	1.4	0.8	1.7	—	—	—	—
(I/ IWT)* 100	27.8	23.7	23.6	23.0	30.4	27.1	27.6	30.7	1.0	1.1	0.9	2.4	—	—	—	—

Sources: (1) The world total exports and imports of the United State, Japan, and Korea are obtained from DOTS yearbook (1982, 1990). (2) Taiwan's world total exports and imports are obtained from TSDB (1990).

The trade between the United States and Japan on the one hand and Taiwan and Korea on the other increased considerably in recent years, ranging between 3% and 6% of American and Japanese total exports and imports (QII). Both Korea and Taiwan rely on the United States as export markets (34% and 36%, respectively, QIII), while they rely on Japan as import markets (29% and 31%, respectively). Both incurred trade surpluses with the United States and trade deficits with Japan (Hsiao and Hsiao, 1990). By contrast, the trade between Korea and Taiwan is relatively small (QIV).

Note that, under the watchful eyes of the US Trade Commission and the Congress, the export ratios of Japan, Korea, and Taiwan to the United States are decreasing while their import ratios are increasing except Taiwan. Both Korea and Taiwan stepped up their exports efforts to Japan, although their imports from Japan also increased in recent years.

In general, Tables 7.1–7.3 suggest that both Taiwan and Korea are small countries compared with the United States and Japan. The trade of both Taiwan and Korea depends heavily on the United States and Japan, but not vice versa. Thus, the trade links among these two sets of countries are very much lopsided.

Furthermore, the USD and the Japanese yen, along with the Deutsche mark, are not only serving as the means of exchange but also held as reserves by Asian countries (see Table 7.4). Thus, changes in the value of dollar and yen have profound effects on the foreign trade performance and domestic economic policy of Taiwan and Korea. The gains from international policy coordination among the four countries should reflect these asymmetries. In the following discussions of the two-country model of policy coordination between Taiwan and the United States, these facts seem to be reflected in our results.

7.3 The Mundell–Fleming–Dornbusch Model

The model we use is generally known as the Mundell–Fleming–Dornbusch two-country macroeconomic model (Cooper, 1985, p. 1215; McKibbin, 1988).

Table 7.4: Official Holdings of Foreign Exchange

1980–1989 (in %)

	1980	1983	1986	1989
Japanese Yen				
All countries	4.4	5.0	7.9	7.9
Selected Asian Countries	13.9	15.5	22.8	17.5
U.S. Dollar				
All countries	68.6	71.4	67.1	60.2
Selected Asian Countries	48.6	55.7	48.4	56.4
Duetsche Mark				
All countries	14.9	11.8	14.6	19.3
Selected Asian Countries	20.6	16.7	16.7	15.2

Reference: Finance and Development, IMF, June 1991, 5.

Sources: IMF annual report 1990 and Finance Development staff estimates. The data for 1989 are preliminary and could be revised.

Small country

$$q = \phi q^* + \gamma(e + p^* - p) - \lambda i, \tag{7.1}$$

$$m - p = \alpha q - \beta i, \tag{7.2}$$

$$p_c = \mu(e + p^*) + (1-\mu)p, \tag{7.3}$$

$$i = i^*. \tag{7.4}$$

Large country

$$q^* = \gamma^*(p - e - p^*)\lambda^* i^*, \tag{7.1*}$$

$$m^* - p^* = \alpha^* q^* - \beta^* i^*, \tag{7.2*}$$

$$p_c^* = \mu^*(p - e) + (1 - \mu^*)p^*, \tag{7.3*}$$

where q is the percentage change in GDP, e is the percentage change in exchange rate (domestic currency price of a unit of foreign currency), p is the percentage change in prices of domestic output (wholesale prices), m is the percentage change in the supply of money (M1), p_c is the rate of inflation (percentage change in consumer price index), and i is the instantaneous change in the interest rate. The asterisk (*) denotes the variables and parameters for the large (and foreign) country.

The model is shown in terms of percentage changes (or growth rate of the variables). The first equation is the IS curve, in which the small country's gross domestic output (GDP) is a function of the large country's GDP, the real exchange rate, and the interest rate (Argy *et al.*, 1989). The LM curve is shown in Eqs. (7.2) and (7.2)*, in which the real money supply is a function of GDP and the interest rate i. The third equation specifies that the inflation rate, that is, the percentage change of the consumer price indexes, is the weighted geometric average of the percentage changes in import price and the domestic price. Finally, Eq. (7.4) shows the interest rate parity between the small and large countries. It assumes free capital movement between the two countries. The interest rates are equalized in the world through foreign investment and perfect substitution between foreign and domestic bonds.

From (7.1) and (7.1)*, we may solve for e and i as

$$e = D_e/D, \quad i = D_i/D, \tag{7.5}$$

where

$$D_e = \lambda^* q - (\phi\lambda^* + \lambda)q^* + (\gamma\lambda^* - \lambda\gamma^*)p + (\lambda\gamma^* - \gamma\lambda^*)p^*,$$

$$D_i = -\gamma^* q + (\gamma^*\phi - \gamma)q^*,$$

$$D = \gamma\lambda^* - \lambda\gamma^*,$$

Thus, the exchange rate e and interest rate i are functions of the outputs and prices of both small and large countries.

Substituting i in (7.5) into the LM Eqs. (7.2) and (7.2)*, we have

$$(D\alpha + \beta\gamma^*)q - \beta(\gamma^*\phi - \gamma)q^* = Dm - Dp,$$

$$\beta^*\gamma^* q + [D\alpha^* - \beta^*(\gamma^*\phi - \gamma)]q^* = Dm^* - Dp^*.$$

These two equations may be solved for q and q^* as

$$q = am + bm^* + cp + dp^*, \tag{7.6}$$

$$q^* = a^* m + b^* m^* + c^* p + d^* p^*, \tag{7.7}$$

where a, b, c, d, a^*, b^*, c^*, d^* are eight constant coefficients of policy instruments in terms of the original parameters in (7.1)–(7.3)*.

Substituting e in (7.5) in (7.3) and (7.3)*, p_c and p_c^* may also be expressed as functions of the same policy instruments:

$$p_c = \bar{a}m + \bar{b}m^* + \bar{c}p + \bar{d}p^*, \tag{7.8}$$

$$p_c^* = \bar{a}^*m + \bar{b}^*m^* + \bar{c}^*p + \bar{d}^*p^*, \tag{7.9}$$

where $\bar{a}, \bar{b}, \bar{c}, \bar{d}, \bar{a}^*, \bar{b}^*, \bar{c}^*, \bar{d}^*$ are eight constant coefficients depending on the original parameters in (7.1)–(7.3)*. These 16 coefficients are arranged in a matrix R in (7A.2) in Appendix 7A and are estimated in (7.19).

Let the utility function of each country be

$$U = -(1/2)[w_1(q - q^{\#})^2 + w_2(p_c - p_c^{\#})^2], \tag{7.10}$$

where $q^{\#}$ is target or desired growth rate of GDP, and $p_c^{\#}$ is the target or desired rate of inflation. Parameters w_1 and w_2 are the weights that the policy maker assigns to the two targets (GDP growth rate and inflation rate).

The policy maker maximizes the utility function U, that is, minimizes the loss function $-U$, for given weights (w_1, w_2). Before we proceed to find the non-cooperative and cooperative equilibria, it will be helpful to review the results from the simplified conventional model.

7.4 Results from the Conventional Model

In the case of symmetric countries, it is generally assumed that $p = p^* = p_0$, and also

$$\alpha = \alpha^*, \; \beta = \beta^*, \; \gamma = \gamma^*, \; \lambda = \lambda^*, \text{ and } \phi = 0.$$

Thus, in this case, because of symmetric relation, both countries are almost the same. Hence, in this section, we will call them *the first country* and *the second country*, respectively. Equations (7.1)–(7.3) then reduce to

$$q = \gamma e - \lambda i, \quad M - p_0 = \alpha q - \beta i, \quad p_c = \mu e + p_0, \tag{7.11}$$

and similarly, for Eqs. (7.1)*–(7.3)*. We call this simplified model the conventional model. In this simple case, Eq. (7.5) reduces to

$$e = (q - q^*)/2\gamma, \quad i = -(q + q^*)/2\lambda.$$

The reduced equations in (7.6) and (7.7) become

$$q = am + bm^* - (a + b)p_0, \tag{7.12}$$

$$q^* = bm + am^* - (a + b)p_0, \tag{7.13}$$

where

$$a \equiv (\beta + 2\alpha\lambda)/2\alpha(\beta + \alpha\lambda),$$

$$b \equiv -\beta/2\alpha(\beta + \alpha\lambda) < 0,$$

$$a^* = b, \quad b^* = a,$$

$$c + d = c^* + d^* = -(a + b) < 0.$$

Furthermore,

$$p_c = p_0 + k(m - m^*), \tag{7.14}$$

$$p_c^* = p_0 - k(m - m^*), \tag{7.15}$$

where $k \equiv \mu/2\alpha\gamma$.

Under simplified assumptions, the policy maker normalizes the target rates to zero, $q^\# = p_c^\# = 0$, and takes $w_1 = 1$ and $w_2 = w$. The conventional model then maximizes $U = -(1/2)(q^2 + wp_c^2)$ with respect to percentage change of money supply m. The reaction function for the first country is

$$m = Am^* + Bp_0, \tag{7.16}$$

where

$$A \equiv (-ab + wk^2)/(a^2 + wk^2),$$

$$B \equiv (a(a + b) - wk)/(a^2 + wk^2),$$

and $(a + b) > 0$, $0 < A < 1$. Due to the symmetry relation, the reaction function for the second country is

$$m^* = Am + Bp_0. \tag{7.17}$$

The Nash equilibrium is at

$$m^N = m^{*N} = Bp_0/(1 - A) < p_0,$$

$$p_c^N = p_0, \quad q^N = (a + b)(m^N - p_0) < 0.$$

The reactions function and Nash equilibrium N is shown in Figure 7.1. At the Nash equilibrium, the money supply growth rates for both countries are the same. They are negative and less than the growth rate of prices. The growth rate of GDP is also negative.

Suppose now that there is a world planner who chooses the growth rates of money supplies m and m^* to maximize the world community welfare:

$$W = hU + h^*U^*$$
$$= -(1/2)h(q^2 + wp_0^2) - (1/2)h^*(q^{*2} + w^*p_c^{*2}), \quad (7.17a)$$

where h and h^* are the weights assigned to the first and the second countries, respectively. For simplicity, we assume $h = h^*, w = w^*$ in the conventional model. Then, the first-order conditions with respect to m and m^* yield:

$$rm + sm^* = (a - b)^2 p_0,$$
$$sm + rm^* = (a - b)^2 p_0,$$

where

$$r \equiv a^2 + b^2 + 2c^2,$$
$$s \equiv -2(ab + c^2).$$

Thus, the cooperative equilibrium of money supply change is

$$m^c = m^{*c} = (a - b)^2 p_0/(r + s) = p_0 > 0,$$
$$q^c = 0, \quad p_c^c = p_c^{*c} = p_0. \quad (7.18)$$

The cooperative equilibrium is shown as C in Figure 7.1. Lastly, we may also find the Stackelberg equilibrium (Cooper, 1985). Suppose the first country is the follower and the second country is the leader, who has complete information on the home country's reaction curve when it maximizes its own utility function. Substituting the first country's reaction curve, $m = Am^* + Bp_0$ into the second country's utility function,

$$U^* = -(1/2)(q^{*2} + wp_c^{*2}).$$

The first-order condition with respect to money supply m^* yields a combination of (m, m^*) which is located on the first country's reaction curve, and shown as S in Figure 7.1.

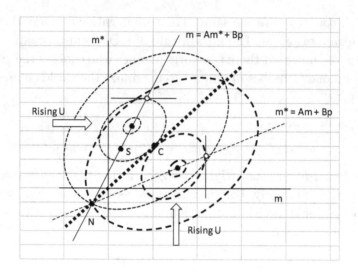

Figure 7.1: An Illustration of Nash and Cooperative Equilibria
Conventional (Symmetric) Model

From Figure 7.1, it is clear that both countries are better-off at the cooperative equilibrium at C than at the Nash equilibrium at N. They are also better-off at the Stackelberg equilibrium at S compared with the Nash equilibrium at N. However, compared with C, the Stackelberg equilibrium is consistently inferior to the leader and superior to the follower. Thus, in this example, countries prefer to be a follower rather than a leader.

In the following sections, we now measure the gains of both countries when the equilibrium point moves from N to C for the general case when the two countries are asymmetric, one country is "larger" than the other, and they do not have the same parameters.

7.5   The Estimation Results

As mentioned above, the simplified model assumes that both countries are symmetric. Such assumption may be allowed among the developed countries like the United States, Japan, and the European Community. However, as we have seen in Section 7.1, it is unrealistic to assume symmetry between Taiwan and Korea on the one hand and the United States and Japan on the other. Thus, in this section, we assume that two countries are asymmetric. The first country, Taiwan, is a small country, and the second country, the United States, is a large country. Without having the symmetric assumptions which lead to Eq. (7.11), the reduced forms of the original model as shown in Eqs. (7.6)–(7.9) depend on very complicated relations among the eight parameters.

The usual simulation method and computable general equilibrium analysis simply assign some plausible values of the parameters, either based on intuition or on some historical observations. In this chapter, we instead estimated the coefficients of the four reduced form equations by the ordinary least squares method. The data for the target variables $T = (q, p_c, q^*, p_c^*)'$ (the prime $'$ denotes the transpose of a row vector), and the instrument variables $y \equiv (x, z)' \equiv (m, m^*, p, p^*)'$, along with the estimated values of the coefficients are reported in Tables 7.7 and 7.8.

To be consistent with the symbols used in the appendixes, we denote T, x, y, and z as column vectors. The data are taken from each country and transformed into percentage changes from 1976 to 1989 for 14 years. The data from 1976 are chosen mainly to avoid irregularity in the data due to the first oil price shock in 1973–1975. Note that, since the variables are in percentage changes, which is given by the model itself, we have suppressed the constant term in each equation.

Since in the recent studies on macroeconometric modeling, it is found that the macroeconomic data are generally non-stationary (see Pindyck and Rubinfeld, 1991, p. 460), we have tested the unit roots of the eight time-series. To test the unit root at the level, we run the test regression for all the eight time-series shown in Table 7.5. For example, q, we first run the regression for

$$\Delta q = \text{cons} + b_1 q(-1) + b_2 \Delta q(-1) + b_3 \Delta q(-2) + b_4 \text{Trend} + u,$$

with both constant term and trend variable (denoted by T in the table), and then without constant term and trend (denoted by N in the table). The Augmented Dickey–Fuller (ADF) t-statistics are shown in the second (T, 2) and the third (N, 1) columns of Table 7.5.

Table 7.5: The Dickey–Fuller Unit-Root Test

Time Series

	Augmented Dickey-Fuller (ADF) t-statistic			
Level Series	U-Root (T,2)	U-Root (N,1)	1st Diff Series	U-Root (N,1)
q	-2.147	-0.877	Δq	-3.769 *
m	-2.648	-1.388	Δm	-2.879 *
p	-3.144	-1.89 ***	Δp	-3.332 *
p_c	-2.422	-1.489	ΔPc	-2.837 *
q*	-2.446	-1.521	Δq*	-2.899 *
m*	-1.35	-0.932	Δm*	-3.219 *
p*	-2.204	-1.143	Δp*	-1.979 **
p_c*	-2.89	-0.941	Δpc*	-2.576 **

Notes: (1) See Table 7.7 for data sources.

(2) In each ADF test, T denotes the inclusion of a constant term and trend variable and N denotes without constant and trend. The parameter 1 or 2 denotes the period(s) of lagged dependent variable in the regression equation.

(3) MacKinnon critical values for the above tests are as follows:

(a) For level series:

Significance level:	1%	5%	10%
U-Root (T,2),			
observations = 11	−5.115	−3.927	−3.410
U-Root (N,1),			
observations = 12	−2.799	−1.973	−1.631

(b) For first difference series:

Significance level:	1%	5%	10%
U-Root (N,1),			
observations = 11	−2.827	−1.976	−1.632

* = Significant at 1% level; ** = Significant at 5% level; *** = Significant at the 10% level.

Table 7.6: The Engle–Granger Cointegration Test

	Augmented Dickey-Fuller(ADF) t-statistic for residual series			
Dep Var	U-Root (T,2)	U-Root (T,1)	U-Root (N,2)	U-Root (N,1)
q	-2.18	-2.918	-2.364	-2.069
Pc	-2.504	-3.582	-2.423	-2.981
p^*	-2.962	-2.626	-2.702	-2.505
pc*	-1.989	-3.037	-2.049	-3.04

Notes: (1) See Table 7.7 for data sources.

(2) In each cointegrating regression, the right-hand side variables are m, m^*, p, and p^*.

(3) In Micro TSP program, version 7, Engle–Granger cointegration test also provided us MacKinnon critical values for ADF t-statistic test for unit-root in residual series, and the critical values for the above tests are as follows:

Significance level:	1%	5%	10%
U-Root (T, 2), observations = 11	−8.078	−6.437	−5.724
U-Root (T, I), observations = 12	−7.818	−6.283	−5.612
U-Root (N, 2), observations = 11	−7.430	−5.909	−5.244
U-Root (N, I), observations = 12	−7.194	−5.774	−5.146

Parameter 1 or 2 denotes the period(s) of lagged dependent variable listed as independent variables at the right-hand side. The MacKinnon critical values for ADF t-statistic test for a unit-root in time-series are readily available from the Micro TSP program (Lilien and Hall, 1991) and are shown in the footnote of Table 7.5. It turns out that the ADF t-statistics for all the level series are smaller than the corresponding critical values. Hence, there is an evidence of the unit roots, and the level series follow random walks and they are non-stationary.

Even the level series follow random walks, if the variables are cointegrated, we may still use the levels to estimate the regression coefficients. To test cointegration, we first estimate the following cointegrating regression,

$$q = const + b_1 m + b_2 m^* + b_3 p + b_4 p^* + b_5 Trend + u.$$

After computing the residuals, we then run the test regression:

$$\Delta u = b_1 u(-1) + b_2 \Delta u(-1) + b_3 \Delta u(-2) + v.$$

The ADF t-statistics for testing unit-root in residual series are given in Table 7.6. Here, we first tested for the cases with both constant term and trend, with two or one period of lagged dependent variables (Column (T, 2) and (T, 1)). We then tested for the case without constant term and trend with a similar lag structure (Column (N, 2) and (N, 1)).

The Engle–Granger cointegration test in Micro TSP program, version 7, also provides the MacKinnon critical values for the above tests. They are shown in the notes of Table 7.6. From the critical values provided, it is clear that all the dependent variables are not cointegrated with the independent variables, m, m^*, p, and p^*. Thus, we are forced to use the differences of the series, instead of the levels, in the estimation of the regression coefficients.

The last column of Table 7.5 shows the ADF t-statistics of the first-difference of the series using the following test regression:

$$\Delta^2 q = b_1 \Delta q(-1) + b_2 \Delta^2 q(-1) + u.$$

We have tested for the case of no constant and no trend $(N, 1)$. Compared with the MacKinnon critical values provided in the notes of Table 7.5, it is clear that all the eight series are significant either at the 1% level (denoted with $*$ in the last column of Table 7.5) or at 5% level (denoted with$**$). Thus, we reject the null hypothesis that the first-difference series contain unit roots and are non-stationary and accept the alternative hypothesis that the first-difference series are stationary.

Using the first-difference, and grouping the equations by the small and the large countries, the regression coefficients are estimated in Table 7.7. The absolute value of the t-statistics (in parentheses), R^2, and the Durbin–Watson (DW) statistics are also reported in Table 7.7. The coefficients of the equations are shown as matrix R in Eq. (7A.2) of the Appendix 7A. More specifically, we have

Table 7.7: Estimated Growth Equations for Real GDP and Consumer Prices

1 $\Delta q = 0.171\Delta m - 0.611\Delta m^* + 0.31\Delta p - 0.947\Delta p^*$
      (2.40)   (2.24)   (1.08)   (1.33)
      $R^2 = 0.491$, DW= 2.53, Se = 3.263

2 $\Delta p_c = 0.078\Delta m + 0.328\Delta m^* + 0.019\Delta p + 1.752\Delta p^*$
      (1.05)   (1.16)   (0.06)   (2.36)
      $R^2 = 0.681$, DW= 2.241, Se = 3.396

3 $\Delta q^* = 0.007\Delta m - 0.371\Delta m^* + 0.003\Delta p - 0.592\Delta p^*$
      (0.07)   (1.08)   (0.01)   (0.66)
      $R^2 = 0.178$, DW= 2.638, Se = 4.089

4 $\Delta p_c^* = -0.012\Delta m + 0.037\Delta m^* + 0.092\Delta p + 0.626\Delta p^*$
      (0.76)   (0.63)   (1.46)   (4.02)
      $R^2 = 0.930$, DW= 1.891, Se = 0.712

Notes and Data Sources:

(1) $q =$ Taiwan annual growth rate (% change) in real GDP, (TSDB, 1990, p. 23).

(2) $q^* =$ US annual growth rate (% change) in real GDP, calculated from the data in U.S. Economic Report of the President, (1990, p. 309).

(3) $m =$ Taiwan annual growth rate (% change) of M1B (TSDB, 1990, p. 151).

(4) $m^* =$ US annual growth rate (% change) of M1 (U.S. Economic Report of the President, 1990, p. 371).

(5) $p =$ Taiwan annual % changes in wholesale price indexes, calculated from the data in TSDB (1990, p. 182).

(6) $p^* =$ US annual % increases in producer price indexes, calculated from the data in U.S. Economic Report of the President (1990, p. 365).

(7) $p_c =$ Taiwan annual % changes in consumer price indexes, calculated from the data in TSDB (1990, p. 188) and TSDB (1987, p. 188).

(8) $p_c^* =$ US annual % changes in consumer price indexes, calculated from the data in U.S. Economic Report of the President (1990, p. 359).

(9) Number of observations, $N = 14$, 1976–1989.

(10) $\Delta q, \Delta q^*, \Delta m, \Delta m^*, \Delta p, \Delta p^*, \Delta p_c$, and Δp_c^* are the first-difference series of $q, q^*, m, m^*, p, p^*, p_c, p_c^*$, respectively. In this case, we use the first-difference series of variables and without a constant term in each OLS regression model. The absolute value of t-ratio is in the parentheses.

estimated that

$$
R = \begin{bmatrix}
a & b & \vdots & c & d \\
\bar{a} & \bar{b} & \vdots & \bar{c} & \bar{d} \\
\cdots\cdots\cdots\cdots\cdots\cdots \\
a^* & b^* & \vdots & c^* & d^* \\
\bar{a}^* & \bar{b}^* & \vdots & \bar{c}^* & \bar{d}^*
\end{bmatrix}
= \begin{bmatrix}
0.171 & -0.611 & \vdots & 0.310 & -0.947 \\
0.078 & 0.328 & \vdots & 0.019 & 1.752 \\
\cdots & \cdots & \cdots & \cdots & \cdots \\
0.007 & -0.371 & \vdots & 0.003 & -0.592 \\
-0.012 & 0.037 & \vdots & 0.092 & 0.626
\end{bmatrix}, \quad (7.19)
$$

where the elements in the matrix are the least-squares estimate of the corresponding parameters in (7.6)–(7.9).

7.6 The Simulation

The above regression coefficients are then used in the model to find the percentage changes in money supply, inflation rate, utility level under Nash, and cooperative equilibrium for both countries. For simplicity, due to the lack of particular information about the relative importance of monetary and inflation policies in both countries, we assume that each country weighs the monetary policy and the inflation rate policy equally ($w_1 = w_2 = 0.5$). We also assume that the weights among different countries are the same ($h = h^* = 0.5$), reasoning that the difference among small and large countries is already reflected in the estimated data. For example, we assume that Taiwan has a much higher GDP growth rate (9%) than the United States (3.7%). (In fact, we have simulated the model with $h = 0.05$ and $h^* = 0.95$, which is roughly the proportion of GDP, the measure of the size of the economies, between Taiwan and the United States. The results were qualitatively the same).

Following the usual convention, we define all the vectors as the column vectors and use the prime to show the transpose of a vector. The vector of the target (or desirable) values are given as

$$
T^{\#} = (q^{\#}, p_c^{\#}, q^{*\#}, p_c^{*\#})' = (9, 5, 3.7, 6.2)', \tag{7.19a}
$$

and the domestic prices are given as

$$
z = (p, p^*)' = (2.860, 4.964)'. \tag{7.19b}
$$

Table 7.8: Average Annual Growth Rates

GDP and Consumer Prices
Determination of the Target Values
(in Parentheses)

Country and Period	GDP[1]	Inflation
Taiwan[3]	$q^{\#}$	$p_c^{\#}$
1965-1980	9.80	-
1980-1988	8.10	4.66
1976-1989	8.97 **(9.0)**	5.10 **(5.0)**
1989	7.4	4.41
USA[2]	$q^{*\#}$	$p_c^{*\#}$
1965-1980	2.70	6.50
1980-1988	3.30	4.00
1976-1989	3.76 **(3.7)**	6.20 **(6.2)**
1989	2.43	4.82

Sources: 1. WDR 1990. 2. U.S. Economic Report
of the President 1990. 3. TSDB 1990.

Equations (7.19a) and (7.19b) are in percentage changes. The value of each variable was chosen as the average of the data on the corresponding variable for 14 years from 1976 to 1989 (see the numbers in parentheses in Table 7.8). To justify the choice of the target values in (7.19a), they are compared with the actual average growth rate of each variable for 1965 to 1980, 1980 to 1988, and 1989 in Table 7.8. Considering the performance of each country during the past decade, the choice of the target values appears to be reasonable.

7.6.1 *Nash Equilibrium*

From Appendix 7A, the reaction curve in (7A.5) for the small country, Taiwan, is given as (see (7B.2) for calculation)

$$0.00883m - 0.01972m^* = 0.47466. \tag{7.20}$$

The reaction curve in (7A.6) for the large country, the United States, is given as (see (7B.3) for calculation)

$$-0.00076m + 0.03475m^* = -0.58877. \tag{7.21}$$

Hence, solving (7.20) and (7.21) simultaneously, the Nash equilibrium money supplies are given as (see (7B.3) for calculation).

$$x^N = (m^N, m^{*N})' = (16.726, -16.576)', \qquad (7.22)$$

in percentage changes.

Now, from Eq. (7A.8), or equivalently, the first and the second equations in Table 7.7, we obtain the target values at the Nash equilibrium as (see (7B.4) for calculation)

$$T_1^N = (q^N, p_c^N)' = (9.174, 4.619)'. \qquad (7.22a)$$

Taiwan's utility at the Nash equilibrium in (7A.9) is computed as (see (7B.5) for calculation)

$$U^N = -0.0219. \qquad (7.22b)$$

They are summarized in Column (3) of Table 7.9.

Similarly, using the Nash equilibrium x^N in (7.22), we may calculate the target values of the United States at the Nash equilibrium as (see (7B.6) for calculation)

$$T_2^N = (q^{*N}, p_c^{*N})' = (3.336, 2.557)', \qquad (7.22c)$$

and the Nash utility as (see (7B.8) for calculation)

$$U^{*N} = -1.676. \qquad (7.22d)$$

They are listed in Column (6) of Table 7.9.

7.6.2   *Cooperative Equilibrium*

Next, we calculate the cooperative equilibrium. Given the world's utility function in quadratic form as shown in (7A.1), the cooperative equilibrium is the solution of Eq. (7A.10) for x. Solving for x, we have (7A.11), namely (see (7B.10) for calculation),

$$x^C = (m^C, m^{*C})' = (16.296, -16.260)'. \qquad (7.23)$$

Table 7.9: Gains from International Cooperation

Assumptions	Taiwan w1 = 0.5 h = 0.5			United States w2 = 0.5 h* = 0.5			Calc of Gain	
Instrument:	Target#	Nash	Coop.	Target#	Nash	Coop.		
(1)	(2)	(3)	(4)	(5)	(6)	(7)	(8)	(9)
Money Supply, %	(avg)	m^N	m^C	(avg)	m^{*N}	m^{*C}		
(7.22), (7.23)	21.90	16.726	16.296	7.600	-16.58	-16.260		
Price Change %	p			p^*				
Calculated, %	2.860	-	-	4.964	-	-	qN-q#	
GDP Gr Rate %	$q\#$	q^N	q^C	$q^*\#$	q^{*N}	q^{*C}	f	f^*
(7.22a) (7.22c)	9.000	9.174	8.907	3.700	3.336	3.216	0.174	-0.364
Inflation Rate %	$p_c^{\#}$	p_c^{N}	p_c^{C}	$p_c^{*\#}$	p_c^{*N}	p_c^{*C}		
(7.22a) (7.22c)	5.000	4.619	4.689	6.200	2.557	2.573		
							$(W^C - U^N)/hw_1$	
Utilities (U)		U^N	W^C		U^{*N}	W^{*C}	= g	g*
(7.22b), (7.22d), (7.25)		-0.022	-1.686		-1.676	-1.686	-6.66	-0.040
Change in Loss (%)			-98.7			-0.593	-f±sqrt(f^2 - 2g)	
=$(U^N - W^C)*100/W^C$							= Δ	Δ*
							(+) 3.479	0.825
Gain or loss in GDP(7A.16)	-3.827			-0.097			(-) -3.827	-0.097

From the cooperative equilibrium, we derive the cooperative targets in (7A.12) as

$$T^C = (q^C, p_c^C, q^{*C}, p_c^{*C})'$$
$$= (8.907, 4.689, 3.216, 2.573)'. \tag{7.24}$$

The cooperative utility in (7A.13) for both countries is calculated as

$$W^C = -1.6864. \tag{7.25}$$

These results are also summarized in Columns (4) and (7) in Table 7.9.

7.6.3 *Comparison of Nash and Cooperative Utilities*

From the Row "Utilities (U)" of Table 7.9, we can see that both Taiwan and the United States will lose by moving from the

Nash equilibrium to the cooperative equilibrium. Clearly, for the United States, the country is so large that the welfare loss due to Nash equilibrium as compared with the cooperative equilibrium is practically the same. However, Taiwan will lose greatly if it moves from its Nash equilibrium to the cooperative equilibrium. Thus, it is indifferent whether the United States cooperates with Taiwan or not. However, for Taiwan, our result shows that, U^N is so small ($= -0.022$) that Taiwan will be better off by not cooperating with the US!

Lastly, we measure the welfare loss of Taiwan, as compared with the non-cooperative Nash equilibrium, in terms of the percentage changes in utilities in terms of GDP. The method is expounded by Oudiz and Sacks (1985) to measure "welfare gain from cooperation measured in units of GNP."

From Eq. (7A.14), it can be shown that the welfare gain or loss Δ in terms of GDP can be calculated from formula (7A.16). We have calculated that for Taiwan,[1] Δ can be either 3.479 or -3.827 (Column (8) of Table 7.9). Thus, the welfare loss for Taiwan by moving from the Nash equilibrium utility ($= -0.022$) down to the cooperative equilibrium utility ($= -1.686$) will make Taiwan worse off by 3.83% of its current GDP. At the 1988 Taiwan's real GDP of US $124 billion (Table 7.1, Column (7)), this amounts to the loss of almost 4 billion.

On the contrary, Column (9) of Table 7.9 shows that for the large country, the United States, Δ can be either 0.825 or -0.097. Thus, the welfare loss of the United States by moving from the Nash equilibrium utility ($= -1.676$) to the cooperative equilibrium utility ($= -1.686$) will make the United States worse off by only 0.1% of its current GDP.

Our conclusion seems unaffected if the coefficient matrix (7.19) is estimated by levels, instead of the first-difference of the percentage changes of the time-series. In that case, Taiwan will gain by policy

---

[1]The original paper gives 2.412 which is obtained by letting $h = 1$ in Column (8) of Table 7.9. Since the weight $\widehat{W}$ in (7A.1) uses $h = 0.5$, we multiply the original g and g^* by 2 to obtain 3.479 in Column (3).

coordination. However, it is calculated that the Taiwan's welfare gain of coordination is a mere 0.06% of GDP at the Nash Equilibrium. In 1988, it amounts to merely US $73 million. Thus, for a small country like Taiwan, it does not seem to matter whether or not she coordinates her economic policy with the United States.

7.7   Some Interpretations and Conclusions

In this chapter, we have found that, using the past decade's average of GDP growth rates and inflation rates as target values (see Table 7.8), the difference between non-cooperative and cooperative values of instruments (money supply) is considerable for the United States, and to a lesser degree, for Taiwan, as shown in the upper part of Table 7.9. However, the calculated optimal target variables between non-cooperative and cooperative equilibrium are very close to each other. We consider that the current *ad hoc* policy formation of each country is neither non-cooperative nor cooperative. The real world is not like the extreme cases depicted by the theoretical model. What we have shown in this chapter is to compare the two extreme cases for the two physically and economically completely different countries.

Both the Nash and cooperative equilibria require deceleration of the growth rates of money supply for both countries. For Taiwan, cooperative money supply growth rate is almost the same as the non-cooperative money supply rate. For the United States, cooperative growth rate of money is also almost the same as the non-cooperative growth rate of money supply, but both are negative, and both growth rates require drastic deceleration from the past experience. We are rather puzzled by these results.

On the contrary, Taiwan's optimal GDP growth rate is slightly higher at Nash than at cooperation (the enclosed cells in Column (3)). However, they are almost the same as the target value, which is the 10-year average of the last decade. Thus, it seems that, so far as our model is concerned, the actual Taiwanese GDP growth rate has already reached its best possible performance. A similar statement can be given for Taiwan's inflation rate, although the equilibrium values are slightly lower than the target value. Both equilibria require the same rate of inflation at 4.6% or 4.7% per year, slightly lower than the target rate of 5.0%.

It is rather difficult to explain the case of the United States. Both Nash and cooperative equilibria require slightly lower GDP growth rates than the target value, and, at the same time, maintaining the inflation rates at about one-third of the target value (see the enclosed cells in Column (6)). For the United States, the current growth rates of GDP seems to have reached the best possible performance like Taiwan. However, her optimal inflation rate is far below the target rate.

A more interesting and significant finding of this chapter is that, compared with the non-cooperative situation, international policy coordination does not improve the welfare of the small country. Although the numerical results shown in our calculation are very small, since the utility functions are ordinal rather than cardinal, we may conclude that our result does show deterioration of the small country's welfare. In cardinal terms, the loss of utility is cut greatly without coordination. In other words, by forgoing coordination, Taiwan can improve her social welfare by almost 100% (see "Change in Loss (%)" row of Table 7.9). On the contrary, as it might be expected, for a large country, policy coordination is practically indifferent, it only improves its utility by 0.6% by moving to non-cooperation.

In general, our results suggest that, like the case of macroeconomic policy coordination among the industrial economies (Oudiz and Sachs, 1984), the policy coordination between industrial economies on the one hand and the developing or "advanced developing countries," like Taiwan, on the other, also faces the same difficulties, if not more so. This probably explains why active policy coordination has only limited success among the industrial countries, and, to our knowledge, has not taken place among the industrial and developing countries.

Naturally, in view of our results, one may argue that it is simply inconceivable that a large country like the United States will even consider to coordinate its economic policy with a small country like

Taiwan. Although our chapter only addresses the relation between Taiwan and the United States, the analysis may equally be applied to the relations between Taiwan, Korea, or other Asian countries on one hand and the United States or Japan on the other. This will be studied in Chapter 8.

In drawing this conclusion, we should note that, in our analysis, the policy coordination is limited only to the monetary policy. For the reasons explained in the introduction, fiscal and exchange rate policies are not considered in this study. Furthermore, international cooperation, and for that matter, international economic integration, can take many other forms. It may take the form of free trade area, custom union, common market, and so forth (Molle, 1990, Part II). Difficulty in policy integration does not preclude the possibility of market integration.

Appendix 7A: A Matrix Derivation of Formulas

To facilitate computation, we rewrite the world welfare functions (7.17a) $W = hU + h^*U^*$ for our model in matrix form, namely,

$$W = -\frac{1}{2}(T - T^\#)'\widehat{W}(T - T^\#), \qquad (7A.1)$$

where

$$T = (q, p_c; q^*, p_c^*)' = (T_1, T_2)',$$
$$T^\# = (q^\#, p_c^\#; q^{*\#}, p_c^{*\#})' = (T_1^\#, T_2^\#)',$$

$$\widehat{W} = \begin{bmatrix} hw_1 & 0 & \vdots & 0 & 0 \\ 0 & hw_2 & \vdots & 0 & 0 \\ \cdots & \cdots & \cdots & \cdots & \cdots \\ 0 & 0 & \vdots & h^*w_1^* & 0 \\ 0 & 0 & \vdots & 0 & h^*w_2^* \end{bmatrix} = \begin{bmatrix} \widehat{W}_1 & 0 \\ 0 & \widehat{W}_2 \end{bmatrix},$$

where T is a 4×1 column vector of the target variables, T_1 is a 2×1 column vector of the domestic (small country) target variables, T_2 is a 2×1 column vector of the foreign (large country) target variables, and $T^{\#}$ is a 4×1 column vector of the target (or desired) values, and $\widehat{W}$ is a 4×4 diagonal matrix consisting of national and international weights (or importance) of policies (w) and countries (h). Prime denotes a transpose. We define all the vectors as column vectors. Equation (7.10) is a particular case when $h = 1$.

Write the reduced form Eqs. (7.6)–(7.9) in matrix form as $\mathbf{T} = \mathbf{R}\mathbf{y}$, or

$$T = \begin{bmatrix} T_1 \\ T_2 \end{bmatrix} = \begin{bmatrix} R_{11} & R_{12} \\ R_{21} & R_{22} \end{bmatrix} \begin{bmatrix} x \\ z \end{bmatrix}, \qquad (7A.2)$$

where

$$R \equiv [R_1; R_2] = \begin{bmatrix} a & b & \vdots & c & d \\ \bar{a} & \bar{b} & \vdots & \bar{c} & \bar{d} \\ \cdots & \cdots & \cdots & \cdots & \cdots \\ a^* & b^* & \vdots & c^* & d^* \\ \bar{a}^* & \bar{b}^* & \vdots & \bar{c}^* & \bar{d}^* \end{bmatrix} = \begin{bmatrix} R_{11} & R_{12} \\ R_{21} & R_{22} \end{bmatrix},$$

$$y = (x, z)' = (m, m^*; p, p^*)'.$$

R is the 4×4 multiplier matrix, R_i is a 4×2 matrix, y is a 4×1 column vector, x is a 2×1 column vector of the policy variables, $x = (m, m^*)'$, and $z = (p, p^*)'$ is a 2×1 column vector of what Tinbergen calls "irrelevant variables."

7A.1: *Nash Equilibrium*

The Nash equilibrium is derived as follows. We choose m such that the quadratic utility function

$$U = -\left(\frac{1}{2}\right)(T_1 - T_1^{\#})'\widehat{W}_1(T_1 - T_1^{\#}) \qquad (7A.3)$$

is maximized, subject to $h = 0.5$, $T_1 = R_{11}x + R_{12}z$.

The first-order condition is[2]

$$\frac{\partial U}{\partial m} = \left[\frac{\partial T_1}{\partial m}\right]' \widehat{W}_1(T_1 - T_1^{\#}) = 0, \tag{7A.4}$$

where $\partial(T_1 - T_1^{\#})/\partial m = (\partial T_1/\partial m)' = (\partial q/\partial m, \partial p_c/\partial m)' = (a, \bar{a})'$.

Substituting the constraint T_1 into the above equation, we have, the reaction function of the first country:

$$(a, \bar{a})\widehat{W}_1 R_{11} x = (a, \bar{a})\widehat{W}_1(T_1^{\#} - R_{12} z). \tag{7A.5}$$

For $h = h^* = 0.5$ and $w_1 = w_2 = 0.5$, (7A.5) is estimated as (7.20) using the results in (7.19) and Table 7.8.

Similarly, the reaction function for the large country is given by

$$(b^*, \bar{b}^*)\widehat{W}_2 R_{21} x = (b^*, \bar{b}^*)\widehat{W}_2(T_2^{\#} - R_{22} z), \tag{7A.6}$$

which is estimated in (7.21). Solving for $x = (m, m^*)'$ in the above two equations, we have the Nash equilibrium solution $x^N = (m^N, m^{*N})'$, which is (7.22) (see (7B.3) for calculation).

Alternatively, the Nash equilibrium can be solved simultaneously by combining (7A.5) and (7A.6) as follows:

$$\begin{bmatrix} a & \bar{a} & 0 & 0 \\ 0 & 0 & b^* & \bar{b}^* \end{bmatrix} \widehat{W} R_1 x = \begin{bmatrix} a & \bar{a} & 0 & 0 \\ 0 & 0 & b^* & \bar{b}^* \end{bmatrix} \widehat{W}(T^{\#} - R_2 z),$$

$$\tag{7A.7}$$

where $\widehat{W}$ is given in (7A.1). Solving for x, the solution is $x^N = (m^N, m^{*N})'$, which is (7.22).

Substituting into the constraint, we have

$$T_1^N = R_{11} x^N + R_{12} z, \tag{7A.8}$$

$$U^N = -(1/2)(T_1^N - T_1^{\#})'\widehat{W}_1(T_1^N - T_1^{\#}). \tag{7A.9}$$

Similarly, we obtain the Nash equilibrium utility for the foreign country (USA), namely, T_2^{*N} and U^{*N}.

---

[2]Many more advanced econometrics textbooks include the method of matrix differentiation. For example, see Johnston (1984, pp. 102–104).

7A.2: *Cooperative Equilibrium*

The cooperative equilibrium is derived as follows. Differentiating the world welfare function (7A.1) with respect to the policy variables $x = (m, m^*)$, we have

$$\frac{\partial W}{\partial x} = \left[\frac{\partial T}{\partial x}\right]' \widehat{W}(T - T^\#) = 0,$$

where the derivative $\partial T/\partial x$ is the 4×2 Jacobian matrix, which is R_1 in (7A.2).

Substituting $T = R_1 x + R_2 z$ of (7A.2) into the above equation and rearranging, we have

$$R_1'\widehat{W}R_1 x = R_1'\widehat{W}(T^\# - R_2 z). \qquad (7A.10)$$

The cooperative equilibrium is then

$$x^C = (m^c, m^{*c})' = (R_1'\widehat{W}R_1)^{-1} R_1'\widehat{W}(T^\# - R_2 z), \qquad (7A.11)$$

which is (7.23).

The corresponding optimal targets are

$$T^C = R_1 x^C + R_2 z, \qquad (7A.12)$$

and the corresponding optimal welfare is

$$W^C = -\left(\frac{1}{2}\right)(T^C - T^\#)'\widehat{W}(T^C - T^\#). \qquad (7A.13)$$

These are estimated in (7.24) and (7.25).

(a) Welfare Gain or Loss

Let

$$W^C \equiv W(T^C) = W(q^C, p_c^C) \text{ and } U^N \equiv U^N(q^N, p_c^N).$$

Then the "welfare gain from cooperation measured in units of GNP" (see Oudiz and Sachs, 1985) is defined as quantity Δ such that

$$W^C = U^N(q^N + \Delta, p_c^N), \qquad (7A.14)$$

where, in general, Δ is positive, since intuitively, $W^C > U^N$, as shown by point C and N in Figure 7.1

In our quadratic utility function (7A.1), the gain Δ is the smallest absolute value of the root of

$$\Delta^2 + 2f\Delta + 2g = 0, \qquad (7A.15)$$

where $f \equiv q^N - q^\#$, and $g \equiv (W^C - U^N)/hw_1$. The two roots are

$$\Delta = -f \pm \sqrt{f^2 - 2g}. \qquad (7A.16)$$

Similarly, we may calculate Δ^* such that

$$W^C = U^{*N}(q^{*N} + \Delta^*, p_c^{*N}).$$

See Appendix 7B for derivation.

Appendix 7B: Expository Notes: A Numerical Derivation of Nash and Cooperative Equilibrium Utilities

Using (7A.1) and (7A.5), namely,

$$(a, \bar{a})\widehat{W}_1 R_{11} x = (a, \bar{a})\widehat{W}_1(T_1^\# - R_{12}z)$$

can be written in detail as

$$(a, \bar{a}) \begin{bmatrix} hw_1 & 0 \\ 0 & hw_2 \end{bmatrix} \begin{bmatrix} a & b \\ \bar{a} & \bar{b} \end{bmatrix} \begin{bmatrix} m \\ m^* \end{bmatrix}$$

$$= (a, \bar{a}) \begin{bmatrix} hw_1 & 0 \\ 0 & hw_2 \end{bmatrix} \left(\begin{bmatrix} q^\# \\ p_c^\# \end{bmatrix} - \begin{bmatrix} c & d \\ \bar{c} & d \end{bmatrix} \begin{bmatrix} p \\ p^* \end{bmatrix} \right). \qquad (7B.1)$$

Substituting the numbers from (7.19), the target value $T_1^\# = (q^\#, p_c^\#)'$ from Table 7.9, and $z = (p, p^*)'$ from Table 7.9), and also by the assumption that $h_1 = h_2 = 0.5$ and $w_1 = w_2 = 0.5$, we have

$$(0.171, 0.078) \begin{bmatrix} 0.25 & 0 \\ 0 & 0.25 \end{bmatrix} \begin{bmatrix} 0.171 & -0.611 \\ 0.078 & 0.328 \end{bmatrix} \begin{bmatrix} m \\ m^* \end{bmatrix}$$

$$= (0.171, 0.078) \begin{bmatrix} 0.25 & 0 \\ 0 & 0.25 \end{bmatrix} \left(\begin{bmatrix} 9 \\ 5 \end{bmatrix} - \begin{bmatrix} 0.31 & -0.947 \\ 0.019 & 1.752 \end{bmatrix} \begin{bmatrix} 2.86 \\ 4.96 \end{bmatrix} \right),$$

$$\qquad (7B.2)$$

where the value of the target vector $T_1^{\#} = (q^{\#}, p_c^{\#})'$ is taken from Table 7.8, and the domestic prices $z = (p, p^{\#})'$ is taken from multiplying out,[3] we have (7.20).

Similarly, we have (7.21). Combining (7.20) and (7.21),

$$
\begin{bmatrix} 0.00883 & -0.01972 \\ -0.00076 & 0.03475 \end{bmatrix} \begin{bmatrix} m^N \\ m^{*N} \end{bmatrix} = \begin{bmatrix} 0.47466 \\ -0.58877 \end{bmatrix}, \tag{7B.3}
$$

Solving for $x^N = (m^N, m^{*N})'$, we have $x^N = (16.726, -16.576)'$, which is (7.22).

7B.1: Derivation of the Nash Equilibrium Utility for Taiwan

To derive the Nash equilibrium target $T_1^N = R_{11}x^N + R_{12}z$ for Taiwan in (7A.8), we first write it as

$$
T_1^N = \begin{bmatrix} q^N \\ p_c^N \end{bmatrix} = \left(\begin{bmatrix} a & b \\ \bar{a} & \bar{b} \end{bmatrix} \begin{bmatrix} m^N \\ m^{*N} \end{bmatrix} + \begin{bmatrix} c & d \\ \bar{c} & \bar{d} \end{bmatrix} \begin{bmatrix} p \\ p^* \end{bmatrix} \right). \tag{7B.4}
$$

Substituting the numbers,

$$
T_1^N = \begin{bmatrix} q^N \\ p_c^N \end{bmatrix} = \left(\begin{bmatrix} 0.171 & -0.611 \\ 0.078 & 0.328 \end{bmatrix} \begin{bmatrix} 16.726 \\ -16.576 \end{bmatrix} \right.
$$

$$
\left. + \begin{bmatrix} 0.31 & -0.947 \\ 0.019 & 1.752 \end{bmatrix} \begin{bmatrix} 2.86 \\ 4.96 \end{bmatrix} \right) = \begin{bmatrix} 9.174 \\ 4.619 \end{bmatrix},
$$

which is (7.22a).

Substituting into the Nash equilibrium utility function (7A.9):

$$
U^N = -\frac{1}{2} \left(\begin{bmatrix} q^N \\ p_c^N \end{bmatrix} - \begin{bmatrix} q^{\#} \\ p_c^{\#} \end{bmatrix} \right)' \begin{bmatrix} h^* w_1 & 0 \\ 0 & h^* w_2 \end{bmatrix} \left(\begin{bmatrix} q^N \\ p_c^N \end{bmatrix} - \begin{bmatrix} q^{\#} \\ p_c^{\#} \end{bmatrix} \right) \tag{7B.5}
$$

---

[3]There are many software to do matrix operations. However, we recommend to use Microsoft Excel program. See Hsiao (2011), or MathLab computer software. Other software programs include the student version or free version of Mathlab by The MathWorks. Note that, due to the number of decimals taken in calculation, and the kind of software, the results of matrix multiplications and inversion may differ slightly.

where $w_1 = w_2 = 0.5$, $h = h^* = 0.5$. Substituting the values from Table 7.9, we have

$$U^N = -\frac{1}{2}\left(\begin{bmatrix} 9.174 \\ 4.619 \end{bmatrix} - \begin{bmatrix} 9 \\ 5 \end{bmatrix}\right)' \begin{bmatrix} 0.25 & 0 \\ 0 & 0.25 \end{bmatrix} \left(\begin{bmatrix} 9.174 \\ 4.619 \end{bmatrix} - \begin{bmatrix} 9 \\ 5 \end{bmatrix}\right)$$

$$= -\frac{1}{2}\begin{bmatrix} 0.174 \\ -0.381 \end{bmatrix}' \begin{bmatrix} 0.25 & 0 \\ 0 & 0.25 \end{bmatrix} \begin{bmatrix} 0.174 \\ -0.381 \end{bmatrix} = 0.02193,$$

which is the Nash equilibrium utility of the small country (Taiwan) as shown in (7.22b) in the text and the Row "Utilities" of Table 7.9.

7B.2:   Derivation of the Nash Equilibrium Utility for the United States

To derive the Nash equilibrium target $T_2^N = R_{21}x^{*N} + R_{22}z$ for the US, we first write it out as

$$T_2^N = \begin{bmatrix} q^{*N} \\ p_c^{*N} \end{bmatrix} = \left(\begin{bmatrix} a^* & b^* \\ \bar{a}^* & \bar{b}^* \end{bmatrix} \begin{bmatrix} m^N \\ m^{*N} \end{bmatrix} + \begin{bmatrix} c^* & d^* \\ \bar{c}^* & \bar{d}^* \end{bmatrix} \begin{bmatrix} p \\ p^* \end{bmatrix}\right). \qquad (7B.6)$$

Substituting the numbers,

$$T_2^N = \begin{bmatrix} q^{*N} \\ p_c^{*N} \end{bmatrix} = \left(\begin{bmatrix} 0.007 & -0.371 \\ -0.012 & 0.037 \end{bmatrix} \begin{bmatrix} 16.726 \\ -16.576 \end{bmatrix}\right.$$

$$\left. + \begin{bmatrix} 0.003 & -0.592 \\ 0.092 & 0.626 \end{bmatrix} \begin{bmatrix} 2.86 \\ 4.96 \end{bmatrix}\right) = \begin{bmatrix} 3.336 \\ 2.557 \end{bmatrix},$$

which is shown in (7.22c).

Substituting into the Nash equilibrium utility function (7A.9) for the United States (not shown),

$$U^{*N} = -\frac{1}{2}\left(\begin{bmatrix} q^{*N} \\ p_c^{*N} \end{bmatrix} - \begin{bmatrix} q^{*\#} \\ p_c^{*\#} \end{bmatrix}\right)' \begin{bmatrix} h^* w_1 & 0 \\ 0 & h^* w_2 \end{bmatrix} \left(\begin{bmatrix} q^{*N} \\ p_c^{*N} \end{bmatrix} - \begin{bmatrix} q^{*\#} \\ p_c^{*\#} \end{bmatrix}\right),$$

$$(7B.7)$$

where $w_1 = w_2 = 0.5$, $h = 0.5$, $h^* = 0.5$. Substituting the values from Table 7.9, we have

$$
U^{*N} = -\frac{1}{2}\left(\begin{bmatrix} 3.336 \\ 2.557 \end{bmatrix} - \begin{bmatrix} 3.7 \\ 6.2 \end{bmatrix}\right)' \begin{bmatrix} 0.25 & 0 \\ 0 & 0.25 \end{bmatrix}\left(\begin{bmatrix} 3.336 \\ 2.557 \end{bmatrix} - \begin{bmatrix} 3.7 \\ 6.2 \end{bmatrix}\right)
$$

$$
= -\frac{1}{2}\begin{bmatrix} -0.364 \\ -3.643 \end{bmatrix}' \begin{bmatrix} 0.25 & 0 \\ 0 & 0.25 \end{bmatrix} \begin{bmatrix} -0.364 \\ -3.643 \end{bmatrix} = -1.6758, \qquad (7B.8)
$$

which is the Nash equilibrium utility of the large country as shown as (7.22d) in the text and the Row "Utilities" of Table 7.9.

7B.3: *Derivation of the Cooperative Equilibrium Utility*

In this case, we first derive the money supply vector $x = x^C$ in (7A.10) as follows:

$$
x^c = (m^c, m^{*c})' = (R_1'\widehat{W}R_1)^{-1}R_1'\widehat{W}(T^\# - R_2 z) \qquad (7B.9)
$$

$$
\begin{bmatrix} a & b \\ \bar{a} & \bar{b} \\ a^* & b^* \\ \bar{a}^* & \bar{b}^* \end{bmatrix}' \begin{bmatrix} hw_1 & & & \vdots & & \\ & hw_2 & & \vdots & & 0 \\ \cdots & \cdots & \cdots & \vdots & \cdots & \cdots \\ & & & \vdots & h^*w_1^* & \\ 0 & & & \vdots & & h^*w_2^* \end{bmatrix} \begin{bmatrix} a & b \\ \bar{a} & \bar{b} \\ a^* & b^* \\ \bar{a}^* & \bar{b}^* \end{bmatrix} x^C
$$

$$
= \begin{bmatrix} a & b \\ \bar{a} & \bar{b} \\ a^* & b^* \\ \bar{a}^* & \bar{b}^* \end{bmatrix}' \begin{bmatrix} hw_1 & & & \vdots & & \\ & hw_2 & & \vdots & & 0 \\ \cdots & \cdots & \cdots & \vdots & \cdots & \cdots \\ & & & \vdots & h^*w_1^* & \\ 0 & & & \vdots & & h^*w_2^* \end{bmatrix} \left(\begin{bmatrix} q^\# \\ p_c^\# \\ q^{*\#} \\ p_c^{*\#} \end{bmatrix} - \begin{bmatrix} c & d \\ \bar{c} & \bar{d} \\ c^* & d^* \\ \bar{c}^* & \bar{d}^* \end{bmatrix}\begin{bmatrix} p \\ p^* \end{bmatrix}\right) \qquad (7B.10)
$$

Substituting the data in (7B.10),

$$
\begin{bmatrix} 0.171 & -0.611 \\ 0.078 & 0.328 \\ 0.007 & -0.371 \\ -0.012 & 0.037 \end{bmatrix}'
\begin{bmatrix} 0.25 & & \vdots & & \\ & & & 0 & \\ & 0.25 & \vdots & & \\ \cdots & \cdots & \cdots & \cdots & \cdots \\ & & \vdots & 0.25 & \\ & 0 & & & \\ & & \vdots & & 0.25 \end{bmatrix}
\begin{bmatrix} 0.171 & -0.611 \\ 0.078 & 0.328 \\ 0.007 & -0.371 \\ -0.012 & 0.037 \end{bmatrix}
\begin{bmatrix} m^C \\ m^{*C} \end{bmatrix}
$$

$$
= \begin{bmatrix} 0.171 & -0.611 \\ 0.078 & 0.328 \\ 0.007 & -0.371 \\ -0.012 & 0.037 \end{bmatrix}'
\begin{bmatrix} 0.25 & & \vdots & & \\ & & & 0 & \\ & 0.25 & \vdots & & \\ \cdots & \cdots & \cdots & \cdots & \cdots \\ & & \vdots & 0.25 & \\ & 0 & & & \\ & & \vdots & & 0.25 \end{bmatrix}
\left(\begin{bmatrix} 9 \\ 5 \\ 3.7 \\ 6.2 \end{bmatrix} - \begin{bmatrix} 0.310 & -0.947 \\ 0.019 & 1.752 \\ 0.003 & -0.592 \\ 0.092 & 0.626 \end{bmatrix} \begin{bmatrix} 2.86 \\ 4.96 \end{bmatrix} \right).
$$

Solving for x^C, we have (7.23).

For simplicity, the cooperative equilibrium target vector $T^C = R_1 x^C + R_2 z$ of (7A.12) may be written as $T^C = (R_1, R_2)(x^C, z)' = Ry$, where R and y are given in (7A.2), in which x should be substituted by x^C. After solving, we have T^C in (7.24).

Using T^C in (7.24), we can find cooperative equilibrium utility (7A.13), where $T^\#$ can be found in (7B.10). After multiplying the matrices out, we have W^C in (7.25).

Appendix 7C: Expository Notes: A Numerical Derivation of Welfare Gain

Since the utility function is quadratic, as in (7.10), the right-hand side of Eq. (7A.14) can be written in detail as, based on the Nash equilibrium utility for the small country in (7A.3),

$$
W^C = U^N(q^N + \Delta, p_c^N) \equiv -(1/2)[hw_1(q^N - q^\# + \Delta)^2
$$
$$
+ hw_2(p_c^N - p_c^\#)^2]. \qquad (7C.1)
$$

Moving $-(1/2)$ inside the bracket and completing the square of the first term, we have

$$W^C = -(1/2)hw_1[(q^N - q^\#)^2 + 2(q^N - q^\#)\Delta + \Delta^2)]$$
$$- (1/2)hw_2(p_c^N - p_c^\#)^2].$$

The first term together with the last term are the Nash Equilibrium utility U^N derived in (7A.9) or (7B.5). Hence,

$$W^C = U^N - hw_1(q^N - q^\#)\Delta - (1/2)hw_1\Delta^2,$$

where W^C and U^N are known numbers. Rearranging, and dividing both sides by $hw_1/2$,

$$\Delta^2 + 2(q^N - q^\#)\Delta + 2(W^C - U^N)/w_1h = 0,$$

we have (7A.15). Applying the quadratic formula, we have the solution (7A.16) for the small country. The gain or loss is taken as minimum of the absolute values of the two solutions.

Similarly, for U^{*N}, we have, similar to (7A.16),

$$\Delta^* = -f^* \pm \sqrt{f^{*2} - 2g^*},$$

where $f^* \equiv q^{*N} - q^{*\#}$ and $g \equiv (W^{*C} - U^{*N})/hw_1$. Δ^* is the welfare gain or loss of the large country by moving from the Nash equilibrium to the cooperative equilibrium.

The calculation of gain Δ for the small country (Taiwan) and Δ^* for the large country (the USA) are shown in the last two columns of Table 7.9.

Acknowledgments

The authors wish to express their sincere appreciation to Professor M. Jan Dutta, the American Committee on Asian Economic Studies, and the Tokai University of Japan for the successful arrangement of the Fifth Biennial Conference on United States–Asia Economic Relations. The authors also would like to thank Drs. Bagestani Hamid and Sukrisno Njoto for allowing them to use their microcomputers and computer software. Postscript: Appendixes 7B and 7C were added for this chapter.

References

Argy, V., W. McKibbin and E. Siegloff (1989). *Exchange-Rate Regimes for a Small Economy in a Multi-Country World*, Princeton Studies in International Finance, December, No. 67.

Branson, W. H., J. A. Frenkel and M. Goldstein (Eds.) (1990). *International Policy Coordination and Exchange Fluctuations*. Cambridge, MA: National Bureau of Economic Research.

Buiter, W. and R. Marston (1985). *International Economic Policy Coordination*. Cambridge, UK: Cambridge University Press.

Canzoneri, M. B. and P. Minford (1988). When international policy coordination matters: An empirical analysis. *Applied Economics* **20**, 1137–1154.

Cooper, R. (1985). Economic Interdependence and Coordination of Economic Policies. In *Handbook of International Economics*, R. Jones and P. Kennen (Eds.). North-Holland, pp. 1195–1234.

Far Eastern Economic Review (FEER) (1990). 11 October, Cover Story. Reports by A. Rowley in p. 74, and by N. Holloway in pp. 72 and 75.

Feldstein, M. (Ed.) (1988). *International Economic Cooperation*. Cambridge, MA: National Bureau of Economic Research.

Hsiao, F. S. T. (1990). Globalization of the Japanese Economy and the Asian NICs-Toward the Asian Economic Community. In *The Globalization of Japanese Economy. International Symposium*, The 40th Anniversary of Economics Faculty. Tokyo: Komazawa University, pp. 129–164.

Hsiao, F. S. T. (2011). *Economic and Business Analysis–Quantitative Methods using Spreadsheets*. Singapore: World Scientific.

Hsiao, F. S. T. and M. C. W. Hsiao (1983). Some development indicators of Taiwan: A comparative study. *Journal of Economic Development* **8** (1), 45–58.

Hsiao, F. S. T. and M. C. W. Hsiao (1989). Japanese Experience of Industrialization and Economic Performance of Korea and Taiwan: Tests of Similarity. In *Taiwan's Foreign Investment, Exports and Financial Analysis, Advances in Financial Planning and Forecasting* [Supplement 1], S. C. Hu and C. F. Lee (Eds.). MA: JAI Press, pp. 157–190.

Hsiao, F. S. T. and M. C. W. Hsiao (1990). Cointegration and Causality in the Trade Relation of a Pacific Triangle. Paper presented at *The Sixth International Congress of North American Economics and Finance Association (NAEFA)*, 7–9 August, Mexico City, Mexico.

Johnston, J. (1984). *Econometric Methods*. New York: McGraw-Hill.

Journal of Commerce and Commercial (JCC). (1990). May 8, 4A, as reported by M. Mangier.

Lilien, D. M. and R. E. Hall (1991). *Micro TSP User's Manual*, Version 7. Irvine, CA: Quantitative Micro Software.

McKibbin, W. J. (1988). The economics of international policy coordination. *Economic Record* **64** (4), 241–253.

Miller, M. and M. Salmon (1990). When does coordination pay? *Journal of Economic Dynamics and Control* **14** (3–4), 553–569.

Molle, W. (1990). *The Economics of European Integration, Theory, Practice, Policy.* Dartmouth, VT: Brookfield.

Oborne, M. W. and N. Fourt (1983). *Pacific Basin Economic Cooperation.* Paris: OECD.

Oudiz, G. and J. Sachs (1984). Macroeconomic policy coordination among the industrial economies. *Brooking Papers on Economic Activities* 1, 1–75.

Pindyck, R. S. and D. L. Rubinfeld (1991). *Econometric Models and Economic Forecasts* (3rd edn.). New York: McGraw-Hill.

Shinohara, M. and F. Lo (Eds.) (1989). *Global Adjustment and the Future of Asian- Pacific Economy.* Tokyo: Institute of Developing Economies, and Kuala Lumpur: Asian and Pacific Development Centre.

Torii, Y. (1989). Asia-Pacific Cooperation and Its Contribution-Historical and Future Perspectives, *Tokyo Symposium on the Present and Future of the Pacific Basin Economy-A Comparison of Asia and Latin America,* 25–27 July. Tokyo: Institute of Developing Economies.

Chapter 8

International Policy Coordination with a Dominant Player — The Cases of the United States, Japan, Taiwan, and Korea

Abstract

This chapter extends the two-country policy coordination model discussed in Chapter 7 to a multicountry model. Consequently, this model is much more complicated. Mathematical derivations are collected in the appendix. Similar to Chapter 7, using a simple asymmetric Mundell–Fleming–Dornbusch static model, this chapter first estimates the parameters of the model with the least squares method, using the data from 1975 to 1990. The results are then utilized to simulate the model. Our results show that, when the United States (or Japan) acts as the dominant player (the Stackelberg leader) by anticipating Taiwan's (or Korea's) reaction functions, the gain from policy coordination is the same as that of the Nash equilibrium. Based on quadratic social welfare function, we show that the small countries lose slightly by cooperating with the large countries, and the large countries are almost indifferent about cooperation or non-cooperation with the small countries. The result is similar to Chapter 7, and it seems to confirm that we return to a neoclassical world of free competition, as cooperation is a type of interference of market mechanism. This probably explains why the active policy coordination only has a limited success among the developed countries, and to our knowledge, has not yet taken place among the developed and developing countries.

Keywords: International policy coordination; game theory; the Mundell–Fleming–Dornbusch two-country model; regression and simulation; the economies of USA, Japan, Taiwan, and Korea

8.1 Introduction

In an interdependent world economy, a country's economic policy exerts externalities on other countries. The policy objective of a country depends not only on its own policy instruments but also on those of other countries. Under the assumption of symmetric economies, it can be shown that Nash non-cooperative equilibrium is not Pareto efficient, and there are gains from policy coordination.

In Chapter 7, using a simple asymmetric Mundell–Fleming–Dornbusch static model, our analysis has shown that Taiwan's losses due to a movement from a Nash equilibrium to cooperative equilibrium with the United States are considerable, and for the United States, the Nash equilibrium and the cooperative equilibrium are practically the same. These results were obtained by using the difference stationary model in estimating the reaction functions. In another paper (Hsiao and Hsiao, 1994b), using the trend stationary model with the logarithm of the variables, we have shown that it is indifferent for the United States whether or not it cooperates with Taiwan or Korea. However, for the small open economies, our results also show that Taiwan and Korea may not gain from coordinating their monetary policy with the United States. These findings are generally consistent with the results obtained for policy coordination among the developed countries (Oudiz and Sachs, 1984; Canzoneri and Minford, 1988).

In Nash equilibrium, both countries are assumed to take the other country's monetary policy as given without recognizing that the other country reacts to its own policy. The purpose of this chapter is to extend the previous analyses to the case when the United States (or Japan) acts as the dominant player (the Stackelberg leader) by anticipating Taiwan's (or Korea's) reaction functions. The

United States announces its policy and maximizes its social utility by taking into account the effects of its policy on Taiwan or Korea (the follower), which takes the decision of the dominant player as given. We then measure gains and losses in social utility from policy coordination under dominant player assumption. The results are then compared with the gains or losses of non-cooperative Nash equilibrium and cooperative equilibrium obtained in the previous chapters.

In what follows, the model is specified and Nash, Cooperative, and Stackelberg equilibria are defined in Section 8.2. The restrictions on parameters are then explained in Section 8.3. Section 8.4 describes the method of estimation and Section 8.5, the method of simulation. The findings of the simulation results are delineated in Section 8.6. Some conclusions are given in Section 8.7. The computational procedures are rather involved and are derived in Appendixes 8A and 8B. We have kept the description of the model, the method of estimation, and simulation of the model to a minimum since a detailed explanation and justification of the model and method are available in Chapter 7 and Hsiao and Hsiao (1994a, 1994b).

8.2   The Mundell–Fleming–Dornbusch Model

As in Chapter 7, the game-theoretic method we use is pioneered by Hamada (1974), and the model we use is generally known as the Mundell–Fleming–Dornbusch two-country macroeconomic model (Cooper, 1985; McKibbin and Sachs, 1991). For convenience, we repeat the model as follows:

Small country

$$q = \phi q^* + \gamma(e + p^* - p) - \lambda i, \qquad (8.1)$$

$$m - p = \alpha q - \beta i, \qquad (8.2)$$

$$p_c = \mu(e + p^*) + (1 - \mu)p, \qquad (8.3)$$

$$i = i^*; \qquad (8.4)$$

Large country

$$q^* = \gamma^*(p - e - p^*) - \lambda^* i^*, \tag{8.1}*$$

$$m^* - p^* = \alpha^* q^* - \beta^* i^*, \tag{8.2}*$$

$$p_c^* = \mu^*(p - e) + (1 - \mu^*)p^*, \tag{8.3}*$$

where q is the real gross domestic product (GDP), e is the exchange rate (domestic currency price of a unit of foreign currency), p is the price index of domestic output (wholesale prices), m is the supply of money (M1), p_c is the consumer price index, and i is the rate of interest.

The asterisk * denotes the variables and parameters for the large country. All the variables, except the rate of interest, are measured in logarithm of the variables. This is different from Chapter 7, in which we represented the variables in percentage change. As in Chapter 7, the difference between small and large countries is shown by the fact that the small country's gross domestic product (GDP) is a function of the large country's GDP in the small country's IS function.

We keep our model as simple as possible so that we may obtain some definite results without being bogged down by computational and data problems. We are interested only in the short-run effects of strategic policy coordination and compare the gains and losses for the small country as well as the large country.

Similar to Chapter 7, the above equations may be solved for q, q^*, p_c, and p_c^* as functions of m, m^*, p, p^*:

$$q = am + bm^* + cp + dp^*, \tag{8.6}$$

$$q^* = a^*m + b^*m^* + c^*p + d^*p^*, \tag{8.7}$$

$$p_c = \bar{a}m + \bar{b}m^* + \bar{c}p + \bar{d}p^*, \tag{8.8}$$

$$p_c^* = \bar{a}^*m + \bar{b}^*m^* + \bar{c}^*p + \bar{d}^*p^*, \tag{8.9}$$

where a, b, c, d, a^*, b^*, c^*, d^*, $\bar{a}$, $\bar{b}$, $\bar{c}$, $\bar{d}$, $\bar{a}^*$, $\bar{b}^*$, $\bar{c}^*$, $\bar{d}^*$ are the 16 coefficients of policy instruments in terms of the original parameters in (8.1) to (8.3) and (8.1)* to (8.3)*. They are called the reduced equations.

The utility function of the small country is

$$U = -(1/2)[w_1(q - q^\#)^2 + w_2(p_c - p_c^\#)^2],   \qquad (8.10)$$

where $q^\#$ is the target or desired GDP, and $p_c^\#$ is the target or desired consumer price index. Parameters w_1 and w_2 are the weights, $w_1 + w_2 = 1$, that the policy makers assign to the two targets (GDP and consumer price) in accordance with their relative importance.

The utility function for the large country is

$$U^* = -(1/2)[w_1^*(q^* - q^{*\#})^2 + w_2^*(p_c^* - p_c^{*\#})^2],   \qquad (8.11)$$

where $w_1^* + w_2^* = 1$.

We now define the following three regimes:

(a) *Nash Non-cooperative Equilibrium*: The policy makers in each country maximize the utility function U or U^*, that is, minimize the loss function $-U$ or $-U^*$, for given weights between the GDP deviation and consumer price deviation from the target values. For the small country, the constraints are (8.6) and (8.8), and for the large country, the constraints are (8.7) and (8.9).

(b) *Cooperative Equilibrium*: The policy makers in both countries jointly choose the money supplies m and m^* to maximize the world community welfare:

$$W = hU + h^*U^*,   \qquad (8.12)$$

where h and h^* are the weights assigned to the small and the large countries, respectively. The constraints are jointly (8.6)–(8.9).

(c) *Stackelberg Equilibrium*: This is known as the dominant player equilibrium. The large country is the leader (the dominant player) and the small country is the follower. In this case, the small country minimizes its loss function subject to its own reduced Eqs. (8.6) and (8.8). The large country minimizes its loss function subject to its own reduced Eqs. (8.7) and (8.9), and the reaction function of the small country. As shown in Appendix 8B, the mathematical property of one country being a leader and the other country being a follower is symmetric. Therefore, just for curiosity and comparison, we also calculated the ludicrous case when the small country is a leader and the large country is a follower. The results are rather surprising.

For convenience, we call the Nash and the Stackelberg regimes the non-cooperative equilibria in contrast with the cooperative regime. Our purpose is to compare utilities and gains or losses measured as the percentage of GDP between non-cooperative regimes and the cooperative regime.[1]

8.3 Restrictions on Parameters

When all the coefficients of (8.6) to (8.9) are estimated without restriction, we call the model the general case. When we explicitly impose the condition that the small country's variables do not affect the large country's variables, that is, when $a^* = c^* = \bar{a}^* = \bar{c}^* = 0$, then we call the model the restricted case. Hence, the system of equation for the restricted case is

$$q = am + bm^* + cp + dp^*,$$

$$q^* = b^*m^* + d^*p^*,$$

$$p_c = \bar{a}m + \bar{b}m^* + \bar{c}p + \bar{d}p^*,$$

$$p_c^* = \bar{b}^*m^* + \bar{d}^*p^*.$$

In both cases, unlike Chapter 7, we assume that the weight of the small country in the world welfare function is $h = 0.1$, and that of the large country is $h^* = 0.9$. The weights are roughly proportional to the ratio of GDP between small and large countries. Throughout this chapter, we also choose the weights between the income policy and the price policy to be 0.8 and 0.2 for small countries, and 0.5 and 0.5 for large countries. This is based on the observation that Taiwan and Korea put more emphasis on economic growth than price stability. In our previous experiments, the variation in weights gives different values of optimum utility functions, but the conclusions are basically the same.

---

[1] For a concise introduction of these three equilibria, see Henderson and Quandt (1971).

8.4 Estimation

We estimated the coefficients of the four reduced-form equations in (8.6)–(8.9) by the ordinary least squares method using the data of each country for 16 years from 1975 to 1990. The summary statistics of the data for the target variables $T = (q, p_c, q^*, p_c*)'$ (the prime $'$ denotes the transpose of a row vector), and the instrument variables $y = (x, z)' = (m, m^*, p, p^*)'$, for the United States, Japan, Taiwan, and Korea are shown in Table 8.1, which is reproduced here from Table 2 of our previous paper (Hsiao and Hsiao, 1994b). The numerical values are measured in the domestic currency to avoid distortion due to fluctuation in the USD during this period.

Due to data availability, all q's for Taiwan, Korea, and the United States are measured in real GDP, and the q for Japan is measured in real GNP. Since Taiwan and Korea are fast-growing countries, we also show the latest 1990 statistics. For comparison, the average and the standard deviation of the data for each variable from 1975 to 1990 are also listed in Table 8.1. We then convert the data for each variable into logarithmic form and calculate their average, standard deviation, maximum, and minimum.

Equations (8.6)–(8.9) are grouped by the small and then the large countries. The regression coefficients of (8.6)–(8.9) are estimated and presented in Table 8.2 in which the US is the large country, and Table 8.3 in which Japan is the large country. Both tables are reproduced from Tables 3 and 4 of Hsiao and Hsiao (1994b), and the method and testing of estimation are the same as those presented in Table 7.7 of Chapter 7.

In Tables 8.2 and 8.3, we first estimated the coefficients of the restricted case, in which the small country does not influence the large country. The absolute value of the t-statistics, R^2, and the Durbin–Watson (DW) statistics are also reported in the tables.

We then estimated all coefficients of the general case, in which both the small and large country's variables influence each other.

The estimates are arranged as a 4×4 coefficient matrix (R) of Eqs. (8.6)–(8.9) for each case, which is similar to the matrix shown in Eq. (7.19) of Chapter 7. Altogether, we have eight R matrices,

Table 8.1: Summary Statistics for Variables
1975–1990

	q	p_c	m	p
USA unit	'87pr US$b	'85=100	US$b	'85=100
1990	4884.9	121	828	113
avg	4046	86.5	539.9	89
std	499.9	22.3	183.4	17.8
avg, in log	**8.3**	**4.4**	**6.2**	**4.5**
std, in log	0.1	0.3	0.3	0.2
max, in log	8.5	4.8	6.7	4.7
min, in log	8.1	3.9	5.7	4.0
Japan unit	'85pr yen b	'85=100	Yen bil	'85=100
1990	404820	106.9	114800	90.6
avg	291481.1	90.4	78760.7	91.1
std	57497.4	13	19546	9.0
avg, in log	**12.6**	**4.5**	**11.2**	**4.5**
std, in log	0.2	0.2	0.3	0.1
max, in log	12.9	4.7	11.7	4.6
min, in log	12.2	4.1	10.8	4.3
Taiwan unit	'86pr NT$b	'85=100	NT$ bil	'85=100
1990	3883.6	110.7	1931.9	94.3
avg	2327.3	87.1	824.7	91.7
std	847.3	19.3	661.1	14.6
avg, in log	**7.7**	**4.4**	**6.4**	**4.5**
std, in log	0.4	0.2	0.9	0.2
max, in log	8.3	4.7	7.6	4.7
min, in log	7.0	4.0	4.9	4.2
Korea unit	'85pr Won b	'85=100	Won bil	'85=100
1990	131263.0	130.0	13952.0	108.0
avg	74334.8	82.9	6114.8	81.1
std	28419.6	30.5	3943.9	26.1
avg, in log	**11.1**	**4.3**	**8.5**	**4.3**
std, in log	0.4	0.4	0.7	0.4
max, in log	11.8	4.9	9.5	4.7
min, in log	10.5	3.5	7.0	3.6

Notes: The USA, Japan, and Korea data, 1975–1989, are obtained from the IFS Tape-(1990), and the 1990 data are obtained from the IFS (1992). The Taiwan data are obtained from TSDB (1992, p. 25, 135, 167). '87pr, etc. means that the variable is in the 1987 prices, etc., b = billion.

Table 8.2: Regression Coefficients for Real Output and Consumer Prices

Taiwan, Korea, and the USA, 1975–1990

Eq.	Dependent Var	Const	m	m*	p	p*	R2	DW
				I. Taiwan-USA: Restricted Case				
1	q	3.212	0.175	0.309	-0.579	0.905		
		(7.75)	(3.25)	(2.84)	(4.00)	(4.59)	0.998	1.783
2	pₑ	-1.397	-0.054	0.247	0.298	0.738		
		(3.06)	(0.91)	(2.06)$	(1.87)	(3.40)	0.994	1.294
3	q*	6.189		0.374		-0.050		
		(43.5)		(7.84)		(0.66)	0.958	0.878
4	pₑ*	-1.134		0.333		0.780		
		(26.2)		(22.9)		(33.8)	0.999	1.264
				II. Taiwan-USA: General Case				
5 and 6. Same as Equations (1) and (2) above								
7	q*	7.117	0.061	0.114	-0.303	0.323		
		(18.1)	(1.20)	(1.10)	(2.20)	(1.73)	0.982	1.237
8	pₑ*	-1.457	-0.045	0.413	-0.064	0.868		
		(9.66)	(2.29)	(10.5)	(1.21)	(12.1)	0.9995	1.728
				III. Korea-USA: Restricted Case				
9	q	2.342	0.155	0.821	-0.887	1.391		
		(2.47)	(1.85)	(6.91)	(5.53)	(3.59)	0.997	2.191
10	pₑ	-2.188	0.119	0.143	0.451	0.599		
		(4.05)	(2.48)	(2.10)	(4.91)	(2.71)	0.999	2.034
11 and 12. Same as Equations (3) and (4) above								
				IV. Korea-USA: General Case				
13 and 14. Same as Equations (9) and (10) above								
15	q*	4.803	0.005	0.315	-0.388	0.710		
		(7.06)	(0.08)	(3.68)	(3.36)	(2.55)	0.983	1.358
16	pₑ*	-1.061	-0.005	0.344	0.028	0.731		
		(3.33)	(0.18)	(8.59)	(0.52)	(5.61)	0.999	1.317

Notes: (1) q, m, p, and p_c are based on either the Taiwan or the Korea data in Table 8.1.
(2) q^*, m^*, p^*, and p_c^* are based on the USA data in Table 8.1.
(3) Number of observations $N = 16$, 1975–1990.
(4) The absolute value of the t-ratio is in the parentheses.

Table 8.3: Regression Coefficients for Real Output and Consumer Prices

Taiwan, Korea, and Japan. 1975–1990

Eq. Var	Dependent Const	m	m*	p	p*	R2	DW
I. Taiwan-Japan: Restricted Case							
1. q	**0.877**	**0.290**	**0.527**	**-0.213**	**0.389**	**0.996**	**1.450**
	(0.42)	(3.77)	(2.24)	(0.83)	(1.08)		
2. pₑ	**-3.167**	**0.084**	**0.264**	**0.623**	**0.289**	**0.989**	**1.035**
	(1.38)	(0.98)	(1.01)	(2.20)	(0.72)		
3. q*	**3.700**		**0.765**		**0.059**	**0.983**	**1.326**
	(9.73)		(25.3)		(0.77)		
4. pₑ*	**-3.452**		**0.493**		**0.532**	**0.99**	**1.245**
	(14.7)		(26.5)		(11.2)		
II. Taiwan-Japan: General Case							
Same as Equations (1) and (2) above.							
5. q*	**6.260**	**0.127**	**0.413**	**-0.310**	**0.498**	**0.987**	**1.142**
	(3.22)	(1.76)	(1.87)	(1.29)	(1.48)		
6. pₑ*	**-2.869**	**0.005**	**0.452**	**0.099**	**0.401**	**0.99**	**1.235**
	(2.16)	(0.10)	(2.99)	(0.60)	(1.74)		
III. Korea-Japan: Restricted Case							
7. q	**5.771**	**0.324**	**0.530**	**0.085**	**-0.821**	**0.992**	**1.420**
	(1.34)	(2.56)	(1.41)	(0.42)	(1.99)		
8. pₑ	**-4.134**	**0.103**	**0.377**	**0.694**	**0.079**	**0.999**	**1.148**
	(2.64)	(2.23)	(2.76)	(9.54)	(0.53)		
Same as Equations (3) and (4) above.							
IV. Korea-Japan: General Case							
Same as Equations (7) and (8) above.							
9. q*	**7.394**	**0.112**	**0.411**	**0.040**	**-0.128**	**0.986**	**1.190**
	(2.47)	(1.27)	(1.57)	(0.29)	(0.45)		
10. pₑ*	**-1.707**	**0.051**	**0.329**	**0.022**	**0.439**	**0.991**	**1.178**
	(0.89)	(0.90)	(1.97)$	(0.25)	(2.39)		

Notes: (1) Same as Notes (1), (2), and (4) in Table 8.2. (2) q^*, m^*, p^*, and p_c^* are for Japan.

four for the restricted case, and four for the general case, as shown[2] in Tables 8.2 and 8.3.

---

[2]Interpretation of Tables 8.2 and 8.3 are given in Hsiao and Hsiao (1994b).

We have found that, as expected, the t-values of the coefficients of the money supply (m) and the wholesale price (p) of the small country are generally not significant in the large country's equations of GDP (q^*) and the consumer price index (p_c^*). In addition, the results of the restricted case are very similar to the general case. Hence, to avoid complication, we only discuss the results of the four general cases, as shown in Table 8.4.

8.5   Simulation

To facilitate simulation in the next steps, we have rewritten the utility maximization problems in matrix form. The calculation is rather involved and is presented in Appendices 8A and 8B. Appendix 8A is basically the same as Appendix 7A of Chapter 7. Appendix 8B shows the computational procedure for calculating Stackelberg equilibrium.

We first calculate the estimated regression line (8.6)–(8.9) for Taiwan and Korea with the United States in Table 8.2, and for Taiwan and Korea with Japan in Table 8.3, for the restricted and the general cases. Thus, we can construct eight coefficient matrix R like (7.19) of Chapter 7.

Using the estimated coefficients and assumptions on the parameters, we calculate the Nash equilibrium money supplies $x^N = (m^N, m^{*N})'$ from (8A.4), cooperative equilibrium money supplies $x^C = (m^C, m^{*C})'$ from (8A.7), and Stackelberg equilibrium money supplies $x^{FL} = (m^F, m^{*L})'$ and $x^{LF} = (m^L, m^{*F})'$ from (8B.19).

Equation (8B.19) calculates simultaneously both money supply for the small country as a leader and also for the large country as a leader, $y = (m^L, m^{*L})'$. The money supplies of the followers may be obtained from the reaction functions. We then calculate the money supplies for the case when the small country is a follower and the large country is a leader.

As mentioned above, since calculation is symmetric, we also calculate the untenable case when the small country is a leader and the large country is a follower. Combining, we have two money supply vectors, $x^{FL} = (m^F, m^{*L})'$ and $x^{LF} = (m^L, m^{*F})'$.

The values of money supply are then rearranged and entered in Table 8.4. For example, in Part I Taiwan and the United States of Table 8.4, we have calculated

$$x^N = (m^N, m^{*N})' = (21.59, 8.23)',$$
$$x^C = (m^C, m^{*C})' = (60.31, 8.64)',$$
$$x^{FL} = (m^F, m^{*L})' = (26.436, 8.22)',$$
$$x^{LF} = (m^L, m^{*F})' = (21.43, 5.23)'.$$

The results are entered in the Row "MS in log" of Part I of Table 8.4.

After the derivation of the money supply vectors, along with the assumption of sticky prices $z = (p, p^*)'$, which are taken from the mean of the data for each country in Table 8.1, we then find the target vectors for Nash equilibrium T^N in (8A.5), cooperate equilibrium T^C in (8A.8), Stackelberg equilibriums T^{FL} in (8B.19), and T^{LF} in (8B.21).

In this study, our calculation yields the following four results. For Part I, Taiwan and the United States, the target vectors are

$$T^N = (q^N, p_c^N, q^{*N}, p_c^{*N})' = (7.778, 5.528, 2.345, 6.044)',$$

$$T^C = (q^C, p_c^C, q^{*C}, p_c^{*C})' = (14.691, 3.539, 4.754, 4.472)',$$

$$T^{FL} = (q^F, p_c^F, q^{*L}, p_c^{*L})' = (7.710, 4.527, 2.334, 6.047)',$$

$$T^{LF} = (q^L, p_c^L, q^{*F}, p_c^{*F})' = (7.756, 5.534, 2.299, 4.789)'.$$

In Table 8.4, T^N is entered in Columns 5 and 11, T^C in Columns 4 and 10 (with bordered cells), T^{FL} in Columns 6 and 12, and T^{LF} in Columns 7 and 13.

Finally, using these results, we estimate the quadratic utilities for the Nash equilibrium (U^N, U^{*N}) in (8A.6), for the cooperative equilibrium W^C in (8A.9), for the Stackelberg equilibrium when the small country is the follower and the large country is the leader (U^F, U^{*L}) in (8B.21), and also when the small country is the leader and the large country is the follower (U^L, U^{*F}) in (8B.23). The results for the general cases are summarized in the Utility row of enclosed cells with bold face font. For Part I, between Taiwan and the United States in Table 8.4, we have

$$(U^N, U^{*N}) = (-0.130, -9.542),$$

$$W^C = -4.793,$$

$$(U^F, U^{*L}) = (-0.002, -9.577),$$

$$(U^L, U^{*F}) = (-0.130, -9.012).$$

While utility is an ordinal number rather than a cardinal number, in many economics textbooks, it has been treated as if it is a cardinal number. Thus, in this chapter, we tried to compare two utilities by calculating percentage changes of utility when the utility changed from cooperative equilibrium to less desirable Nash and Stackelberg equilibriums. When a country moves from cooperative equilibrium utility to the Nash equilibrium utility, we define the percentage change of utility r as

$$r = (U^X - W^C) * 100/W^C, \tag{8.13}$$

where X may take N, FL, or LF. Since both U^X and W^C are negative, a positive value of (8.13) means that the country is better-off at the cooperative equilibrium than at non-cooperative equilibrium, and the number measures the percentage gain relative to a cooperative utility when a country changes policy from non-cooperative to cooperative. On the other hand, a negative value means that the country is worse-off at the cooperative equilibrium than at a non-cooperative equilibrium, and the number measures the percentage loss of utility relative to the cooperative utility when a country changes its policy from cooperative to non-cooperative.

We also calculated Oudiz and Sachs' welfare gain from cooperation measured in units of GDP. The method is presented in Appendix 7A of Chapter 7. The computational results are shown as "Gain Δ to Coop, log" of each of four parts in Table 8.4. The method of calculation is the same as that in Chapter 7 (see Appendix 7C).

Since we already know the gain of moving from non-cooperation to cooperation in logarithm, we may calculate the actual amount of real GDP which is required to increase (if Δ is positive) so that the economy may move from the non-cooperative equilibrium to the cooperative equilibrium. This is calculated by taking anti-logarithm. For example, in Part I of Table 8.4, "Gain Δ to Coop, log," that is, the gain to move to cooperative equilibrium from Nash equilibrium is -3.328, from a follower is -3.451, and from a leader is -3.359, all in logarithm.

In terms of real GDP, this is equivalent to $-\exp(\text{abs}(-3.386)) = -27.890, -31.539$, and -28.753, all in NTD billion. These are actual loss of real GDP by moving from non-cooperative equilibrium to cooperative equilibrium. For Taiwan, the gain is all negative, and for the USA the gain is all positive.

Table 8.4: Gains or Losses from Policy Coordination

The General Cases, Taiwan with the USA and Japan

Weights	$w_1=$ 0.8 $h=$ 0.1					$w_1^*=$ 0.5 $h^*=$ 0.9				
	for Taiwan and Korea					for the USA and Japan				
		Tgt	Coop	Nash	Follr	Ldr		Tgt	Coop	Nash	Follr	Ldr
1	2	3	4	5	6	7	8	9	10	11	12	13
I. Taiwan and the United States												
	Twn **p = 4.5**						**USA p* = 4.5**					
MS in log	m	**6.4**	60.310	21.590	26.436	21.430	m*	**6.2**	8.639	8.226	5.231	8.216
GDP in log	q	**7.7**	14.691	7.787	7.710	7.756	q*	**8.3**	4.754	2.345	2.299	2.334
p_c in log	pc	**4.4**	3.539	5.528	4.527	5.534	pc*	**4.4**	4.472	6.044	4.589	6.047
Utility			**-4.793**	-0.130	-0.002	-0.130			**-4.793**	-9.542	-9.012	-9.577
		$T^\#$	W^C	U^N	U^F	U^L	$T^{*\#}$	W^{*C}	U^{*N}	U^{*F}	U^{*L}
% change in Utility@				-97.3	-100.0	-97.3				99.1	88.0	99.8
Gain Δ to Coop, log				-3.328	-3.451	-3.359				1.897	1.627	1.910
Gain,GDP (NT$b)	3884			-27.890	-31.539	-28.758	(US$b)		4885	6.666	5.086	6.747
% of 1990 GDP				-0.718	-0.812	-0.740				0.136	0.104	0.138
II. Taiwan and Japan												
	Twn **p = 4.5**						**Jpn p* = 4.5**					
MS in log	m	**6.4**	38.864	-7.506	3.065	-7.196	m*	**11.2**	7.726	16.758	11.027	16.713
GDP in log	q	**7.7**	16.134	7.447	7.492	7.513	q*	**12.6**	8.972	6.814	5.789	6.834
p_c in log	pc	**4.4**	9.408	7.898	7.273	7.912	pc*	**4.5**	5.936	9.787	7.249	9.768
Utility			**-6.521**	-1.249	-0.842	-1.247			**-6.521**	-15.358	-13.486	-15.249
%, Utility@				-80.8	-87.1	-80.9				135.5	106.8	133.8
Gain Δ to Coop, log				-3.386	-3.566	-3.449				4.420	2.507	4.474
Gain,GDP (NT$b)	3884			-29.548	-35.359	-31.456	(Yen b)		404820	83.061	12.263	87.692
% of 1990 GDP				-0.761	-0.910	-0.810				0.021	0.003	0.022

(Continued)

Table 8.4: (*Continued*)

The General Cases, Korea with the USA and Japan

Weights	w_1= 0.8	h=	0.1				$w_1{}^*$= 0.5	h*=	0.9			
	for Taiwan and Korea						for the USA and Japan					
		Tgt	Coop	Nash	Follr	Ldr		Tgt	Coop	Nash	Follr	Ldr
1	2	3	4	5	6	7	8	9	10	11	12	13
III. Korea and the United States												
	Kor₁ p = 4.3						USA p* = 4.5					
MS in log	m	**8.5**	2.709	-5.934	-2.742	-5.930	m*	**6.2**	10.855	11.369	10.700	11.369
GDP in log	q	**11.1**	11.778	10.859	10.805	10.860	q*	**8.3**	4.960	5.078	4.883	5.078
pc in log	pc	**4.3**	6.510	5.554	5.839	5.555	pc*	**4.4**	7.131	7.350	7.104	7.350
Utility			**-4.255**	-0.181	-0.272	-0.181			**-4.255**	-4.771	-4.747	-4.771
		$T^\#$	W^C	U^N	U^{FL}	U^{LF}		$T^{*\#}$	W^{*C}	U^{*N}	U^{*FL}	U^{*LF}
%, Utility@				-95.8	-93.6	-95.8				12.1	11.5	12.1
Gain Δ to Coop, log				-2.960	-2.874	-2.961				0.338	0.301	0.338
Gain, GDP (Won, b)		131263		-19.30	-17.72	-19.31	(US$b)		4885	1.40	1.35	1.40
% of 1990 GDP				-0.0147	-0.0135	-0.0147				0.0287	0.0277	0.0287
IV. Korea and Japan												
	Kor p = 4.3						Jpn p* = 4.5					
MS in log	m	**8.5**	37.893	10.191	14.874	12.340	m*	**11.20**	11.749	19.858	17.080	19.371
GDP in log	q	**11.1**	15.176	10.498	10.543	10.936	q*	**12.6**	8.669	8.899	8.282	8.940
pc in log	pc	**4.3**	11.672	11.876	11.311	11.914	pc*	**4.5**	7.868	9.123	8.448	9.073
Utility			**-7.237**	-5.885	-5.040	-5.808			**-7.237**	-8.768	-8.558	-8.577
%, Utility@				-18.7	-30.4	-19.8				21.1	18.3	18.5
Gain Δ to Coop, log				-1.333	-1.852	-1.734				0.949	0.663	0.825
Gain, GDP (Won b)		131263		-3.792	-6.373	-5.661	(Yen b)		404820	2.582	1.940	2.281
% of 1990 GDP				-0.003	-0.005	-0.004				0.00064		0.00056
											0.00048	

Notes: MS = Money Supply. @ "% change in Utility" = $(U^X - W^C) * 100/W^C$.

What is the actual gain or loss in terms of real GDP? Since we already know Taiwan's GDP in 1990 was NT $3,384 billion (see Column q of Table 8.1, Taiwan), which is listed again in the bordered cell for each country in Table 8.4, we may estimate the percentage of 1990 GDP required to move from non-cooperative to cooperative equilibrium based on the current real GDP.

For the case of Taiwan, her loss of utility moving from the Nash equilibrium is NT $27.890 billion. Since Taiwan's 1990 real GDP was NT $3,884 billion (see the box), the loss is mere 0.718% of its real GDP. Similarly, we can calculate the other losses in terms of the "% of 1990 GDP" from follower to cooperative, 0.812%, from leader to cooperative, 0.740%, respectively.

As for the restricted cases, the optimal money supply and the utility at the Stackelberg equilibrium of a small country, whether the small country acts as a follower or a leader, is the same as the utility at the Nash non-cooperative equilibrium. Similarly, the optimal money supply and the utility at the Stackelberg equilibrium of a large country, whether the large country operates as a leader or a follower, also coincides with the utility at the Nash non-cooperative equilibrium. Thus, all the utilities at non-cooperative equilibria are the same. Since the relations between the Nash utility and cooperative utility have been explored in Chapter 7 (see also Hsiao and Hsiao, 1994b), we skip the restricted cases for the sake of brevity in this chapter.

8.6   The Findings

The calculations in Appendixes 8A and 8B are so involved and the results in Table 8.4 are so complicated and entangled that it is best to illustrate them in a figure. Figure 8.1 illustrates the main results of Table 8.4, which is similar to the summary table of Table 7.9 of Chapter 7.

In Figure 8.1, utilities are measured on the negative axes (the third quadrant). The horizontal axis measures the utility at Nash and Stackelberg equilibria. The right vertical axis measures the utility at cooperative equilibrium. Its origin is located well above the upper right corner of the diagram, and only the range between -4 and -7.5 along the vertical axis and 0 and -10 along the horizontal axis are shown. The LL line is the 45-degree line from the hidden origin and shows utilities at the cooperative equilibrium. The left-hand-side axis of the diagram shows the part number of Table 8.4.

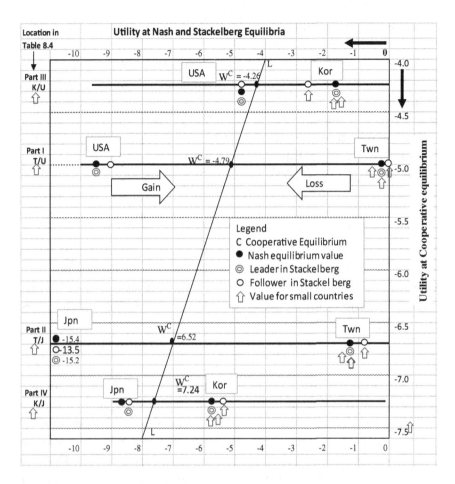

Figure 8.1: Gains or Losses from Policy Cooperation
From Table 8.4, Row "Utility"

The double white circle shows the utility of the country as a leader, and the single white circle represents the utility of a country as a follower in relation to the other country presented. The position of Nash utility is shown by a black filled circle. The utility of the small country is indicated by upward arrow. Any point on the left side of the LL line moving toward the LL (45-degree) line will be utility gaining and a point on the right side of the LL line moving toward it will be utility losing. The size of utility gain or loss by moving to the cooperative equilibrium is proportional to the distance from the LL line.

For convenience, Part I (Taiwan with the USA) of Table 8.4 may be illustrated in Figure 8.1 as follows: Given a cooperative utility at $W^C = -4.793$ on the LL line, we may find the utility of USA as a leader at $U^{*L} = -9.577$ (double white circle) and as a follower (single white circle) at $U^{*F} = -9.012$ (overlapped in the figure). We also find Taiwan as a follower (single white circle with an arrow) at $U^F = -0.002$ and as a leader (double circle with an arrow) at $U^L = -0.130$. The Nash utility for the US is located at $U^{*N} = -9.542$ (the black circle) and that for Taiwan at $U^N = -0.130$ (the black circle with an arrow).

Note that in Part II, the utility of Japan for Nash equilibrium and leader and follower of Stackelberg equilibrium (in dealing with Taiwan) should be much longer toward the left side of the diagram than the position shown (as indicated by numbers). They are outliers of our estimates.

Several interesting characteristics appear from the diagram.

(1) All the three non-cooperative utilities of small countries are located to the right of the LL line, and most of them are close to zero. This shows that the small countries will lose by moving to the cooperative equilibrium and most will lose considerably. The exception is the case of Korea and Japan in Part IV. The Nash utility and utilities of Korea as a leader or as a follower are close to the LL line, showing that the losses of moving from non-cooperative equilibria to cooperative equilibrium are relatively small.

(2) All non-cooperative utilities of large countries are located to the left of the LL line, and most of them are close to the LL line, except the case of Japan in Part II. This shows that the large country will gain by moving to the cooperative equilibrium, and the gain is relatively small. The exception is Part II, which shows that Japan will gain considerably in cooperation with Taiwan by moving from non-cooperative equilibria to cooperative equilibrium with Taiwan.

(3) For simplicity, we did not show the four restricted cases in the diagram. They would be in the middle part of the diagram. They are clustered in the range from −5.5 to −6.0 of cooperative utilities. In these restricted cases, it can be shown that the Nash, leader, and follower equilibria coincide for each country. In our model, the restriction of the parameters of the small country in the large country's regression equations makes the three non-cooperative equilibria indistinguishable. Hence, we may ignore the four restricted cases.

(4) In all four general cases, as shown in Figure 8.1, when we make a direct comparison between a small country and a large country, the small country is better-off in non-cooperative equilibria than in the cooperative equilibrium, and a large country is better-off in cooperative equilibria than in the non-cooperative equilibrium.

(5) For the general cases shown in Table 8.4, the utilities of Nash and leader equilibria tend to be the same, but both tend to be different from the utility of the follower equilibrium, which generally has higher utility.

(6) All the three non-cooperative equilibria tend to cluster together. Thus, the results of Chapter 7 hold without additional discussion of the Stackelberg equilibrium, the derivation of which is much more difficult.

(7) Among the large countries (the US and Japan), cooperation with Taiwan will generally bring higher utility gain than the cooperation with Korea. Thus, the large countries would more likely cooperate with Taiwan than with Korea.

(8) Among the small countries, the losses in utilities by moving from non-cooperative equilibria to the cooperative equilibrium with the United States and Japan are generally higher for Taiwan and lower for Korea. Thus, Korea seems to be easier to cooperate with the United States and Japan.

(9) For the large countries, the Nash and Stackelberg utilities of non-cooperation are generally higher with Korea than with Taiwan. In other words, in terms of cooperation, for both the United States and, especially, Japan, the gain in utilities

by moving from non-cooperative equilibria to the cooperative equilibrium with Taiwan is generally higher than that with Korea. Thus, the United States and Japan are rather eager to cooperate with Taiwan than with Korea. This seems to be consistent with the actual observation of triangular trade relations between Japan, Taiwan, and the United States (Hsiao and Hsiao, 1995).

(10) In all cases, however, the large countries generally gain slightly from cooperation with the small countries as compared with non-cooperation.

(11) In all cases, if anything, for the small countries, cooperation with the United States will yield higher utility than that with Japan.

(12) It may be interesting to note that, in the general cases, except Part III (Korea with the United States), the small countries lose more by acting as followers in the Stackelberg equilibrium as compared with the Nash equilibrium or acting as leader, and the large countries gain slightly more by acting as leaders in the Stackelberg equilibrium.

In summary, since it is simply out of the question that a small country acts as a leader, or a large country acts as a follower, the fact that the utilities of all three different non-cooperative equilibria tend to be the same seem to suggest that, whether acting as a follower or as a leader, the small countries are better-off if they act independently. This probably indicates that the best policy for the small countries is to pursue their own interests and follow their own judgments, and minimize the influence of specific policies of the large countries, which, in addition, may be predatory.

The gains or losses of cooperation is one thing, their relative magnitude is another. In terms of actual gain or loss of real GDP due to moving from non-cooperative equilibrium to the cooperative equilibrium, the actual gain or loss is very small, all are less than 1% of real GDP, and for Korea with the United States, the gain or loss is even less than 0.03% of real GDP.

8.7   Some Concluding Observations

In this chapter, we have shown that even if a dominant player is introduced into a game of international policy coordination, the gain from policy coordination is almost the same as that of the Nash equilibrium. The small countries lose by cooperation with the large countries, and the large countries gain slightly by cooperating with the small countries. Thus, the large countries are almost indifferent about cooperation or non-cooperation with the small countries. Our results are consistent with the findings in the literature. Oudiz and Sachs (1984) found the gains from policy coordination among the United States, West Germany, and Japan in mid-1970s to be about 0.5% of GNP in each county. Other studies on the gains of policy coordination among the developed countries using larger and more sophisticated models show similar results (Currie and Levine, 1993; also see Appendix 8C).

The empirical implications derived here seem to suggest that we return to a neoclassical world of free competition. Cooperation is a type of interference of market mechanism. Social welfare is maximized when each agent acts in accordance with his/her own benefits. The merit of policy coordination lies on information exchange, rather than all aspects of policy objectives and instruments (Currie and Levine, 1993, p. 63). If recent trade imbalances between Taiwan and Korea with the United States and Japan are manifestations of market failure, then our model does not seem to reflect such short-run adjustment problems.

Furthermore, as a practical problem, many conditions are required to make economic cooperation effective. The policy makers of each country must have a reputation for pre-commitment of the agreed policy, the agreement must be binding, policy information can be exchanged freely, and small-country policy makers should not feel overwhelmed or even threatened by the large countries. These are some of the difficulties faced by the policy makers in small countries. As we have observed in Chapter 7, this probably explains why the active policy coordination has only a limited success among the developed countries, and to our knowledge, has not taken place yet among the developed and developing countries (see Appendix 8C).

Appendix 8A: Calculation of Nash and Cooperative Utilities

We use the same notations of vectors and matrices as appendixes in Chapter 7. For convenience, we use braces $\{a, b\}$ or $\{A, B\}$ to denote a diagonal matrix with scalars a and b or submatrices A and B along the diagonal.

8A.1: *Nash Equilibrium*

As shown in Appendix 7A of Chapter 7, for the first (small) country, we choose m such that

$$U = -(1/2)(T_1 - T_1^{\#})'\widehat{W}_1(T_1 - T_1^{\#}), \qquad (8A.1)$$

is maximized, subject to the constraints $h = 1$, $T_1 = R_{11}x + R_{12}z$.

After deriving the first-order condition as in Eq. (7A.4), the reaction function of the small country is

$$(a, \bar{a})\widehat{W}_1 R_{11}x = (a, \bar{a})\widehat{W}_1(T_1^{\#} - R_{12}z), \qquad (8A.2)$$

which is the same as (7A.5).

Similarly, the reaction function for the large country is

$$(b^*, \bar{b}^*)\widehat{W}_2 R_{21}x = (b^*, \bar{b}^*)\widehat{W}_2(T_2^{\#} - R_{22}z), \qquad (8A.3)$$

which is the same as (7A.6).

Combining (8A.2) and (8A.3) for easy calculation, the Nash equilibrium money supply for both countries will then be given by solving the combined expression of (8A.2) and (8A.3) for $h = h^* = 1$,

$$A\widehat{W} R_1 x = A\widehat{W}(T^{\#} - R_2 z), \qquad (8A.4)$$

where

$$A = \begin{bmatrix} a & \bar{a} & 0 & 0 \\ 0 & 0 & b^* & \bar{b}^* \end{bmatrix}.$$

Denote the solution x of (8A.3) as $x^N = (m^N, m^{*N})'$. Combining the two constraints for the small and large countries, namely,

$T_1 = R_{11}x + R_{12}z$ and $T_2 = R_{21}x + R_{22}z$, and substituting x^N into the constraints, we have

$$T^N = Ry = R(x^N, z)'. \tag{8A.5}$$

The Nash utilities, expressed as a 2×2 diagonal matrix $\{U^N, U^{*N}\}$ for small and large countries are computed simultaneously from

$$(U^N, U^{*N}) = (-1/2)(T^N - T^\#)'\widehat{W}[\{T^N - T^\#\}], \tag{8A.6}$$

which is a 1×2 vector. Note that $(T^N - T^\#)'$ is a 1×4 vector, and

$$\{T^N - T^\#\} = \begin{bmatrix} (T_1^N - T_1^\#) & 0 \\ 0 & (T_2^N - T_2^\#) \end{bmatrix}_{4 \times 2}$$

is a 4×2 diagonal matrix. Note that we use braces $\{\cdot\}$ to denote a diagonal matrix.

After this simplification, we find (8A.6) for the four pairs of Nash equilibrium, between Taiwan and the US, Taiwan and Japan, Korea and the US, and Korea and Japan. The four pairs are shown in the four parts of Columns 5 and 11 of Table 8.4.

8A.2: *Cooperative Equilibrium*

Differentiating the world welfare function (7A.1) with respect to the policy variables $x = (m, m^*)$ and solving for x, we have (see (7A.11)):

$$x^C = (m^c, m^{*c})' = (R_1'\widehat{W}R_1)^{-1}R_1'\widehat{W}(T^\# - R_2z). \tag{8A.7}$$

The corresponding optimal targets are

$$T^C = R_1x^C + R_2z, \tag{8A.8}$$

and the corresponding optimal welfare is

$$W^C = -(1/2)(T^C - T^\#)'\widehat{W}(T^C - T^\#). \tag{8A.9}$$

8A.3: *Derivation of Welfare Gains*

The derivation of this part is the same as that in Appendix 7A of Chapter 7. The welfare gain from cooperation measured in units of GNP (see Oudiz and Sachs, 1985) is defined as quantity Δ such that

$$W^C = U^N(q^N + \Delta, p_c^N). \tag{8A.10}$$

Here, the weights w_1, w_2, h, and h^* are taken differently, as shown in the upper part of Table 8.4.

Appendix 8B: Calculation of Stackelberg Utilities

In this section, we first show that the small country is a follower and the large country is a leader. Since theoretically we may treat the two countries symmetric, we also discuss the case when the small country is a leader and the large country a follower. Lastly, we show that the two cases can be treated simultaneously in computation of the lost functions (Hsiao, 1993).

Case I. The small country is a follower, the large country is a leader

Small country's reaction function is the same as (8A.2) with m^* given by the large country.

The large country maximizes

$$U^* = -\frac{1}{2}(T_2 - T_2^\#)'\widehat{W}_2(T_2 - T_2^\#), \tag{8B.1}$$

with respect to m^*, subject to the small country's reaction function (8A.2) and the large country's own constraint

$$T_2 = R_{21}x + R_{22}z.$$

We may simplify the constraints by eliminating the reaction function. For convenience, rewriting the coefficient $(a, \bar{a})\widehat{W}_1 R_{11} \equiv (\alpha, \beta)$ on the LHS of (8A.2) as $\alpha = (a, \bar{a})(w_1 a, w_2 \bar{a})'$, $\beta = (a, \bar{a})(w_1 b, w_2 \bar{b})'$ (see (7B.1)), we have

$$\alpha m + \beta m^* = \gamma, \tag{8B.2}$$

where γ is the right-hand side of (8A.2).

Solving (8B.2) for m in terms of m^*, and substituting into $x = (m, m^*)'$. Then

$$T_2^L = R_{21} x^{*L} + R_{22} z, \qquad (8B.3)$$

where $x^{*L} = ((\gamma - \beta m^*)/\alpha, \ m^*)'$, a 2×1 column vector.

Thus, we only need to maximize (8B.1) with respect to m^* subject to (8B.3).

The result of maximization is similar to (8A.3), with $(b^*, \ \bar{b}^*)$ now substituted by $(b_s^*, \ \bar{b}_s^*)$:

$$(b_s^*, \ \bar{b}_s^*) \, \widehat{W}_2 R_{21} x^{*L} = (b_s^*, \ \bar{b}_s^*) \widehat{W}_2 (T_2^\# - R_{22} z), \qquad (8B.4)$$

where

$$(b_s^*, \ \bar{b}_s^*) \equiv \left(b^* - \left(\frac{\beta a^*}{\alpha} \right), \ \bar{b}^* - \left(\frac{\beta \bar{a}^*}{\alpha} \right) \right).$$

To solve for m^* in (8B.4), we decompose x^{*L} into two vectors,

$$x^{*L} = x^{*L1} + x^{*L2} m^*,$$

where $x^{*L1} = (\gamma/\alpha, 0)'$, $x^{*L2} = (-\beta/\alpha, 1)'$, the 2×1 column vectors. Substituting into (8B.4) and rearranging, we have the money supply of the large country when the large country is the leader:

$$(b_s^*, \ \bar{b}_s^*) \widehat{W}_2 R_{21} x^{*L2} m^{*L} = (b_s^*, \ \bar{b}_s^*) \widehat{W}_2 (T_2^\# - R_{22} z - R_{21} x^{*L1}). \qquad (8B.5)$$

Substituting m^{*L} into the small country's reaction function (8B.2), we obtain the money supply m^F of the small country when the small country is the follower:

$$m^F = (\gamma - \beta m^{*L})/\alpha. \qquad (8B.6)$$

Using m^F and m^{*L}, the policy variable x^{*L} is now rewritten as

$$x^{FL} \equiv (m^F, m^{*L})',$$

where x^{FL} denotes the vector of the policy variables in which the small country is a follower and the large country is a leader (note that FL is ordered from small to large country).

The large country's target can be derived from (8B.3),

$$T_2^L = (q^{*L}, p_c^{*L})',$$

and its utility function is

$$U^{*L} = -\frac{1}{2}(T_2^L - T_2^{\#})' \widehat{W}_2 (T_2^L - T_2^{\#}). \qquad (8B.7)$$

The small country's target as the follower will be

$$T_1^F = (q^F, p_c^F)' = R_{11} x^{FL} + R_{12} z, \qquad (8B.8)$$

and its utility function is

$$U^F = -\frac{1}{2}(T_1^F - T_1^{\#})' \widehat{W}_1 (T_1^F - T_1^{\#}). \qquad (8B.9)$$

Case II. The small country is a leader, and the large country is a follower

In this case, large country's reaction function is the same as (8A.3). Again, we take $h = h^* = 1$. Write (8A.3) as

$$\alpha^* m + \beta^* m^* = \gamma^*, \qquad (8B.10)$$

and substituting into T_1, we have the target variable when the small country is a leader:

$$T_1^L = R_{11} x^L + R_{12} z, \qquad (8B.11)$$

where

$$x^L = (m, (\gamma^* - \alpha^* m)/\beta^*)'.$$

Substituting T_1^L for T_1 in (8A.1), the small country then maximizes U in (8A.1) subject to (8B.11). The first-order condition is similar to (8A.2):

$$(a_s, \bar{a}_s) \widehat{W}_1 R_{11} x^L = (a_s, \bar{a}_s) \widehat{W}_1 (T_1^{\#} - R_{12} z), \qquad (8B.12)$$

where

$$(a_s, \bar{a}_s) \equiv \left(a - \frac{\alpha^* b}{\beta^*}, \bar{a} - \frac{\alpha^* b}{\beta^*} \right).$$

As in Case I, let

$$x^L = x^{L1} + x^{L2} m,$$

where $x^{L1} = (0, \gamma^*/\beta^*)$, $x^{L2} = (1, -\alpha^*/\beta^*)$. Substituting into (8B.12), we have the money supply m^L of the small country when the small country is the leader:

$$(a_s, \bar{a}_s)\widehat{W}_1 R_{11} x^{L2} m^L = (a_s, \bar{a}_s)\widehat{W}_1 (T_1^\# - R_{12}z - R_{11}x^{L1}).$$

$$(8\text{B}.13)$$

Finally, substituting m^L into (8B.10), we have the money supply m^{*F} of the large country when the large country is the follower:

$$m^{*F} = (\gamma^* - \alpha^* m^L)/\beta^*. \qquad (8\text{B}.14)$$

Using m^L and m^{*F}, x^L is now rewritten as

$$x^{LF} \equiv (m^L, m^{*F})',$$

where x^{LF} denotes the vector of the policy variables in which the small country is a leader and the large country is a follower.

The small country's target is given by $T_1^L = (q^L, p_c^L)'$ in (8B.11), and its utility function is

$$U^L = -\frac{1}{2}(T_1^L - T_1^\#)'\widehat{W}_1(T_1^L - T_1^\#). \qquad (8\text{B}.15)$$

Similarly, for the large country as the follower, we have

$$T_2^F = (q^{*F}, p_c^{*F}) = R_{21}x^{LF} + R_{22}z, \qquad (8\text{B}.16)$$

and

$$U^{*F} = -\frac{1}{2}(T_2^F - T_2^\#)'\widehat{W}_2(T_2^F - T_2^\#). \qquad (8\text{B}.17)$$

Computational Procedure

To facilitate numerical computation, similar to the Nash Equilibrium case in which (8A.2) and (8A.3) are combined into (8A.4), we may combine (8B.5) and (8B.13) as follows:

$$A_s \widehat{W} \widehat{R}_1 \hat{X} y = A_s \widehat{W}(T^\# - R_2 z - \widehat{R}_1 v), \qquad (8\text{B}.18)$$

where

$$A_s = \begin{bmatrix} a_s & \bar{a}_s & 0 & 0 \\ 0 & 0 & b_s^* & \bar{b}_s^* \end{bmatrix}_{2\times 4}, \quad y = \begin{bmatrix} m^L \\ m^{*L} \end{bmatrix}_{2\times 1},$$

$$R_1 = \begin{bmatrix} R_{11} & 0 \\ 0 & R_{21} \end{bmatrix}_{4\times 4}, \quad \hat{X} = \begin{bmatrix} x^{L2} & 0 \\ 0 & x^{*L2} \end{bmatrix}_{4\times 2},$$

and $v = (x^{L1}, x^{*L1})' = (0, \gamma^*/\beta^*, \gamma/\alpha, 0)'_{4\times 1}$.

The right-hand side of (8B.18) is a 2×1 vector and (m^L, m^{*L}) can be derived simultaneously by matrix inversion. The corresponding money supply, m^F and m^{*F} can be derived from (8B.6) and (8B.14), respectively. Thus, we have the pairs

$$x^{FL} \equiv (m^F, m^{*L})', \quad \text{and} \quad x^{LF} \equiv (m^L, m^{*F})'. \qquad (8\text{B}.19)$$

Again, to facilitate computation of the estimated targets and utilities, we may combine the results in Case I and Case II as follows. For Case I, using (m^F, m^{*L}), we have

$$T^{FL} = \begin{bmatrix} T_1^F \\ T_2^L \end{bmatrix} = R(x^{FL}, z)', \qquad (8\text{B}.20)$$

and from (8B.7) and (8B.9),

$$U^{FL} \equiv (U^F, U^{*L}) = -\frac{1}{2}(T^{FL} - T^{\#})' \widehat{W}_2 \{T^{FL} - T^{\#}\}, \qquad (8\text{B}.21)$$

where the 4×4 quadratic coefficient matrix is pre-multiplied by a 1×4 vector and post-multiplied by a 4×2 diagonal matrix:

$$\{T^{FL} - T^{\#}\} = \begin{bmatrix} (T_1^L - T_1^{\#}) & 0 \\ 0 & (T_2^L - T_2^{\#}) \end{bmatrix}_{4 \times 2}.$$

Similarly, for Case II,

$$T^{LF} \equiv \begin{bmatrix} T_1^L \\ T_2^F \end{bmatrix} = R(x^{LF}, z)', \qquad (8\text{B}.22)$$

and from (8B.15) and (8B.17),

$$U^{LF} \equiv (U^L, U^{*F}) = -\frac{1}{2}(T^{LF} - T^{\#})' \widehat{W} \{T^{LF} - T^{\#}\}, \qquad (8\text{B}.23)$$

where

$$\{T^{LF} - T^{\#}\} = \begin{bmatrix} (T_1^L - T_1^{\#}) & 0 \\ 0 & (T_2^F - T_2^{\#}) \end{bmatrix}_{4 \times 2}.$$

Hence, the computational procedure simplifies to find matrix multiplication of (8B.18), (8B.20), (8B.21), and (8B.23).

Oudiz–Sachs' welfare gain from cooperation measured in units of GDP under Stackelberg regime may be defined as in (8A.10), in which superscript N should be substituted by superscripts FL or LF.

Appendix 8C: Policy Coordination or Economic War?

Note that, if we do not consider the monetary policy, the extreme opposite side of policy coordination is economic war, as exemplified by the recent trade war between the United States and China.

As we have mentioned in the Introduction of this book, since the beginning of 2017 under the Trump Administration, we see the rapid rise of the US protectionist policy, resulting in the US and China Trade War.

Using static multicountry multisector computable general equilibrium (CGE) model, Bouët and Laborde (2018) studied the impact of trade war on the welfare (GDP) of both countries. Their method is different from our open macroeconomic model based on Mundell–Fleming–Dornbusch analysis with econometric techniques.

Bouët and Laborde found that, overall, the literature concludes that (a) in global trade wars, all countries lose in terms of welfare; (b) a trade war between a large country and a small country can result in gains for the large country, but losses for the small one; and (c) all countries cannot gain from a trade war, and cooperation may lead to a better solution for all countries. However, their own conclusion of the study is that trade war systematically decreases global welfare. Considering our conclusions of Chapters 7 and 8 that welfare gain from policy coordination results in small gain for large countries and loss for small countries, with a risk of oversimplification, we may point out again that the neoclassical economic system of free competition is still the best modus operandi among the world economies. More theoretical and empirical studies are called for. Note that our presentation is based on the basic international open economy macroeconomic model and differs from the CGE method.

Acknowledgments

We thank Professor M. Jan Dutta and the Brandeis University for arranging the successful Sixth Biennial Conference on United States–Asia Economic Relations. This chapter consists of part of the paper given at the *Post-Conference Workshop on New Frontiers in Economic Theory*, the 1993 Far Eastern Meeting of the Econometric Society, at Chung-Hua Institute for Economic Research, Taipei, Taiwan, June 1993. We have explored the dynamic discrete version of the Mundell–Fleming–Dornbusch macroeconometric model in the 1993 paper. Comments, suggestions, and hospitality of Professors M. Jan Dutta, Tzong-Shian Yu, and Joseph C. Lee, and other participants of the Conference and the Workshop are greatly appreciated. Postscript: The tables, figure, and conclusions of this chapter had been rearranged for clarity. Appendix 8C was added for this chapter.

References

Bouët, Antoine and Laborde, David (2018). US trade wars in the twenty-first century with emerging countries: Make America and its partners lose again. *The World Economy* 41 (9), 2276–2319. Downloaded in September 2018 from SSRN: https://ssrn.com/abstract=3245483 or http://dx.doi.org/10.1111/tw ec.12719.

Canzoneri, M. B. and P. Minford (1988). When international policy coordination matters: An empirical analysis. *Applied Economics* 20, 1137–1154.

Cooper, R. (1985). Economic interdependence and coordination of economic policies. In *Handbook of International Economics* (Vol. II.), R. Jones and P. Kennen (Eds.). Amsterdam: Elsevier Science Publishers, B.V., pp. 1195–1234.

Currie, D. and P. Levine (1993). *Rules, Reputation and Macroeconomic Policy Coordination.* Cambridge, UK: Cambridge University Press.

Hamada, K. (1974). Alternative exchange systems and the interdependence of monetary policies. In *National Monetary Policies and The International Financial System*, R. Z. Aliber (Ed.). Chicago, IL: The University of Chicago Press.

Henderson, J. M. and R. E. Quandt (1971). *Microeconomic Theory: A Mathematical Approach* (2nd edn.). New York: McGraw-Hill, Inc.

Hsiao, F. S. T. (1993). International policy coordination and strategy in small open economies. Presented at the post-conference workshop on New Frontiers in Economic Theory, the 1993 Far Eastern Meeting of the Econometric Society, Chung-Hua Institution for Economic Research, Taipei, Taiwan.

Hsiao, F. S. T. and M. C. W. Hsiao (1994a). Gains from policy coordination between Taiwan and the United States-On the games governments play. In M. Dutta and R. Shiratori (Eds.), *Asia-Pacific Economies: 1990s and Beyond*, Research in Asian Economic Studies (Vol. 5). Greenwich, CT: JAl Press, Inc., pp. 239–264.

Hsiao, F. S. T. and M. C. W. Hsiao (1994b). Monetary policy coordination between large and small countries: An empirical study. *Journal of Economic Development* **19** (2), 7–46.

Hsiao, F. S. T. and M. C. W. Hsiao (1995). Taiwanese Economic Development and Foreign Trade. In *Economic Development of Taiwan–Early Experiences and the Pacific Trade Triangle*. Singapore: World Scientific.

Hsiao, F. S. T. and M. C. W. Hsiao (2015). *Economic Development of Taiwan–Early Experiences and the Pacific Trade Triangle*. Singapore: World Scientific.

International Financial Statistics (IFS) (1993). *On Tape*. Washington, D.C.: International Monetary Fund.

McKibbin, W. J. and J. D. Sachs (1991). *Global Linkages, Macroeconomic Interdependence and Cooperation in the World Economy*. Washington, D.C.: The Brookings Institution.

Oudiz, G. and J. Sachs (1984). Macroeconomic policy coordination among the industrial economies. *Brooking Papers on Economic Activities* **15** (1), 1–75.

Taiwan Statistical Data Book (TSDB) (1992). Taipei, Taiwan: Council for Economic Planning and Development.

Chapter 9

Epilog — The Global Economy, Economic Policy, and Development Strategies

9.1 Introduction

In the previous chapters, our studies of development strategies of open economies, namely, trade, FDI, and growth in the real sector and stock markets and monetary system in the financial sector, were based on the experiences of the East and Southeast Asian countries some decades ago. It may be appropriate to consider what are the recent conditions of the world economy and the development strategies of open economies in this age of globalization today. In this epilog, with a risk of some repetitions of the previous conclusions in each chapter, we show the relevance of our research results in the broader comparative perspectives of the current global economy and world economic development, as well as from the vantage points of the evolution of economic policy and recent financial development.

In Sections 9.2–9.4, we follow the World Bank's classification of economic development by income level, and review the condition of the three strategies in the real sector, namely, trade, FDI, and growth in the world economy as a whole. Note that trade consists of exports, imports, and balance of trade, and FDI consists of inward- and outward-foreign direct investment. As we explained in the Introduction of this book, in our economic analysis of relations among trade,[1] investment, and growth, we choose exports and inward FDI as the variables of our analysis. We then review these three strategies with economic growth in Section 9.5, discuss them from vantage points of evolution of economic policy in Section 9.6, and relate them with the importance of causality analysis in Section 9.7.

The second half of this book deals with the interactions among the financial system and the real economy. The financial development is also seen as a development strategy of open economies. We first study the causality among the volatilities of the financial and real variables in Section 9.8 and the role of the United States in the Asia-Pacific Region through the stock markets in Section 9.9. We then discuss the possibility of international monetary policy coordination in Section 9.10. We show that the conclusions of our analysis are still valid in current financial development. Section 9.11 concludes.

9.2   The Global Economy and Economic Groups

According to the World Bank (2018), as shown in UNCTADSTAT (2019), the world economies can be classified into four groups based on annual Gross National Income (GNI) per capita in US dollars. They are as follows: (1) low-income economies (GNI per capita less than or equal to \$995), (2) lower-middle-income economies (\$996–3,895), (3) upper-middle-income economics (\$3,896–12,055), and (4) high-income economies (above \$12,055). Figure 9.1 shows the long-run trend of aggregate world GDP from 1970 to 2018, along with

---

[1]Note that trade consists of exports, imports, and balance of trade. As we have explained in the Introduction of this book, in our economic analysis of relations among trade, investment and growth, we choose exports as the variable of our analysis Most of the studies on openness use trade volumes as a measure of openness. However, it is noted that "trade volumes are affected by trade policies, distance to neighbors and trading partners, country size, exchange rate movements, terms of trade changes, and barriers to entry. Consequently, simply using trade volumes to proxy for changes in trade policy may be misleading," and trade shares in GDP are suggested (Harrison and Rodrigues-Clare, 2015, pp. 4081–4082, 4084). Since our variables include GDP separately, we use exports value to measure openness in our causality analysis.

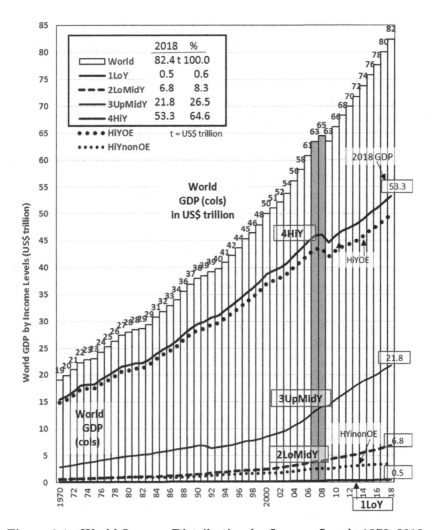

Figure 9.1: World Income Distribution by Income Levels 1970–2018, in US dollar trillion

aggregate GDP of each of these four groups of economies, denoted in the figure as 1LoY, 2LoMidY, 3UpMidY, and 4HiY for easier reading. We may define high-income countries as the developed countries and others as the developing countries, based on the differences in per capita income.

According to UNCTADSTAT (2019), in 2018, the number of economies in the above four groups and their percentage composition in the world were 37 (16.5%) for 1LoY, 48 (21.4%) for 2LoMidY, 58 (25.9%) for 3UpMidY, and 81 (36.2%) for 4HiY, out of a total of 224 countries and regions or economies[2] (not shown in Figure 9.1). Thus, in 2018, there were twice as many high-income economies than low-income economies in the world.

Among them, as of 2019, the economies we studied in this book, namely, the four Asian Newly Industrializing Economics (NIEs: South Korea, Taiwan, Singapore, and Hong Kong), Japan, and the United States are currently in the 4HiY group; China, Malaysia, and Thailand are in the 3UpMidY group; and Indonesia and the Philippines are in the 2LoMiY group. However, as we have observed in the book, the four Asian NIEs (ANIEs) were in the 2LoMidY group during the 1970s and 1980s, and they were in the 3UpMidY group during the 1990s and the 2000s. Similarly, the four ASEAN (ASEAN-4) were in the 1LoY and 2LoMidY during the 1970s to the 1980s and 3UpMidY during the 1990s to the 2000s. Thus, in Chapter 4, we called the four Asian NIEs the first-generation NIEs, and the ASEAN-4 the second-generation Asian NIEs. The development status of these countries was evolving over time and they emerged as developed countries in the last decade (Hsiao and Hsiao, 2017, Chapters 7 and 9).

Based on the data from UNCTADSTAT (2019), Figure 9.1 shows that the 2018 world Gross Domestic Product (GDP) at constant price (of 210) was 82.4 trillion, distributed among the four economic groups as 1LoY 0.5 (0.6%), 2LoMidY 6.8 (8.3%), 3UpMidY 21.8 (26.5%), and 4HiY 53.3 (64.6%) in US dollar trillion (see the numbers next to the legend box and also in the square boxes on the right-hand side edge of Figure 9.1).

---

[2]These numbers are slightly different from the World Bank (2018), which lists only 218 countries and economies, with the composition of 1LoY, 34 (15.6%); 2LoMidY, 47 (21.6%); 3UpMidY, 56 (25.7%); and 4HiY, 81 (37.2%). Note that the data in Figures 9.1–9.3 are taken from UNCTADSTAT (2019), which conveniently provides a complete dataset in Microsoft Excel form.

Figure 9.1 shows that, world GDP has been increasing steadily almost every year since 1970, with the exception of the year 2009, immediately after the global financial crisis of 2007–2008 (see the shaded columns and the data labels above the columns). However, the GDP of 1LoY stayed flat in the last 50 years, maintaining at about US $0.5 trillion or less during those years. The major sources of global economic growth came from the growth of the 4HiY and 3UpMidY, and to a lesser degree, 2LoMidY. Thus, 3UpMidY and 2LoMidY can be considered as the emerging developing countries, which consist of 106 countries (47.3%) in the world. Our analysis in this book studies the development strategies related to exports, FDI, and GDP (and financial development) of the successful and comparatively homogeneous Asian NIEs and ASEAN-4, and shows how their early experiences can be valuable paradigms for these developing countries to advance to a higher level of development.

For reference, Figure 9.1 also shows the total GDP of high-income OECD countries (HiYOE) and high-income non-OECD countries (HiYnonOE), which consist of 37 and 44 economies, respectively. Japan, South Korea, and the US are in the HiYOE economies, and Taiwan, Singapore, and Hong Kong are in the HiYnonOE economies. These two groups are plotted in Figure 9.1 for their GDP (and also in Figure 9.2 for Exports and Figure 9.3 for FDI) as a heavy dotted line in the upper part of the figure and a light dotted line in the lower part, respectively.

Note that 4HiY and HiYOE are very close to each other and also grew together, except during the past two decades. It shows that the 4HiY economies consist mostly of OECD countries, and the rest of the high-income economies are in the non-OECD group. Apparently, these two groups have quite different total GDP levels.

9.3   World Exports and Economic Groups

Through the exchange of goods and services between countries, foreign trade, either in developing countries or developed countries, gives us more goods and services than a country's own domestic goods and services. It enhances efficient production of goods and services through comparative advantage of resources among countries.

Under free trade, better qualities and lower prices will be available for the people, and thus increase the social welfare of a country and promote growth and development. Thus, foreign trade is closely related to economic growth.

Figure 9.2 shows the world exports by income levels defined in Section 9.2, which is taken from UNCTADSTAT (2019) exports data with the World Bank classification of the world economies. The data for 2018 are shown inside the table next to the legend box. It shows that the world exports value was US $19.5 trillion in 2018. Among them, 1LoY economies exported 70 billion (0.3% of total); 2LoMidY economies, 1.3 trillion (6.6%); 3UpMidY economies, 5.1 trillion (26.5%); and 4HiY economies, 13 trillion (66.6%). Thus, in 2018, almost 93% of world exports were performed by the upper-middle-income (3UpMidY) and high-income (4HiY) economies.

Note that the pattern of the time-series trend for the world exports and that for the four groups of economies are very similar during the early period (1970–1980) and also during the following period from 1981 to the mid-2000s. The series were very well "behaved." The pattern after 2008, namely, after the great global financial crisis of 2007–2008, has been quite irregular and fluctuating, which is similar to the pattern experienced by the NIEs and ASEAN-4 as discussed in Chapters 3 and 4 (see Figure 4.1). The synchronization of the time-series pattern during the two periods indicates that the world exports were heavily influenced by the global economic environment and world business cycles, but not so much by the world trend of GDP, as GDP increased steadily.

Compared with Figure 9.1, the fluctuation in exports in the past decade since the financial crisis did not seem to have an impact on the GDP growth for all the four income level economies. At first glance, this apparently belies the conventional wisdom that trade is the engine of growth or is the handmaiden of growth.

Note the consistent sequence of income groups in Figure 9.2. It moves from 1LoY to 2LoMidY to 3UpMidY, and then to 4HiY. The pattern of upward movement in exports value of these four groups of economies is the same as Figure 9.1. It shows clearly that the higher the GDP level, the higher the exports level. Conversely, we may also

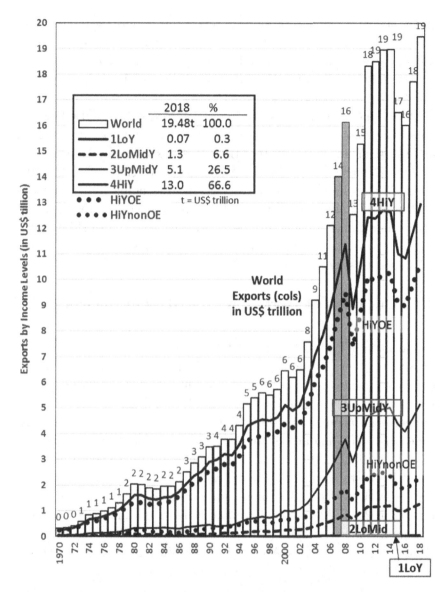

Figure 9.2: World Exports Distribution by Income Levels 1970–2018, in US$ trillion

state that the higher the exports level, the higher the GDP level. This relationship holds for all income levels. Thus, visually, it is very difficult to ascertain whether GDP growth causes exports or exports causes the GDP growth. Note that 1LoY economies are completely isolated from global trade.

The same causality observation can be said about OECD countries. The close parallel between the HiYOE, the upper dotted line, and the 4HiY line indicates that the world's exports were done mostly by OECD members before the global financial crisis of 2007–2008. After 2009, however, exports of high-income non-OECD countries (HiYnonOE), along with 3UpMidY countries, also increased along with other higher income groups, contributing to the world exports. On the other hand, the exports of the low-income economies (1LoY) continued to stay flat for over 50 years.

9.4   The Trend of World Inward FDI and Economic Groups

While inward FDI are important in developing countries for technology transfer,[3] stimulating domestic investment and increasing employment, among others, it is also important in developed countries for the same reasons for efficient allocation of resources through mergers and acquisition to maximize global profit, and at the same time raise the standard of living in the host countries. In fact, the UNCTADSTAT (2019) data charted in Figure 9.3 show that (also listed in the table next to the legend in Figure 9.3), in 2018, global total FDI was US \$1.3 trillion, down from the highest of US \$2.0 trillion in 2015. Among \$1.3 trillion FDI, \$810 billion (62.3%) went to high-income economies (4HiY), and only \$49 billion (38%) went to the developing countries. Although the low-income economies (1LoY)

---

[3]Some economists and policy makers question whether there could be technology transfer, instead of "stealing" technology, like the US accused Chinese firms in recent years. We have shown elsewhere that, in the case of Taiwan, the 1970s surveys showed what we called "the slanted structure" of technology transfer to local firms, namely, the higher the foreign share in manufacturing firms, the higher the adaptation of foreign technology as compared with completely native-owned firms (Hsiao and Hsiao, 2015, pp. 432–434, 558–560).

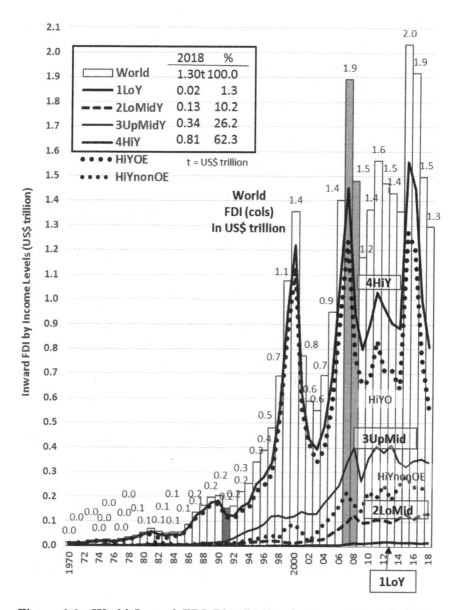

Figure 9.3: World Inward FDI Distribution by Income Levels 1970–2018, in US$ trillion

need FDI the most for development, only as little as US$ 20 billion (namely, 0.02 trillion, only about 1.3% of total FDI)[4] went to low-income economies in 2018.

Note the extreme volatility of the FDI over the years. It is more pronounced after the year 2000, especially after the global financial crisis of 2007–2008. This is the same as the volatility we found in the individual Asian NIEs and ASEAN-4 between 1981 and 2005 in Chapters 3 and 4. The volatility is more pronounced in the high-income economies (4HiY), and at a lesser degree upper-middle-income economies (3UpMidY). By comparison, the volatility only slightly affects the lower-middle-income (2LoMidY) and low-income (1LoY) economies.

Like exports, Figure 9.3 also shows that, in general, the higher the income level of the economies, the higher the FDI, or vice versa, although the correlation between them is rather loose. The data also show that before the global financial crisis of 2007–2008, based on the closeness of the 4HiY and HiYOE lines most of the world's inward FDI was performed by the high-income OECD (HiYOE in Figure 9.3) countries. However, after the crisis, high-income non-OECD (HiYnonOE) and upper-middle-income (3UpMidY) economies started being active, but they were still far behind the OECD countries.

Figure 9.3 also shows that FDI is increasing over time, although very unevenly. This is quite different from the relatively smoothly increasing pattern of world exports shown in Figure 9.2, and is also quite different from the continuously smoothly increasing pattern of world GDP in Figure 9.1.

From the pattern of the time-series trend of income, exports, and FDI, as we have seen in Figures 9.1–9.3, so far as the macro data are concerned, it is rather difficult to ascertain any strong relationship,

---

[4]Before the rounding of the numbers, the amount of FDI that went to 1LoY was $0.017 trillion and the world total FDI was $1.297 trillion, thus we have the 1.31% figure. Note also that, on the left-hand side of Figure 9.3, the total FDI being US $0.0 trillion means that world FDI of that year was, since the vertical axis scale is 0.1 trillion, less than 0.05 trillion. For example, in 1971, the world FDI was 0.014 trillion, which is shown in the figure as 0.0.

except a vague long-run upward pattern among income, exports, and investment of the world economy.

Thus, in conclusion, the volatility of exports and FDI aside, Figures 9.2 and 9.3 show that the increase in exports and inward FDI by upper- and lower-middle-income economies (3UpMidY and 2LoMidY, respectively) during the past two decades indicates the progress of opening up of the economies among these countries. In view of the success of East and Southeast Asian countries, Japan, the Asian NIEs, and China, and to a lesser degree, the ASEAN-4, through exports and inward FDI, scholars and policymakers are interested in finding valuable paradigms for other developing countries and look for development strategies and policies through the relation among exports, FDI, and growth.

9.5 Trade, Investment, and Growth as Development Strategies

As amply shown by the five volumes of the *Handbook of Development Economics*, and pointed out by Rodrik and Rosenzweig (2015) in the Preface of Volume 5, "The policies that impact development are wide ranging" and intricate. In this book, we only considered the relations among three development strategies, namely, promoting foreign exports, attracting foreign direct investment (FDI), and stimulating economic growth, what we called TIG, as the basic development strategies in an open economy (Chapters 3–5). We illustrated these three factors in a basic income determination framework of macroeconomics. As such, the importance of these three factors is not limited to the developing emerging economies. It is also relevant to developed countries.

Economic growth is generally measured by annual change of real GDP. In the 1950s, the Prebisch–Singer thesis observed that, due to lower prices of primary commodities (raw materials and agricultural products produced by the developing countries) and higher prices of industrial goods (produced by developed countries), in the long run, foreign trade will reduce the real GDP of developing countries. Thus, they proposed the import substitution policy as a development strategy, casting a doubt on the export-promotion policy as the engine of growth.

However, as we have pointed out elsewhere (Hsiao and Hsiao, 2017, pp. 206–208), the decade of the 1970s was the beginning of the era of energy saving and high-tech industries. It was the era of electronics, computers, and information equipment. Since the mid-1980s, the developed countries, especially the United States, and the countries in the Asia-Pacific region have increasingly formed a new international vertical division of labor between the United States and advanced European countries in the New Economy of Information and Computer Technology (ICT) or simply information technology (IT). We have seen the rapid economic growth of the Asian countries, especially the newly industrializing economies (NIEs), through exports as the new development strategy. The Asian NIEs were followed by ASEAN, and then China and India through international trade and investment.

The new economy raised the question of whether foreign trade and investment can promote or deteriorate economic growth, whether economic growth enhances trade and FDI, whether foreign trade stimulates FDI, or whether FDI induces foreign trade. Thus, the question of causality among trade, FDI, and economic growth has become the concern among the economists and policymakers.

Government role in promoting economic growth and attracting FDI or encouraging foreign trade (TIG) is part of what we call economic policy, namely, the role of government in economic activities. Historically, government economic policy could not be taken for granted. We would like to review briefly the evolution of government role in economic activities and find the context of these three factors, TIG, in government economic policy.

9.6   Evolution of Economic Policy and Development Strategies

Government economic policy evolved a long way. Adam Smith (1776) considered three functions of the government — simply stated, (1) National defense, (2) Justice (law and order), and (3) Certain public works — in which the cost is so large and the profit is so small that we cannot expect the member(s) of the society to engage. Other than these three functions, Smith pointed out that, as individuals pursue their own interests, the invisible hand of markets would lead to optimal allocation of resources (efficient) without interference from the government. This view prevailed in France in the 18th century as laissez-faire capitalism and spread to the US in the early 19th century during the period of industrial revolution.

As it turned out, the invisible hand applies only when the market is perfectly competitive. In reality, the market is generally not perfect. It is imperfect and inefficient due to oligopoly and monopoly of firms and businesses. By the mid-19th century, problems of unemployment, extreme poverty and inequality, inflation, and unsafe factories appeared and were prevalent, with recurring business cycles. Thus, in 1926, Keynes proclaimed "The End of Laissez-faire" (Keynes, 1926) and called for rethinking of economic policy. His 1936 General Theory (Keynes, 1936) provided the theoretical basis of government spending in general. In particular, it supported job programs as economic policy for solving high unemployment, and the use of monetary and fiscal policies to counter business cycles.

Since the end of WWII, after former colonies gained independence, and especially after the late 1970s, the concern of economic policy shifted to economic growth and development. In addition, after the 2000s, the problems of negative externalities (the spillover effects) like pollution or global warming also become prominent with calls for government regulations. Today, governments play a very important role in economic activities, especially when related to economic strategies for development and growth.[5]

---

[5]In their classic textbook, Samuelson and Nordhaus (2010, pp. 40, 306–308) listed four major functions of the government: (1) Improving economic efficiency (microeconomic issues); (2) stabilizing the economy and boosting economic growth (macroeconomic issues); (3) reducing economic inequality; and (4) conducting international economic policy. In addition, we may add Smith's three roles of government. Boulding (1958, p. v) argued that "Policy is not one thing and principles another; the principles of economic policy are principles of

While there are many functions of the government and categories of economic policy, this book has dealt with the economic policy related to promoting growth through foreign trade and foreign direct investment in open economies, and vice versa, namely, their causal relations in the emerging developing countries in East and Southeast Asia. Cohn (2012) called these three factors the development strategies. He also included other institutional settings like official development assistance (ODA) and the role of international organizations, like World Bank and WTO. But these institutional settings are not a concern in this book.

As usual, every economic policy has its pros and cons, involving different value judgments, and they may result in different or even opposite conclusions. Furthermore, if the purpose of an economic policy is, in general, to promote economic stabilization, economic growth and development, income and wealth equality, or increase social welfare in general, then among the different policies, one policy may be complimentary, or substitutable, or independent to another, especially under the limited resources and government budget constraints.

As an example, in the area of trade policy, a government may choose an import substitution policy with tariffs and quotas, other trade barriers, industry subsidies, and protection. It may also choose an export-promotion policy with export credit, tax incentive for exports, encouraging duty-free raw material imports, etc.[6] In general, these two policies are substitutes to each other, but some specific policies may be complimentary, like industry subsidies and duty-free material imports. The implementation of these policies may also be sequential. Many countries started from the import substitution policy and then evolved into the export-promotion policy, depending on the stage of development, like Taiwan and South Korea in the 1950s and 1960s[7] (Hsiao and Hsiao, 2015, 90, Figure 2.12).

---

economics." However, this is untenable. From the evolution of economic policy, we see policy IS one thing and principles are another.

[6]In an extensive review of the three factors, Harrison and Rodrigues-Clare (2015, pp. 40–41) call these sets of government interventions as industrial policy (IP).

9.7 Importance of Causality Relations in Development Strategies

Under these circumstances, it is important to sort out the causes and effects of different economic policies. However, every country has different social and institutional settings. Therefore, the consequence of economic policy differs with the development stages, social background, and international economic conditions. Thus, the countries we have chosen and studied are more or less homogenous in economic, social and institutional setting as compared with other cross-section groups, to avoid heterogeneity problems and derive some meaningful conclusions. Because of this consideration, in this book, we choose the Asian NIEs and ASEAN-4 as the countries of emerging economies to study and compare.

We have pointed out that, so far as Asian NIEs and ASEAN-4 are concerned, as Figure 3.2 clearly demonstrates, the causality relations among these three development strategies for any individual country are very erratic at best. Thus, it is untenable, if not wrong, to conclude any causality relations from an individual country and extend the conclusions to any other country. Only when we analyze a group of more or less similarly developing country by using panel data analysis are we able to find meaningful causality relations, as

---

[7]Elsewhere (Hsiao and Hsiao, 2015, pp. 157–160) we pointed out that export-promotion policy is not a popular economic strategy or policy even among the developing countries. If we interpret export-promotion policy as an outward-oriented (OO) policy and import substitution policy as the inward-oriented (IO) policy, then according to the World Bank (1987, p. 83), among the 43 countries and areas, in period (A), 1963 to 1973, only the Asian NICs (South Korea, Taiwan, Singapore, and Hong Kong) maintained a strongly outward-oriented policy (SOO); 10 countries, mostly the ASEANs, took a moderately outward-oriented policy (MOO); 12 countries, mostly Latin American countries, took a moderately inward-oriented policy (MIO); and 16 countries, mostly the African countries, maintained a strongly inward-oriented policy (SIO).

However, in period B, 1973–1983, 6 MOO changed to MIO, 3 MIO even changed to SIO, and only one country changed from MIO to MOO. Thus, unlike the popular notion that an outward-oriented (OO) trade policy promotes economic development, many countries stay at MIO or SIO. It appeared that, among the developing countries, the SOO policy of NIEs after the 1970s was rather an exception (Hsiao and Hsiao, 2015, pp. 157–160).

shown in Figures 3.3 and 4.2 for Asian NIEs, ASEAN-4, and China, and also in Figure 4.3 for ANIEs 1 countries and Figure 4.4 for ANIEs 2 countries.

In all these cases, we found that, in general, exports and GDP have bidirectional Granger causality relations (Figures 3.3, 4.2, 4.3, and 4.4), not unidirectional from exports to GDP, as conventional wisdom will predict. This result is also consistent with the Sims' exogeneity test (but not the Granger test) between exports and GDP in Chapter 1. Furthermore, the relations are stronger when the developing countries are advanced (Figure 4.3), and the relations are weaker when the developing countries are less advanced (Figure 4.4). Extending this observation to Figures 9.1–9.3, our findings may explain why GDP of the low-income (1LoY) and lower-middle-income (2LoMidY) economies has stayed very low for many decades since the end of WWII. It also explains why the upper middle-income (3UpMidY) and high-income (4HiY) economies can continue to grow through interaction between exports and the growth of GDP. It also explains that the conventional exports-promotion policy alone by a developing country (through tax breaks, tariffs, or subsidies) may not explain economic growth without considering the effects of growth on exports.

Like exports, the amount of inward FDI generally depends on income level. The higher the income level, the higher the FDI, and almost no FDI went to low-income countries (1LoY) and a very small amount, almost none of the FDI before the global financial crisis of 2007–2008, went to lower middle-income countries (2LoMidY) (Figure 9.3).

Similar to the case of exports, the relations between FDI and GDP for individual countries for Asian NIEs and ASEAN-4 and China are mixed and erratic, as shown in Figure 3.2. A bidirectional causality was seen only in Thailand, and a strong unidirectional causality relation was seen from GDP to FDI in China. However, the results of Chapter 2 on FDI in China indicate that FDI, among other variables, is also a strong explanatory variable of Chinese GDP.

When all three strategies, exports, FDI and GDP, were introduced in causality analysis, an interesting relation appeared. While, as might be expected, FDI unidirectionally causes GDP in the panel data analysis (see Figures 3.3 and 4.2), if the panel data analysis is restricted only to the Asian NIEs (ANIEs 1), GDP also causes FDI. In fact, there is rather strong bidirectional causality between FDI and GDP in the more advanced first-generation ANIEs (ANIEs 1, Figure 4.3), but FDI has no causality relations with GDP among the ASEAN-4, the second-generation ANIEs (ANIEs 2). For ANIEs 2, the FDI is completely isolated (see Figure 4.4). This indicates that FDI could cause GDP growth, and vice versa, in the high-income countries, and have no effect on exports and growth in the low-income countries. This might be because too few and too little FDI went to low-income countries (1LoY and 2LoMidY economies in Figure 9.3). Thus, when we study the effects of FDI on GDP, the level of development and the size of FDI should be considered.

Furthermore, we also found that there is bidirectional causality relation between FDI and exports among more advanced developing economies (Figure 4.3), but no causality relation whatsoever between FDI and exports in the less advanced developing countries (Figure 4.4), This indicates that FDI is most effective on GDP among the higher income countries, and that since higher income countries have strong bidirectional relation between exports and GDP, we found "reinforcing effects" of FDI through exports to GDP (Figures 3.3, 4.2, and 4.3). Thus, the effect of FDI on economic growth is more powerful in the advanced countries (4HiY and 3UpMidY) than the lower developing countries (2LoMidY and 1LoY). The clear result of these reinforcing effects of sequential causality apparently is missing in economic literature.

9.8 Financial Development and the Real Sector

Along with the theory of the invisible hand (Section 9.6), classical economics considered money as a veil. Change in money supply only affects prices and wages, with no effect on the real sector of the economy (output or the structure of economy) in the long run. The dominant topics of economic analysis before WWII were the relations among the real variables like income, taxes, investment, trade, capital, etc. While some economists (for example, Schumpeter (1949, originally published in Germany, 1911)) pointed out the importance of finance in economic development long before WWII, only after the war, and much later, had the importance of money and finance in economic growth been recognized widely as financial development,[8] an important topic on development strategies for open economies.

Financial development is the development of the financial sector, which is a set of financial institutions, instruments, and markets, to reduce the "cost" of the sector. The costs are related to transaction, information, enforcement of regulations and contracts, etc. (World Bank, 2016). Financial development is one of development strategies to promote economic growth and technological progress through pooling savings into investment, facilitating investment decision and foreign investment, optimizing allocation of capital, etc. In this way, financial development contributes to economic growth, but growth also contributes to financial development (World Bank, ibid; Levine, 2005).

The emergence of the New Economy of Information Technology (IT) Revolution intensified the role of money and finance in globalization and in the process of economic development (see Chapters 5 and 6). Since the new IT firms are mostly burgeoning firms, they have to raise capital fund from stock markets rather than from banks. Thus, in addition to the improved banking system, the sound operation of stock markets becomes an important part of financial development. Stock price volatility affects consumer and business confidence, influences consumer spending and business investment, and in turn, impacts on the overall economy and growth. Theoretically, this relationship also works the other way. Other financial factors, like interest rate, money supply, consumer price, and exchange rate, also influence the economy.

In view of the growing importance of these financial variables in developing economies, Chapter 5 uses volatilities (or variations) of these five financial variables. They were specifically chosen from

---

[8]For an extensive survey, see, among others, Beck (2011).

the well-known Mundell–Fleming–Dornbusch model of open economy macroeconomics. The volatilities of GDP and exports were the two real variables. We then went to find the pairwise causalities among these seven variables. The data were once again chosen from the three similarly developed Asian Newly Developed Countries (NDC-3): South Korea, Taiwan, and Singapore. The volatilities of the seven variables were measured by the square root of time-varying conditional variance series derived from the best-fitted ARCH or GARCH models.

The estimation results are very similar to those of TIG in the previous chapters. They are explained in detail in Chapter 5. Here we summarize the results from the broader perspective of financial development, which was not available at the time of writing.

As expected, the causality relations vary with country (Figure 5.9). For Korea, the stock price volatilities unidirectionally cause volatilities of exchange rate, GDP, money supply, consumer price, and interest rate, but not exports. However, the volatility of GDP does not cause volatilities of any other variables. For Singapore, stock price volatility is isolated, with no relations with volatilities of any other variables, but there is a bidirectional causality between the volatilities of GDP and exports. For Taiwan, the volatility of stock price has bidirectional causality with GDP volatility, and has strong unidirectional causality with money supply volatility.

When the three countries are combined into panel data analysis (Figure 5.10), we see that the stock price volatility has strong unidirectional causality with the volatilities of exchange rate, GDP, and money supply, showing the importance of the stock price volatility on the real sector. Conversely, the GDP volatility does not cause stock price volatility, but does have unidirectional causality with volatilities of exports, and also with volatilities of exchange rate and money supply, but the relations are rather weak. Like the case of Taiwan, interest rate and consumer price volatilities are totally isolated, and neither has any causality relation with the volatilities of any other variables.

The importance of financial development and interactions continues to grow in East and Southeast Asia. According to Allianz Global

Wealth Report (2018, pp. 159, 163), if a country is classified based on average net per capita financial assets, then, in 2018, among the 53 countries surveyed, the US (#2, in the world ranking, same below), Japan (#6), Singapore (#7), and Taiwan (#8) are in the high-wealth group[9] (greater than €45,600); South Korea (#21), China (#30), and Malaysia (#35), in the middle-wealth group (between €7,600 and €45.600); and Thailand (#44) and Indonesia (#52) in the low-wealth group (less than €7,600).[10] Thus, there is a call for studies on the financial interactions among NIEs, ASEAN-4, the US, Japan, and China. Our studies in Chapters 5 and 6 are a step toward this direction.

In summary, we find that, for the Asian newly developed countries under the IT revolution, volatilities of the financial sector and the real sector influence each other (like the case of Taiwan, see Figure 5.9(b)), but, in general, the stock price volatility appears to have a strong impact on GDP, exchange rate, and money supply volatilities. Thus, financial development is important for these countries. The government policy and regulation should not ignore the movement of stock price index, as it has an impact on both the real and financial sectors.

9.9 The Role of the United States in the Asia-Pacific Region

The United States has played a very important role in the economic development of East and Southeast Asia. Through vertical division of labor, the IT revolution under open economies enabled East Asia,

---

[9]Some other countries in this group are Switzerland (#1), Sweden (#3), Netherlands (#4), Canada (#10), UK (#12), France ($15), Italy (#16), and Germany (#18). The positions of Singapore (#7) and Taiwan (#8) should be noted.

[10]Similarly, according to the Credit Suisse Global Wealth Report (2018), as listed in Wikipedia (2019), the world ranking of gross financial wealth per adult in 2017 among 174 countries in the world was as follows: the US (#2, US $320 K, K = 1,000, same below), Singapore (#9, $179 K), Japan (#13, $154 K), Taiwan (#16, $143 K), Hong Kong (#17, $127 K), and South Korea (#26, $74K). Note the very high financial wealth per adult among the Asian NIEs.

and then Southeast Asia to integrate with the US economy and the world economy in general. Integration took place not only in the real sector though the US outsourcing of products and services but also in the financial sector through the movement of capital and investment. As we have seen in the previous section on financial development, the financial sector played an important role in the Asian Newly Developed Countries (NDC-3). Thus, it is natural to find a relationship between GDP and stock prices among these countries.

Chapters 6 analyzes the causality relations of the linkages between the real sector (GDP) and also the financial sector (stock price index) among the closely related countries linked by the IT Revolution, namely, the US, Japan, Korea, Taiwan, and China, using the methods of pairwise Granger causality and VAR Granger causality. Both methods yield very similar results. In terms of GDP, the GDP of Japan (instead of the US), had strong unidirectional impact on Taiwan and Korea, but not the other way around. China was more or less isolated. China's GDP was only slightly influenced by Korean GDP, but not the other way around, probably reflecting China's late developing economic status during the 1980s and the 1990s (the data period).

In terms of stock price, the US (but not Japan) had a strong unidirectional influence on the stock prices of Japan, Taiwan, and Korea, but not vice versa. Similar to GDP, China is also isolated in this case, except that Japanese stock price weakly unidirectionally caused that of China. Somehow, Chinese stock price in turn unidirectionally caused that of the US. The results also show that the stock price of Korea strongly unidirectionally causes Taiwan's stock price, but a very weak causality direction from Taiwan to Korea exists.

The prominent influence of the US stock market on these countries implies that both Taiwan and Korea should closely watch the fluctuations in the US stock market to avoid any undesirable influence on their own stock markets, and prevent unwanted secondary impact on their GDP through the domestic link between stock price and GDP, which we had already alluded to in Chapters 5 and 6.

9.10   International Monetary Policy Coordination

In the previous two sections, we have seen that financial development plays a dominant role in promoting economic development in emerging open economies led by the US economy (Chapter 6). The volatility of the US stock price index had strong unidirectional influence on the stock prices of Taiwan and Korea (Chapter 6), and the stock price volatilities of Taiwan, Korea, and Singapore subsequently have strong unidirectional causality with the volatilities of GDP, exchange rate, and money supplies of these countries (Chapter 5).

In view of the important role of the US in the economies of the Asia-Pacific region, Chapters 7 and 8 applied an asymmetric Mundell–Fleming–Dornbusch model of open economies, which included both real variable (GDP) and financial variables (money supply, exchange rate, wholesale and consumer prices) to study the gains from monetary policy coordination between the advanced countries and the emerging developing countries during the 1970s and the 1980s.

Here, we adopt the definition of the international monetary coordination as "policy actions formally agreed upon and taken by groups of policymakers ... aimed at achieving beneficial outcomes ..." (Bordo and Schenk, 2017) for the countries involved. The countries we are interested in are the US and Taiwan (Chapter 7), the US and Japan (large countries), and Taiwan and Korea (small countries) (Chapter 8).

Chapter 7 is a limited preliminary investigation and empirical study of international monetary policy coordination, a prelude to a larger empirical study in Chapter 8. Both chapters use a game theoretic approach. After setting up an asymmetric Mundell–Fleming–Dornbusch model, we estimated the coefficients of the reduced equations of the model empirically, using the 1975–1989 dataset. The policy coordination is shown as a cooperative equilibrium, and non-coordination or non-cooperation is shown as a Nash equilibrium. We then measure welfare gain from cooperation measured in units of GDP (instead of GNP, see Oudiz and Sachs, 1984).

The results in Chapter 7 show that both Taiwan and the US would lose their social welfare or their GDP by moving from Nash equilibrium to cooperative equilibrium. The difference is that the loss for Taiwan is much larger (3.83% of its 1988 GDP), as compared with the loss for the US (mere 0.1% of its 1988 GDP). Thus, Taiwan will shun monetary policy coordination with the US and the US is indifferent to whether it will coordinate or not.

Even if we extend the analysis to two large countries, the US and Japan, and two small countries, Taiwan and Korea, the results are similar. In this case, in addition, we considered the Stackelberg equilibrium, namely, one country can be either the follower or the leader in a bilateral relation. Thus, in Chapter 8, each country has the possibility of three moves: moving from Nash, follower, or leader non-cooperative equilibrium position to cooperative equilibrium position. The reduced equations of the model for each country were estimated from the slightly expanded data from 1975 to 1990.

For Korea with either the United States or Japan, any of the above three moves from the non-cooperative equilibrium to cooperative equilibrium will cause them to lose a little (less than 0.02% of Korea's 1990 GDP).[11] On the other hand, for Japan or the US with Korea, any of the above three moves to cooperative equilibrium will cause them to gain very little (less than 0.03% of 1990 GDP of Japan or the US). Thus, regardless of the monetary policy coordination of Korea with the US or Japan, or the US or Japan with Korea, all three countries will be indifferent or neutral to a move to cooperative equilibrium.

The magnitude of loss for Taiwan for any of the above three moves from the non-cooperative equilibrium to the cooperative equilibrium with the US or Japan is larger compared with Korea but still very small (loss up to 0.9% of Taiwan's 1990 GDP).[12] On the other hand, the US will gain only slightly (up to 0.14% of the US GDP) from any of the three moves to the policy coordination with Taiwan, although

---

[11]See the last row of Parts III and IV, "% of 1990 GDP" in Table 8.4.

[12]See the last row of Parts I and II, "% of 1990 GDP" in Table 8.4.

the gain is larger than Japan's same three moves to cooperation with Taiwan (up to 0.02% of Japan's GDP).

In general, our study shows that international monetary policy coordination will benefit the large countries negligibly, but will incur larger loss to the small countries. Our findings seem still valid today, and they are consistent with the current observations from the International Monetary Fund that "as far as international monetary policy coordination is concerned, the traditional view of domestically oriented monetary policy is still seen as the optimal arrangement" (Mohan and Kapur, 2014), meaning that the Nash equilibrium is the best solution (Taylor, 2013). Thus, "if each central bank in a flexible exchange rate system follows a monetary policy rule that was optimal for its own country's price stability and output stability, then there would be little additional gain from the central banks' joint optimizing policy" (Taylor, 2013). Hence, "International policy coordination is like the Loch Ness monster: much discussed but rarely seen. Going back over the decades ... coordination efforts have been episodic" (Blanchard *et al.*, 2013). While our study on international monetary coordination was done decades ago, it shed some light on the current problem of international monetary policy coordination.

9.11 Conclusions

In general, in view of the current economic development, we have shown that, although our research was done decades ago, our studies of development strategies of open economies on exports, FDI, and growth, along with causality analysis of the real and financial sectors and monetary policy coordination, are still very much relevant and useful for the understanding and analysis of the current global economy, financial development, and the international monetary system. For researchers as well as policy makers, the cases from the emerging East and Southeast Asian countries can be valuable paradigms for the emerging middle-income and low-income countries in other part of Asia, Africa, and Latin America in this age of globalization and open economies.

Note that the time span of the data on GDP, exports, FDI and the financial system we have analyzed in this book was before the global financial crisis of 2007–2008. As shown in Figures 9.1–9.3, before 2007–2008, the time trend of the data for GDP, exports, and FDI was rather smooth and predictable, namely, the data were "well-behaved". Similar to any other historical and empirical studies, we should note that the global economy has changed since the crisis. Thus, while we believe that the development strategies of the open economies we have analyzed in this book are valuable and still applicable to the current world economy, the applicability and validity of our results and conclusions should take into account the different characteristics of recent data and latest advancement of the analytic methods.

References

Allianz Global Wealth Report (2018). Allianz SE Economic Research, München. Downloaded in August 2019 from https://www.allianz.com/en/economic_re search/publications/specials_fmo/agwr18e.html.

Beck, T. (2011). The Role of Finance in Economic Development: Benefits, Risks, and Politics. European Banking Center Discussion Paper, no. 2011-038. Downloaded in August, 2019 from https://poseidon01.ssrn. com/delivery.php?ID=959114027008111126100097087065071023001092026 034079086085025026118066084006118098096020058018036060032020101031 000771170931040240480220930360921200810751240021161070670430381040 890640150960900750301240690940660941131001030221201161130871071010 11064095&EXT=pdf.

Blanchard, O., J. D. Ostry, and A. R. Ghosh (2013). International Policy Coordination: The Loch Ness Monster. INF Blog. Downloaded in August 2019 from https://blogs.imf.org/2013/12/15/international-policy-coordinat ion-the-loch-ness-monster/.

Bordo, M. D. and C. Schenk (2017). Monetary Policy Cooperation and Coordination. An Historical Perspective on the Importance of Rules. In *Rules for International Monetary Stability: Past, Present, and Future* [Chapter 5], Michael D. Bordo and John B. Taylor (Eds.). CA: Hoover Institution Press.

Boulding, K. E. (1958). *Principles of Economic Policy*. New Jersey: Prentice Hall, Inc.

Cohn, T. H. (2012). *Global Political Economy* (6th edn.). Boston, MA: Longman/Pearson.

Credit Suisse Global Wealth Report (2018). Research Institute, Credit Suisse AG. Switzerland. Downloaded in August 2019 from https://www.credit-sui sse.com/about-us/en/reports-research/global-wealth-report.html.

Harrison, A. and A. Rodriguez-Clare (2010). Trade, Foreign Investment, and Industrial Policy for Developing Countries. Chapter 63 in *Handbook of Development Economics* (Vol. 5), Dani Rodrik and Mark R. Rosenzweig (Eds.). Development Economics and Policy, 2010, Elsevier, pp. 4039–4214.

Hsiao, F. S. T. and M.-C. Wang Hsiao (2015). Economic Development of Taiwan: Early Experiences and the Pacific Trade Triangle. In *Advanced Research on Asian Economy and Economics of Other Continents* (Vol. 9). Singapore: World Scientific.

Hsiao, F. S. T. and M.-C. Wang Hsiao (2017). *Economic Development of Emerging East Asia: Catching Up of Taiwan and South Korea.* Anthem Press. London. Cambridge University Press Cambridge Core, 2018.

Keynes, J. M. (1926). *The End of Laissez-faire.* London: Hogarth Press.

Keynes, J. M. (1926). *The General Theory of Employment, Interest, and Money.* London: Palgrave Macmillan.

Levine, R. (2005). Finance and Growth: Theory and Evidence. In *Handbook of Economic Growth* 1A, Philippe Aghion and Steven Durlauf (Eds.), pp. 865–934.

Mohan, R. and M. Kapur (2014). Monetary Policy Coordination and the Role of Central Banks, IMF Working Paper WP/14/70. International Monetary Fund. Downloaded in August 2019 from https://www.imf.org/external/pub s/ft/wp/2014/wp1470.pdf.

Oudiz, G. and J. Sachs (1984). Macroeconomic policy coordination among the industrial economies. *Brooking Papers on Economic Activities* **I**, 1–75.

Rodrik, D. and M. R. Rosenzweig (2010). Preface: Development Policy and Development Economics: An Introduction. In *Handbook of Development Economics* (Vol. 5), Dani Rodrik and M. R. Rosenzweig (Eds.), Development Economics and Policy. Elsevier, pp. xv–xxvii.

Samuelson, P. A. and W. D. Nordhaus (2010). *Economics* (29th edn.). NY: McGraw-Hill Irwin.

Schumpeter, J. A. (1949). *The Theory of Economic Development, An Inquiry into Profits, Capital, Credit, Interest, and the Business Cycle.* Translated from the German edition (1911) by Redvers Opie. Cambridge, MA: Harvard University Press.

Smith, A. (1776). *An Inquiry into the Nature and Causes of the Wealth of Nations.* Edited with an Introduction, Notes, Marginal Summary, and Enlarged Index by Edwin Cannan. 1937. The Modern Library, NY: Random House.

Taylor, J. B. (2013). International Monetary Policy Coordination: Past, Present, and Future. Monetary and Economic Department, Bank for International Settlements. BIS Working Papers, No. 427.

UNCTADSTAT (2019). Economic Groups and Composition, Economic Groups, Classifications. File name: DimCountries_EconomicsGroupings_Hierarchy, in Excel. Downloaded from UNCTADSTAT, CLASSIFICATION, in August 2019, from the website: https://unctadstat.unctad.org/EN/Classifications. html.

Wikipedia (2019). List of Countries by Financial Assets per capita. Downloaded in August 2019, from https://en.wikipedia.org/wiki/List_of_countries_by_fin ancial_assets_per_capita.

World Bank (1987). *World Development Report, 1987.* World Bank. New York: Oxford University Press.

World Bank (2016). Financial Development. Downloaded in August 2019, from https://www.worldbank.org/en/publication/gfdr/gfdr-2016/backgrou nd/financial-development.

World Bank (2018). Classifying Countries by Income. Story, October 4, 2018. Downloaded in August 2019, from https://datatopics.worldbank.org/ world-development-indicators/stories/the-classification-of-countries-by-inco me.html.

Index

Printed in the United States
By Bookmasters